business research methods

a managerial approach

business research methods

2 EDITION

a managerial approach

A. J. Veal

Pearson Education Australia
Unit 4, Level 2
14 Aquatic Drive
Frenchs Forest NSW 2086

www.pearsoned.com.au

Senior Acquisitions Editor: Simone Bella
Senior Project Editor: Kathryn Fairfax
Editorial Coordinator: Roisin Fitzgerald
Copy Editor: Jane Tyrrell
Proofreader: Terence Townsend
Cover design by Jason Gemenis
Cover illustration by Getty
Typeset by Midland Typesetters, Maryborough, Vic.

Printed in Malaysia (CTP-VVP)

3 4 5 09 08 07

National Library of Australia
Cataloguing-in-Publication Data

Veal, Anthony James.
Business research methods : a managerial approach.

2nd ed.
Includes index.
ISBN 1 74103 253 9.

1. Management – Research – Methodology. 2. Management – Research. I. Title.

658.0072

An imprint of Pearson Education Australia
(a division of Pearson Australia Group Pty Ltd)

Contents

Detailed contents

APPENDICES

List of figures

List of case study examples

Preface

This second edition of *Business Research Methods* has been updated and reshaped in a number of ways. A new chapter has been added on the case study method and a number of chapters have been divided into two, so that data collection and data analysis are addressed in separate chapters. This division is not always easy to achieve, particularly in some qualitative research methods, but it is hoped that the new arrangement will assist in the teaching and learning process. A further enhancement is the addition of Case Study Examples of the use of various research methods throughout. The chapters dealing with quantitative and qualitative analysis have been updated and demonstrate the use of the most recent versions of the two software packages *SPSS* and *NVivo*. At the end of most chapters, 'Test questions' are presented, which should be answerable entirely from reading the chapter, while 'Exercises' require some further reading or research.

Information is the lifeblood of contemporary business, whether in commercial, public or not-for-profit settings. The ability to gather, analyse, evaluate, present and utilise information is an essential competency for the modern manager and the essence of business research. But business research is not just a set of disembodied skills; it exists in a variety of social, political, organisational and economic contexts. With these issues in mind *Business Research Methods: a Managerial Approach* was designed to assist in the development of the skills necessary to conduct business research, to gain a critical understanding of the value of existing research and to appreciate the role of research in strategic and day-to-day management processes.

The book has been written for undergraduate and postgraduate business students who are required to understand business research methods and undertake research projects as part of their studies. It is also suitable for practising managers who are required to conduct business research and prepare management reports. The book provides a complete guide to the basics of business research processes in its own right, but also provides an extensive guide to further reading.

My experience and that of my former collaborator, Bill Ticehurst, in teaching research methods at university level and conducting industry research convinced us of the need for a book such as this which is comprehensive in its coverage and crosses the boundaries between critical and empirical research paradigms. It is our view that no one research approach is necessarily superior to another. Rather, research methods should be judged in terms of their appropriateness to the research problem at hand, the rigour with which the method is applied, and the insights and understandings provided by the methodology in relation to the business research problem.

Modern information technologies enhances business research effectiveness and to this end emphasis has been placed on the use of electronic databases and the Internet in searching both the business literature and other resources, while not neglecting more traditional methods. Also highlighted are the use of software packages such as *NVivo* and *SPSS* to facilitate deeper insights into management issues which might not be possible without the assistance of modern information technologies. However, the surfeit of data which can be generated using such software packages places even more emphasis on the role of critical reflection in business research to determine the meanings of the findings and their relevance to the research question at hand.

The first edition of the book resulted from a collaboration between myself and my colleague at the University of Technology Sydney, Professor Bill Ticehurst. Bill has now retired from UTS and academic life and, having decided to embrace retirement fully, he decided not to be involved with the production of the second edition. Needless to say, his influence on the book is still very strong.

In addition to the fruits of the partnership with Bill Ticehurst, I am appreciative of the support and insights that have been provided by colleagues and students in the further development of *Business Research Methods: a Managerial Approach.* To the readers of this book, both students and managers, I wish you the enduring satisfaction that arises from a challenging business research project carefully carried out and continued to completion.

A support website for the book is available at: (www.pearsoned.com.au/veal), containing updates and copies of downloadable data for exercises.

Tony Veal
April 2005

preparation

PART 1

CHAPTER 1

The research process

Knowledge and understanding of natural, social and economic environments have become the basis of modern societies and organisations. The outcomes of research affect modern life fundamentally, and the importance of research into science and technology and into people and organisations and their relationships is widely acknowledged. Understanding how knowledge is generated and used, and having the ability to generate valid and useful information about the management environment can be considered a key skill for modern managers. It is therefore also an important part of business education. The purpose of this book is to provide an introduction to business research and its application in private, public and not-for-profit sector organisations from a managerial point of view. The aim is to assist the development of skills in the conduct of management-related research, and to provide a critical understanding of the value of existing research and an appreciation of the role of research in strategic and day-to-day management processes.

Research is not just a set of disembodied skills: it exists in a variety of social, political, organisational and economic contexts. This first chapter therefore addresses preliminary questions concerning the nature of research, who does it and why, and briefly examines the history of management research.

WHAT IS MANAGEMENT? WHAT IS RESEARCH?

Management

There is considerable debate regarding the nature of management and little consensus concerning its definition. For example, Robbins and Mukerji (1994: 6) define management as 'the process of getting activities completed efficiently with and through other people', while Van Fleet (1991: 8) defines management as 'a set of activities directed at the efficient and effective utilisation of resources in the pursuit of one or more goals'. The definition proposed by Richard Daft (1994: 8) tends to combine these two views, describing management as 'the attainment of organisational goals in an effective and efficient manner through planning, organising, leading, and controlling organisational resources'.

According to these definitions the primary activity of a manager involves coordinating and facilitating the management of people and resources in an organisation. This can involve just a small number of people in a voluntary group or small business, or it may involve many thousands of employees in a large corporation or government department. It can also take place in differing contexts, for example delivering social services in a small town, managing a high technology company in a city, sales promotion in an overseas branch or managing employee communications in company headquarters.

Stewart Clegg (1996: 1) suggests that the nature of management is much more complex than is implied by the definitions quoted above. He argues that management is whatever it is made to be, according to the social fabric from which it is constructed and the extent to which it is embedded in various social contexts. What managers do is *what managers know to do*. They know in many ways, through example, training, experience, intuition, reading, education, instinct and more. The sources of knowledge are many and varied. The effects of knowledge are complex, often contradictory, but always situated in practice—in what managers do.

We can conclude from these definitions that management is certainly a complex process. In the light of Clegg's description it seems unlikely that any one definition will entirely capture the range of management processes, and the nature of management will remain a matter for debate. Such debate is of long-standing and is reflected in the history of management thinking and research.

Research

In *The Management Research Handbook*, Roger Bennett (1991: 68) defines research as 'a systematic, careful inquiry or examination to discover new information or relationships and to expand/verify existing knowledge for some specified purpose'. The 'specified purpose' of research refers to some problem of concern to the researcher or manager, which may be theoretical or practical in nature.

The 'discovery of new information and relationships for a particular purpose' covers a number of investigatory activities, for instance the work of journalists, detectives or even auditors. However, the *methods* and *purposes* of research as defined above distinguish it from these other forms of professional inquiry.

Scientific research is research that is conducted within the rules and conventions of science. This means that it is based on logic, reason and the systematic examination of evidence. Ideally, within the scientific model it should be possible for research to be replicated by the same or different researchers and for similar conclusions to emerge. Scientific research should also contribute to a cumulative body of knowledge about a field or topic. This model of scientific research applies most aptly in the physical or natural sciences, such as physics or chemistry. *Biological science* differs somewhat from the purely physical sciences because the natural world is in a constant state of evolution. In the area of *social science*, which deals with people as social beings, in groups and in organisations, the scientific model frequently needs to be modified, or even, in some cases, abandoned.

Social science research is carried out using the methods and traditions of social science. Social science differs from the physical or natural sciences because it deals with people and groups of people and their behaviour, and people are much less predictable than non-human phenomena. People and organisations can be aware of the research being conducted about them and are therefore not always purely passive subjects; they can react to the results of research and change their behaviour accordingly. Another difference between social science research and natural science research is the fact that the social world is constantly changing, so it is rarely possible to replicate research at different times or in different places and obtain identical results.

In its simplest form, research can be seen as a process of *discovery* or *finding out*. However, to advance human knowledge it is also necessary for research to provide *explanation*—to explain *why* things are as they are. There is also a third function of research, namely *evaluating*—judging the success or value of management policies, programs and strategies, as discussed above.

Three types of research can therefore be distinguished which correspond to these three functions. In some cases research projects concentrate on only one of these functions, but often two or more of the approaches are included in the same project.

Three types of research:

- *Descriptive research*—finding out, describing *what is*.
- *Explanatory research*—explaining *how* or *why* things are as they are (and using this to *predict* demand, sales, impacts, etc.).
- *Evaluative research*—evaluation of policies, strategies, programs and practices.

Descriptive research seeks to find out and describe, but not necessarily to explain. This will typically arise in the 'environmental appraisal' process discussed later in the chapter. It is also the nature of much research produced by government statistical agencies—such as the census of population and surveys of household expenditure. Such descriptive research is conducted on a regular basis to monitor social and economic change; the researchers in the government agencies collect the data, others use it for academic, policy or political purposes.

Explanatory research moves beyond description to seek to explain the patterns, relationships and trends observed or discovered. Why is a particular product or service falling in popularity? How do staff bonuses bring about increases in efficiency? Such questions raise the thorny issue of *causality*. The aim of explanatory research is to be able to say, for example, that there has been an increase in A because of a fall in B. It is one thing to discover that A has increased while B has decreased, but to establish that the rise in A has been *caused* by the fall in B is often a much more demanding task. To establish causality, or the likelihood of causality, requires the researcher to be rigorous in the collection, analysis and interpretation of data, and it typically requires some sort of theoretical framework in order to relate the phenomenon under study to social, psychological, economic or political processes. In general, the purpose of establishing causal relationships is to be able to *predict*. For example, if we know that demand for a certain product is largely determined by a relationship with levels of disposable income then we can predict levels of demand for the product using predictions of future levels of disposable income and population. The issues of causality, prediction and the role of theory in research are discussed in later chapters.

Evaluative research arises from the need to make judgements on the success or effectiveness of policies, practices, strategies or programs—for example, whether a particular practice or program is meeting required performance standards or whether a particular advertising campaign has been cost-effective. In the private sector this can often be determined in relation to profitability, but in the public sector it is generally more complex. Again, this is a topic that is discussed in more detail later in the book.

A further division can be made between a *pilot* or *exploratory* study and a full-scale study. It is often the case that the researcher wishes to explore the field or test methodology before committing resources to a full-scale study. Sometimes the results of such pilot or exploratory studies are sufficiently revealing to be worthy of publication in their own right, but for the most part they are used only as a basis for the design of the full-scale study.

Contemporary business research is a very wide-ranging activity. It can take place in large multinational organisations, in universities, in government agencies, or in a single local community organisation or small business. The kinds of research undertaken can range from a single interview or series of observations made by a single researcher, to a decade-long investigation using multiple research methods and conducted around the world by a large team of investigators.

WHO DOES RESEARCH?

This book is mainly concerned with how to conduct research, but it also aims to provide an understanding of the research process that will help the reader to become a knowledgeable and critical consumer of research carried out by others. When reading research reports it is useful to bear in mind *why* the research has been done. To a large extent this is determined by *who* did the research and who *paid* for it to be done. Who does research and who funds it is important because it affects the kind of research conducted and the outcomes of research. It has a significant impact on what constitutes the *body of knowledge* that students need to learn and which managers use.

Management research is undertaken by a wide variety of individuals and organisations. The respective roles of these 'actors' are discussed in turn below.

Who does research?

- Academics
- Students
- Government and business organisations
- Consultants
- Managers

Academics

In most universities, professors and lecturers are expected to engage in both research and teaching, and there are also some full-time researchers. Some academic research, for example theory building, requires little or no financial support beyond the acadmic's own time. However, other research requires financial support for employment of research assistants, interviewers or market research firms, and to cover the costs of travel or equipment. The main sources of academic research funding are universities themselves, government research councils, and privately funded trusts and foundations. Funds may also come from the world of practice—for example, from government agencies, commercial companies, professional bodies or not-for-profit organisations—to fund research to solve particular problems or to inform sponsors about particular issues relevant to their interests. In this case research directions will be more practically orientated.

Generally academics seek to communicate the results of their research to their peers by publication. Publication of research can take various forms, including: articles in refereed journals; articles in non-refereed journals, such as professional magazines; books; published reports; and conference papers. All of these can be in 'hard' copy or on the Internet. Publication of research in refereed journals is considered the most academically prestigious because of the process of *peer review*. This involves two or three anonymous scholars reviewing articles which have been submitted to journals in order to ensure their level of quality and scholarship. In addition, an editorial board of experts oversees the editorial standards for such journals.

Academics may use funds to employ one or more research assistants who may also be registered for a higher degree—usually a Masters or a PhD. This leads to the second academic source of research—students.

Students

The conduct of small research projects, or assistance in larger projects, is an important learning experience for students. In universities the business area is not generally well-endowed with research funds, so research conducted by students can often make a significant contribution. A survey conducted by a group of students on a particular business problem or on a market segment may be especially appreciated by the organisation for which it is conducted. Similarly a thorough review of an area of literature may be of considerable use to others.

The work of doctoral, masters research and honours students makes a significant individual and collective contribution to management research. Theses from most Australian, American and British universities are available commercially on microfiche, from the library of the university where the research was supervised and, increasingly, electronically.

Government and business organisations

Government organisations often have their own 'in-house' research agencies. The Australian Bureau of Statistics, the Department of Workplace Relations and Small Business, the Bureau of Tourism Research and the CSIRO (Commonwealth Scientific and Industrial Research Organisation) are all examples of government research agencies. Business organisations tend to rely on external consultants for their social, economic and market research, although there are exceptions, such as banks and some of the very large companies which tend to conduct their research in-house.

Research conducted by government agencies is generally available to the public, but research conducted by commercial bodies is usually confidential. Research reports from government organisations can be important sources of knowledge, especially research of a more practically orientated nature. For example, the Australian government takes responsibility for conducting the nationwide census of population. This is descriptive research which no other organisation would have the resources to undertake. Further information on similar information sources is presented in Chapter 5.

Consultants

Consultants provide research and advisory services to industry and government. Some consultancy organisations are large, multinational companies involved in accountancy, finance, management and business consultancy generally. Examples of large consultancy companies are PriceWaterhouseCoopers and Ernst and Young. There are also many smaller, specialised organisations in the consultancy field. Some academics offer their specialist knowledge through consultancies, and self-employed consultancy activity is common among practitioners who have taken early retirement.

Managers

Managers who understand the full extent of the management process see research as part of their job. Successful management depends on high quality information. A great deal of information—for example, sales figures—is routinely available to the manager and does not require research. However, the creative utilisation of such data—for example, to establish market trends—can be a form of research. Other types of information can only be obtained by specific management research. A range of research areas that concern managers is shown below.

Research areas of concern to managers:

- Clients
- Potential clients
- Staffing
- Performance
- Competitors
- Legal issues
- Sales
- Products
- Culture
- Productivity
- Strategy
- Quality
- Policy
- Finance
- Training and staff development
- Information technology
- Industrial relations
- Organisational environment
- Managerial effectiveness
- Communication
- Organisational development

Most managers need to conduct—or commission—research if they require information and understanding to aid in their decision-making. It might be argued that managers do not themselves need research skills since they can always commission consultants to carry out research. However, managers who are familiar with the research process will be better able to commission research and evaluate the results. It is also the case that managers sometimes need to conduct research themselves because funds are insufficient to commission outsiders to do the work.

WHY RESEARCH?

To a large extent the 'why?' of research is explained by the above discussion of who does research. Each type of researcher has different motivations, although they may often coincide. Since our belief is that the research can and does contribute to the management process, we consider here the relationship between research and the management process, and then the relationship between academic research and business.

Research in the management process

The research process can be studied for a variety of reasons, including social or political criticism and the pursuit of knowledge 'for its own sake'; here it is viewed as an essential tool of management. Many managers find it necessary to conduct or commission research for professional reasons and some become specialists in research—for example, as management consultants or marketing researchers. It is therefore particularly appropriate to consider the role of research in the management process.

While there are many models of the management process, the traditional 'rational-comprehensive' model, a version of which is depicted diagrammatically in Figure 1.1, is used here as a framework for examining the part played by research in the management process. Alternatives to the rational-comprehensive model may call for varying amounts and types of research and for varying emphases on different parts of the process, but they invariably involve some sort of research input. Nine steps in the rational-comprehensive

FIGURE 1.1 The rational-comprehensive planning/management process

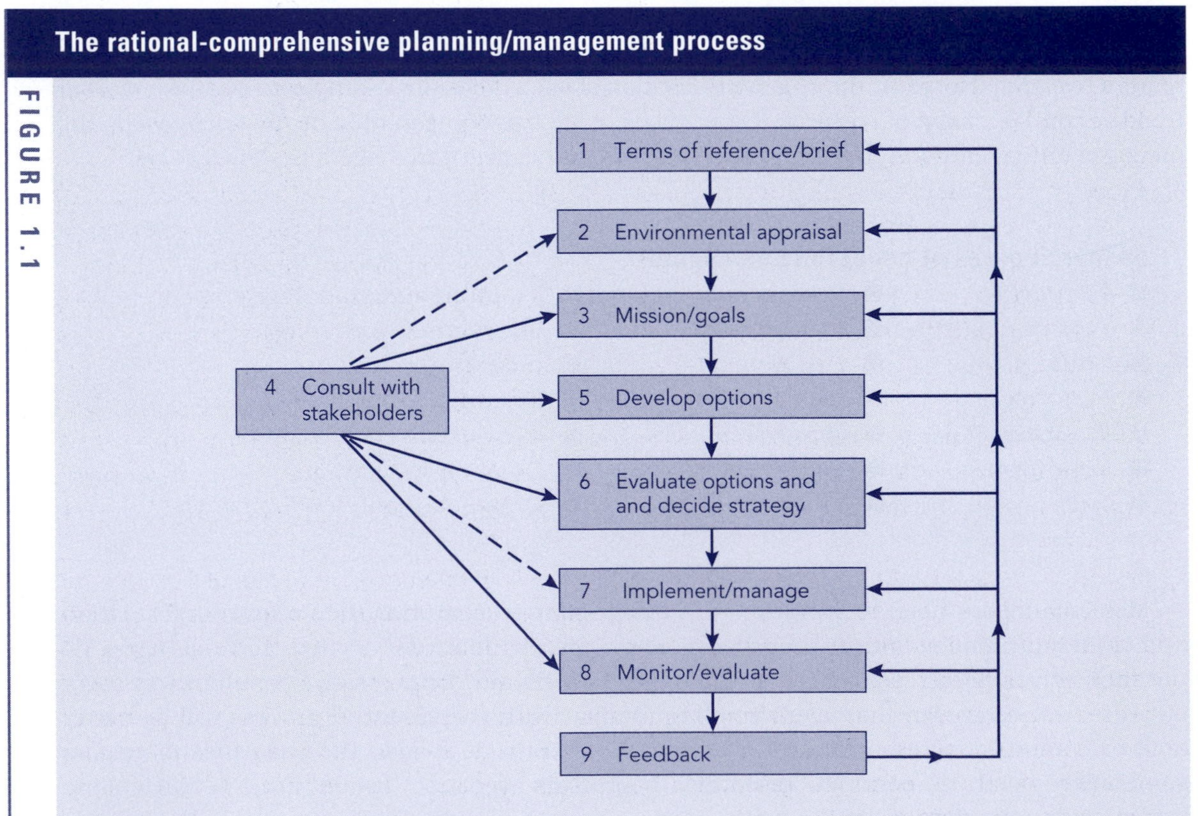

model of the process are shown in Figure 1.1, and these steps and their relationship with research are discussed briefly in turn below.

1 *Terms of reference/brief*: The 'terms of reference', or brief, for a particular planning or management task sets out the scope and purpose of the exercise, which might relate to a specific, limited project or to strategic planning for the whole organisation. Research can be involved right at the beginning of this process by assisting with the establishment of the terms of reference. For example, research on working conditions in a corporation may result in a policy initiative to seek to *improve working conditions*, or customer research might reveal a need for a *re-branding exercise*.
2 *Environmental appraisal*: An environmental appraisal involves the gathering of all information necessary for, and relevant to, the task in hand. Information may relate to the organisation's internal workings and structure or to the outside world. It may be organised to address *Strengths*, *Weaknesses*, *Opportunities* and *Threats* (commonly called a *SWOT* analysis). An environmental appraisal may involve an analysis of such phenomena as: changes in technology; past trends in sales and costs; labour relations; profiles of actual and potential customers; the activities of competitors; and government policies and regulations. This information may be readily available in the form of what is referred to later in the book as 'secondary data', or it may require extensive gathering of new data. In either case, gathering, collating and analysing the data into a usable form can be termed 'research'.
3 *Mission and goals*: Statements of the mission or goals of the organisation may already be in place if the management task is a relatively minor one. If the task is a major undertaking, such as the development of a strategic plan for the whole organisation, then the development of, or revision of, *statements of mission and goals* may be involved. Research is unlikely to be directly involved in this stage unless it is required in the consultation process, as discussed under step 4.
4 *Consult*: Consultation with 'stakeholders' is considered vital by most organisations and is a statutory requirement in many forms of public sector planning. Stakeholders include: employees; shareholders; clients; members of the public; members of boards and councils; and neighbouring organisations. Consultation can take place in a number of ways, including formal research processes, such as surveys and focus groups.
5 *Develop options*: In order to develop a plan, strategy or course of action, consideration must be given to the range of possible courses of action—the options—available. Often such options emerge from informal processes such as 'brainstorming', but research can also be involved—for example gathering information on how similar tasks have been undertaken by the organisation in the past, or by competitors or similar organisations overseas.
6 *Evaluate options and decide strategy*: Options must be *evaluated* in terms of their costs, feasibility, likely contribution to the achievement of the organisation's goals and the best method of implementation. Typical formal evaluation techniques include: financial viability analysis; cost-benefit analysis; economic impact analysis; importance-performance analysis; and environmental and organisational impact analysis. Deciding on a strategy involves selecting a course of action from among all the options identified and taking into account the evaluative appraisals available. This process of choice may involve a complex procedure which also requires research input.

7 *Implement and manage*: Implementing a plan or strategy is the ultimate task of management. Research can be involved in the day-to-day management of implementation in a variety of ways, including investigation of improved ways of deploying resources and by providing continuous feedback about the management process—for example in the form of customer surveys. The line between this kind of ongoing monitoring research and the next step, the monitoring and evaluation process, is difficult to draw.

8 *Monitor and evaluate*: Monitoring progress and evaluating the implementation of strategies is clearly a process with which research is likely to be involved. In commercial organisations the data for the monitoring and evaluation of a project is likely to consist primarily of sales, income and cost information, requiring little if any research input. Additional information, such as customer and dealer attitudes, may also be involved. In the public and not-for-profit sectors, non-financial data related to clients or the environment—which can often only be collected by means of research—are often more important than financial data.

9 *Feedback*: The process comes full circle with the feedback step. The data from the monitoring and evaluation process are fed back into the planning or management cycle and can lead to a revision of any or all of the decisions previously made. The monitoring and evaluation process might report complete success, it might suggest minor changes to some of the details of the policies and plans adopted, or it might result in a fundamental re-think of the approach—going 'back to the drawing board'.

Case Study Example 1.1 provides a hypothetical example of how the above process might give rise to research in a car manufacturing company.

THE RELEVANCE OF PUBLISHED RESEARCH TO PRACTICE

Management research can be initiated by academic interest or because of practical problems faced by organisations or a mixture of the two. Much *academic research* is governed by the concerns of theoretical disciplines such as sociology, economics or psychology, which may not coincide with the immediate concerns of business. However, part of the role of academic research is to 'stand apart' from the rest of the world and provide detached analysis. Research seen as critical or irrelevant by some may be seen as insightful and constructive by others. There is also a great deal of *applied research* that focuses specifically on practical aspects of business in areas such as finance, training and marketing. While research in these applied areas can also be theoretical and critical rather than immediately practical or supportive, it is more likely to be driven by the sorts of issues that concern organisations and practitioners.

In each of these theoretical and applied areas there is a fairly distinctive body of business research. Some of the research that draws on more than one discipline is described as *multi-disciplinary*, while research that occupies a niche somewhere between disciplines is described as *inter-disciplinary*. There is also research that recognises no particular disciplinary allegiance.

When using published research for your own purpose it is important to consider carefully the context and relevance of the research in relation to your needs. For example, the results of a survey of the leading journals in management indicate that 30 per cent of the studies reported had findings that were based solely on samples of students (Hubbard & Lindsay 1995). A researcher or manager would therefore need to be very careful about extending the findings of such studies to employees or customers in practical situations.

CASE STUDY EXAMPLE 1.1

Research in the management process

Source: Hypothetical.
Methods/approaches: Multiple
Topic: Rational-comprehensive model

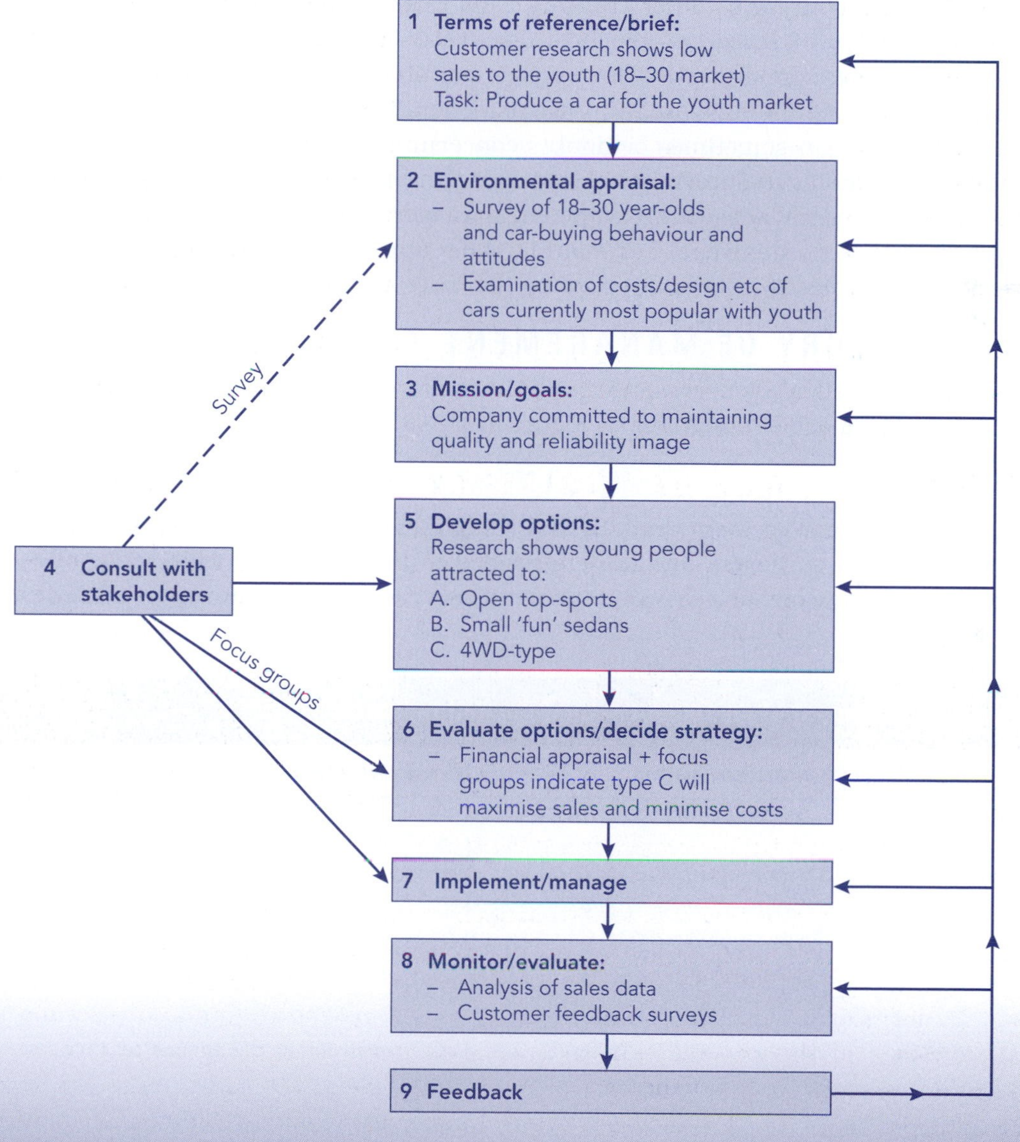

Culture can also influence the outcomes of research. Up to 80 per cent of management research published to date has been conducted by North American researchers on Americans and in American organisations. The findings of this research may or may not be applicable to organisations in other countries. For example, Dewhirst (1989) suggests that three kinds of management behaviour appear to be influenced by cultural differences between Australia and the US, namely entrepreneurship, participation, and patience and persistence. Australian managers have been found to be less entrepreneurial and less participative, but more patient and persistent than American managers.

Clearly, great care needs to be taken when extending the findings of business research conducted in one country to other cultures. This raises concerns regarding the *reliability* and *generalisability* of research, which is discussed later in this chapter. However, this issue also suggests opportunities for replication of research in different countries to establish whether the findings are, in practice, generalisable.

Although there can sometimes be doubts concerning the relevance of much research to frontline management, the processes of managing and business research should ideally be seen as interdependent activities. Competent managers should always take the outcomes of research into account when formulating their approach to managing and, likewise, business research needs to be influenced by the daily and strategic needs of the manager.

THE HISTORY OF MANAGEMENT THINKING AND RESEARCH

The review which follows is necessarily brief: the main periods covered and key researchers/thinkers and ideas are summarised in Figure 1.2.

Pre-industrial

The beginnings of management thinking and research are lost in the mists of time. However, it seems clear that managers and leaders needed to think about a wide range of complex and challenging management issues in projects such as the development of ancient armies

FIGURE 1.2 Historical development of management thinking and research

School of thought	Researchers/thinkers	Management ideas
Pre-industrial		
Ancients	Sumerians (3500 B.C.) Babylonians (2000–1700 B.C.) Egyptians (4000–2000 B.C.) Romans (300 B.C.–300 A.D.) Chinese (1500 B.C.–1300 A.D.)	Planning/coordination for cities, armies, government, etc.
European Middle Ages	Venetians (450 A.D.–1500 A.D.)	Legal frameworks for sea commerce, early assembly line for ships
Renaissance	Machiavelli (1469–1527)	Politics and power
Industrial Revolution	Adam Smith (1723–93)	Division of labour, market forces

FIGURE 1.2

Historical development of management thinking and research *continued*

School of thought	Researchers/thinkers	Management ideas
Classical School		
Scientific Management	Frederick Taylor (1856–1915) Frank Gilbreth (1868–1924) Lilian Gilbreth (1878–1972) Henry Gantt (1861–1919)	Principles of scientific management Time and motion studies, welfare of employees important Production scheduling, Gantt chart
General Administrative Theorists	Henri Fayol (1841–1925) Max Weber (1864–1920)	Fourteen general principles of management Introduced concept of bureaucracy and professional management
Behavioural Approaches		
	Hugo Munsterberg (1863–1916) Mary Parker Follett (1868–1933) Chester Barnard (1886–1961) Elton Mayo (1880–1949)	Founded industrial psychology Important role of individuals and groups in organisations Importance of communication and social relationships in organisations Importance of human factors in work behaviour, Hawthorne studies 1927–1932
Human Relations Approaches		
	Abraham Maslow (1908–1970) Douglas McGregor (1906–1964)	Hierarchy of needs Theory X: workers lazy; theory Y: workers need full potential developed
Modern Approaches		
Quantitative Approaches (also called management science, operations research)	Robert McNamara, Charles Thornton, various others post-World War II	Application of statistics, mathematical modelling, computers to planning and management)
General Systems Theory	Von Bertalanffy (1972)	Organisation seen as a series of interdependent parts—a system
Contingency Approach	Frederick Fiedler (1974)	Every situation is unique—no one best way of managing
Japanese Management	William Ouchi (1981)	Theory Z—hybrid US/Japanese influences management style
Culture and Power Approaches	French and Raven (1959), Clegg and Dunkerley (1980), Clegg (1989)	Recognises role and importance of power, politics and culture in organisational functioning

and walled cities, the building of the Great Wall of China and the building of the pyramids of Egypt. Some of the earliest management activities can be traced back to the Sumerians, who settled along the Euphrates River around 3500 B.C., the Egyptians from about 2000 B.C. and the Greek and Roman empires (Barney & Griffin 1992: 39–42). Records about production management are found in the work of the Chinese philosopher Mencius, written in 300 B.C. (Easterby-Smith, Thorpe & Lowe 1991: 3).

Concerns with the problems of management clearly continued over the centuries as city-states developed into nations, and complex organisational structures such as the Catholic Church developed further and became more specialised. In the European Middle Ages the successful maritime trading activities of the Venetians led to the establishment of a legal framework for commerce (1300 A.D.) and the development of early assembly line systems in shipyards (1500 A.D.). In the sixteenth century Niccolo Machiavelli produced his treatises on politics and personal power, *The Prince* (Vecchio, Hearn & Southey 1992: 11).

In 1776 Adam Smith published his landmark text, *The Wealth of Nations*, which marked the move from pre-industrial to an industrial economy in Europe. He suggested that great productivity advantages could be gained through the division of labour in manufacturing organisations. The division of labour involved specialisation, which required the breakdown of jobs into a series of simple repetitive tasks each carried out by a specialised individual, rather than one person doing the entire job. Experimentation with management was stimulated by the advent of the Industrial Revolution during the eighteenth century, which saw the shift of production from cottage-based industries to purpose-built factories. The factory system posed managerial problems that earlier organisations had not encountered, such as controlling large-scale organisations and increasing industrial efficiency in the context of rapid technological change and the development of a competitive capitalist environment. This resulted in the need to organise and manage large numbers of people, transport, raw material, production processes and products.

However, it was not until the end of the nineteenth century and the beginning of the twentieth century that researchers started formally to develop theories of management which sought to provide new insights into management and to improve management processes. The new theories and approaches to management developed at this time are known as the *classical school* of management.

The classical school

Scholars in the classical school of management emphasised a rational and scientific approach to the study of management and tried to make organisations more efficient. They attempted to develop universal principles or models that would apply in all management contexts. The approach often focused on the factors that affected the efficiency of job inputs and outputs. Their approach was practical rather than theoretical, drawing upon their own business experiences. The classical school included two major subgroups of researchers: those concerned with *scientific management* and those concerned with *administrative theory*. These subgroups are best described in terms of the work of their founders and major proponents.

The major advocates of scientific management were Frederick Taylor, Frank and Lilian Gillbreth, and Henry Gantt. Scientific management concerned the use of scientific method to define the 'one best way' for a job to be done so as to maximise employee output (Robbins & Mukerji 1994: 38).

Taylor (1856–1915) has been described as the 'father' of this school. His ideas are contained in his two major works, *Shop Management* and *The Principles of Scientific Management.* Taylor's scientific management was primarily concerned with factory management and production workers. He sought to increase output by discovering the fastest, most efficient and least fatiguing production methods (Shafritz & Oh 1987: 25). Taylor identified four major principles of management. The first principle was that the manager should develop a science for each component of the job (one best way of working). Second, the manager should scientifically select the best person for the job and train the worker. The third principle involved cooperation with the workers to ensure work was done in accordance with the scientific steps already developed. Finally, the manager should assume all management activities, leaving the workers to get on with their jobs (Van Fleet 1991: 41). Taylor believed that if these principles were adhered to, prosperity could be achieved—management would earn more profits and workers would earn more pay.

Taylor's four principles of scientific management:

1 The manager should develop a science (one best way of working) for each component of the job.
2 The manager should scientifically select the best person for the job and train the worker.
3 The manager should cooperate with the workers to ensure work is done in accordance with the scientific steps developed.
4 The manager should assume all management activities, allowing workers to get on with their jobs

Frank and Lilian Gilbreth (1868–1924 and 1878–1972) were primarily interested in time and motion studies in industry. In particular, the Gilbreths studied the bricklaying industry, seeking ways to eliminate wasteful hand and body motions. They applied the principles of scientific management by studying the steps involved and then standardising them. The Gilbreths also experimented with optimising work performance through the design and use of proper work equipment. They took a broader view than Taylor in one respect, arguing that organisations must take the welfare of individuals into consideration as well as the organisation as a whole (Van Fleet 1991: 42).

Other theorists, such as Gantt (1861–1919), also made significant contributions to the study of scientific management. He was an associate of Taylor and was interested in control systems for shop-floor production scheduling as well as pay systems. He developed the 'Gantt Chart' that is used for scheduling work over a span of time. Gantt also developed a bonus system that supplemented basic wage rates when workload targets were achieved (Robbins & Mukerji 1994: 40).

Classical *administrative theory* deals with the anatomy and structural relationships within formal organisations. The most prominent theorists in this area were Henri Fayol and Max Weber.

Fayol (1841–1925) drew on his own extensive industrial experience with his efforts directed towards the activities of all managers. His most important book, *General and Industrial*

Fayol's five basic functions of management:
- Planning
- Organising
- Commanding
- Coordinating
- Controlling

Management, contained fourteen general principles of management. Some of these principles included the division of labour, authority, unity of command and remuneration. Fayol believed that his concept of management was applicable to every kind of organisation. Fayol also described five basic functions of management: planning, organising, commanding, coordinating and controlling. These functions were to underlie the further development of a great deal of management theory up to the present time (Daft 1994: 49).

The research of Max Weber (1864–1920) was concerned with developing a theory of authority, structures and relations in organisations. Weber described an ideal type of organisation called a *bureaucracy* that possessed a rational set of structuring guidelines. He believed that organisations would be more effective if they were based on rational–legal authority, where authority is based on official position rather than personal status. Weber's ideal bureaucracy system involved the division of labour, an authority hierarchy, detailed rules and regulations, impersonal relationships and career-oriented managers. Weber believed that his model could remove the inefficiencies that characterised most organisations at the time, and it has become the prototype for many of today's large organisations (Robbins & Mukerji 1994: 42–3).

The different ideas which were used to develop scientific management and classical administrative theories came from a variety of sources which reflected the various backgrounds and experiences of these early researchers and thinkers. However, a number of common themes can be identified which characterise their work. These include the ideas that:

- there are general principles of management that are universally applicable;
- there should be unity of purpose in an organisation;
- management methods should be based on rational scientific principles; and
- the best form of organisation is bureaucratic, and management should be viewed as a profession regardless of the organisation or industry involved.

Behavioural approaches

Researchers and theorists belonging to the behavioural school recognised the complexity of human behaviour and became concerned with individual employee needs and motivation in the workplace. Their approach represented a rejection of the prescriptive supervisory procedures proposed by scholars of the classical school. Some of the main contributors to this school were Mary Parker Follett, Chester Barnard and Elton Mayo.

Mary Parker Follett (1868–1933) was one of the earliest writers to recognise that organisations could be considered from individual and group perspectives. She considered that an individual's talents and potential could be best utilised by groups working together. The manager needed to see him or herself as a member of the group along with the employees. The manager's role was to act as a harmoniser and coordinator of group efforts, rather than exercising a formal authority role.

Chester Barnard (1886–1961) was a management practitioner and President of the New Jersey Bell Telephone Company. In his text, *The Functions of the Executive*, he was the first to identify the importance of planned and intentional communication in organisations directed towards the achievement of strategic goals (Barnard 1938). In defining the functions of the executive, Barnard took a further conceptual step by linking communication to organisational structure, recognising the role of communication in shaping 'the form and internal economy of organisation' (1938: 90). He presented a theory of organisational structure that focused on the organisation as a communication system, proposing that: 'an organisation comes into being when (1) there are persons able to communicate with each other (2) who are willing to contribute action (3) to accomplish a common purpose' (1938: 82).

Elton Mayo (1880–1949) was an Australian-born academic who became involved in a series of studies at the Hawthorne Plant of the Western Electric Company near Chicago (Roethlisberger & Dickson 1939). The *Hawthorne studies* began in 1924 as a series of small-scale management experiments which concerned the relationship between the intensity of lighting in the workplace and productivity. As expected, productivity increased as illumination was increased. However, as brightness was decreased productivity also rose. Traditional scientific management theorists could not explain the results and Mayo was commissioned to investigate the matter further. Mayo and his co-researchers conducted an extensive series of studies extending over a six-year period. By the time the Hawthorne studies were concluded in 1933 it was recognised that employee attitudes and workplace relationships were more important determinants of workplace efficiency than more physical and scientific factors. The Hawthorne studies are discussed further in Chapter 10 as an example of reactive effects in experimental settings.

Human relations approaches

The human relations movement developed following the findings of the Hawthorne studies described above. Two important contributors to the human relations movement were Abraham Maslow and Douglas McGregor.

Abraham Maslow's (1908–1970) work was one of the earliest contributions to the field of human relations. He suggested that there is a range of human basic needs that must be met, and that organisations which rely solely on monetary rewards for employees may be ignoring important aspects of human behaviour. He proposed a hierarchy of needs, starting with physical and physiological needs, then safety and security needs, love and social needs, ego and status needs, and finally self-fulfilment needs. Lower level needs should be met before the fulfilment of higher level needs can act as an incentive for employees. Although Maslow was an academic theorist, his proposed hierarchy was an important factor in the increased attention that practising managers started to give to the work of academics.

Douglas McGregor (1906–1964) challenged traditional management thinking concerning the characteristics of employees, and his ideas provided the theoretical foundations for the human relations movement. He suggested that there are two opposing sets of assumptions that managers can make about their employees. One view, *Theory X*, takes a negative view of employees, assuming that they do not like working, need to be directed, avoid responsibility and have little ambition. Managers need to coerce and control these employees to achieve their organisational goals. The alternative view, *Theory Y*, assumes that work is a natural part of people's lives. People are internally motivated and will seek responsibility under favourable conditions. Under most organisational conditions, people have the capacity to be innovative and an employee's full potential is usually underutilised. McGregor proposed that Theory Y is the most appropriate and productive approach for managers to take. Like Maslow, McGregor's work was particularly influential among practising managers.

Modern approaches

Management thinking and research has continued to develop in recent times. Many of the issues that concern management scholars and researchers today are similar to those faced hundreds of years ago, however, improvements in information technologies and globalisation have raised new challenges and issues.

The *quantitative approach* to research is also known as *management science* or *operations research*. The quantitative approach grew out of mathematical modelling and statistical approaches that were first developed during the Second World War. The approach is used to improve the allocation of resources, work scheduling and management decision-making, and relies heavily on computer-based applications.

Systems theory considers an organisation as a system of interrelated and interdependent parts that function as a unit. Closed systems are seen to operate independently of their environment and these models closely reflect the perspectives adopted by the earlier scientific management scholars. Open systems are seen to interact with their external environment. The role of the manager from a systems perspective is to coordinate all the inputs and outputs within the system to achieve the organisation's goals.

The *contingency approach*, associated with Frederick Fiedler (1974), takes the view that organisations and management are complex entities and that no universal principles can be applied to their operation and conduct. The underlying philosophy of this approach is that optimal organisational outcomes depend on the context and situation in which a manager is operating—there are no universal rules for management.

One outcome of the increasing globalisation of business and management has been the development of theory based on *Japanese approaches* to management. Ouchi (1981) developed his theoretical model by examining the characteristics of typical American management approaches (Type A) and typical Japanese approaches (Type Z), and integrating the best features of both models. Type Z model organisations offer employees the prospect of long-term employment, collective decision-making, relatively slow evaluation and promotion, cross-functional career paths, individual responsibility, balanced implicit and explicit control measures, and a holistic concern for employees and their family members.

More recent approaches in management research have examined the role of the manager in the context of *organisational culture, organisational politics and power*. In this approach, the organisation is seen as comprising overlapping coalitions of groups and stakeholders competing with each other in a sometimes hostile organisational environment. The role of management involves managing the interface between these different coalitions. Bargaining, negotiating and conflict management are seen as important management skills from this perspective.

Management trends and 'fads'

One characteristic of contemporary management research is the rapid emergence and subsequent disappearance of management *fads*. There are normally organisational pressures on practising managers to provide speedy and profitable solutions to organisational problems. These pressures can arise from commercial imperatives such as the need for profits, from changes in the organisational environment, or from performance appraisal requirements. Regardless of the cause, the manager needs to be 'seen to be doing something'.

When the manager's need for action combines with the ability of private and public sector organisations to provide significant funds for management research, a common outcome is for applied research to be focused on particular areas or management 'fads' for intense periods. This phenomenon is usually accompanied by wide coverage in the business media and the emergence of numerous consultants promising significant benefits arising from the new practices.

The novice researcher planning a research project needs to be critically aware of these characteristics of management research. Although the theoretical underpinnings and goals of trendy research areas are often sound and worthwhile, the original research goals frequently become distorted, with disappointing results for participating organisations. Examples over the past decade have included concentrations on T-group training, business ethics, downsizing, business process re-engineering, quality circles, management by objectives, 360 degree feedback and total quality management (Dreilinger 1994; Daft 1994: 54; Waldman, Atwater & Antonioni 1998). Of course, this does not imply that these areas are not worthy concerns for well-planned future research.

The diversity of contemporary business research

Contemporary business research is a diverse activity because of the complex processes it seeks to explore. The field of inquiry crosses a range of disciplinary boundaries including psychology, sociology, communication, engineering, finance, computing, mathematics, economics and education. An indication of this diversity is provided in the range of research and professional interest groups of the Australian and New Zealand Academy of Management, as shown below.

Interest groups of the Australian and New Zealand Academy of Management:

- Accounting and finance
- Communication
- Economics
- Ethics
- Human resource management
- Industrial relations
- Innovations and technology
- International business/management
- Leadership
- Management education
- Marketing
- Management information systems
- Operations management
- Organisational behaviour
- Public sector management
- Qualitative methods/qualitative management
- Small business/entrepreneurship
- Strategy
- Women in management/gender issues

FIGURE 1.3

Dimensions of business research

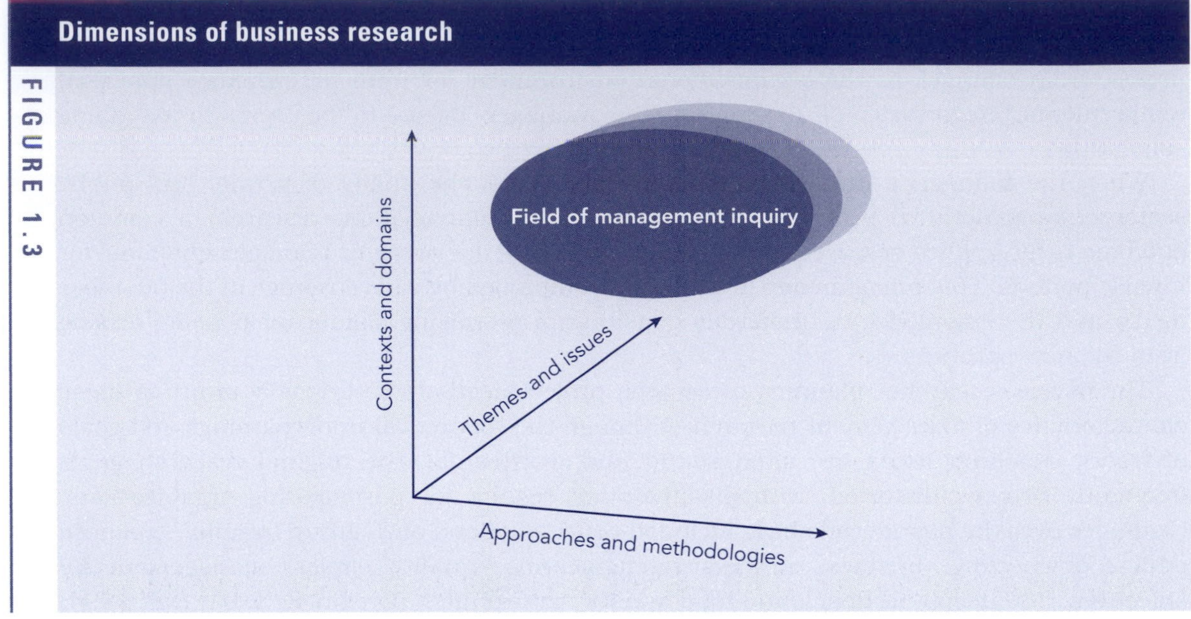

As indicated in Figure 1.3, contemporary business research can be described in terms of three dimensions, namely:

- the *context* or *domain* in which the research takes place;
- the *themes* or *issues* addressed by the research; and
- the research *approaches* or *methodologies* adopted in the project.

The *context* or *domain* dimension locates the environmental or organisational conditions of the research and where it is applied in practice; examples are listed below. Of course, the contexts are not exclusive, and business research may involve more than one domain or application. For example, a research project may be conducted in an industrial relations context within the public sector.

The *themes* or *issues* dimension describes the concerns, subject or purpose of the research; some examples are listed below. The themes may overlap, for example a research project may well concern issues of gender, ethics and power. We would expect these themes and issues to change with time as the concerns of business researchers and practitioners develop. This dimension also encompasses research concerned with *theory building* that may have no immediate practical application in terms of contexts or domains.

Contexts and domains:

- Human resources
- Economics, finance and accounting
- Social services (health, employment, etc.)
- Industrial relations
- Information technology
- International management
- Training and development
- Marketing
- Not-for-profit
- Operations/manufacturing
- Private sector
- Public sector
- Law

Themes and issues:

- Climate
- Communication
- Conflict
- Culture
- Entrepreneurship
- Environment
- Ethics
- Gender
- Leadership
- Learning organisations
- Managerial effectiveness
- Motivation
- Organisation development and change
- Organisational behaviour

The *approaches* or *methodologies* dimension is concerned with the broad range of overlapping approaches, or epistemologies, which may be used by a business researcher. Sometimes a study might use two or more approaches in one investigation. These issues are discussed in Chapter 2.

SUMMARY

This chapter has presented an overview of the what, who and why of business research that shows it to be a varied and complex process that crosses a number of disciplinary boundaries. The conduct of business research requires a combination of research skills, an understanding of current research and research methods, and an appreciation of the relevance of research outcomes to strategic and day-to-day management.

For managers, various kinds of business research can be seen as an integral part of the strategic management process. An understanding of business research methods is an essential tool in management practice, in policy development and in understanding research and consultancy reports.

The chapter outlined the history of business research, from its origins in pre-industrial periods. The field of business research overlaps a number of other areas, such as sociology, psychology, economics, education, engineering and communication, although the field has a number of features which make it distinctive. These include its *eclectic* character, the limited access to managers and organisations, and the expectation of action as a research outcome. Stakeholders in business research include academics, consultants, managers, students, and government and private organisations. The business research literature provides a broad body of knowledge that seeks to inform contemporary management practice.

EXERCISES

1
   a. Define business research.
   b. List five purposes of business research in an organisation with which you are familiar.
   c. Describe three management issues in your workplace or field of interest that would be suitable topics for business research.
2. Examine the *strategic plan* of an organisation with which you are familiar and indicate the points in the plan where research has been used or where it could be used.
3. Popular management books and business magazines frequently advocate new strategies

or solutions for more effective management, for example, *business process re-engineering, quality circles, management by objectives, total quality management, downsizing* and *benchmarking*. Review one such book or article and identify the research bases for the management outcomes that are claimed.

4 Find three research articles from the business research literature (refer to Chapter 4) and describe them in terms of:

a the domain or context of the research;

b the themes or issues addressed in the research;

c the research approach or methodology adopted by the researchers.

5 Review the contents of one or two issues of an academic management research journal (see Chapter 4) and critically evaluate the authors' claims about the usefulness of their research for practice.

FURTHER READING

The bibliography at the end of the book includes a number of research methods texts, some of a general social science nature and some applied to business. Each of these includes a general introduction and overview of research methods, generally in their opening chapters. The reader is encouraged to sample these texts for contrasting views or alternative presentations of the same basic message.

Relevant general texts: Bouma (1993); Burns (1994); Leedy (1993).

Business-specific texts: Cooper and Emory (1995); Davis and Cosenza (1993); Easterby-Smith, Thorpe and Lowe (1993); Gay and Diehl (1992); Ghauri, Gronhaug and Kristianslund (1995); Gill and Johnson (1997); Hussey and Hussey (1997); Kervin (1992); Metcalfe (1996); Punnett and Shenkar (1996); Saunders, Lewis and Thornhill (1996); Sekaran (1992); Smith and Dainty (1991); Veal (1997); Wass and Wells (1994); Zikmund (1991, 1997).

On consultancy: Garratt (1991).

CHAPTER 2

Approaches to research

In this chapter the research approaches and methodologies touched on briefly in Chapter 1 are explored in more detail. First some theoretical/philosophical, or 'paradigmatic', issues are discussed; this is followed by an examination of 'data issues' and an outline of the range of research methods available to the business researcher and the consideration of how to select an appropriate research method for a particular research task.

PARADIGMATIC ISSUES

A *paradigm* is a shared framework of assumptions held within a discipline, subdiscipline or school of thought within a discipline. It reflects a basic set of philosophical beliefs about the nature of the world, the scientific problems which it presents and the types of solutions which arise from research. It therefore provides guidelines and principles concerning the way research is conducted within the discipline. Thomas Kuhn (1962), in *The Structure of Scientific Revolutions*, noted how science, often with great difficulty, drops one dominant paradigm and adopts another—for example the displacement of Newtonian physics with Einstein's theory of relativity. The history of management research outlined in Chapter 1 suggests that comparable displacement processes have taken place in the field of management and management research. Indeed, Clarke and Clegg (2000) have recently suggested that significant paradigmatic 'shifts' were already taking place in management practice in developed economies at the close of the twentieth century.

In the social sciences, rival, and sometimes complementary, paradigms often coexist and these are reflected in competing or alternative approaches to research. Some of these dichotomies are discussed in turn below.

Paradigmatic issues

- Positivist and critical/interpretive approaches
- Quantitative and qualitative methods
- Induction and deduction
- Experimental and non-experimental approaches

Positivist and critical/interpretive research

Two of the central paradigms in social science research are known as the *positivist* and the *critical/interpretive* approaches. The *positivist* paradigm takes the view that the world is external and objective to the researcher—the position adopted in the natural sciences. Researchers are seen as independent of the research they are conducting and the approach focuses on objective description and explanation. Behaviour of individuals, groups or organisations under study is explained on the basis of the facts and observations, generally of a quantitative nature, gathered by the researcher, using theories and models developed in advance of the empirical part of the study. The positivist paradigm is also referred to as *scientific*, *empiricist*, *quantitative* or *deductive*, although these terms have their own specific meanings, as discussed in the rest of this chapter.

The contrasting position is known as the *critical* or *interpretive* paradigm. It rejects the idea that human behaviour can be studied in the same way as non-human phenomena and emphasises the view that the social world is socially constructed and subjective, and that the 'reality' which should be studied is the perceptions of the actors involved in a given social milieu, rather than a model of reality imposed by the researcher.

Researchers are seen to be part of the research process, rather than being independent of it. Critical researchers seek to uncover meanings and understandings of the broad interrelationships in the situation they are researching. This approach places more reliance on the people being studied to provide their own explanation of their situation or behaviour. The interpretive researcher therefore tries to 'get inside' the minds of his or her subjects and see the world from their point of view. This of course suggests a more flexible approach to data collection, usually involving qualitative methods and an inductive approach. The critical/interpretive position also has a range of alternative names that includes *hermeneutic, qualitative, phenomenological, interpretive, reflective, inductive, ethnographic* or *action research*. As with positivist approaches, these terms also have different shades of meaning depending on their use.

In the history of management research, as discussed in Chapter 1, the earlier schools of thought, such as scientific management and a number of the behavioural approaches, involved positivist research methods, while a number of the more recent modern approaches have adopted a critical/interpretive approach.

Despite their differences positivist and critical interpretive perspectives can sometimes coexist in the same study and complement one another. The characterisation of any one piece of research becomes a matter of degree, rather than a clear distinction. For example, a study comparing workers' incomes might involve the gathering and analysis of quantitative data on income and expenditure with conclusions which form part of a critical/interpretive analysis also drawing on data on workers' perceptions and feelings about money and work.

The important point to recognise is that both positions make significant assumptions concerning approaches to research that need to be carefully weighed before choosing a research methodology. Researchers are generally free to pick and choose the best techniques from either perspective for their own research use. In fact, it has been argued that researchers should try to mix research methods because the findings provide broader insights into the issues being investigated (Easterby-Smith, Thorpe & Lowe 1991: 31). Further discussion of this idea is presented below in relation to *triangulation*.

As indicated above, the positivist and critical/interpretive paradigms tend to be associated with other dichotomies, including quantitative and qualitative methods, induction and deduction, and experimental and non-experimental methods. These are discussed briefly below.

Quantitative and qualitative research

Much business research involves the collection, analysis and presentation of statistical information. Sometimes the information is innately quantitative—for instance the number of sick days taken by employees in a year, the level of sales of a particular product, or the average income of an occupational group. Sometimes the information is qualitative in nature but is presented in quantitative form—for example, numerical 'scores' calculated by asking clients to indicate levels of satisfaction with different services, where the scores might range from 1, indicating 'very satisfied', to 5, indicating 'very dissatisfied'.

The *quantitative* approach to research involves the gathering and analysis of numerical data. It relies on numerical evidence to draw conclusions or to test hypotheses. To be sure of the reliability of the results it is often necessary to study relatively large numbers of people or organisations—subjects—and therefore to use computers to analyse the data. Typically the aim is for the sample studied to be representative of some wider population, so that the results can be generalised to that wider population. The data might be derived from questionnaire-based surveys, from observation or from secondary sources, such as sales data.

The *qualitative* approach to research is not concerned with this sort of statistical analysis. It involves gathering a great deal of information about a relatively small number of subjects rather than a limited amount of information about a large number of subjects. The information collected is generally not presentable in numerical form and conclusions are not based on statistical analysis. While representative samples are possible in qualitative research, it is often the case that no claim is made for representativeness—the findings may be presented as case studies of a few individuals or organisations with no indication as to how typical or representative they might be. The approach is based on belief in the value of a full and rounded understanding of the experiences and situations of a few individuals.

The methods used to gather qualitative information include observation, informal, unstructured and in-depth interviewing, and participant observation. Research which studies groups of people using non-quantitative, anthropological approaches is often referred to as *ethnographic*. Qualitative methods are considered further in Chapters 7 and 15.

While there is a tendency for qualitative research approaches to involve the gathering of large amounts of 'rich' information from a few subjects, and for quantitative research approaches to involve the gathering of relatively small amounts of data from large numbers of subjects, it should be emphasised that this is only a *tendency*. It is possible, for example, for a *quantitative* research project to involve the collection of 500 items of data on only 20 people or for a *qualitative* research project to involve the collection of relatively little information on 200 people. The main difference between the two approaches lies in the nature of information collected and the way it is analysed.

Although there is a vigorous debate between proponents of qualitative and quantitative research methods, and some researchers are 'wedded' to just one approach, it is widely held that the two approaches complement one another and even that quantitative research should be based on initial, exploratory qualitative work. It can be argued that the two approaches are moving together, as computers are increasingly being used to analyse qualitative data, as indicated in Chapter 15.

Induction and deduction

As noted in Chapter 1, research can be descriptive or explanatory. Description and explanation can be seen as part of a circular model of research, as shown in Figure 2.1. This process can work in two ways: *inductively* or *deductively*. If the research process begins with *observation/description/data collection* at point A in Figure 2.1, and moves from there via point B (*analysis*) to point C (*explanation*), the process is described as *inductive*. The explanation is *induced* from the data—the data come first and the explanation comes later. If the process starts at point C in Figure 2.1, and moves to A and then to B, it is described as *deductive*—the process is based on prior logical reasoning: a possible explanation comes first and the data are collected later to confirm or negate the explanation.

In the case of deduction, the initial explanation is referred to as a *hypothesis*—a proposition suggesting how something might work or behave—a potential explanation that may be supported or negated by data, or possibly by more detailed or rigorous argument. A hypothesis can arise from informal observation and the experience of the researcher, or

Circular model of the research process (induction and deduction)

FIGURE 2.1

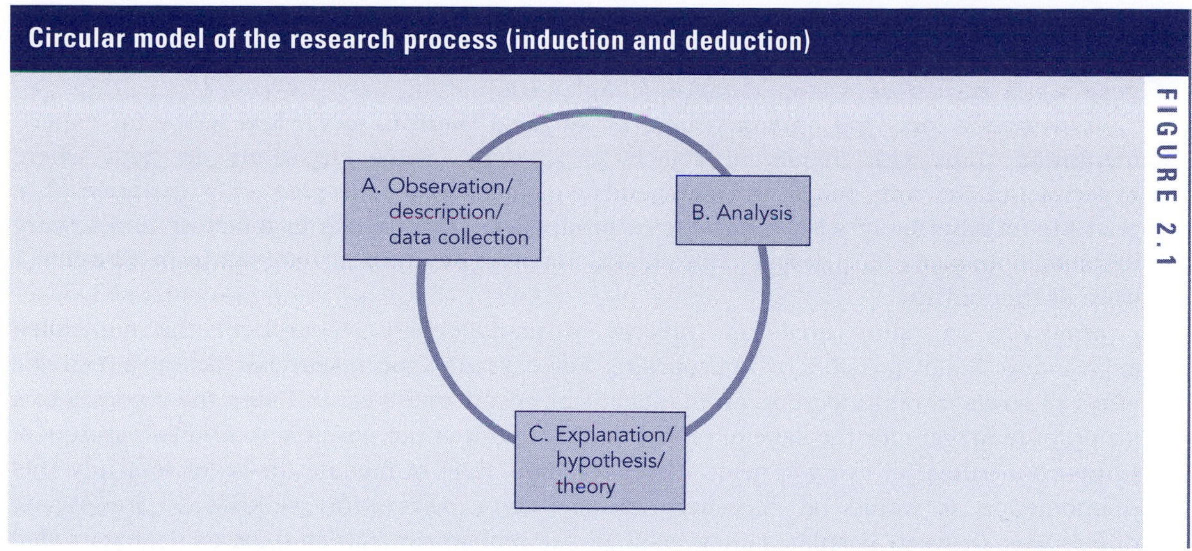

Based on Williamson *et al.* (1982: 7).

from examination of the literature. The deductive process is used to test the hypothesis against the data.

The term 'theory' is used when more elaborate hypotheses, or a number of interrelated hypotheses, are involved. A theory can be similar to a hypothesis, in that it can be propositional, or it may have been subjected to empirical validation.

In practice, data are rarely collected without *some* explanatory model in mind—otherwise how would we know what data to collect? Thus, there is always *some* element of deduction in any research. Conversely, it is not possible to develop hypotheses and theories without at least some initial information on the subject in hand, however informally or indirectly obtained, so there is always *some* element of induction. Thus, most research is partly inductive and partly deductive. In general terms, positivist researchers tend to place more emphasis on deduction than induction in their approach to research, while critical/ interpretive researchers tend to place more emphasis on induction.

Whether hypotheses or theories containing the explanation are put forward at the start of the project or emerge as a result of data analysis, they represent the key creative part of the research process. Data collection and analysis can be quite mechanical, but the *interpretation* of data and development of explanations requires at least creativity and, at times, inspiration.

A research project may involve a single circuit of the research model or a number of circuits, possibly in both directions.

Experimental and non-experimental research

Experimental research involves the researcher in attempting to control the environment of the subject of the research and in measuring the effects of controlled change. It is the approach traditionally associated with research in the physical, natural and biological/ medical sciences. Scientific knowledge progresses on the basis that any change in X in a *controlled* experiment must have been brought about by a change in Y, because everything except X and Y was held constant. The researcher therefore aims to produce controlled conditions so that the research will fulfil the requirements for *causality*. Experimental research is discussed in more detail in Chapter 10.

In research involving human beings as subjects there is much less scope for experimentation than with inanimate objects or animals. Some situations do exist where experimentation with people in management contexts can take place. For instance, it is possible to experiment with variations in production line settings in a factory and to vary working hours or office design. The classic 'Hawthorne studies' referred to in Chapter 1 were of this nature.

However, in many areas of interest to management researchers the controlled experiment is not possible or appropriate. For example, the researcher interested in the effect of levels of remuneration on management effectiveness cannot vary the incomes of a group of managers for the sake of research. Further, it is not possible to find two groups of humans identical in every respect except for their level of income. In order to study this phenomenon it would be necessary to use *non-experimental* methods to investigate differences between people as they exist in the real world, rather than in the controlled world of the experiment.

Thus to study the effects of income on management effectiveness it would be necessary to gather information on the management behaviour patterns of a number of managers with different levels of income. But people differ in all sorts of ways, some of which may be related to their level of income and some not. For example, two people with identical income levels can differ markedly in terms of their personalities, family situation, physical health, and so on. In comparing the behaviour of two groups of people, it would be difficult to be sure which differences arose as a result of income differences and which resulted from these other differences. The results of such non-experimental research are therefore likely to be less precise than the results from a controlled experiment.

Paradigmatic awareness

While business research in the past was largely positivistic and deductive, interpretive and inductive research has now become more common—particularly in the academic realm. Experimental research has always been, and remains, comparatively rare in business. The purpose in raising these abstract issues is to encourage the reader to be aware of, and to have a broad understanding of, the variety of approaches to business research and to be conscious of this diversity when reading, commissioning or conducting research. Key features of the paradigmatic issues discussed above are summarised in Figure 2.2.

DATA ISSUES

Primary and secondary data

In planning research it is necessary to decide whether to collect new information or whether existing data are suitable to answer the research questions. New information collected as part of a research project is referred to as *primary* data. Existing data that has been collected by someone else for some other purpose are called *secondary* data. Large quantities of information are collected and stored by companies, as well as government and other organisations, as routine functions of management or policy monitoring, including sales figures and population numbers, income and expenditure, staffing levels, accident

FIGURE 2.2

Paradigmatic and data issues: key features

Paradigmatic issues		
Positivist—Critical/interpretive	Positivist: —Researcher seeks objectivity/detachment —World to be researched is 'external' —Deductive, quantitative methods common—similar to natural science model	Critical/interpretive: —Researcher accepts subjectivity —Researcher engages with research subject —Inductive, qualitative methods common
Quantitative—Qualitative	Quantitative: —Involves numerical data —Often involves large numbers of cases —Seeks to generalise to whole population	Qualitative: —Generally does not involve numerical data —Generally involves small number of cases —Findings typically not generalisable
Induction—Deduction	Deduction: —Begins with hypothesis/theory and gathers data to test the hypothesis/theory	Induction: —Interrogates data to discover meanings/theoretical propositions
Experimental—Non-experimental	Experimental: —Research conducted in an environment (e.g. laboratory) in which the researcher has control over a limited number of variables	Non-experimental: —Research conducted in a 'real world' environment where the researcher has no control over variables
Data issues		
Primary—Secondary	Primary: —Data collected for the purposes of the research in hand—researcher is primary user	Secondary: —Data already collected by other researchers for other projects or for non-research (e.g. administrative) purposes—researcher is secondary user
Self-reported—Observed	Observed: —Research is based on observation of subjects' behaviour	Self-reported: —Research based on information provided by subjects—e.g. in an interview

reports, crime reports and health data. An important part of any research project is to search existing sources of information in order to avoid replication of possibly expensive and time-consuming data collection.

Secondary data need not be quantitative. Historians, for example, use diaries, official documents or newspaper reports as sources. In policy research, documents such as company reports or minutes of meetings of organisations can be seen as secondary data.

Even if a research project is to be based mainly on primary data, it is invariably also necessary to make use of existing information, such as government statistics, annual reports or stock exchange data. Sources of secondary data are discussed in Chapter 5 and their analysis in Chapter 12.

Self-reported and observed data

Sometimes the only sources of information about people's behaviour and attitudes are their own reports about themselves. Much management research involves asking people about their past, recent and possibly future behaviour, and current attitudes and aspirations. The information that is provided is called *self-reported* data and is usually gathered by means of interviews or surveys.

While such an approach clearly has merits and may be the only method available for collecting some types of data, it has some disadvantages. The researcher can never be sure how honest or accurate people are in responding to questions. In some cases people may, deliberately or unwittingly, distort or 'bend' the truth—for example, in understating the amount of alcohol they drink or overstating the number of hours they work. In other instances there may be problems with recall—for example, in remembering just how much money they have spent on a particular product over the last year.

The alternative to relying on people to provide the researcher with information about themselves is to *observe* their behaviour. To find out how employees interact in an office facility area it would probably be better to observe them than to try to ask them about it. Patterns of movement and usage can be observed. Sometimes people leave behind evidence of their behaviour—for example, the most used section of an office will be the area where the carpet is most worn and the terminals most used on a network will have the highest log-on hours. These data collection methods are referred to as *observational* or *unobtrusive* methods and are discussed in more detail in Chapter 6.

Other alternatives to self-reported data are some of the secondary data sources discussed above. In the financial and economic area, financial transactions—for example in the stock market or in retail—are a form of evidence of people's past behaviour. Data items of this sort are often referred to as 'observations' in research. Economists refer to people's actual patterns of expenditure as 'revealed preference'.

A summary of the key features of the data issues discussed here is presented in Figure 2.2.

THE RANGE OF RESEARCH APPROACHES

Introduction: horses for courses

This section discusses the broad range of available research methods and criteria for their use as an introduction to the more detailed presentation on individual methods presented in later chapters.

The use of methods that are appropriate to the research issues being addressed is vital for successful research. The principle espoused here is that every research approach has its place; the important thing is for the researcher to be aware of the limitations of any particular approach, to use appropriate criteria to select research methods, and not to make claims that cannot be justified for the methods used.

There is a tendency in the research literature for commentators to defend the methods in which they themselves are skilled. It is rare to find a researcher who is experienced in the full range of techniques discussed in this book. It is hoped that the new generation of researchers in management and related fields will be competent in a wide range of skills and will therefore adopt a balanced and non-partisan approach to their use.

In this book a *horses for courses* philosophy is adopted—research approaches are not considered to be intrinsically good or bad, but are considered to be *appropriate* or *inappropriate* for the task in hand. Further, it is maintained that it is not a question of good or bad methods that should be considered, but of good or bad *use* of methods. The range of approaches to be discussed is listed below and discussed briefly in turn. They are divided into 'major' approaches or methods and 'cross-cutting or subsidiary' techniques. The latter are techniques which generally use one or more of the major approaches in particular ways or particular contexts. Some of what follows revisits issues discussed above, but here particular approaches are presented in their own right, rather than as a counterpoint to a contrasting approach. The major approaches are examined in more detail in subsequent chapters.

Range of research approaches:

- Scholarship
- 'Just thinking'
- Using the existing literature
- Using secondary data
- Observation
- Qualitative methods
- Questionnaire-based surveys
- The case study method
- Experimental methods
- Cross-cutting/subsidiary techniques:
  - Textual analysis
  - Longitudinal studies
  - Panel surveys
  - Projective techniques
  - The use of scales
  - Meta-analysis
  - Action research
  - Historical research
  - Media-sponsored surveys
  - Delphi technique

Scholarship

Although the dividing line between *scholarship* and research can be difficult to draw, it is useful to consider the differences between the two. Scholarship involves being well-informed about a subject and also thinking critically and creatively about a field and the accumulated knowledge about it. Scholarship therefore involves knowing the literature and being able to synthesise, analyse and critically appraise it. Scholarship is traditionally practised in the role of teacher, but when the results of scholarship are published they effectively become a contribution to research, which involves the generation of *new* knowledge. Traditionally this has been thought of as involving the gathering and presentation of new data, but clearly this is not a necessary condition for something to be considered 'research'. Examination of academic journals in business will reveal that many contributions to the literature do not involve presentation or analysis of what is conventionally seen as 'data'. New insights, critical or innovative ways of looking at old issues, or the identification of new issues or questions, are also contributions to knowledge. Indeed, the development of a new framework or paradigm for looking at a field can be far more significant than a minor piece of empirical work using an old, outmoded paradigm. Recognising therefore that research does not have to be empirical, the first method discussed below is *'just thinking'*.

'Just thinking'

There is no substitute for thinking. It is possible for creative and informed thinking about a topic to be the only process involved in the development and presentation of a piece of research, but it is more usual also to involve consideration of the literature, as discussed below.

When data collection is involved, the difference between an acceptable piece of research and an exceptional or significant piece of research is usually the quality of the creative thought that has gone into it. The researcher needs to be creative in identifying and posing the initial questions or issues for investigation, creative in conceptualising the research and developing a research strategy, creative in analysing data and creative in interpreting and presenting findings. Texts on research methods, such as this text, can provide a guide to mechanical processes, but creative thought must come from within the individual researcher—in the same way that the basics of drawing can be taught but *art* comes from within the individual artist.

Using the literature

There is virtually no research that can be done which would not benefit from some reference to the existing literature. For most research, such reference is essential. In fact, it is possible for a research project to consist entirely of a review of the literature. In broad and diverse areas of study such as management, there is a great need for the consolidation of existing knowledge through thorough literature reviews.

A review of the literature often plays a key role in the formulation of research projects—it indicates the state of knowledge on a topic and is a source or stimulator of ideas, both substantive and methodological.

A review of the literature can be important, even when it uncovers no literature on the topic of interest. To establish that *no* research has been conducted on a particular topic, especially when the topic is considered to be of some importance to the field, can be a research finding of some significance in its own right. The literature review process is discussed in detail in Chapter 4.

Using secondary data

If information is already available to answer the research questions posed, then it is wasteful to collect new information for the purpose. As discussed earlier in the chapter, large quantities of secondary data area are available—awareness of the existence of such data and the ability to access and analyse them when appropriate is a key research capability. Even when secondary data are not ideal for the research at hand, they can often provide answers to some questions more quickly and at less cost than new data.

In some cases data are collected for research purposes but not fully analysed, or analysed only in one particular way for a particular purpose, or not even analysed at all. Secondary analysis of under-exploited research data is therefore a potentially fruitful, but widely neglected, activity. Types of secondary data are discussed further in Chapter 5 and their analysis in Chapter 12.

Observation

Observation has the advantage of being unobtrusive—indeed, as indicated above, the techniques involved are sometimes referred to as *unobtrusive* techniques (Kellehear 1993). Unobtrusive techniques involve gathering information about people's behaviour without their knowledge. While this may raise ethical questions (see Chapter 2), it clearly has advantages over techniques where the subjects are aware of the researcher's presence and may therefore modify their behaviour, or where reliance must be placed on subjects' own recall and description of their behaviour, which can be inaccurate or distorted.

For example, observation may be the only possible technique to use when researching an illicit activity that people may be reluctant to talk about, or when researching the situation where employees find a manager's communication style threatening and the manager is unaware of those perceptions.

Observation is capable of presenting a perspective on a situation that is not apparent to the individuals involved. For example, the users of a crowded part of an office space or a retail area may not be aware of the way their patterns of movement interact with the design of the space to produce congestion. Taylor's (1911) historic time and motion study of work practices could only have been achieved through observation of people at work. Observation is therefore an appropriate technique to use when knowledge of the presence of the researcher is likely to lead to unacceptable modification of subjects' behaviour and when mass patterns of behaviour not apparent to individual subjects are of interest. Observation methods are discussed further in Chapter 6.

Qualitative methods

Qualitative approaches are used when the researcher accepts that the concepts, terms and critical issues should be defined by the subjects of the research and not by the researcher; they are often used for the study of groups, particularly where interaction between group members is of interest. They are also used when exploratory theory building, rather than theory testing, is undertaken. Qualitative techniques are also useful when the focus of research is on people's attitudes and the meanings they attribute to people and events, although these can also be studied quantitatively. Qualitative techniques are not appropriate when the aim of the research is to make general statements about large populations.

Five approaches to qualitative research are examined further in Chapter 7, namely:

- *informal and in-depth interviews*, which usually involve relatively small numbers of individuals being interviewed at length, possibly on more than one occasion;
- *group interviews or focus groups* that apply the informal in-depth interview approach to groups of people rather than separate individuals;
- *participant observation* that involves the researcher being a participant in the phenomenon being studied and making observations based on his or her own experiences;
- *ethnography*, which utilises a number of the above techniques, rather than being a single technique—borrowed from anthropology;
- *biographical research*, which focuses on individual full or partial life histories and may involve in-depth interviews but also documentary evidence and subjects' own written accounts.

It should be noted that here the term 'informal' or 'in-depth interview' is used deliberately to describe qualitative research involving lengthy interviews. In some texts the term 'interview' is used alone, particularly in the context of 'interviews' versus 'questionnaires'. This can be confusing since many questionnaire surveys involve an interview; it is only when questionnaires are completed by the respondent, for example in a mail or hand-out survey, that no interview is involved.

Chapter 15 examines techniques used in analysing qualitative data.

Questionnaire-based surveys

Questionnaire-based surveys are the most commonly used approach in management research. They come in a variety of forms and are discussed in detail in Chapter 8. This diversity is partly because the basic concepts are relatively easily understood and mastered, but also because much management research calls for general quantified outcomes. For example, governments need to know how many people engage in training, managers want to know how many people are dissatisfied with a service, and marketers need to know how many people are in a particular market segment. These research needs arise from practical management or policy requirements in the public and private sectors.

Questionnaire-based surveys require researchers to be very specific about their data requirements early in their research. Questions omitted from a questionnaire inevitably mean that this data can never be easily retrieved because of the costs involved. In contrast, qualitative researchers may begin data collection in a tentative way, can return to subjects for additional information, and can gradually build their data, research concepts and explanation.

A further feature of questionnaire-based surveys is that they depend on respondents' own accounts of their behaviour, attitudes or intentions. In some situations this can raise questions about the validity of the approach, since accuracy and honesty of responses may be called into question. Examples include exaggeration in relation to activities that are socially approved (such as frequency of consultation with staff, level of income) and understatement of activities that are disapproved of (such as days of sick leave, alcohol consumption).

Consequently, questionnaire-based surveys should only be used when quantified information is required concerning a specific population and when individuals' own accounts of their behaviour and attitudes are acceptable as a source of information.

The design and conduct of questionnaire-based surveys is discussed in Chapter 8 and their analysis in Chapter 13.

Case studies

A *case study* involves the study of a single example—a case—of the phenomenon being researched. The aim is to seek to understand the phenomenon by studying single examples. A case might consist of a single individual, a community, a country, an organisation, a place, an event or a project. Often a research project using the case study method will involve a number of contrasting cases, but each is separately identified and studied in a similar manner. Case studies can range from small-scale vignettes to major projects in their own right. The case study as research method can encompass any or all of the data collection approaches discussed in this text and is examined further in Chapter 9.

Experimental methods

While experimental methods are usually associated with natural science and laboratories, it is possible for some experiments to be conducted in the social world. The essence of the experiment is that the researcher ideally controls all the relevant variables in the experiment. Selected variables are manipulated while others are held constant and the effects on 'subjects' are then measured. In social settings the researcher does not have the same level of control that is available in a scientific laboratory. Nevertheless, in some areas, such as psychology and product testing, experimental approaches can be used. Experiments in management research are rarely as precise as scientific experiments, because people are involved—they are in effect *management* experiments. For example, an employer might experiment with an incentive bonus scheme or a different physical layout of the workplace. To qualify as an experiment the measure should be reversible so that if it is not effective it can be changed back to the way it was. If this is not possible, the experiment is simply a change in management practice, the performance of which should be monitored in the normal way using evaluative research. The research tools available to the researcher in experimental research are the same as for non-experimental approaches—observation, use of secondary data, and questionnaire surveys—and the overall approach is evaluative. Experimental research is discussed further in Chapter 10.

Cross-cutting and subsidiary techniques

The methods and techniques discussed below are variations on some of the major approaches discussed above, or specialist techniques which cut across some of the above approaches. They are not followed up in detail in the rest of the book, but an indication is given as to which chapters are relevant and additional information can be found in the Further Reading section.

Textual analysis

In some fields of inquiry the focus of research is *textual*—for example, the content of annual reports, politicians' speeches or operation manuals. The analysis and interpretation of the content of published or unpublished texts is referred to as *content analysis* (generally when the analysis is quantitative) or *hermeneutics* (generally when the analysis is of a more qualitative nature). The technique has not traditionally been widely used in management studies, but with the deepening interest in organisational culture and climate and the widening of the scope of *text* to include a wide variety of *cultural products* such as company documents, advertising material, websites and letters, the approach is attracting increasing attention. Further reference to this approach is made in Chapter 7.

Longitudinal studies

Longitudinal studies involve a sample of individuals or organisations being studied periodically over a number of years. Such studies are of course expensive because of the need to keep track of the sample members over the years and the need to have a large enough sample at the beginning to allow for the inevitable attrition of the sample over time. Longitudinal studies are, however, ideal for studying organisational change and the combined effects of social change, age and experience. Longitudinal studies are not common in the general business field but are common in areas such as health and education, as the listing by the UK Longitudinal Studies Centre (ULSC 2004) indicates. While some medically-based longitudinal studies involve such procedures as physical health tests, typically they involve periodic questionnaire surveys. Longitudinal studies are therefore not explicitly discussed further in this book, but the chapters on questionnaire surveys and sampling are relevant. Further information sources are given in the guide to further reading.

Panel surveys

A type of research which is similar to longitudinal research is the panel study. In this type of study, a 'panel' of respondents is subject to questioning on a periodic basis, for example once a month, but any one individual's membership of the panel will be of fixed duration—say one year. The panel membership is 'refreshed' periodically, with those whose term has been completed dropping off and new members being added, in such a way as to maintain the representativeness of the panel as a whole, in terms of such factors as age, gender and geographic distribution. This type of technique is common among market research firms which conduct 'omnibus' surveys on a continuous basis. Typically, panel members are remunerated in cash or kind. The most well-known use of panels is in audience research for television; since the research involves the cost of installing hardware to monitor a household's viewing habits, it makes sense for households to remain members of a panel for a reasonable period of time. As with longitudinal studies, since they are basically a form of questionnaire survey, panel studies are not explicitly discussed further in this book, but further information sources are given in the guide to further reading.

Projective techniques

Projective techniques are extensively used in psychological research and might be termed 'what if?' techniques, in that they involve subjects responding to hypothetical—projected—situations. For example, subjects might be asked to indicate how they would spend a particular sum of development money if given a free choice, or how they would utilise additional staff if they were made available, or they might be invited to respond to photographs depicting particular business situations. While this technique can become elaborate and specialised, in this text it is considered as an extension of questionnaire-based surveys and focus group interviews.

Use of scales

Scales are numerical indexes used to measure constructs or variables which are generally not intrinsically quantitative. Typically, subjects are asked to respond to questions using rating scales (as discussed in Chapter 8) and the scores are combined to produce a scale or index of the phenomenon of interest. Case Study Example 2.1 describes an investigation which used three such scales: one related to self-esteem, one to job satisfaction and one to family environment.

The use of such scales is widespread, particularly in psychology and related disciplines; thus Bruner and Hensel (1992) list no less than 588 scales used in marketing research. The advantage of the use of published scales means that researchers are not continually 'reinventing the wheel' by devising their own measure of a particular phenomenon. Widely used scales have generally been subject to considerable testing to ensure validity—that is that they measure what they are intended to measure. Further, the use of common measures facilitates comparability between studies. The disadvantage is, of course, that any fault in the scale validity may be replicated across many studies and a fixed scale may not fully reflect different socio-economic environments or change over time.

Meta-analysis

One approach to research combines the feature of a literature review and secondary data analysis and involves a quantitative appraisal of the findings of a number of projects on the

CASE STUDY EXAMPLE 2.1

Scales/mail survey: family men—job satisfaction and self-esteem

Source: Ada L. Sinacore and F. Özge Akçali 2000, Men and families: job satisfaction and self-esteem. *Journal of Career Development*, 27(1), 1–13.
Methods/approaches: Use of scales, mail survey, regression
Topic: Family environment, job satisfaction and self-esteem

This study seeks to assess the effect of family environment on men's job satisfaction and self-esteem, based on a mail survey sent to a 'convenience' sample of fathers recruited through advertisements in community organisations and churches, and 'posted around' in a US midwest suburban area. Of 120 men who responded and were sent a questionnaire, 72 (60 per cent) returned completed questionnaires. The sample was therefore small and doubly 'self-selecting', limitations which the authors recognise, so the study can be considered a pilot, indicative, study rather than a representative one. Of particular interest is the use of three pre-existing scales:

- The *Job Descriptive Index* (JDI) (Smith, Kendall & Hulin 1975), based on scores relating to six job components (1. Work, 2. Pay, 3. Promotion opportunities, 4. Supervision, 5. Fellow workers, 6. Job in general), was used to measure job satisfaction.
- The *Four Component Self-Esteem Scale* (FCSS) (Hampilos 1988) was based on respondents' assessment of: 1. Inner (own opinion) worth; 2. Inner competence; 3. External (assessment of opinions held by others) worth; 4. External competence.
- The *Family Environment Scale, The Real Form* (FES, Form R) (Moos & Moos 1974) measures the 'socio-environmental characteristics' of families on the basis of 10 sub-scales: 1. Cohesion; 2 . Expressiveness; 3. Conflict; 4. Independence; 5. Achievement orientation; 6. Intellectual-Cultural orientation; 7. Active recreational orientation; 8. Moral-Religious reasoning; 9. Organisation; 10. Control.

Regression analyses were performed between the three scales and their components, but few significant relationships were found. It is concluded that, while family involvement is generally accepted as being 'highly beneficial in contributing towards men's psychological wellbeing', the men in this study were 'failing to reap these benefits'.

same topic. The technique, known as *meta-analysis* (Glass, McGaw & Smith 1981), is suitable for the sort of research where findings are directly comparable from one study to another—for example, where the key findings are expressed in terms of correlation and regression coefficients between particular variables (see Chapter 14). In a meta-analysis, the reported findings of a large number of individual research projects in the same area provide the basis for further exploration and analysis of the area. Typically, because many studies are involved and must be compared on a common basis, only relatively simple relationships can be examined. Figure 2.3 indicates the topics of a sample of recent studies using meta-analysis.

FIGURE 2.3

Meta-analysis: recent examples

Reference	Study/variables compared	No. of studies reviewed
Brewer and Shapard 2004	Employee burnout and age/years of experience	**
Daniel *et al.* 2004	Slack resources and firms' financial performance	66
Garcia-Quevedo 2004	Public funding of R&D and private spending on R&D	39
Hosoda, Stone-Romero & Coats 2003	Effects of physical attractiveness on job-related outcomes	27
Judge, Colbert & Illies 2004	Intelligence and leadership qualities	96
Robbins *et al.* 2004	Psychosocial/study skills and students' college outcomes	109

Action research

The common image of research is as a detached, 'clinical' process reporting objectively on what is discovered. When a researcher is personally committed to the topic under investigation, whether that be self-interest-related, such as the fortunes of a company, or a social cause, like saving the environment, efforts are still generally made to abide by the rules of science, for ethical reasons or because of the general belief that 'good research' is more effective research. Some types of research can, however, be deliberately designed to involve the researcher in the topic and to be part of the process of bringing about change—such research is termed 'action research'. This type of research is unusual in the business context but there are contexts where it is conceivable. Thus, for example, research on questionable labour or marketing practices by Western companies in Third World countries can often be seen as 'action research'—the research is part of the process of seeking to bring about change, not only by using the research findings to influence the companies but also even to the extent of the research act itself encouraging resistance by Third World workers or consumers. McDonagh and Coghlan (2001) report on a case study of a consultant being brought into a large company to solve the problem of lack of communication and trust between senior management and technical IT staff over the development of IT infrastructure for the firm. They report on a slow and painstaking process of the researchers gathering information on the views and needs of the two groups and building their trust so that information could begin to flow and a suitable model for IT infrastructure could be developed. The researcher was not a disinterested observer but someone committed to the achievement of change on behalf of the company.

Historical research

History is a major discipline with its own approaches to research. Historical research arises in the business research environment in at least two contexts: biographical research, discussed as a qualitative approach in Chapter 7, and in case study research, discussed in Chapter 9. It can also be seen as a form of secondary data analysis, since historians are invariably dependent on documents contemporary to a period, which were compiled for purposes other than historical research. Historical methods are not pursued in this book, but some sources are indicated in the Further Reading section.

Media-sponsored surveys

Newspapers, magazines and radio and television stations often run opinion-poll-style surveys among their readers, listeners and viewers. At the local level the public's views on an issue may be canvassed by the inclusion of a form in a newspaper, which readers may fill in and return. Radio and television stations often run 'phone-in' polls on topical issues. The results of these exercises have entertainment value, but should not generally be taken seriously. This is mainly because there is no way of knowing whether either the original population (the readers/listeners/viewers who happen to read, hear or view the item) or the self-selected sample of respondents are representative of the population as a whole. In most cases they are decidedly unrepresentative, in that only those with pronounced views, one way or the other, are likely to become involved in the process.

However, not all surveys reported in the media are of this nature. A number of newspapers and broadcasting organisations sponsor regular political opinion polls and business surveys conducted by reputable market research organisations and these are generally reliable.

Delphi technique

The Delphi technique, named after the classical Greek 'Delphic oracle', is a procedure involving the gathering and analysing of information from a panel of experts on future trends in a particular field of interest (Linstone 1978). The experts in the field (for example, human resource management) complete a questionnaire indicating their views on the likelihood of certain developments taking place in the future. These views are then collated and circulated to panel members for further comment, a process that might be repeated a number of times before the final results are collated. The technique is used in some areas of business and technological forecasting, and has been used to a limited extent in management. In this book, the technique is not examined explicitly, but the basic data collection method used is the mail questionnaire survey, which is covered in Chapters 8 and 13. Examples of the use of the Delphi technique are given in the Further Reading section.

MULTIPLE METHODS: TRIANGULATION

Triangulation gets its name from the land surveying method of fixing the position of an object by measuring it from two different positions. In research, the triangulation method involves the use of more than one research approach in a single study to gain a broader or more complete understanding of the issues being investigated. The methods used are often complementary in that the weaknesses of one approach are complemented by the strengths of another. Triangulation often utilises both qualitative and quantitative approaches in the same study. Duffy (1987: 131) has identified four different ways that triangulation can be used in research, namely: analysing data in more than one way; using more than one sampling strategy; using different interviewers, observers and analysts in the one study; and using more than one methodology to gather data.

If triangulation methods are to be used in a study the approaches taken will depend on the imagination and the experience of the researcher. However, it is important that the research question is clearly focused and not confused by the methodology adopted, and that the methods are chosen in accordance with their relevance to the topic. In particular, the *rationale* for using triangulation should be outlined, that is, the possible weaknesses of one method and the ways in which the additional method might overcome such a weakness might be explained. This is clearly relevant to the issue of validity and reliability discussed in later chapters.

Often 'triangulation' is claimed in a study because more than one data source and/or analytical method is used to address different aspects of the research question, or even different research questions. It is when the different data/methods address the *same* question that true triangulation can be said to have occurred. Consequently, a research report on a project where triangulation is claimed should compare and contrast the findings from the multiple methods. Whether the multiple methods produce similar or different findings should then be an issue for discussion.

CHOOSING A METHOD

The process of choosing appropriate research methods for a research task is part of the whole process of planning and designing a research project, as discussed in Chapter 3. Here a number of considerations are discussed, which should be borne in mind.

Considerations in selecting a research method:

- The research question or hypothesis
- Previous research
- Data availability/access
- Resources
- Time
- Validity, reliability and generalisability
- Ethics
- Uses/users of the findings

The research question or hypothesis

Much of the decision on how to research a topic is bound up in the basic research question or hypothesis. As discussed in Chapter 3, the 'research question' can take a variety of forms, but generally it will point the researcher in the direction of certain data sources—for example in relation to employees, customers or organisations. Certain types of data also suggest certain types of analysis. There are no hard and fast rules in this area, but real examples illustrate the process at work, as shown in Figure 2.4, which summarises information from the various Case Study Examples presented in the text.

Previous research

If the proposed research is closely keyed into the literature and previous research, then the methods used in that research are likely to influence the choice of methods. The aim may be to replicate the methodology in previous studies to achieve comparability, to improve on the methods used, or to deliberately adopt a contrasting methodology.

Data availability/access

In some cases an obvious existing data source presents itself, and may even have prompted the research in the first place. For example, a set of archives of an organisation can provide the basis for historical research. Published but superficially analysed official data can be

FIGURE 2.4

Research questions and methods

Case Study Example No.	Research question (paraphrased)	Main data required	Data source	Methods/ approaches used	Quantitative/ qualitative
1.1	How does research relate to the management process in product development?	Knowledge of a firm's product development process and research activity	Hypothetical	Descriptive	—
2.1	What is the effect of family environment on men's job satisfaction and self-esteem?	Data on men's: a. family environment b. job satisfaction c. self-esteem	a. Job Descriptive Index (JDI) b. Four Component Self-Esteem Scale (FCSS) c. Family Environment Scale (FES)	Mail survey; scales	Quantitative regression
3.1	How do potential online customers view the purchase experience?	Data on online purchasers' assessment of various aspects of the online provider and purchase experience	Student survey	Respondent-completed questionnaire; captive group	Quantitative, regression
4.1	What are the key issues in entrepreneurial ethics?	Research on entrepreneurial ethics	Published literature	Literature review	Qualitative
5.1	What is the relationship between employee turnover and a firm's performance?	Employee turnover rates Firm's performance levels	Staffing records Financial records	Secondary data analysis	Quantitative (multiple regression)
7.1	Can one company accommodate two apparently contradictory cultures/ discourses?	Company cultures/discourses	Staff of one company	Case study; interviews	Qualitative
7.2	To what extent do cultural cues in advertising/websites reflect or contradict dominant national cultural values?	Advertising in different markets Cultural values of markets	Company websites	Textual/content analysis	Quantitative (Chi square ANOVA)
9.1	Do Nike's management practices towards women reflect their advertising rhetoric?	Data on management practices Data on advertising rhetoric	Historical Print and TV ads	Historical method Textual/content analysis	Qualitative
9.2	What explains the Hong Kong manufacturing sector's contribution to GDP over the period 1983–99?	Data on the HK manufacturing sector's value added, investment, capital stock and labour	Official government data	Case study	Quantitative, multiple regression
9.3	What is the relationship between successful leadership style and a company's life cycle stage?	Data on leadership style and stage in the company life cycle.	Biographies and media reports	Biographical Case study	Qualitative
10.1	To what extent does packaging shape/size influence consumer behaviour?	Consumer behaviour when faced with varying packaging shapes/sizes	Subjects attending residential camps Subjects at workplace	Experimental	Quantitative

analysed in depth. Access to a sample of people, such as the workforce or customer-base of a company, can be seen as an opportunity too good to miss. In other cases lack of access shapes the research—for example, ethical or practical issues may preclude some research on children, so data may have to be gathered from parents.

Resources

Clearly the resources of staff and money will have a major effect on the type and scale of the research to be conducted.

Time

Time is also often a limitation. Research using the current year's sales data must be completed quickly if it is to be used to influence next year's marketing strategy.

Validity, reliability and generalisability

Validity is the extent to which the data collected truly reflect the phenomenon being studied. Business research faces difficulties in this area, especially in the measurement of attitudes and behaviour, as there are always doubts about the true meanings of responses made in surveys, interviews and self-reported accounts of behaviour. The concept of validity is discussed further in Chapter 6.

Reliability is the extent to which research findings would be the same if the research were to be repeated at a later date or with a different sample of subjects. Caution should be exercised when making general statements on the basis of just one study.

Generalisability refers to the probability that the results of the research findings apply to other subjects, other groups and other conditions. While measures can be taken to ensure a degree of generalisability, strictly speaking, any research findings relate only to the subjects involved, at the time and place the research was carried out.

Ethics

Ethical issues also limit choices of research method. Reference has already been made to ethical issues surrounding research on children; further examples of ethical issues in business research are discussed in Chapter 3.

Uses/users of the findings

The uses and users of the research are often taken for granted, but they are an important factor in shaping research. If substantial investment will depend on the results of the research then a more extensive and thorough-going project will be required than if the research is to be used only to generate ideas. When life and death issues are at stake—for example in medical research on the effects of a treatment for a disease—much more precision is needed in the results than if, for example, a company merely wishes to know the socioeconomic characteristics of its customers.

SUMMARY

This chapter has examined some generic theoretical and taxonomic issues concerning social science research in the business context. It has outlined a number of paradigmatic and data issues with which researchers and the users of research should be familiar. A paradigm is a way of looking at the world which influences the way research is conducted. In the social sciences there are competing paradigms in play, although they may also be complementary. Among these are: the positivist and the critical/interpretive approaches to research; qualitative and quantitative approaches; inductive and deductive approaches; and experimental and non-experimental methods. The chapter provides a brief overview of the range of research methods available to the business researcher and discusses their nature and situations for their use. A major message of the chapter is that research methods should be selected to address the research questions or hypotheses of the project in hand, based on careful consideration of a range of factors.

TEST QUESTIONS

1 What are the differences between positivist and critical/interpretive approaches to research?
2 What is the difference between deduction and induction?
3 Why is experimental research not common in business?
4 What are the distinguishing features of primary and secondary data?
5 What are the distinguishing features of self-reported and observed data?
6 What is triangulation in the context of research?
7 What are the main considerations to be used when selecting a research method?

EXERCISES

1 Examine the articles in the latest issue of two management/business research journals and classify them according to which dominant research paradigm they adopt.
2 Consider the same collection of articles and present an analysis of the research questions, data needs, and sources and methods used, similar to that presented in Figure 2.4.

FURTHER READING

On paradigms *in business research:* Evered and Reis Louis (1991); Hassard (1991).

On qualitative/quantitative issues: see Bryman and Bell (2003: 465–478), Chapter 21, 'Breaking down the quantitative/qualitative divide'.

On main research methods: Further Reading in subsequent chapters.

- *Textual analysis*: in general: Prior (2003); websites: Okazaki and Rivas (2003), see Example 5.1; television and print advertising: Carty (1997), see Example 10.2.
- *Longitudinal surveys*: in the social sciences see Young *et al.* (1991); NB. despite its title, *The Australian Business Longitudinal Survey* (Australian Bureau of Statistics 1997) is not a longitudinal survey as defined in this chapter because the sample of firms studied is drawn afresh each year.

For a UK study which has followed a sample of 17 000 individuals born in 1958, interviewing them at ages 7, 11, 16, 23, 33 and 42, see the National Child Development Study (Ferri 1993).

- *Panel surveys*: Kasprzyk *et al.* (1989); Rose (2000).
- *Projective techniques*: Semeonoff (1976).
- *Action research*: Reason and Bradbury (2001); McDonagh and Coghlan (2001); McNiff and Whitehead (2002); Zuber-Skerritt (1996).
- *Delphi technique*: General introduction: Linstone (1978); in regional economic planning: Gibson and Miller (1990); for consultative purposes: Critcher and Gladstone (1998).
- *Historical research*: Story (2004); Williams (2003).

CHAPTER 3

Planning and designing research projects

This chapter examines the processes involved in the planning and design of research projects. The process of developing a research *plan* is first addressed. The formulation of self-generated and responsive research *proposals* is then examined, including consideration of the research/consultancy tendering process. A research plan or proposal must consider how a research project is to be conducted in its entirety, involving examination of the research process from beginning to end. Finally, the chapter addresses the range of ethical issues which must be taken into account in planning and conducting any research project.

THE RESEARCH PROCESS

The research process can be divided into eight main elements, as shown in Figure 3.1. However, the variety of approaches to research suggests that not all research projects will follow precisely the same sequence of procedures. In particular, the first four elements—selecting the topic, reviewing the literature, devising a conceptual framework and deciding the key research questions—rarely happen in the direct, linear way that the numbered sequence implies. There is generally a great deal of interaction between the elements. Hence, in Figure 3.1 these elements are located within a circle, implying that more than one circuit may be necessary before proceeding to element 5. Each of the eight elements is discussed in turn below.

1. Selecting the topic

How do research topics arise? They can arise from a range of sources, as shown in Figure 3.2.

Personal interest

Personal interest can give rise to a research project in a number of ways. For example, the researcher may be personally responsible for a particular function in an organisation. He or she may be a member of a particular social group, based on gender, ethnicity or occupation, or may live in a particular location and be aware of certain local issues or problems. Using such an interest as a focus for research has advantages and disadvantages. The advantages lie in the knowledge of the phenomenon that the researcher already has, the possibility of access to individuals and further information, and the likely high level of

FIGURE 3.1 Elements of the research process

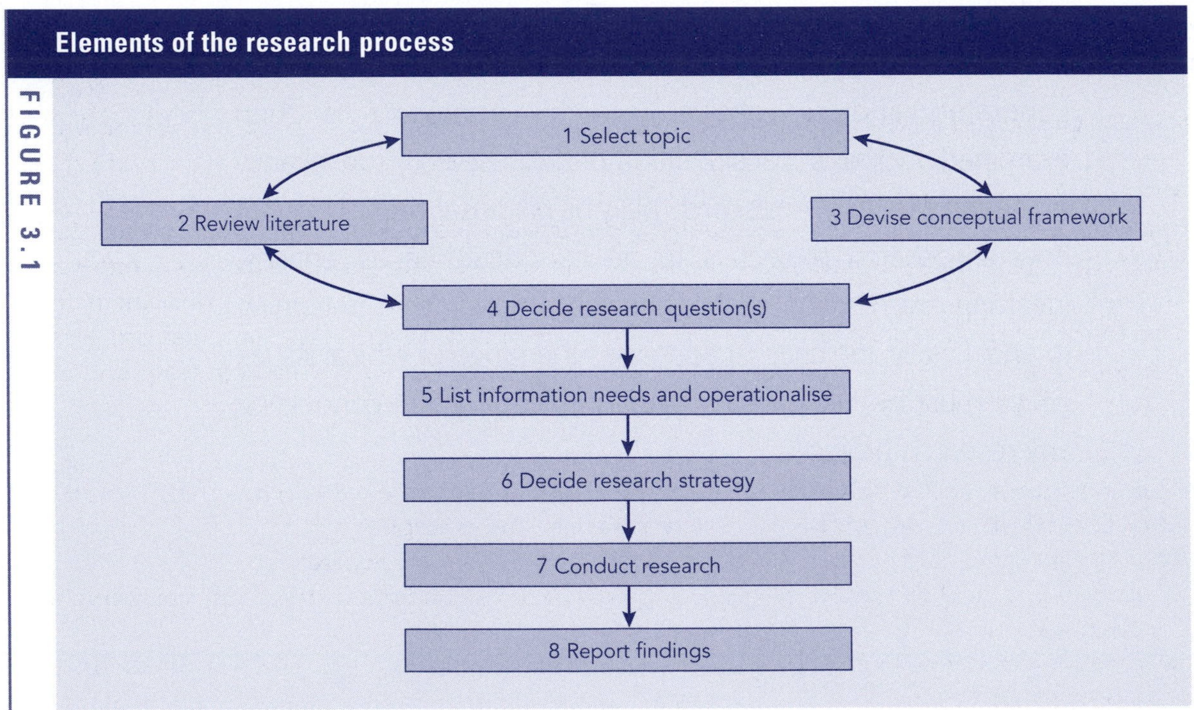

FIGURE 3.2

Examples of research topics from different sources

Source of topic	Examples of topics
1 Personal interest	■ Trends in a particular business sector ■ Workplace needs of a particular ethnic or age group ■ A professional organisation—ethos, history and future
2 The literature	■ Do Downs' (1988) dimensions of communication satisfaction apply to cultures outside the United States? ■ What are the perceived differences between the organisational 'climate' and 'culture' constructs (Schneider 1990)? ■ What is the relationship between job satisfaction and organisational commitment (Mathieu & Zajac 1990)?
3 Policy or management	■ Why are sales figures falling in the Victorian branch of this organisation—is this happening in other parts of the industry? ■ Should the IT function in this organisation be outsourced? ■ What are the effects of performance bonuses in this organisation? ■ What are the advantages of TQM as an organisational policy?
4 Social	■ Child care needs of single parents working in this department ■ Role of this organisation in a Third World community ■ The environmental impact of this industry on global warming
5 Popular issues	■ Are Aboriginal land claims having an effect on mining development? ■ The impact of the strength of economic rationalist philosophies on management attitudes towards staff

motivation which can be brought to the research. The disadvantages are that the researcher may be biased and may be unable to view the situation as objectively as someone with no prior interest or knowledge. Personal interest is usually just a starting point in selecting a topic. If the selected topic area is initially fairly broad, deciding on a specific focus for the research will usually depend on consideration of one or more of the other four criteria discussed below. In the research report, discussion of personal interest or involvement in the topic being researched should generally be confined to a *Preface* or *Foreword* (see Chapter 16). In the main body of the report the research should be justified using one or more of the following criteria.

The literature

The literature is the most common source of ideas for academic research. A researchable idea from the literature can take a variety of forms. For example:

- a certain theory may have been tested in the US but not elsewhere;
- a theory may have been developed in relation to manufacturing, but not service organisations;
- a widely accepted theory may be based on research conducted solely on men, thus ignoring women;

- a widely quoted theory may never have been tested empirically;
- a theory may have last been tested twenty years ago and so may be out of date;
- a certain theory or methodology may be developed in one area of management but may never have been applied to your area of interest; or
- a certain concept may not have been fully investigated in a historical context.

Clearly, if the literature is to be the main source of ideas for a research topic then the first two elements of the research process—selecting a topic and reviewing the literature—are effectively combined. Identifying a topic from the literature requires a special approach to reading, in that the aim is not just to identify what the literature says, but also what it does *not* say. The process of critically reviewing the literature is further discussed in Chapter 4.

Policy or management

Decisions to undertake policy or management research can be made on behalf of organisations or by academics interested in a particular policy or management area. The difference between these situations is that the results of research carried out for a specific industry organisation will often remain confidential and the wider implications of the research may not be examined. Academic research is usually made public and is generally presented to highlight its more general implications, rather than the particular application to the organisation being studied. In addition, academic studies are often as concerned with methodology as with the substantive findings of the research. Research sponsored by government bodies lies somewhere in between these two approaches—the results of the research may be very specific, but widely disseminated.

It is common for policy or management topics to be outlined by an organisation in a *brief* for a funded research or consultancy project. Research organisations—usually consultants, who may include academics—are invited to respond in the form of a competitive tender to conduct the project. This type of procedure has its own set of practices and conventions, as discussed later in this chapter under 'Responsive proposals: briefs and tenders'.

Social concern

Social concern can give rise to a wide range of research topics. Concern for certain deprived or neglected groups in society can lead to research, for example, on the health needs of outworkers in the garment industry. Concern for the environment can lead to research on the environmental or social impact of industry practices. Often such research is closely related to policy issues, but may have a more limited role, seeking merely to highlight problems rather than devising solutions.

Popular issues

Finally, a popular issue can inspire research that seeks to explore popular beliefs or conceptions, especially where it is suspected that these may be inaccurate. 'Popular' usually means 'as portrayed in the media'. For example, this might be the motivation for much research on media portrayals of the 'dole bludging' unemployed, or of the waterfront as 'overstaffed and inefficient'.

2. Reviewing the literature

The process of reviewing the existing literature is sufficiently important for a whole chapter (Chapter 4) to be devoted to this topic. *Reviewing the literature* is a somewhat academic term referring to the process of identifying and engaging with previously published research relevant to the topic of interest. The process can play a number of roles.

The roles of the literature review in research:

- The entire basis of the research
- A source of ideas on topics for research
- A source of information on research already done by others
- A source of methodological or theoretical ideas
- A source of comparison between your research and that of others
- A source of information that is an integral or supportive part of the research (for example, data on a local market)

In many cases the review undertaken in the early stages of the research needs to be seen as an 'interim' literature review only, since time does not always permit a thorough literature review to be completed before a project begins. Part of the research project itself may be to explore the literature further. When the literature has been investigated as thoroughly as possible, it is usually necessary to proceed with the proposed research in the hope that all relevant material has been identified. Exploration of the literature will generally continue for the duration of the project.

Researchers always run the risk of coming across a previous—or contemporaneous—publication which completely negates or upstages their work just as they are about to complete it. But that is part of the process of research. In fact, unlike the situation in the natural sciences, the risk of this happening in the area of management is minimal, since research in this area can rarely be replicated exactly. In the natural sciences, research carried out in Los Angeles can reproduce exactly the findings of research carried out in Sydney. In business research, however, this is not the case. A set of research procedures carried out in Los Angeles would be expected to produce different results from identical procedures carried out in Sydney, or even New York. This is because the research is involved with unique people in unique organisational and cultural settings. In fact, replication of research in different environments, sometimes referred to as *comparative* research, is an important motive for social science research.

Where possible, attempts should be made to explore not just published research—the *literature*—but also unpublished and ongoing research. This process is very much 'hit and miss'. Knowing what research is ongoing, or knowing about completed but unpublished research, usually depends on having access to informal networks, although some organisations produce registers of continuing research and the Internet has assisted greatly, through the websites of research organisations. Once a topic of interest has been identified it is often clear from the literature where the major centres for such research are located. The researcher can then uncover, from direct approaches or from annual reports, newsletters or websites, what research is currently being conducted at those centres. This process can be particularly important if the topic is a 'fashionable' one. If this is the case, the communication networks are usually very active, which makes this process easier. Papers from recent conferences and seminars are usually better sources of information on current research than books and journals. The latter tend to have long preparation periods, so that the research reported in them is generally based on work carried out two or more years prior to publication.

A review of the literature should be concluded by a *summary and conclusions*. In an academic study this would provide an overview of the relevant research and indicate its substantive and methodological merits and deficiencies or gaps, and give an indication of how such conclusions are related to the research task at hand. In a management consultancy report the review will generally be briefer and will be more concerned with relevant and useful findings than with methodological issues. This is discussed further in Chapter 4.

3. Devising a conceptual framework

The development of a conceptual framework is arguably the most important part of any research project and the most difficult—and it is often the weakest element in research proposals. A *conceptual framework* involves *concepts*. These are general representations of the phenomena to be studied—the 'building blocks' of a study. Figure 3.3 lists some

FIGURE 3.3

Concepts: examples

Concept	Definition	Operationalisation
Communication	A multidimensional construct 'summing up' a person's satisfaction with information flow and relationship variables within an organisation.	Factor scores on Communication Satisfaction Questionnaire developed by Downs and Hazen (Downs 1988).
Organisational commitment	A state in which an individual identifies with a particular organisation and its goals, and wishes to maintain membership in order to facilitate these goals.	Score on Organisational Commitment Questionnaire (Mowday, Steers & Porter 1979).
Organisational culture	A pattern of assumptions that an organisation has discovered or developed in learning to cope with external adaptation and internal integration.	Organisational Culture Index (OCI) (Wallach 1983).
Social class	Socioeconomic and political position of a group of people in society.	Composite of: occupation, income, education level, occupation of parents.
Job satisfaction	An attitude that individuals have about their jobs, which results from their perception of their jobs and the degree to which there is a good fit between the individual and the organisation.	Score on Job Diagnostic Survey (JDS) (Hackman & Oldham 1975).
Attitude	Person's feelings towards something or someone.	Response on Likert scale (agree strongly, disagree, etc.) to a number of statements on a given topic.
Profit	Surplus after all costs have been met.	Difference between annual revenue and annual costs, as a percentage of annual revenue.

examples of concepts encountered in management research, their definitions and how they might be *operationalised*, or communicated, in a qualitatively or quantitatively assessable or measurable form.

A conceptual *framework* indicates how the researcher views the concepts involved in a study, especially the *relationships between* concepts. The concepts identified, and the framework within which they are set, determine the whole course of the study. Thus the development of a conceptual framework involves four elements: identification of concepts, definition of concepts, exploration of relationships between concepts and operationalisation of the concepts—as depicted in Figure 3.4. Examination of the relationships between concepts is discussed further below. The *operationalisation* of concepts involves deciding how they might be measured, if quantitative in nature, or recognised or assessed, if qualitative in nature. Identification of concepts is usually the starting point, but the exercise is generally *iterative*, that is, it involves going backwards and forwards between the various elements until a satisfactory outcome is reached.

It is necessary to decide upon the kinds of research being conducted in order to determine how elaborate the conceptual framework needs to be—that is, it is necessary to decide whether the research is, using the terms explained in Chapter 1, descriptive, explanatory or evaluative.

Descriptive research rarely requires an elaborate conceptual framework, but clear definitions of the concepts involved are required. In some cases this can be a considerable undertaking, for example determining the job categories in an organisation.

Both *explanatory* and *evaluative* research call for a well-developed conceptual framework that forms the basis for the explanation or evaluation required from the research. Explanation usually involves the idea of cause and effect—the relationship between one variable and another. Evaluation involves examination of the relationships between inputs and outputs or actions and outcomes.

The key element for most research is therefore the exploration of *relationships between concepts*. One approach to this process is to use a *concept map*, sometimes referred to as a

Development of a conceptual framework

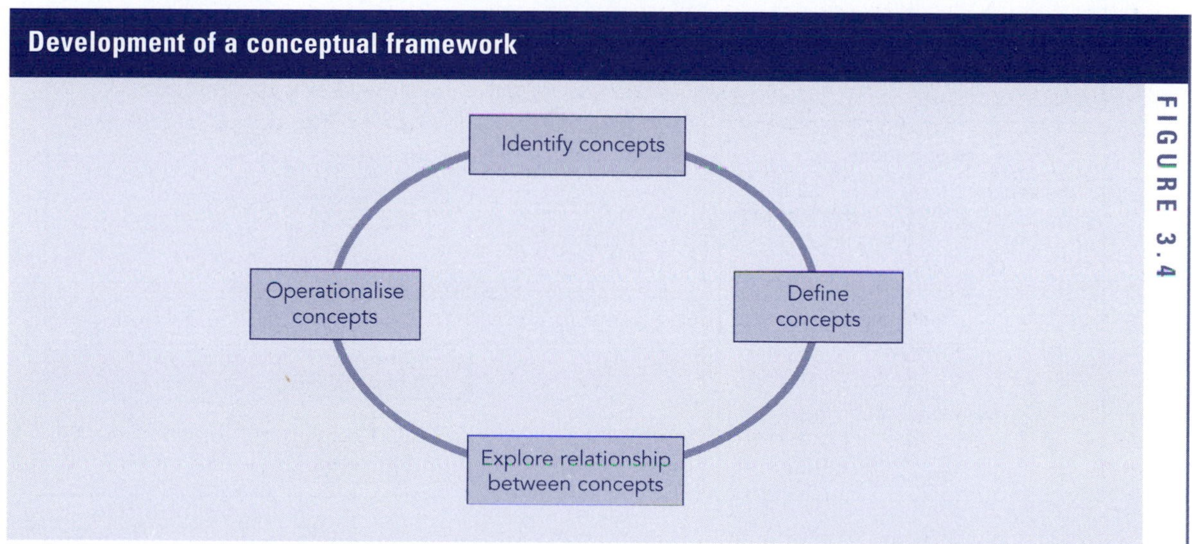

FIGURE 3.4

mind map. Concept mapping can be seen as a form of visual 'brainstorming' and can be undertaken alone or as part of a group exercise. It involves writing down all the concepts that appear to be relevant to a topic in any order that they come to mind, then spatially grouping the concepts that seem to be related. Finally, the perceived relationships between groups of concepts and individual concepts can be indicated by a series of lines and arrows. An example of concept mapping used in research seeking to explain the high staff turnover in an organisation is shown in Figure 3.5. Three stages in the process are shown, with the diagram becoming more complex with each stage. In practice there are likely to be many more stages and a much more 'messy' process before a framework suitable for guiding the research is arrived at.

The concepts and suggested relationships do not come out of 'thin air', but should reflect the participant researchers' understanding or informed speculation based on direct observation of the phenomenon to be studied—in this case a workplace—and/or on reading of relevant literature.

The term *conceptual framework* has been used here to cover a wide range of research situations. Such a term can be used in applied research when the framework adopted might relate to activities such as planning or marketing within an organisation. In this case, ready-made ideas for conceptual frameworks may be found in the planning or marketing

FIGURE 3.5 Concept mapping for a project on staff turnover

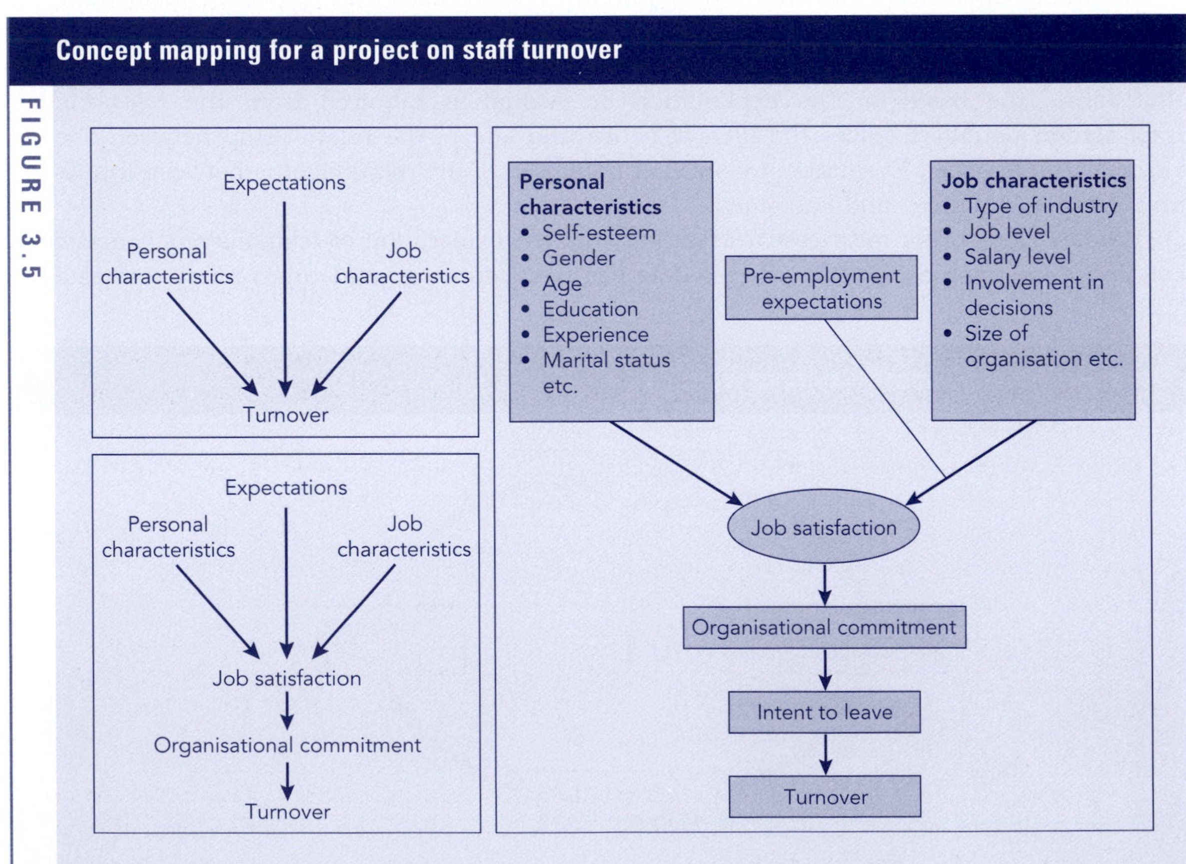

literature. When the research is more academically orientated, the term *theoretical framework* might equally be used. A theoretical framework might also be called a *model*, particularly when the research is quantitative in nature. For example, the idea that the level of turnover of an organisation is directly related to the size of the organisation in terms of number of employees could be expressed in quantitative modelling terms as follows:

$$T = a + bE$$

where T is the concept *staff turnover* and E is the concept *size of organisation*, as operationalised by the number of employees. By analysing the level of staff turnover and size of a number of organisations, or the same organisation over a period of time, research would seek to find values for the 'parameters' a and b, so that the level of turnover could be predicted once the number of employees was known. This modelling process is discussed further in Chapter 14, where the technique of regression analysis is examined.

4. Deciding research questions

From concept map to research questions

Research questions are the questions to which researchers seek answers in the research project. Deciding on the research questions is one of the most difficult tasks in the whole research process. The concept mapping exercise discussed above is intended to aid this process. The connecting arrows in the concept map suggest relationships between concepts/variables. Thus, for example, in Figure 3.5, a number of research questions present themselves:

What are the relative influences of '*Personal characteristics*', '*Pre-employment expectations*' and '*Job characteristics*' on '*Job satisfaction*'?

To what extent does '*Job satisfaction*' affect '*Organisational commitment*'?

To what extent does '*Organisational commitment*' influence the level of '*Staff turnover*'?

In this case three research questions are identified, although the first could be seen as three questions. In most cases this is manageable, but a complex conceptual framework may result in a large number of potential questions which would be impossible to pursue in one project. In that case, the researcher must either simplify the conceptual framework or be selective in the questions to be addressed.

Research questions must not only be relevant in terms of the topic and the justification for studying it, but must also be *researchable*, that is, it must be possible to produce answers to the questions by means of a research strategy which is feasible within the time scale and resources available to the researcher. Two aspects of this process can be identified: first the *scale and scope* of the implied research program and, second, the *answerability* of the questions posed. These two aspects are discussed in turn below.

Scale and scope

A common failing of research proposals, particularly with respect to self-generated research projects, is for the researcher to pose research questions which are too ambitious. In this case the scope of the question is too great, so that the implied program of research resembles a 'royal commission' that gathers masses of material from numerous sources, resulting in a report which is potentially a magisterial overview of the topic with a definitive list of solutions and recommendations. The problem with this approach is that, unlike royal commissions, researchers rarely have millions of dollars worth of resources at their disposal and years to complete their work. While the initial topic or problem may seem large and unwieldy, the typical researcher must match the research task to the resources available. This generally involves deciding to address just one or two aspects of the wider problem or issue, or proposing a case study or exploratory project which could provide a basis for more detailed or extensive research. Figure 3.6 presents some examples of researchable questions abstracted from bigger issues or topics. In each case it is possible for the conceptual framework outlined in the proposal to encompass all the dimensions of the larger topic or issue. A comprehensive research project is able to address all the subprojects indicated and more. However, for a single-person or small team research project a choice has to be made as to which aspects of the wider problem or issue to tackle.

Answerability

The test of answerability is simply whether it is possible to answer the questions posed by means of research. This can be viewed in both theoretical and practical terms. Thus, for

FIGURE 3.6

Researchable questions

Big issue	Researchable questions/manageable subprojects
Why are sales of a firm's products declining?	**a** What is the level of public awareness of the firm's *advertising*? **b** What are the public's views of the firm's product *quality*? **c** What are the demographic trends in the firm's main *customer* segments? **d** What are *wholesalers'* views of the firm's performance as a supplier? **e** How does the firm's *pricing* structure compare with those of competing firms?
Feasibility of developing a new product/service	**a** What is the *market environment* or *social need* for the product/service? **b** What is the likely level of *demand* for such a service? **c** What are the *costs* of producing the product/service? **d** What are the *technical/staffing/resource/planning* requirements to produce the product/service? **e** What should the *marketing* strategy for the service be?
Produce a strategic plan for an organisation	**a** What are the stakeholders' views of the organisation's *vision*? **b** What are the organisation's *Strengths*, *Weaknesses*, *Opportunities* and *Threats*? **c** What has the organisation's level of *performance* been over the last five years, against key performance indicators? **d** What *objectives* should the organisation adopt? **e** How should *performance* in the newly adopted objectives be evaluated?
How can employee turnover be reduced?	**a** What are the pre-employment *expectations* of employees? **b** How *satisfied* are employees with their job? **c** What is the level of *organisational commitment* of employees? **d** Is high turnover a *characteristic* of this industry?

example, in theoretical terms it is widely accepted that it is almost impossible to assess the effectiveness of advertising (because a pattern of sales may have been the same in the absence of advertising, due, for example, to word of mouth, editorial coverage or point-of-sale impact). So the first 'researchable question' indicated in Figure 3.6 is not 'How effective has the firm's advertising been?', but a more modest: 'What is the public's level of awareness of the firm's advertising?'. The advantage of the latter question is that it is answerable using available research techniques. The practical dimension of the answerability issue involves the resources available to the researcher. For example, a two-person research team with a time limit of three weeks may not even be able to tackle the question just discussed. The scope of the question might need to be reduced even more, for example, 'What is the Sydney North Shore public's level of awareness of the April advertising campaign for product X?'.

In each of the cases discussed above, it is necessary to make choices among a range of research possibilities. Such choices should, of course, be explained and justified in any research proposal or research report. Often such explanations or justifications argue that the selected product, market segment, time period or event is 'typical' or 'indicative' or 'the most important', or simply that despite its limitations it was the only feasible option within the resource constraints.

In some cases the research topic selected by the researcher is quite specific from the beginning of the research process, and the literature review and conceptual framework are the means by which the specific issue is placed in the context of existing knowledge. In other cases the topic is initially quite vague and is an area of interest without a specific focus. In such cases the literature review and process of developing a conceptual framework help to focus the topic and determine what exactly should be researched.

Primary and subsidiary questions

In most situations the idea of *primary* and *subsidiary* questions is helpful. The subsidiary questions are necessary steps towards answering the primary question. Thus, in the case of research questions arising from the concept map in Figure 3.5, subsidiary questions might consider the lists of variables in the 'Personal characteristics' and 'Job characteristics' boxes:

What '*Personal characteristics*' are influential in determining '*Job satisfaction*'?

What '*Job characteristics*' are influential in determining '*Job satisfaction*'?

Research questions vs objectives

It is possible to express research questions in the form of *objectives*. Thus the primary research questions listed above could be expressed as follows:

The objectives of the research are to determine:

1. the relative influences of '*Personal characteristics*', '*Pre-employment expectations*' and '*Job characteristics*' on '*Job satisfaction*';
2. the extent to which '*Job satisfaction*' affects '*Organisational commitment*'; and
3. the extent to which '*Organisational commitment*' influences the level of '*Staff turnover*'.

Using this format rather than the question format is a matter of personal choice, but is more common in consultancy style research.

Research questions vs hypotheses

In the natural sciences, and in some areas of the social sciences, rather than pose research *questions to be answered*, it is more customary to consider *hypotheses to be tested.* A hypothesis is a statement or proposition that can be tested by reference to empirical study. Thus, for example, a *research question* might be expressed in the form:

What is the relationship between advertising expenditure and revenue?

A hypothesis dealing with the same topic might be expressed as:

There is a positive relationship between advertising expenditure and revenue.

A hypothesis can be shown to be true or false as a result of empirical research. The question format lends itself more to descriptive and inductive research, while the hypothesis format is more appropriate for explanatory and deductive research.

Hypotheses are usually stated in a form that predicts there is a difference between two groups in relation to some variable, or that there is a relationship between two variables. For example:

There is a difference between the organisational commitment of male employees and female employees.

There is a relationship between job satisfaction and salary level.

These hypotheses are called *non-directional* hypotheses because they do not predict the direction of the difference or relationship. *Directional* hypotheses are used if the researcher is more confident about the direction of a relationship, or if the literature reports that previous studies found differences to be in a particular direction. In such cases the researcher might propose the research hypotheses as directional hypotheses. For example:

Female employees have a higher level of organisational commitment than male employees.

There is a positive relationship between job satisfaction and salary level.

In each of these hypotheses the direction of the differences or relationship being studied is predicted by the hypothesis, that is a *higher level* of commitment and a *positive relationship.*

In experimental research researchers typically begin with a *null* hypothesis which predicts that there is *no difference* between two groups in relation to some variable, or that there is *no relationship* between two variables. For example:

There is no difference between the organisational commitment of male employees and female employees.

There is no relationship between job satisfaction and salary level.

A null hypothesis is usually indicated by the symbol H_0. The *alternative* hypothesis to the null hypothesis is indicated by symbol H_1. For example:

H_0	There is no relationship between job satisfaction and salary level (null hypothesis).
H_1	There is a positive or negative relationship between job satisfaction and salary level (alternative hypothesis).

Statistical analysis is used to conclude the null hypothesis is *probably* true or *probably* false and, if it is probably false to accept the alternative hypothesis as the logical alternative. This approach to framing the research task is explored in more detail in the context of statistical analysis discussed in Chapter 14.

An example from the literature which presents a particularly clear outline of the relationship between concepts, a conceptual framework and a set of hypotheses to be tested is summarised in Case Study Example 3.1.

CASE STUDY EXAMPLE 3.1

Conceptual framework: perceived customer value

Source: Chen Zhan & Alan J. Dubinsky 2003, A conceptual model of perceived customer value in e-commerce: a preliminary investigation. *Psychology and Marketing*, 20(4), 323–347.
Methods/approaches: Respondent-completed questionnaire
Topic: Perceived customer value—online purchasing

This study sought to examine the phenomenon of *perceived customer value* in relation to online purchasing. Perceived customer value (PCV) is a 'consumer's perception of the net benefits gained in exchange for the costs incurred in obtaining the desired benefits' from a purchase—a concept similar to the economist's notion of 'utility'. A conceptual framework is put forward suggesting a range of eight variables/concepts which influence and determine a customer's PCV, which in turn influences the decision to purchase. The variables/concepts are:

- Ease of use of the website
- Relevant information
- Customer service
- Valence of experience ('customer's emotional or attitudinal state aroused by the pre-purchase online shopping experience')
- Perceived product quality
- 'E-tailer' reputation
- Perceived risk
- Product price.

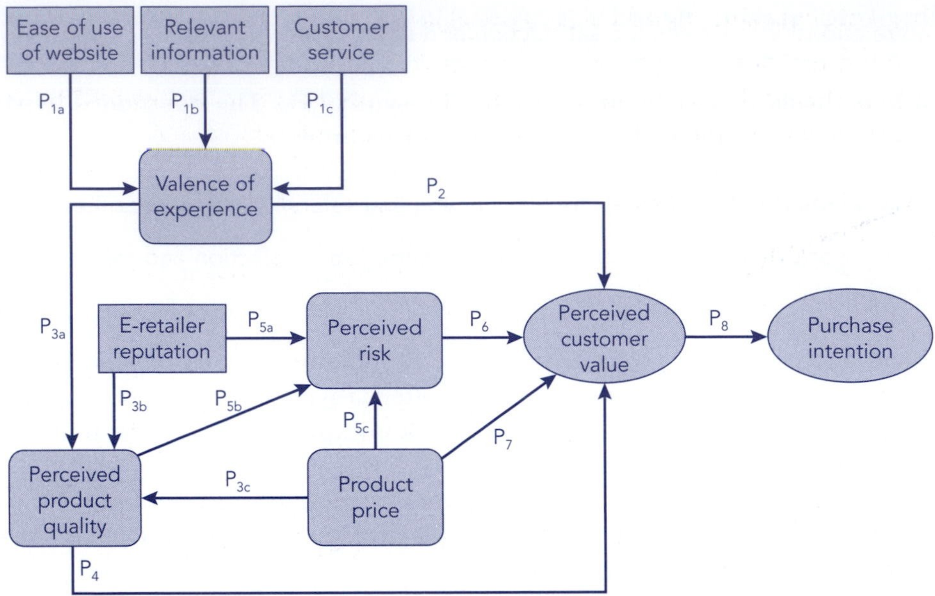

Figure A. Conceptual framework of perceived customer value in an e-commerce context

Each of these eight concepts is discussed and defined and, based on previous research on PCV, adapted for the online environment, a conceptual framework linking them is put forward as in Figure A.

Each link is labelled $P_1 - P_8$ and each gives rise to a proposition or hypothesis, as follows:

P_1 (a) The degree of relevant information provided, (b) The ease of use of the website, and (c) The degree of customer service offered are positively related to the online shopper's valence of experience.

P_2 Valence of experience of the online shopper is positively associated with his or her perceived customer value.

P_3 (a) Valence of experience of the online shopper, (b) E-retailer reputation, and (c) Product price are positively related to perceived product quality.

P_4 Perceived product quality is positively associated with perceived customer value.

P_5 (a) E-retailer reputation is negatively related to perceived risk, (b) Perceived product quality is negatively associated with perceived risk, (c) Product price is positively related to perceived risk.

P_6 Perceived risk is negatively associated with perceived customer value.

P_7 Product price is negatively related to perceived customer value.

P_8 Perceived customer value is positively related to online purchase intention.

A sample of students who were active online shoppers responded to a questionnaire asking them to rate, using five-point scales, each of the eight factors in regard to their most recent online shopping experience where they seriously considered buying a product. The propositions/hypotheses were explored using regression analysis (see Chapter 14). Readers are referred to the original article for the findings: the purpose of describing this example here is to note the clear and methodical way in which concepts, a conceptual framework and hypotheses are related.

5. Listing information needs and operationalising

The research questions or objectives should give rise to a list of information needs. At this stage the information is expressed in general terms, for example, in Figure 3.5 there will be a need for information on each of the items listed in the boxes, such as employees' pre-employment expectations, self-esteem, gender, salary level, and so on. Just how the information might be collected is not yet determined. No item should appear on the list unless it is related to the research questions and the conceptual framework.

The question of *operationalising* concepts or variables can begin to be considered here, although the process is an iterative one, depending on the data-gathering methods which make up the research strategy. Operationalisation means deciding how a concept or variable is to be measured. In the case of qualitative research 'measurement' may not be the correct word, 'identified' or 'assessed' would be more appropriate. Figure 3.7 lists the concepts/variables and possible operationalisation for the project depicted in Figure 3.5. It should be noted that reference is made in three cases to existing scales, a phenomenon discussed in Chapter 2. When operationalising concepts it is sensible to make use of existing scales if they are suitable, rather than 'reinventing the wheel'.

6. Developing a research strategy

Development of a *research strategy* involves making decisions on a number of aspects of the research process.

Research strategy:
- Information-gathering methods
- Data analysis methods
- Budget and timetable

Information-gathering methods

It is at this stage that alternative information-gathering methods are considered. The process of *operationalising concepts* will generally have indicated certain types of information sources—it is here that the detail is determined. For each item of information listed in step 5 above, a range of sources may be possible. Judgement is required in order to determine just what methods to use, particularly in light of the time and resources available.

A further review of the literature can be valuable at this stage, concentrating particularly on data-gathering techniques used by previous researchers and asking such questions as: Have their chosen methods been shown to be limiting or even misguided? What lessons can be learned from past errors? What research methods have been particularly productive? In Figure 3.7 at a number of points it is suggested that previous research may provide suitable data formats which, if replicated, would provide a basis for comparison.

The range of information-gathering methods which are most likely to be considered at this stage are those discussed in Chapter 2 and covered in detail in the following chapters of this book, namely:

- utilisation of existing information, including published and unpublished research and secondary data (Chapters 4 and 5);
- experimental and observation methods (Chapter 6);
- qualitative methods including ethnographic methods, participant observation, informal and in-depth interviews, group interviews or focus groups (Chapter 7); and
- questionnaire-based surveys including household surveys, face-to-face surveys, street surveys, telephone surveys, user/site/employee surveys and mail surveys (Chapter 8).

FIGURE 3.7

Concepts/variables, operationalisation and possible sources for staff turnover project

Concept/variable	Operationalisation	Likely data source
Pre-employment expectations	Scores on Likert scales regarding expectations re specified job characteristics (see below)	Questionnaire
Personal characteristics		
Self-esteem	Use existing measure of self-esteem, eg, Core Self-evaluation scale (Judge *et al.*, 2003)	Questionnaire
Gender	M/F	Questionnaire/staff records
Age	Age last birthday	Questionnaire/staff records
Education	Highest qualification achieved	Questionnaire/staff records
Experience	Number of years in employment since leaving full-time education	Questionnaire/staff records
Marital status	Married, de facto, single, divorced, widowed	Questionnaire
Job characteristics		
Type of industry*	Suitable classification from previous research or national statistics agency	Questionnaire
Job level	Suitable classification from previous research or national statistics agency	Questionnaire/staff records
Salary level	Suitable classification from previous research or national statistics agency	Questionnaire/staff records
Involvement in decisions	Suitable scale from previous research or ad hoc classification	Questionnaire
Size of organisation*	Number of employees	Questionnaire
Job satisfaction	Use existing scale, eg, Job Description Index (Smith, Kendall & Hulin 1975)	Questionnaire
Organisational commitment	Use existing scale, eg, British Organisational Commitment Scale BOCS) (see Mathews & Shepherd 2002)	Questionnaire

These variables not relevant if only one firm is involved in the study.

Once the data collection methods to be used have been decided it is necessary to plan the data collection process. Where the process of information gathering involves going out into the *field*, for instance to conduct interviews or to undertake observation, the *planning of fieldwork* needs to be considered. In the case of experimental research, rather than fieldwork, the proposed program of experiments would be considered here. Where extensive data collection is involved then the organisation of fieldwork may be complex, involving recruitment and training of field staff (for example, interviewers), obtaining permission—including ethics committee clearance in universities and hospitals—and the organisation of data processing and analysis. It is often the case that a pilot study is a necessary part of the planning process, not just to test such things as the wording of a questionnaire, but also to discover how long certain processes, such as sampling and interviewing, will take. This will affect the budget or the scale of data gathering which can be undertaken within a given budget. The conduct of pilot studies is discussed in Chapter 8. If the proposed research does not involve primary data collection then this is not a consideration, but the availability of secondary information sources and the time likely to be needed to access them and compile the information will need to be considered. These practical aspects of planning particular data-gathering exercises are considered in the relevant chapters of the book.

Development of a research strategy may become an iterative process in which the use of certain methods or the pursuit of certain aspects of the research are precluded by their cost, so that the range of research questions addressed may have to be restricted.

Data analysis methods

Data analysis may be simple and straightforward and may follow fairly logically from the type of information collection technique to be used. This is particularly the case when the research is descriptive in nature. In some cases, however, the analysis of data may be complex, and thought needs to be given to the time and the skills required to undertake the analysis. Consideration must be given to the format of the data that will be collected and just how it will be used to answer the research questions posed. Where qualitative data are to be collected, for example using in-depth interviews, thought must be given as to how the results of the interviews will be analysed. Details of analysis methods which are appropriate and possible for different data collection techniques are discussed in subsequent chapters, but it must be borne in mind that when planning a project, full consideration should be given not only to the collection of data but also to their analysis.

Budget and timetable

In some situations key aspects of the budget and timetable are fixed. For example, students generally have available only their own labour and may be required to submit a report by a specified date. Research consultancies usually have an upper budget limit and a fixed completion date. In other situations, for example, when seeking a grant for research from a grant-giving body or permission to conduct an 'in house' project, the proposer of the research is called upon to recommend both budget and timetable. Whatever the situation, the task is never easy, since there is rarely enough time or money available to conduct the ideal research project, so compromises invariably have to be made.

7. Conducting the research

Conducting the research is what the rest of this book is about. However, it must be stressed that good research outcomes will only result if the preparatory processes discussed in this chapter are carefully followed. Sound preparation can ease the rest of the research process considerably.

Inexperienced researchers often move too rapidly from selecting the topic to conducting the research. This can result in the collection of data of dubious use and the researcher being presented with the problem of making sense of information which has been laboriously collected, but does not fit into any framework. If the above processes are followed then every item of information collected should have a purpose, since it will have been collected to answer specific questions. This does not mean that the unexpected will not happen and serendipitous findings may not arise, but at least the core structure of the research should be under control.

8. Reporting findings

The question of writing up research results is not discussed in detail here since the final chapter (Chapter 16) is devoted to this topic. Unlike the conduct of the research, which inexperienced researchers invariably rush into too quickly, the writing up of results is usually delayed too long, so that insufficient time is left for satisfactory completion of the task. An outline of the research process, as presented here, can itself be part of the problem, since it implies that the writing process comes at the end. In fact, the writing of a research report can begin almost as soon as the project begins, since all the early stages, such as the review of the literature and the development of the conceptual framework, can be written up as the project progresses.

RESEARCH PROPOSALS

Two kinds of research proposal are discussed here. The first is the *self-generated* proposal prepared by academics seeking funding for a research project they have devised, or by students seeking approval for research for a project or thesis on a selected topic. The second type of proposal is the *responsive* proposal prepared by consultants responding to research briefs prepared by clients wishing to commission research. Students may also be required to prepare responsive proposals when they conduct projects for real or hypothetical clients. Planners and managers seeking 'in house' resources to conduct research fall somewhere between these situations.

In each case the proposal is a written document, which may be supported by a *live* presentation, that attempts to demonstrate the worth of the research to the person or group of people who will decide whether it should go ahead. Writers of a research proposal are faced with the difficult task of convincing the decision-makers of the value of the research, the valuable and original insights they will bring to the project, and their personal capability to conduct the research. In some cases the decision-makers will be experts in the field, while they may not be in other cases, so care must be taken to ensure that the proposal can be understood by all concerned. Clarity and succinctness of expression are often the key qualities of research proposals.

Self-generated research proposals

Academic research proposals for student theses or projects, or for academics seeking funding, need to describe the research to be done and provide a rationale for the choice of topic. The topic and its treatment must be appropriate—in terms of scale and complexity—to the level of the research project, which may be an undergraduate project, a PhD thesis or a funded project involving a team of researchers over a period of months or even years.

In general, an academic research proposal must cover the material discussed in this chapter. In some cases considerable work will already have been completed before the proposal is submitted. This could apply in the case of a PhD proposal or a proposal from an experienced academic who has been working in a particular field for a number of years. In such cases the proposal may present considerable detail on the literature and conceptual/theoretical elements of the research process, with funding being sought to actually conduct the fieldwork part of the research and write up the results. In other cases, little more than the selection of the topic may have been completed and the proposal will outline a program to undertake procedures from the review of the literature to the final report. Some proposals contain a preliminary review of the literature with a proposal to undertake more as part of the project. Some proposals are very clear about the conceptual framework to be used; in other cases just speculative ideas are presented.

While bearing in mind that there can be substantial differences between proposals of various types, the checklist presented overleaf is offered as a guide to the contents of a proposal. It covers all the stages outlined in this chapter. In addition, ethical issues are introduced and these are discussed at the end of the chapter.

Responsive proposals: briefs and tenders

A *brief* is an outline of the research that an organisation wishes to be undertaken and is sometimes referred to as the 'terms of reference' of a study. Consultants seeking to undertake a research project must submit a written proposal or *tender*. Briefs are usually prepared by an organisation with a view to a number of consultants competing to obtain the contract to do the research. In some cases potential consultants are first asked, possibly through an advertisement, to indicate an *expression of interest* in the project. This will involve a brief statement of the consultants' capabilities, their experience in the field and staff available. In some cases public bodies maintain a register of accredited consultants with particular interests and capabilities who may be invited to tender for particular projects.

In the light of such expressions of interest or information in the register, a *short list* of consultants is sent the full brief and invited to submit a detailed tender. Successful tenders are not usually selected on the basis of price alone (the budget is often a fixed sum), but on the quality of the submitted proposal and the 'track record' of the consultants.

Briefs vary in the amount of detail they give. Sometimes they are very detailed, leaving little scope for consultants to express any individuality in their proposals. In other cases they are very limited and leave a great deal of scope to consultants to indicate proposed methods and approaches. Client organisations that are experienced in commissioning research can produce briefs that are clear and 'ready to roll'. In other situations it is necessary to clarify the client's meanings and intentions. For example, a state rail authority might ask for a study of 'management practices' in its organisation. In this case it would be necessary to clarify what the authority means by 'management', that is whether they wish to include supervisory practices on railway stations, in their maintenance workshops, in track maintenance gangs, or whether they simply refer to senior management in their central offices. If a client asks for the 'effectiveness' of a program to be assessed it may be necessary to clarify whether a statement of objectives or a list of performance criteria for the program already exists, or whether that must be developed as part of the research.

Paradoxically, problems can arise when client organisations are over-specific about their requirements. An organisation may ask for a 'customer survey' to be conducted, but it is

Research proposal checklist: self-generated research

1. Background and justification for selection of topic.
2. (Preliminary) review of the literature.
3. Conceptual/theoretical framework.
4. Statement of research problems, questions or hypotheses.
5. Outline of data requirements and overall research strategy. Division of project into elements, stages and tasks.
6. Details of information collection methods:
   - types of information collection
   - sample or subject selection methods—measures to ensure data quality
   - justification of sample size (where appropriate)
   - data and information to be generated by each method
   - outline of any ethical issues and how they will be addressed.
7. Details of data analysis methods.
8. Timetable (NB some tasks will be concurrent):
   - preparatory work
   - ethics approval if required
   - fieldwork—data collection tasks
   - analysis
   - draft report or thesis
   - feedback on draft
   - final report or thesis presentation.
9. Budget, where applicable—costing of each element, stage and task:
   - project staff costs (n days at $x per day)
   - permissible overheads
   - fieldwork or data collection costs
   - additional items—travel, printing, telephone, postage, &c.
10. Report or thesis chapter outline or indication of number and type of publications.
11. Resources, skills and experience available (necessary when seeking funds):
    - researchers' curricula vitae, especially experience relevant to the proposed project
    - availability of computers, equipment, library resources, &c.

not easy to decide what should be included in such a survey without information on the management or policy questions which the data are intended to answer. Is the organisation concerned about a decline in the number of customers? Does it want to change its 'marketing mix'? Is it concerned about future trends in demand? It would be preferable in such a situation for the client to indicate the nature of the management problem and leave the researcher to determine the most suitable research approach to adopt, which might or might not include a customer survey.

Sometimes there is a hidden agenda that the researcher would do well to become familiar with before embarking on the research. For example, research can sometimes be used as a means to defuse or delay difficult management decisions in an organisation. An example of this is a situation in which a service is suffering declining sales because of poor maintenance of facilities and poor staff attitudes to customers. This is very clear to anyone who walks in the door, but the management decides to commission a 'market study' in the hope that the answer to their problem can be found 'out there' in the market. In fact, the problem is very much 'in there' and their money might be better spent on improving maintenance and staff training than on customer research.

A situation where the client's requirements may seem vague is when the research is not related to immediate policy needs but to possible future needs or simply to satisfy curiosity. For example, a manager of a service facility may commission a customer survey (perhaps because there is spare money in the current year's budget) without having any specific policy or management problems in mind. In this case the research will need to specify hypothetical or potential policy and management issues, and match the data specifications to them.

What should a proposal contain? The first and most important principle is that it should *address the brief*. It is likely that the brief will have been discussed at great length in the commissioning organisation. Every aspect of the brief is likely to be of importance to some individual or section in the organisation, so every aspect of the brief should be considered in the proposal. For example, if the brief lists four objectives, the proposal must indicate how each of the four objectives will be met. A proposal must therefore indicate clearly:

- what is to be done;
- how it is to be done;
- when it will be done;
- what it will cost; and
- who will do it.

A typical research proposal might include ten elements, as indicated overleaf.

It can be helpful to present aspects of the proposal in diagrammatic form, particularly the conceptual approach, the various stages or elements of the project and the timetable. Examples of the latter are shown in Figures 3.8 and 3.9. Computer programs such as *Microsoft Project* and *ABC Flowcharter* can assist in the organisation of complex projects and their graphical presentation.

RESEARCH ETHICS

Ethical behaviour is important in research, as in any other field of human activity. Certain ethical considerations, concerned with such matters as plagiarism and honesty in reporting of results, arise in all research, but additional issues arise when the research involves human subjects, in both the biological and social sciences. The principles underlying 'research ethics' are universal—they concern issues such as honesty and respect for the rights of individuals. Insofar as research is part of business activity, research ethics become an aspect of business ethics.

Professional groups such as market researchers have established explicit *codes of ethics* to which members are obliged to adhere. Most universities now have codes of ethics enforced by 'ethics committees', which must approve all research projects involving humans or animals. These codes of ethics have intrinsic value in protecting the rights of humans and animals who may become involved in research, but they also serve a professional

Research proposal checklist: responsive research

1 Brief summary of key aspects of the proposal, including any unique approach and particular skills or experience of the consultants.
2 Re-statement of the key aspects of the brief.
3 Interpretation of key concepts in the brief.
4 Overall 'approach' to the problem.
5 Division of project into elements, stages and tasks related to structure of brief.
6 Information collection methods:
   - information collection tasks
   - sampling methods where appropriate—measures to ensure data quality
   - sample sizes where appropriate
   - information to be generated by each method used
   - outline of any ethical issues and how they will be addressed.
7 Timetable (NB. some tasks will be concurrent):
   - meetings with clients
   - other meetings with interested parties
   - preparatory work
   - fieldwork—data collection
   - analysis
   - draft report
   - feedback on draft
   - final report.
8 Budget: Costing of each element, stage and task:
   - project staff costs (n days at $x per day; gross costs, including normal office, overheads and support)
   - fieldwork and data collection costs
   - additional items—eg travel, printing
   - report preparation costs if significant (for example, if multiple copies are required).
9 Chapter outline of report and, if appropriate, details of other proposed reporting formats—interim reports, working papers, articles.
10 Resources available:
   - project and supervisory staff—curricula vitae, especially experience relevant to the proposed project
   - support staff, backup resources, organisation capability, experience.

and organisational function. Researchers may be subject to litigation and could lose professional indemnity if they are not seen to have adhered to the appropriate code of ethics. A related consideration is the question of public relations and the public standing within the community of organisations responsible for the research. Some practices might be ethical, but they may still give offence, so the value of the data collected using such practices must be weighed against the ill will that could be generated. The Academy of Management, which is the largest international association of management teachers and

Example of a research program: diagrammatic representation

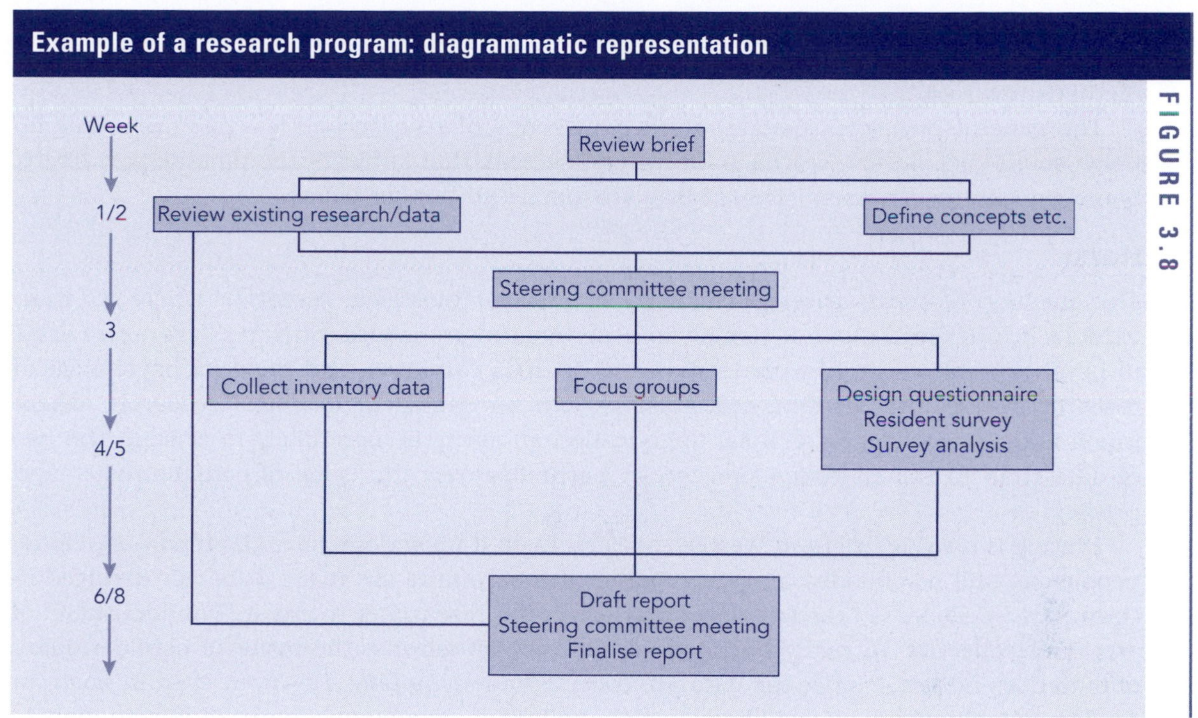

FIGURE 3.8

Example of a research project timetable

Week:	1	2	3	4	5	6	7	8
Review literature	■	■	■					
Secondary data analysis			■	■	■			
Conduct survey			■	■	■			
Analyse survey						■		
Focus groups			■					
Meetings with clients	*			*		*		*
Write report				■			■	■

FIGURE 3.9

researchers, publishes its *Code of Ethical Conduct* annually in the December issue of the *Academy of Management Journal.*

Ethical issues arise in the design and conduct of research and in the reporting of results. With regard to the design and conduct of research, many codes of ethics deal with practices in laboratories, but this discussion is concerned with ethical issues in the 'field'. As far as the reporting of results is concerned, the same ethical principles apply, regardless of the methods involved.

The general principles usually invoked in codes of research ethics are, first, that no harm should befall the research subjects, and second, that subjects should take part freely, based on informed consent. These ideas are discussed further below.

Harm

The question of harm arises particularly in medical/biological research, where an individual's health may be put at risk by an experimental procedure. Such risks can also arise in psychological research, where stress and distress can arise, and in social psychological research where interpersonal relationships can be damaged. In social research, where much management research falls, the question of 'harm' is more likely to arise in the *use* of data than in the collection process, in particular over the issue of confidentiality and privacy.

Privacy is a valued right in Western society. Even if no serious harm is *apparently* done, people can still be offended and suffer stress if their affairs are made public or divulged to third parties. There is therefore an obligation on the researcher to ensure confidentiality of any data collected. In many questionnaire survey situations, the issue of confidentiality of data does not arise since the data are collected anonymously. However, even in such an anonymous situation, informants may be reluctant to give certain types of information to 'a complete stranger'. Where such sensitivity is encountered, the usual approach is to stress the voluntary nature of the information-giving process.

In some research projects named individuals are inevitably involved—for example, where the number of subjects is small and they are important figures associated with particular organisations or communities. In this case the issue of confidentiality does arise. Where data are collected directly from the individual, care must be taken to adopt the journalist's practice of checking whether information is being given 'on the record' or 'off the record'. Thus, in interviews where sensitive matters arise, it is wise to ask informants whether they are prepared to be quoted. However, some information is obtained from third parties, and the researcher, like the journalist, must give careful consideration to just how such information is to be used. Unlike newspapers, few research organisations can afford to take the risk of publishing defamatory material.

When data are confidential, measures must be taken to protect that confidentiality through ensuring the security of the raw data such as interview tapes, transcripts and completed questionnaires. Care must also be taken in the way the results are written up. Data can be stored with code numbers or false names, with a key to the code numbers or names being kept securely in a place apart from the data. Surveys conducted by mail are an 'in between' case. If returns cannot be identified, then there is no way of identifying non-respondents in order to send reminders. Sending reminders to *everyone* is costly and an irritation to those who have already responded. One solution is to place an identifying number on the return envelope rather than on the questionnaire, with an assurance that the number will not be transferred to the questionnaire.

In reporting results, the use of false names or numbers to identify individuals, organisations, events, places and communities is an obvious solution, although it is often not sufficient. For those 'in the know', the places and the people involved in the research project may be all too easily identifiable. This is often the case when only a small group of employees are involved in a company research project. Occasionally the problem is exacerbated by the author's own list of 'acknowledgments', which may clearly identify people and places.

Confidentiality issues often arise with regard to the relationship between the researcher and the sponsoring organisation. In particular, if the sponsoring organisation 'owns' the data, the researcher may wish to protect the confidentiality of informants by *not* passing on to the sponsoring organisation any information that could identify informants by name.

Free choice

It seems obvious that subjects should not be coerced to participate in research projects, but there are some grey areas. Some of these are institutional and some are intrinsic to the design and nature of the research.

In universities, students are often used as subjects in research. In some universities, students are required to be available for a certain amount of experimental or survey work conducted by academic staff, and sometimes they receive credit for this involvement. Although students can 'opt out' of such activities, there is moral pressure on them to conform and they possibly fear sanctions if they do not. It is clearly unethical for the university to allow such undue moral pressure to be brought to bear.

Other 'captive group' cases involve groups of apprentices or members of organisations whose participation in a study is agreed to by the person in charge. Again, while opting out may be possible, it may be difficult in practice and the subject is, to all intents and purposes, coerced. Research in prisons and mental and other hospitals raises similar questions about genuine freedom of choice on the part of the subject.

Governments constantly infringe the principle of freedom of choice: it is an offence, for example, not to complete the population census forms or to refuse cooperation with a number of other official surveys. In these cases, the social need for accurate data is considered to outweigh the citizen's right to refuse to give information.

In some types of research, choice on the part of the subject is virtually impossible—such as observational research where large numbers of subjects are involved—for example, studies of traffic flows, pedestrian movements or crowd behaviour. In many observational research situations, if the subjects knew that they were being observed they might well modify their behaviour and thus invalidate the research. This would apply particularly in situations where anti-social and even illegal behaviour may be involved. These considerations might apply in research ranging from people's interpersonal behaviour in a workplace through to research on the milieux of bribery, gambling or drinking.

The problem of freedom to participate arises particularly in research using participant observation (Bulmer 1982). The whole basis of such research may rely on the researcher being accepted and trusted by the group being investigated—this acceptance and trust may not be forthcoming if it is known that the participant is a researcher. If the researcher does 'come clean', there is the risk—even the likelihood—of the subjects modifying their behaviour, thus invalidating the research. To what extent is it ethical for researchers to disguise their identity to the people they are interacting with and studying—in effect to lie about their identity? When researchers are involved with groups engaging in illegal or antisocial activities—for example, pilfering from work or exaggeration of production reports—where do their loyalties lie?

If it is accepted that research of this type is permissible, despite the lack of freedom of consent, then the issue of confidentiality in reporting, as discussed above, becomes even more important.

Informed consent

Where there is a risk, however remote, of harm to the subject (for example, where stress might be involved, or a risk of heart attack or psychological trauma), it is clearly necessary for the subject to be fully aware of the risks involved in order to give their *informed consent* to participate in the research. The level of risk of harm is a matter of judgement, and often only the researcher is fully aware of the extent of risk involved in any given research procedure. This raises the question of the extent to which the subject can be fully 'informed'. Subjects can never be as fully informed as the researcher. A judgement has to be made about what is reasonable. In the traditional science laboratory setting, verbal and written explanations of the nature of the research are given to the potential subjects and they are asked to sign a document indicating their agreement to being involved in the research. A researcher could of course 'go through the motions' of following this procedure, but abuse it by providing misleading information about the level of risk—hence the need for clear guidelines and monitoring of these matters.

Physical or mental risks do not generally arise in management research, but they are only one aspect of being informed. There may be a moral dimension also. For example, some people may object to being involved in research that is being conducted for certain public, political or commercial organisations. Thus, being informed also involves being informed about the purpose of the research and the nature of the sponsor or beneficiary. In some cases the status of the researcher is ambivalent, for example, when students conduct a project on behalf of a client organisation. This is also the case when part-time students conduct research for a university assignment in their workplaces using their fellow employees as subjects, or conduct research on competitors. It is clearly unethical for students to identify themselves only as students, and not to inform their subjects as to which organisation will be the beneficiary of the research.

However, there are some grey areas. In some instances, research is invalidated if subjects know its full purpose. Examples of such instances include quasi-experimental research on people's attitudes based on reactions to pictures, or to interviewers of differing race or gender. In some attitudinal research on potentially sensitive topics, such as racism or gender bias, it may be thought that responses will be affected if respondents are told too much about the research and therefore placed 'on their guard'. Such deception clearly raises ethical issues, and judgements have to be made about whether the value of the research justifies the use of mild deception.

Sometimes providing detailed information to informants or obtaining their written consent is neither practicable nor necessary. For example, a management survey may well:

- be anonymous;
- involve only a short interview (eg three or four minutes);
- involve fairly innocuous, non-personal questions; and
- take place at a business or site with the agreement of the management or authorities.

In this type of situation, most respondents are not interested in detailed explanations of the research. Most people are familiar with surveys and their main concern is that the interview should not take up too much of their time. Potential respondents can become impatient with attempts to provide detailed explanations of the research and would prefer to 'get on with it'. Often, questions about the purpose of the survey, if they arise at all, do so later during an interview process, when the respondent's interest has been stimulated.

A suggested set of guidelines for such surveys is as follows:

1 Interviewers should be identified with a badge bearing their name and the name of the organisation involved (the host organisation or university).
2 Interviewers should be fully briefed about the project so that they can answer questions if asked.
3 If a self-completion questionnaire is used, a brief description of the purpose of the project should be provided on the questionnaire (it should not take a long time to read) with telephone numbers for those requiring more information.
4 Interviewers approaching potential respondents should introduce themselves and seek cooperation using the following words, or similar: 'We are conducting a survey of ...., would you mind answering a few questions?'
5 Telephone numbers of supervisors should be available and be given to respondents if requested.
6 A short printed handout should be available with more information for those respondents who are interested.

General research ethics

The discussion so far has been concerned with the relationship between the researchers and subjects or informants and, to some extent, with client organisations. We should not leave this topic without considering a number of other issues, some of which might be considered 'obvious' to the moral person but which are nevertheless included for completeness.

Competence

Researchers should not embark on research involving the use of skills in which they have not been adequately trained. To do so may risk causing harm to subjects, may be an abuse of subjects' goodwill, may risk damaging the reputation of the research organisation and may involve waste of time and other resources.

Literature review

Any research should be preceded by a thorough review of the literature to ensure, as far as possible, that the proposed research has not already been done by others.

Plagiarism

The use of others' data or ideas without due acknowledgment and permission, where appropriate, is unethical.

Appropriate acknowledgement

Due acknowledgement should be made of individuals who have assisted in the research, even when—as in the case of research assistants and some participants in focus groups and panel surveys—they have been paid for their services. Such acknowledgement may be made individually by name or collectively, as appropriate. Even when a client organisation has commissioned research and owns the copyright, the researchers or consultants retain certain 'moral rights' (Sainsbury 2003) in the research and have a right to public acknowledgement of their inputs, and to expect that the research will not be unduly distorted or misreported.

Falsification of results

The falsification of research results or the misleading reporting of results is clearly unethical.

SUMMARY

This chapter has examined a range of issues associated with the planning and design of research projects. Undertaking a *research project* is a broad and exacting task that extends well beyond simply conducting fieldwork. The research process involves a number of steps, beginning with the selection of the *research topic* and ending with a report of the *research findings*.

The choice of a *research topic* can arise from personal interest, from the literature describing existing theory and research in the area, from social concern or as the outcome of some currently popular issue. Irrespective of the reason for choosing a particular topic, a *literature review* of previous research in the topic area is an essential component of the research process. Following the literature review, a *conceptual framework* for the research project needs to be developed. This conceptual framework indicates how the researcher views the concepts involved in the study and the relationships between those concepts.

Once a conceptual framework is established, specific *research questions* or *hypotheses* can be developed which will be directly addressed in the study. A list of *information needs and the operationalisation of concepts/variables* can then be developed.

The next step is the development of an appropriate *research strategy* for the project. This involves making decisions about the information-gathering methods to be used, the approach to data analysis, and the budget and timetable for the project. A substantial proportion of this book is devoted to a discussion of the range of available information-gathering processes such as the utilisation of existing information, observation, qualitative methods and questionnaire-based surveys.

The preceding steps will have provided the foundations for the actual *conduct of the research*. The final step in the research process is *reporting the findings* of the research. The final chapter of this book is devoted to that topic.

Research proposals can take two forms. The first is the *self-generated* proposal prepared by academics seeking funds for a research project they have devised, or by students seeking approval for research for a project or thesis on a selected topic. The second type of proposal is the *responsive proposal* prepared by consultants in response to research briefs prepared by potential clients. A *self-generated* research proposal will usually describe the proposed research in terms of the steps involved in the research process up to the point of actually conducting the research, namely:

- topic selection;
- literature review;
- conceptual framework;
- research questions;

- information needs; and
- research strategy.

A *responsive proposal* must first of all address the brief and indicate clearly:

- what is to be done;
- how it is to be done;
- when it will be done;
- what it will cost;
- who will do it.

Research ethics play an important part in the planning, design and conduct of research projects. Ethical considerations such as plagiarism and honesty occur in all research, but additional issues arise when the research involves human subjects. The principles underlying *research ethics* are universal—they concern issues such as honesty and respect for the rights of individuals. The general principles usually invoked in codes of research ethics are, first that *no harm* should befall the research subjects, and second that subjects should participate in research projects freely, based on *informed consent*.

EXERCISES

1. Select three research articles from a business journal and identify the basis of their choice of research topic. Identify the key concepts used in the articles and draw a simple concept map for each article to show how the concepts are related. Identify the research approaches used in each of the studies.
2. The senior management of a national Australian company is considering moving its headquarters from the present site in the central business district of Sydney to a new site in Parramatta, 23 km from the CBD. The new site is in a modern air-conditioned building with every facility and is a short walking distance from the busy Parramatta railway station. The management is concerned that the move may result in staffing instability, manifesting itself in increased frequency of staff turnover, absenteeism and sick leave. You have been asked to prepare a research proposal to assist management in deciding whether or not to move. Prepare a bullet point summary of items to be included in your research proposal under the following headings.
   - **a** key concepts in the proposal
   - **b** stages of the project
   - **c** information collection methods
   - **d** timetable
   - **e** budget
   - **f** structure of final report.
3. The outcomes of business research can sometimes be potentially harmful to two groups of people:
   - **a** employees within an organisation whose performance is seen to be inadequate by the research
   - **b** outside suppliers or customers of the organisation who may be adversely affected by the findings of the research.

   Outline the ethical challenges faced by a business researcher whose research may have these potential outcomes. Provide details of the actions the researcher should take in response to these challenges.

FURTHER READING

Planning and design of research projects: Easterby-Smith, Thorpe and Lowe (1993), Chapters 2 & 3; Jankowicz (1991), Chapters 2, 3, 4, 6 and 7; Kervin (1992), Chapters 1 & 2; Raimond (1993); Sekaran (1992), Chapters 1 and 2; or Zikmund (1991), Chapter 3.

Preparation of a research plan: Gay and Diehl (1992), Chapter 3.

Mental mapping: Buzan (1994).

Example of a conceptual framework: For a study of consumer food-store loyalty: Huddleston, Whipple and Van Auken (2004); in e-commerce: Zhan & Dubinsky (2003)—see Case Study Example 3.1.

Research ethics: Bulmer (1982); Cooper and Emory (1995), Special section: Ethics in business research; Davis and Cosenza (1993), Chapter 14; Kimmel, (1988); Sieber (1992); or Zikmund (1997), Chapter 4.

CHAPTER 4

Using the literature

The purpose of this chapter is to explain the importance of reviewing previous research and writing as part of the research procedure. Previous research and writing is known as *the literature*. This chapter considers the *processes* of reviewing the literature. It discusses general sources of information relevant to management research and sets out the mechanics of compiling bibliographies, or lists of references, in the management area.

Reviewing the work of earlier researchers is an important step in the research process. The literature relating to management research is extensive since the management field is wide-ranging and multidisciplinary in nature. Reports of relevant studies can be found in a number of areas related to business as well as in the mainstream business literature. Finding the work that has been already been done by others can be a challenging task.

As indicated in Chapter 3, a literature review can fulfil a number of different roles in relation to research. It is important to note that more than one role can apply to a particular research project.

The roles of the literature review:

- The entire basis of the research, ie there is no intention of collecting new data in the current project and it will be based entirely on the literature—see Case Study Example 4.1.
- The source of ideas on what topics need researching.
- An exercise to ensure that the proposed research has not already been done by someone else.
- A source of ideas about the proposed topic of research, whether in terms of theories or methodology.
- A source of comparison, where findings from previous related studies are compared with those of the proposed project.
- An integral or supportive part of the research, complementing the newly collected data—for example, the use of population census data or business customer records in conjunction with survey data.

CASE STUDY EXAMPLE 4.1

Literature review: entrepreneurship and ethics

Source: Francis T. Hannafey 2003, Entrepreneurship and ethics: a literature review. *Journal of Business Ethics*, 46(2), 99–110.
Method: Literature review
Topic: Entrepreneurial ethics

This does not set out to be a comprehensive review but to 'identify and prioritise key ethical issues and important patterns in the present research and discuss new directions for future study'. The author draws on an existing conceptual framework for the field to divide the review into two sections, one dealing with the collective issue of 'the entrepreneur and society' and the other dealing with individual issues under the heading 'ethics and the entrepreneur'. The latter is subdivided into four sections: the individual entrepreneur; the entrepreneurial organisation; the entrepreneurial environment; and the new venture creation process. A final section of the paper discusses 'future directions' for research and lists a large number of topics requiring research, including: more empirical research on actual entrepreneurs with larger sample sizes; research with a global/cross-cultural and cross-industry focus; cross-disciplinary research including the humanities as well as the social sciences; research on changing ethical concerns over time; the influence of educational curricula and other formative institutions on entrepreneurs' ethical standards; the frequency with which entrepreneurs confront ethical issues; and what motivates individuals to become entrepreneurs and how these motives relate to ethics.

This paper provides an example of a research outcome which consists entirely of a literature review, but with just 50 references it is limited and focused. It makes a contribution to the field by summarising and evaluating a distinctive body of research.

The aim of *academic* research is to add to the body of knowledge that forms the literature. To add to the body of knowledge it is necessary to be familiar with that knowledge base and to indicate precisely how the proposed or completed research relates to the existing work. The aim of *consultancy*, on the other hand, is to use research to assist in the solution of immediate problems. A familiarity with the existing body of knowledge is nevertheless important. Reference to the literature can save much time and resources by finding research methods that have been tried and validated by others. Inexperienced researchers often try to 're-invent the wheel' by devising their own methodologies and conducting research with inadequate methodologies, when reference to the literature would have provided information on well-proven approaches.

THE LITERATURE SEARCH: PREPARING A BIBLIOGRAPHY

The literature search is a vital part of the research process. It involves the following steps: a careful search for information on relevant published work and, if necessary, unpublished work; obtaining copies of relevant items and reviewing them; making a list of useful items to form a *bibliography;* and assessing and summarising salient aspects for the research proposal, research report or article. Researchers often write short summary notes or abstracts following each item in their bibliographic list to remind themselves or inform others of the content and relevance of each particular reference. This form of bibliography is called an *annotated bibliography.*

Although this chapter focuses on reviewing the literature in relation to planned research projects, the development of bibliographies can be a useful exercise in itself. It might be thought that modern electronic search methods, as discussed below, have made the compilation and publication of bibliographies obsolete, but this is not the case. Electronic databases are still incomplete, especially with regard to older published material and 'ephemeral' material such as conference papers, reports and working papers not published by mainstream publishers.

In addition, electronic databases do not provide an evaluation of material; they do not usually distinguish between a substantial research paper and a lightweight commentary that provides no original material. Electronic systems generally identify items on the basis of their titles, keywords and abstracts. Many existing databases do not indicate, for example, whether a report on *management activities* includes data on a specific activity, such as leadership or performance reviews, or whether a report on *management communication patterns* addresses issues such as written communication, non-verbal communication or supervisor-subordinate communication.

A great deal of useful work can therefore still be done in compiling bibliographies on specific topics, which identify items that may not be listed electronically and weed out items of limited value, thus helping to consolidate the 'state of the art' and saving other researchers' time and effort in searching out relevant material.

LITERATURE SOURCES

The researcher interested in a particular topic should be constantly alert for sources of material on that topic. Sometimes key items are encountered when they are least expected. The researcher should be like a bloodhound, searching out anything of relevance to the topic of interest. In a real world research situation the process of identifying as much

Sources of information:

- Library catalogues
- Published indexes
- Electronic databases
- The Internet
- General management books
- Reference lists
- Published bibliographies
- Library browsing
- Asking (librarians and academics)

literature as possible can take months or even years. While particular efforts should be made to identify material at the beginning of any research project, this should also continue throughout the course of the research project. Where can the researcher look for information on existing published or unpublished research on a topic? In this section a number of sources are examined.

Library catalogues

A library catalogue is a listing of all the holdings of a library, whether the material is in print, audio-visual or electronic form. Modern libraries have computerised catalogues that are accessed via terminals within the library and can also be accessed from remote locations via the Internet. The Internet makes it possible to access the catalogues of many libraries, worldwide. Searches can be made using the titles of publications, authors or keywords that have been included in the catalogue by the librarians. Searching library catalogues can be very helpful as a starting point in establishing a bibliography, but it is only a starting point, particularly for the researcher with a specialist interest.

Library catalogues themselves do not generally contain references to:

- individual articles in journals;
- individual chapters in books which are collections of readings; or
- individual papers in collections of conference papers.

A library catalogue may not indicate whether a general publication includes any reference to a subject of specific interest within that area—for example, whether a publication on marketing covers psychographics. A catalogue will only identify publications by their main substantive subject, so they will not identify publications that, while they are not concerned with the researcher's topic of interest, may provide a suitable *methodology* for studying the topic. Such material can only be identified by actually reading—or at least perusing—original texts and following up leads.

To identify more detailed items, other sources of information need to be used, as discussed below.

Published indexes

Published *indexes* are specialist listings of bibliographic material that are updated on a regular basis by specialist libraries or research centres. Indexes reference the contents of a large number of journals and other resources such as books, reports, newspaper articles, conference papers and magazines. Some indexes also provide a short summary or *abstract* of each article that is referenced or *cited* in the index. Indexes containing abstracts of articles are sometimes called 'Abstracts' themselves (eg *Psychological Abstracts*).

The following are examples of indexes available in printed format.

- The *Business Periodicals Index* is a cumulative index of English language journals. Subject areas covered include management, industrial relations, accounting, banking, marketing, computer technology and applications, personnel administration, finance and investment.

- The *Social Science Citation Index*, available in most university libraries, is a comprehensive listing of papers from thousands of social science journals, cross-referenced by author and subject. In addition, cited authors are cross-referenced and can be followed up.

Appendix 1 provides a list of additional print and electronic resources in the management and business area.

An index will generally focus on materials associated with a broad field of study such as business, education, psychology, sociology or chemistry. It is not uncommon to find considerable overlap between different indexes—for example, references to management might be found not only in indexes concerned with business (eg *ABI/INFORM*) but also in those concerned with psychology (*Psychological Abstracts*), social sciences (*Sociological Abstracts* or *Sociofile*), communication (*Communication Abstracts*) or education (*ERIC*) indexes.

Indexes which were originally published in hard copy are now often also available online, so they become part of the *electronic databases* discussed below.

Electronic databases

Indexes readily lend themselves to production in electronic formats as large electronic databases held on a library or company computer. Electronic databases generally provide great advantages over print indexes by virtue of the speed and range of searches that they can conduct. These indexes may be accessed and searched directly through computer terminals in a library or remotely via the Internet, and some are also available in CD-ROM format.

In general, an index or database will provide the title, author and publication details that are referred to as the citation for an article. Keywords and a summary or abstract of an article are also often included. Most electronic indexes provide a facility for conducting keyword searches, which locate a selected word in any part of the citation including the title, descriptors and abstract, and, in some cases, the full text of articles. This is especially useful for finding material relevant to a particular area of interest and greatly enhances the power of the search. It may also produce irrelevant material where the keyword is used in an inappropriate context. For example, as part of a management research project on organisational climate, a search on the keyword 'climate' would uncover a large number of irrelevant references from fields such as biology, geography, oceanography and meteorology. However, electronic databases offer flexibility in allowing searches that involve more than one search term. In the given example, irrelevant references could be avoided by searching for the terms 'organisation' and 'climate' where they appear together in a reference.

Libraries subscribe to a variety of journal index services, such as EBSCO and ABI/INFORM, which provide access to certain sets of journals. The contents of these services are then incorporated into the library's own catalogue so that, if the library does not have a hard copy subscription to a journal, the user is referred to the electronic source. Since these services cost money, access is only available to registered users of the library, such as enrolled students or academic staff.

The following electronic databases focus on management or business in international and Australian contexts:

- The *ABI/INFORM* (American Business Index) database, established in 1990, indexes international business journals. Online subscriptions give approximately 50 per cent in full text. However, *BPOD* (Business Periodicals On Disc), which is provided on CD-ROM, provides full text of articles indexed by *ABI/INFORM* and includes graphics, pictures and tables.
- *ABIX* (Melbourne, Vic., Royal Melbourne Institute of Technology & Business Intelligence Australia) is an Australian database available on CD-ROM. This is a major source of Australian business information. It provides information on Australian companies, industries, government developments, and a wide range of topics in the business and financial sector, including telecommunications, information technology, marketing and advertising from major Australian newspapers and business journals.
- *Business Australia* is a CD-ROM which includes coverage of industrial relations, management and training.

Related databases

Because of the diversity of business research, useful material is likely to be indexed on a number of databases that overlap the business field.

- The *APAIS* (Australian Public Affairs Information Service) CD-ROM covers Australian political, economic, social and cultural affairs. It is part of a collection of twelve Australian databases known as *AUSTROM.*
- *Dissertation Abstracts* lists masters and doctoral theses internationally in all academic areas and is available on CD-ROM.
- *Periodical Abstracts* is a complete general reference resource that contains indexing and abstracting for significant articles appearing in general and academic periodicals, as well as full text from more than 600 journals from 1986 to the present day. Topics covered include current affairs, business and industry news and analysis, cultural events and issues, and academic topics of general interest.
- *IDEAL* (International Digital Electronic Access Library) *Academic Press* (www.janet.idealibrary.com/index.html) includes areas such as economics, business, finance, psychology and social science.
- *Sociological Abstracts* and *SOCIOFILE* are online databases concerning sociology and related disciplines. *Sociological Abstracts* includes subfiles covering citations and abstracts from more than 2000 indexed journals, plus relevant dissertation listings, abstracts of conference papers and selected books, and citations of book reviews and other media.
- *PsycINFO* is an online database concerning psychology and related disciplines. It is a development of *Psychological Abstracts*, which is a related print index. It covers journal articles and book chapters in fields such as psychology, educational psychology, consumer behaviour, adolescence, adoption, ageing, psychiatry and counselling.

The Internet

The Internet was first established in the late 1960s, and most computers around the world are now connected to this network, which is becoming an important source of information for business researchers. The content of the Internet is known as the *World Wide Web*. The World Wide Web provides individual *web pages* that can be displayed on a computer screen. Web pages have the capacity to display text, pictures, sound and video clips.

Various organisations and individuals have established *websites* on the Internet which provide information on a wide range of business-related topics and issues. Topics include biographies, conferences, journals, ongoing research and cross references to other websites.

To view the World Wide Web, an application called a *browser* is needed. Two commonly used browsers are *Microsoft Internet Explorer* and *Netscape Navigator.* A browser connects the user's computer to a remote website that has a unique Uniform Resource Locator (URL), or 'web address', which directs the browser to the location of the resource on the Internet. The address of a website generally appears in a form similar to: (http://www.orgname.com.au), where:

- *http* stands for 'hypertext transfer protocol' (this is often omitted when giving URL details);
- *www* stands for 'World Wide Web';
- *orgname* is an organisational or company name;
- *com* is the code used to indicate that the organisation maintaining the website is a commercial organisation (alternatively, *gov* is used by government organisations, *org* or *net* is used by non-profit organisations and *edu, ed* or *ac* by educational institutions); and
- *au* represents the country name, in this case Australia (*uk* is the United Kingdom, *kr* Korea, *jp* Japan and *fr* France. The US has no country code).

For example, the web address of the *Australian Financial Review* is (www.afr.com.au), while the University of Technology, Sydney's address is (www.uts.edu.au).

Information on the Internet is found by using a *search engine*, the most commonly used being 'Google'. A word or phrase is typed into the search engine, much in the same way key phrases and words are entered into an electronic library catalogue. The search is initiated by clicking on the 'Search' button with the mouse. The search engine will then provide a list of relevant website addresses. One useful site, located at (www.dogpile.com), integrates a number of popular search engines, providing a very broad search facility.

Information found on the World Wide Web can either be printed immediately or saved as a file for later reference. It is important to note that the Internet is not a structured database like the electronic databases described above, and the user must carefully evaluate the quality of the information found.

Appendix 1 (p. 327) provides the addresses of some websites that may be useful in business research.

General management books

The researcher should be aware of general information sources that contain information on specific business topics. For example, general textbooks on 'management' contain numerous references to literature on particular aspects of management, such as human resource management, ethics, management theory, planning and decision-making, strategic planning, organisational structure, culture, communication management, leadership, motivation, teamwork, change management and international management.

Reference lists

The lists of references in the books and articles identified in initial searches, and in course handouts, will generally lead to other material.

Published bibliographies

Libraries usually have a number of bibliographies relevant to more specific management areas. These can be found in associated subject areas where it may be worth 'browsing' to find items of interest, especially when the topic is interdisciplinary. Bibliographies are generally catalogued in the reference section of the library.

Library browsing

While browsing library shelves is not generally recommended as a systematic process of identifying literature, it can often yield results, particularly if the researcher is drawing on material from an unfamiliar disciplinary area. Browsing a particular section of the library shelves and the contents of particular journals can give an indication of the extent to which a topic is addressed in that particular field and the emphasis and terminology used.

Asking (librarians and academics)

Librarians and academics can be sources of advice in searching the literature. When engaged in assignments or theses students will be under the supervision of an academic who will generally give at least a starting point for a literature search. If other academics are approached by students, perhaps because of their known expertise in an area, there is an expectation that students will have already made some efforts to identify material and that a request for guidance will be specific rather than general. Similarly, given the considerable resources for searching catalogues and databases available in most modern libraries, librarians would expect a student to have utilised these before seeking their help in relation to a specific search.

OBTAINING COPIES OF MATERIAL

If material is not available in a particular library or via the Internet, it can often be obtained through an *inter-library loan*. This is a system through which loans of books and reports can be made between one library and another. In the case of journal articles, the system usually involves the provision of a photocopy. In theory, any item published in a particular country should be available through this system since it is connected with national copyright libraries, such as the National Library in Canberra, the British Library or the Library of Congress, where, by law, copies of all published items must be lodged. Practices vary from library to library, but in academic libraries the service is usually only available to postgraduate research students and academic staff.

For researchers working in metropolitan areas, an obvious source of material is specialist libraries, particularly those of government agencies. Access conditions to these libraries vary.

COMPILING AND MAINTAINING A BIBLIOGRAPHY

What should be done with reference material once it has been identified? The researcher is strongly advised to start an index of everything identified. This can be of use not only in the current research project, but also for future reference—a personal bibliography can be built up over the years. The index can be established and maintained using a database or word-processing program. This has the advantage that when there is a need to compile a bibliography on another topic in the future, a start can be made from your personal bibliography by copying designated items into a new file.

Specialist software packages, such as *Endnote* or *Pro-Cite*, can be used to store references in a database in a standard format. The database can be cross-referenced and will automatically compile a reference list in appropriate formats to meet the needs of varying report styles and the requirements of different academic journals. Such packages are highly recommended for researchers starting out on a research career. Their use means that any one reference will only ever have to be typed out once!

It takes only seconds to copy out the *full* details of a reference *when it is first identified*. It is advisable to have a notebook or a supply of reference cards handy for such a purpose. If this practice is adopted, many hours of time and effort can be saved by not having to chase up details of references at a later date. Not only should all the details be recorded accurately, as set out below, but a note should also be made on the card or in the database about the availability of the material. For example, it should be noted that the item is a library catalogue reference, or that the item is *not* in the library, or that a photocopy has been taken. When taking a photocopy, ensure that *all details of the reference are included* by photocopying such items as title pages of books and/or noting the year of publication.

REVIEWING THE LITERATURE

Writing a review of the literature on a selected topic can be one of the most rewarding—and one of the most frustrating—of research tasks. It is a task where a range of skills and qualities needs to be employed, including patience, persistence, insight and lateral thinking. The review of the literature can play a number of roles in a research project, as outlined above, and this leads to a variety of approaches to conducting a review.

Types of literature review:
- Inclusive
- Inclusive/evaluative/meta-analysis
- Exploratory
- Instrumental
- Content analysis/hermeneutics

Inclusive

The *inclusive* approach simply seeks to identify and list everything that has been written on a particular topic. Judgement is made as to what to include and what not to include, for example in regard to non-academic materials. Abstracts may also be provided, in which case the outcome is referred to as an *annotated* bibliography. The compilation of such a bibliography can be an achievement in itself and may even serve as a resource to be drawn on by the researcher or by others.

Inclusive/evaluative/meta-analysis

The *inclusive/evaluative* approach takes the inclusive approach a stage further by providing a commentary on the literature in terms of its coverage and its contribution to knowledge and understanding of the topic.

One approach to this style of review involves a systematic, quantitative appraisal of the findings from the literature on a number of projects, sometimes in the hundreds, focused on the same topic. The technique, known as *meta-analysis*, was discussed in Chapter 2 and falls somewhere between a literature review and secondary data analysis. Examples of studies using meta-analysis are included in Figure 2.4 in Chapter 2 (p. 41).

Exploratory

The *exploratory* approach is more focused than the inclusive or evaluative approach and seeks to discover existing research that might throw light on a specific research question or issue. This is the classic literature review that is the norm for academic research and best fits the model of the research process outlined in Chapter 3. Comprehensiveness is not as important as being focused on the particular question or issue. The skill in conducting such a review lies in keeping the question or issue in sight, while 'interrogating' the literature for ideas and insights which may help shape the research. The reviewer needs to be open to useful ideas, but should not be sidetracked into areas that stray too far from the question or issue of interest.

Instrumental

In an *instrumental* review the primary focus is the issue being researched; the literature is used as a source of suitable ideas on how the particular research question might best be tackled. The criterion for selection of literature is not to present a picture of the state of knowledge on the topic, but merely to identify a useful methodology or suitable research instruments which can provide appropriate insights or an effective approach to research the issue. The methodology or instruments identified may provide quantitative or qualitative data on the topic, or the basis of a conceptual framework. This approach is more common in consultancy or project reports.

Content analysis and hermeneutics

Content analysis and *hermeneutics* are techniques that involve detailed analysis of the content of a certain body of literature, or other documentary sources, which are viewed as *texts*. The text becomes a focus of research in its own right rather than merely as a report of research. The texts might be, for example, company reports, the speeches of CEOs, policy statements or the contents of advertising. *Content analysis* tends to be quantitative, for example, counting the number of occurrences of certain phrases in certain documents or speeches. *Hermeneutics* tends to be more qualitative in nature, the term being borrowed from the traditional approach to analysis and interpretation of religious texts. The essence of this approach is discussed in Chapter 7 in relation to the analysis of in-depth interview transcripts.

Reading critically and creatively

Reviewing the literature for research purposes involves reading the literature in a certain way. This differs from the way literature might be read in other contexts, for example in an essay in an established field of knowledge. It involves being concerned with the methodological aspects of the research (which are not always well reported), as well as in the substantive content, that is, with *how* the conclusions are formed as well as with the conclusions themselves. It involves being particularly critical and questioning what is being read. Importantly, the task is to ascertain what is *not* known, as well as to determine what *is* known. As material is being read, a number of questions might be asked, such as those listed below, while bearing in mind that not all the questions will be appropriate for all types of research.

Questions to ask about individual literature items:

- What is the (empirical) basis of this research?
- How does the research relate to other research writings on the topic?
- What theoretical framework is being used?
- What geographical area does the research refer to?
- What social group does the research refer to?
- When was the research carried out and is it still likely to be empirically valid?

A major challenge is to provide a framework to classify and analyse the content of the literature reviewed. This can be similar to the development of a conceptual framework for the research project as a whole and is where creativity particularly enters the process. Some sort of diagrammatic, concept map approach, as indicated in Figure 4.1, may be helpful. This example, which is not meant to be definitive, contains four sorts of inputs from the literature: data sets, theories, subthemes related to the main issue; and a related issue. A diagram might be devised before starting a review, or may be developed, inductively, as the review progresses.

Summarising the literature review

A review of the literature should draw *conclusions* and identify *implications* for the proposed research program. It is therefore advisable to complete a review by presenting a *summary* that addresses the sorts of questions listed below. This summary should logically be linked to the research project at hand and it should be clear to a reader just how the proposed research relates to the existing body of literature. It should be readily apparent whether the research is seeking to add to the existing body of knowledge, to fill a gap, or to bring it up

Making sense of the literature

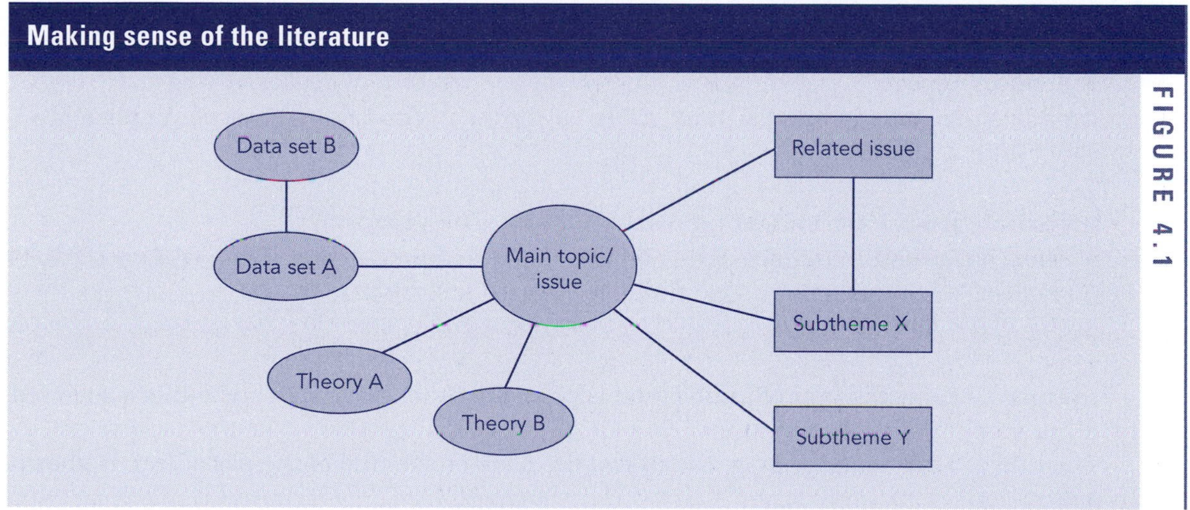

FIGURE 4.1

to date, or whether it is simply using the existing literature as a source of ideas, or for comparison purposes.

Questions to ask in summarising and drawing conclusions about the literature review:

- What is the range of research that has been conducted?
- What *methods* have generally been used and what methods have been neglected?
- What, in summary, does the existing research tell us?
- What, in summary, does the existing research *not* tell us?
- What contradictions are there in the literature—either recognised or unrecognised by the authors concerned?
- What are the *deficiencies* in the existing research, in substantive or methodological terms?
- Which particular contributions from the literature will be most relevant to the research at hand and how will they shape the research?

RECORDING REFERENCES TO THE LITERATURE

A number of standard or conventional formats exist for recording references to the literature. The conventions have been established by leading academic organisations and publishers. Guides are produced by organisations such as the *Australian Government Publishing Service* and the *American Psychological Association*. The formats outlined below are acceptable in most academic contexts if followed consistently. In what follows, the word 'text' refers to the main body of the research report or article.

The general format recommended for recording references is shown below. In some systems the date is put at the end, but when using the *author/date* system, as discussed below, the date should follow the name(s) of the author(s).

Standard reference formats:

A book or report:

Author surname(s), Initials Year, *Title of Book or Report (in italics)*, Publisher, City/State of publication.

An article from a periodical (journal/magazine/newspaper):

Author surname(s), Initials Year, Title of article (lower case). *Title of Periodical (in italics)*, Volume number(Issue number), Page number(s).

In some systems the year of publication is placed in brackets and in some this is followed by a full stop.

The title of a reference, that is, the title of the book or the title of the periodical, is shown in italics.

Note that the *publisher* of a book is not the same as the *printer* of the book; references do not need to refer to the printer. It is customary to indicate only the *city* of the publisher in a reference, although in the case of United States' cities it is customary to include the abbreviated state name as well—for example, San Francisco, CA. Elsewhere, where the city is obscure or its location ambiguous, the state and/or country of publication should also be included. It is not necessary to refer to the publisher in the case of periodicals.

Some examples of references are set out here to illustrate these principles. Numerous other examples appear in the bibliography of this book. Note that it is common practice to indent the second and subsequent lines of the reference to give emphasis to the author name.

A book

Easterby-Smith, M., Thorpe, R. & Lowe, A. 1993, *Management Research: An Introduction.* Sage, London.

An edited book of readings

Clegg, S.R., Hardy, C. & Nord, W.R. (eds) 1996, *Handbook of Organization Studies.* Sage, London.

A paper or chapter from an edited book of readings

Alvesson, M. & Deetz, S. 1996, Critical theory and postmodern approaches to organizational studies. In S. R. Clegg, C. Hardy, & W. R. Nord (eds), *Handbook of Organization Studies.* Sage, London, pp. 191–217.

A published conference report

Gibson, B., Newby, R. & Morris, R. (eds) 1996, *Changing Business Relationships, Small Business Growth and Other Challenges: Proceedings of the Small Enterprise Association of Australia and New Zealand, and the Institute of Industrial Economics, Joint Small Enterprise Conference.* Fremantle, WA, Institute of Industrial Economics, University of Newcastle, Newcastle, NSW.

A published conference paper

Ticehurst, G.W. & Winfield, I. 1997, The global march of Toyota: from rhetoric to reality. In *Restrategising the Asia-Pacific Region: Towards a New Millenium, Proceedings of the 14th Pan-Pacific Conference, Kuala Lumpur, Malaysia.* Pan-Pacific Business Association, University of Nebraska, Lincoln, NB, pp. 40–3.

A government agency report, authored and published by the same agency

Environment Protection Authority 1993, *Waste Minimisation: Assessments and Opportunities for Industry: A Practical Guide to Cleaner Production.* Environment Protection Authority, Melbourne, Vic.

continues

A government report published by the government publisher

Industry Task Force on Leadership and Management Skills 1995, *Enterprising Nation: Renewing Australia's Managers to Meet the Challenges of the Asia-Pacific Century. Report of the Industry Task Force on Leadership and Management Skills.* (David S. Karpin, Chairman), AGPS, Canberra. (NB. Abbreviation normally used: AGPS—Australian Government Publishing Service.)

A journal article

Ticehurst, G.W. 1991, The role of communication in the development of organisations to the year 2000 and beyond. *Australian Journal of Communication,* 18(3), 59–72.

A newspaper article with named author

Davies, A. 1997, Proposal for panel on takeovers. *Sydney Morning Herald,* 13 Nov., p. 27.

A newspaper item without a named author

Sydney Morning Herald 1997, Hong Kong rattled by bank scare. 13 Nov., p. 26.

REFERENCES AND REFERENCING SYSTEMS

What is the purpose of referencing? Firstly, referencing is evidence of the writer's scholarship—it indicates that the report is related to the existing body of knowledge. This is not only of importance to teachers marking student assignments, it is part and parcel of the development of knowledge. Secondly, references enable the reader to check sources—either to verify the writer's interpretation of previous research, or to follow up areas of interest.

There are two commonly used referencing systems: the *author/date* system and the *footnote* or *endnote* system. These two systems are discussed in turn below.

The author/date system

Basic features

In the author/date or 'Harvard' system, references to an item of literature are made within the text by using authors' names and the year of the publication. Thus, a sentence in a report might look something like this:

> *Concepts of leadership in corporations include the trait approach of the 1940s (Stogdill 1948), the style approach of the 1950s and 1960s (Korman 1966), the contingency approach of the 1970s (Fiedler 1967), and the newer contemporary leadership approach from the 1980s up to the present (Bryman 1992).*

Note that authors' initials are not used in these references (unless there are two authors with the same surname and references in the same year). At the end of the report a list of references is provided, arranged in alphabetical order, as follows:

References:

Bryman, A. 1992, *Charisma and Leadership of Organisations*. Sage, London.

Fiedler, F.E. 1967, *A Theory of Leadership Effectiveness*. McGraw Hill, New York, NY.

Korman, A.K. 1966, 'Consideration', 'initiating structure', and organisational criteria—a review. *Personal Psychology*, 19(3), 349–61.

Stogdill, R.M. 1948, Personal factors associated with leadership: a survey of the literature. *Journal of Psychology*, 25(1), 35–71.

Style variation

The style of presentation of referenced material can vary depending on the writer's intention. For example, the above statement could be made in the following alternative ways: first, de-emphasising the authors:

> *There has been ongoing interest in concepts of leadership in companies since the 1940s, including the trait approach, the style approach, the contingency approach and the newer contemporary leadership approaches, as shown in the work of a number of authors (Stogdill 1948; Fiedler 1967; Korman 1966; Bryman 1992).*

Second, drawing more explicit attention to the authors:

> *Concepts of leadership in corporations have included Stogdill's (1948) work on the trait approach, Korman's (1966) study of style approaches, Fiedler's (1967) contingency approach, and more recent work by Bryman (1992) involving new leadership approaches.*

Specifics and quotations

When referring to specific points from an item of literature, rather than making a general reference to the whole item as above, page references should be given to the specific aspect of interest. For example:

> *There is a large literature associated with 'critical theory' and 'postmodernism' and it is generally difficult to read (Alvesson & Deetz 1996: 191).*

When quoting directly from a source, page references should also be given:

> *Alvesson and Deetz (1996: 191) make the point that 'most of the various critical theory and postmodernist positions are still relatively new to management studies'.*

A longer quotation of four lines or more would be indented in the page and handled like this:

> *Alvesson and Deetz argue a case for the adoption of critical theory and postmodernist approaches in management studies and note:*
>
>> *The general projects of critical theory and postmodernism do not represent fad or simple fascination. Certainly some popular accounts on postmodernism invite such a critique, and we do not believe that this label is necessarily the best or will last. We believe that postmodernism—and critical theory for that matter—should be studied not because they are new and different, but because they provide unique and important ways to understand organisations and their management (Alvesson & Deetz 1996: 191).*

Advantages and disadvantages of the author/date system

The author/date system is an *academic* style. The referencing is very 'up front', even obtrusive, in the text. It is not an appropriate style for some practically orientated reports, particularly where the readership is not academic. Large numbers of references using this style tend to clutter up the text and make it difficult to read. The author/date system also has the disadvantage that it does not accommodate footnotes or endnotes. However, one view is that footnotes and endnotes are undesirable—if something is worth saying, it is worth saying in the body of the text. If notes and asides are nevertheless considered necessary, it is possible to establish a footnote system for this purpose in addition to using the author/date system for references to the literature only. This of course becomes somewhat complex. If extensive notes are considered necessary then it is probably best to use the footnote style for everything, as discussed below.

The advantages of the author/date system are that it saves the effort of keeping track of footnote numbers, it indicates the date of publication to the reader, the details of any one item of literature have to be written out only once and it results in a tidy, alphabetical list of references at the end of the document.

Footnote and endnote systems

Basic features

The *footnote* style involves the use of numbered references in the text and a list of corresponding numbered references at the foot of the page. The term footnote originates from the time when the notes were invariably printed at the foot of each page. This can be seen in older books. However, printing footnotes at the bottom of the page came to be seen as too complex to organise when typing and too expensive to set up for printing. As a result, the practice was generally abandoned in favour of providing *endnotes*: a list of notes at the end of the text. Consequently endnotes are now more common, even though computer software has automated the process of numbering and locating both footnotes and endnotes. The term *endnote* is therefore used below, but the comments apply equally to footnotes.

The endnote style involves the use of numbered references in the text and a list of corresponding numbered references at the end of a chapter or article, or at the end of a book. The system also allows authors to add notes or comments which appear in the endnote list.

The actual numerical reference in the text can be given in brackets (1) or as a superscript:[1]. Using the endnote system, the paragraph given above would therefore look like this:

> *Concepts of leadership in corporations have included Stogdill's[1] work on the trait approach, Korman's[2] study of style approaches, Fiedler's[3] contingency approach and more recent work by Bryman[4] involving new leadership approaches.*

The list of notes at the end of the report would then be listed in the numerical order in which they appear in the text:

Notes

1 Stogdill, R.M. 1948, Personal factors associated with leadership: a survey of the literature. *Journal of Psychology*, 25(1), 35–71.

2 Korman, A.K. 1966, 'Consideration', 'initiating structure', and organisational criteria—a review. *Personal Psychology*, 19(3), 349–61.
3 Fiedler, F. E. 1967, *A Theory of Leadership Effectiveness*. McGraw Hill, New York.
4 Bryman, A. 1992, *Charisma and Leadership of Organizations*. Sage, London.

This format is less obtrusive in the text than the author/date system. It can be made even less obtrusive by using only one endnote, as follows:

Concepts of leadership in corporations include the trait approach of the 1940s, the style approach of the 1950s and 1960s, the contingency approach of the 1970s, and the newer contemporary leadership approach from the 1980s up to the present.[1]

At the end of the document the reference list would look something like this:

Notes

1 Trait approach: Stogdill, R.M. 1948, Personal factors associated with leadership: A survey of the literature. *Journal of Psychology*, 25(1), 35–71.
Style approach: Korman, A.K. 1966, 'Consideration', 'initiating structure', and organisational criteria—a review. *Personal Psychology*, 19(3), 349–61.
Contingency approach: Fiedler, F. E. 1967, *A Theory of Leadership Effectiveness*. McGraw Hill, New York.
Contemporary approach: Bryman, A. 1992, *Charisma and Leadership of Organizations*. Sage, London.

Multiple references

It should never be necessary to write a reference out in full more than once in a document. In the endnote system, additional references to a work already cited can be made by using the phrase *op. cit.* or by references to previous endnotes. For example, the previous paragraph of text might be followed by:

Fiedler was the best known proponent of the contingency approach to leadership.[2]

The endnote would then be:

2 Fiedler, *op. cit.* **or** 2 See endnote 1.

Specifics and quotations

Page references for specific references or quotations are given in the endnote, rather than the text. So the Alvesson and Deetz quotation given above would look like this:

Alvesson and Deetz make the point that 'most of the various critical theory and postmodernist positions are still relatively new to management studies'.[3]

The endnote would then read:

3 Alvesson, M. & Deetz, S. 1996, Critical theory and postmodern approaches to organisational studies. In S. R. Clegg, C. Hardy & W. R., Nord (eds). *Handbook of Organization Studies*. Sage, London, p. 191.

Further quotations from the same work would have endnotes as follows:

4 Alvesson and Deetz, *op. cit.* p. 194.

Advantages and disadvantages of the footnote/endnote system

One of the advantages of the footnote/endnote system is that it can accommodate notes and comments other than references to the literature. A disadvantage of the system is that it does not result in a tidy alphabetical list of references. This diminishes the convenience of the report as a source of literature references for the reader. Some writers therefore resort to producing a bibliography in addition to the list of endnotes. This results in extra work, since it means that references have to be written out/printed a second time. Keeping track of footnotes or endnotes and their numbering is much less of a disadvantage than it used to be, since this can now be taken care of by word-processing applications. When large numbers of endnotes are used and extensive use of *op. cit* is used, it can be difficult to trace the original point at which the full details of a reference are given.

The best of both worlds

The features, advantages and disadvantages of the two systems, author/date and footnote/endnote are summarised in Figure 4.2.

FIGURE 4.2

Reference systems: features, advantages, disadvantages

	Author/date	Footnote/endnote
Reference in text	Author (date)	Number, for example . . . [1]
Reference format	Author date, *Title*, publishing details	1 Author date, *Title*, publishing details
Reference list format	Alphabetical list at end of report	Numbered list at: ■ foot of pages ■ end of chapters, or ■ end of report or book
Advantages	■ alphabetical bibliography ■ easy to use	■ unobtrusive in text ■ can add notes and comments
Disadvantages	■ obtrusive in text ■ can't add notes	■ difficult to use without a computer ■ no alphabetical list

One way of combining the advantages of both systems is for the list of notes in an endnote system to consist of author/date references and then to provide an alphabetical list of references at the end of the report. So the list of endnotes for the paragraph on pp. 90–91 would look like this:

Notes

1 Stogdill, 1948.
2 Korman, 1966.
3 Fiedler, 1967.
4 Bryman, 1992.

An alphabetical bibliography would then follow which would be the same as for the author/date system. This approach is particularly useful when making several references to the same document. Its use is not common, but does exist (see, for example, Hannafey 2003, the basis of Case Study Example 4.1).

OTHER REFERENCING ISSUES

Internet and electronic references

The need to cite reference material obtained from the Internet or other electronic sources is increasing. These sources include the World Wide Web, list servers, newsgroups, electronic journals, electronic databases and CD-ROMs. These electronic media are still developing but standard formats for referencing are now becoming established.

As a general guide, all references to electronic media should begin with as much as possible of the information that would be provided for a print source, followed by the date of retrieval and details of the source of the electronic information. The date of retrieval is important since websites can be moved, changed or deleted. The full name of the organisation responsible for the website and its geographical location can be important information for those wishing to follow up the reference at a later date when the website address may have changed.

Basic components of an electronic citation are:
Author, Initials. Year, Further details as for print media. Retrieved: date, from: address/URL

Emails received from individuals which others cannot retrieve should be treated in the same form as a personal communication cited in the text, for example personal communication, June 25, 1998, and should not appear in the list of references. A reference to a *website* appearing in the text which does not refer to a specific document should not appear in the list of references.

Further information concerning references to the Internet and other electronic sources can be obtained from Lester (2000), Walker (1996 n.d.) or Li and Crane (1996). Some examples of Internet and electronic reference formats are shown below.

Examples of Internet and electronic references:

World Wide Web sites:

Working paper

Chiarella, C. 1992, *The Dynamics of Speculative Behaviour*, Working Paper Series No. 13, School of Finance and Economics, University of Technology, Sydney. Retrieved Sept 23, 2004 from: (www.business.uts.edu.au/finance/research/wpapers/wp13.pdf)

continues

Online journal

Clinch, G. & Verrechia, R. 1997, Competitive disadvantage and discretionary disclosures in industries. *Australian Journal of Management*, 22(2), 125-38. Retrieved Sept 23, 2004 from: (www.agsm.edu.au/eajm/9712/clinch.html)

Newspaper

Marr, M. 2004, Comcast a latecomer in Sony's MGM deal, *Australian Financial Review*, 25 Sept. Retrieved Sept 23, 2004, from <http://afr.com/articles/2004/09/24/1095961855771.html) (NB. Articles from newspaper archives—ie prior to current week—generally only available to paying subscribers.)

CD-ROM

Microsoft Encarta Encyclopedia 1997, Trade Union, World English edition, Microsoft Corporation, Seattle, WA, [CD-ROM].

Wessel, D. 1995, Fed lifts rates half point, setting four-year high. *Wall Street Journal*, 2 February, p. A2+. From UMI-ProQuest file: *Wall Street Journal Ondisc* [CD-ROM] Item 34561.

Further information about citing information from the World Wide Web can be found on the Internet at (www.apastyle.org/elecref.html), and in the former Australian Government Publishing Service's *Style Manual for Authors, Editors and Printers* (Snooks and Co 2002).

Second-hand references

While it is always best to go back to original sources when possible, occasionally reference is made to an item of literature that you have not read directly, but which is referred to in another document that you have read. This can be called *second-hand* reference. In such situations it is misleading, somewhat unethical and risky to give a full reference to the original source, implying that you have read it directly yourself. Your reference should instead refer to the 'second-hand' source, not to the original. This is an example:

> *Peters and Austin see vision as an important component of leadership, noting that 'You have got to know where you are going, to be able to state it clearly and concisely—and you have got to care about it passionately' (quoted in Bryman 1996: 281).*

The writer of this sentence has not read Peters and Austin in the original, but is relying on Bryman's quotation. Peters and Austin are therefore *not* listed in the references; only the Bryman reference is listed. It is ethical to treat the second-hand reference this way and it is also safe, since any inaccuracy in a quotation then rests with the second-hand source.

Excessive referencing

A certain amount of judgement must be used when a large number of references are being made to a single source. It becomes very tiresome when repeated reference is made to the same source on every other line of a report. One way to avoid this is to be 'up front' about the fact that a large section of your literature review is based on a single source. For example, if you are summarising Clegg's work on power, create a separate section of your report and begin it as follows:

> *The Work of Clegg*
> This section of the review summarises Clegg's (1989) seminal work, *Frameworks of Power . . .*

In such instances, detailed references need only be given when using specific quotations; just page references will be adequate in most cases.

Latin abbreviations

A number of Latin abbreviations are used in referencing. They are generally italicised. Examples are as follows.

- If there are more than two authors of a work, the first author's name and *et al.* may be used in text references instead of the full list of authors, but all authors should be listed in the bibliography. The abbreviation stands for *et alia*, meaning 'and the others'.
- The abbreviation *op. cit.*, discussed earlier, stands for *opere citato*, meaning 'in the work cited'.
- In the endnote system, if reference is made to the same work in consecutive footnotes, the abbreviation *ibid.* is sometimes used, short for *ibidem*, meaning 'the same'.

SUMMARY

This chapter has discussed the processes of *reviewing* previous research and writing as part of the research procedure; a process known as a *literature review*. It also discussed referencing procedures and referencing systems.

An important part of the *literature review* is the preparation of a *bibliography*, which involves a search for relevant information, obtaining copies of relevant items and reviewing them, making a list of useful items to form the *bibliography*, and assessing and summarising salient aspects for the research proposal, research report or article. Useful sources of information for a bibliography include *library catalogues*, *indexes*, *electronic databases*, and various *specialised management and business resources*. The use of the *Internet* is becoming an indispensable skill for obtaining information relevant to management research.

Writing a *literature review* on a selected topic is a critical part of the research process. It is a task where a range of skills and qualities needs to be employed, including patience, persistence, insight and lateral thinking. The literature review can play different roles in a research project and this leads to a number of different approaches to writing the review.

The *inclusive* approach to a literature review seeks to identify everything that has been written on a particular topic. An *inclusive/evaluative* approach goes further than the inclusive approach by providing a commentary on the relevant literature that is uncovered. The *exploratory* approach is more focused than the inclusive or evaluative approach and seeks to discover existing research that might throw light on a specific research question or issue. This is the form of the classic literature review that is the norm for academic research.

In an *instrumental* review, the primary focus of the research is a business issue and the literature is used as a source of suitable ideas on how the research question might best be approached. The criterion for selection of literature is to identify a useful *methodology* or suitable research *instruments* which can provide appropriate insights or an effective approach to research into the business issue. *Content analysis* and *hermeneutics* are techniques that involve detailed analysis of the contents of a certain body of literature, or other documentary sources, which are viewed as texts. The text becomes a focus of research in its own right rather than merely a report of research.

A key feature of a literature review is the summary and conclusions drawing out implications for the research study at hand.

There are two commonly used *referencing systems*: the *author/date* system and the *footnote* or *endnote* system. Referencing evidences the researcher's scholarship and indicates that the particular report is related to the existing body of knowledge. References also enable the reader to check sources—either to verify the writer's interpretation of previous research or to follow up areas of interest.

EXERCISES

1 Compile an *inclusive* bibliography on a topic of your choice, using the sources outlined in this chapter. If your topic is too broad you will find hundreds of references. Conversely, if your topic is too narrow you will find very few references. The appropriateness of your topic will become apparent as you conduct your search.

2 Choose a research topic and:
   a investigate the literature using a computerised library catalogue and any other electronic database available to you;
   b explore the literature via literary sources such as reference lists and indexes in general textbooks, journal contents and lists of references in articles;
   c compare the nature and extent of the bibliography arising from the two sources.

FURTHER READING

Conduct of a literature review: Easterby-Smith, Thorpe and Lowe (1993: 145–56); Gay and Diehl (1992: 56–71); Hussey and Hussey (1997), Chapter 4; Jankowicz (1991), Chapter 8; Leedy (1993), Chapter 4, pp. 87–107; and Sekaran (1992: 47–61).

In-depth treatment of referencing procedures: the Australian Government Publishing Service *Style Manual* (Snooks & Co 2002) and American Psychological Association (1994).

Electronic referencing procedures: Walker (nd), Lester (1997) and Li and Crane (1996).

PART 2

data collection methods

CHAPTER 5

Secondary data sources

While most of this book deals with the collection of new data, this chapter concentrates on using existing sources of data. It examines potential resources for acquiring company information, the use of company management data, statistical sources such as the census, management sources in related disciplines and Internet-based information sources. This and subsequent chapters in Part II of the book concentrate on data sources and collection, leaving the discussion of analysis of data to corresponding chapters in Part III.

A good policy when undertaking research is to use existing information wherever possible rather than embarking on new information collecting exercises which can be expensive and time-consuming. When treated as part of the literature review and used for background information only, the use of secondary data in a study can be seen as part of the 'preparation' stage. Similarly, when such information is used to provide context when reporting the results of a study its use becomes part of the report preparation stage. Here secondary data is viewed as a significant research method in its own right, contributing a major part of the empirical side of a study, and sometimes even the whole of it.

One aspect of this form of data collection has already been touched on in Chapter 4 in relation to reviewing the literature. In searching the literature the researcher may come across references to statistical or other data which may not have been fully analysed or exploited by their original collectors, perhaps because of their particular interests or because of limitations of time or money. It may be that the available data are open to additional or alternative analyses and interpretations. In other cases information may exist which was not originally collected for research purposes, but would be a potential source of useful research information if tapped.

Primary data are new data specifically collected in a current research project—the researcher is the primary user. *Secondary* data are data that already exist and which were collected for some other (primary) purpose but which can be used a second time in the current project—the researcher is the *secondary user*. Further analysis of such data is referred to as *secondary analysis*.

As with the literature, secondary data can play a variety of roles in a research project, from being the whole basis of the research to being a vital or incidental point of comparison. If existing information can wholly or partially answer the research question at hand there is a certain professional obligation for the researcher to utilise it, rather than going to the expense of collecting new data.

Some of the main sources of secondary data available to the business researcher are examined here.

Sources of secondary data:

- Company information (internal and external)
- Government agencies
- Educational institutions and specialist centres
- Professional organisations
- Management-related fields
- Archival material
- Internet-based resources

COMPANY INFORMATION

Sources of information about companies or corporate organisations can be both *internal* and *external*. Internal data are generated within a company and may or may not be readily available for research purposes. External data are available from sources other than the company through such organisations as stock exchanges. These two types of data are discussed in turn below.

Internal sources

The internal record-keeping of a company or organisation can be a significant source of data for secondary research. Companies necessarily keep either electronic or hard copy records of their day-to-day transactions which can represent decades of business activity. Among the types of records/data available are:

Internal data/records:

- Financial accounts
- Sales data
- Prices
- Product development
- Advertising expenditure
- Purchase of supplies
- Human resources records
- Customer complaint logs

An issue in many larger organisations is that the data collected within different functional or departmental areas may not be visible to the whole organisation. This can be due to a lack of internal communication between departments or because there is no electronic data or *management information system* in place to provide an opportunity for a systematic exchange of information. Researchers should try to gain awareness of all potentially useful existing internal records in companies they are researching.

CASE STUDY EXAMPLE 5.1

Secondary data: Employee turnover and company performance

Source: Arie C. Glebbeek and Erik H. Bax (2004) Is high employee turnover really harmful? An empirical test using company records. *Academy of Management Journal*, 47(2), 277–286.
Methods/approaches: Secondary data analysis; quantitative; hypothesis-testing; multiple regression analysis
Topic: Employee turnover and company performance

On the basis of a review of the literature on the relationship between employee turnover and company performance, the authors of this study put forward the hypothesis that: 'The overall relationship between employee turnover and firm performance has an inverted U-shape'. This posits that a high a level of employee turnover and a low level of employee turnover are both likely to be associated with low performance.

Using company records from 100 offices of a Dutch temporary job agency over the period 1995–98, the authors compiled data, for each year and for each office, on employee turnover, various measures of the performance of the office (sales, profitability, etc.) and other possible influential variables such as absenteeism, the average age of the employees and the geographic region of the office. Multiple regression analysis was used to test the hypothesis. Various regression models were tested, the most successful ($R^2 = 0.34$) using *change* in performance over three years as the dependent variable to produce an equation as follows:

$$Y = \text{Constant} + 0.38\,X_1 + 0.32\,X_2 - 0.14\,X_3 - 0.07\,X_4 + 0.44\,X_5 - 0.56\,X_6$$

where: X_1 = Performance in 1995; X_2 = Employee turnover; X_3 = Absenteeism; X_4 = Age; X_5 = Region; and X_6 = Employee turnover squared.

The positive coefficient for X_1 and the negative coefficient for X_6 confirm the inverted U-shaped curve (see Chapter 14). While the significance of the coefficients makes the results ambivalent, the authors suggest that the findings provide some support for the hypothesis.

An example of research using existing internal data sources is the study of employee turnover and company performance by Glebbeek and Bax (2004), as described in Case Study Example 5.1. This simply used data on staff turnover and profitability from 100 branches of an employment agency over a four-year period.

One of the major obstacles to external researchers gaining access to these valuable research resources is the issue of commercial and personal confidentiality. Where access is provided by an organisation, a strict adherence to research ethics (discussed in Chapter 3) is of course essential.

External sources

A distinction needs to be drawn between public and private companies when seeking information about companies. *Public* companies are required by law to disclose detailed information concerning their finances and structure. Annual reports and other company data are lodged annually at stock exchanges. This material is a major source of company information for business researchers. However, these rules of disclosure do not apply to *private* companies. As a result, information on private companies can be difficult to locate and, when it is available, a fee may be involved to access the information. A search of the periodical literature, including newspapers, the financial press and trade journals may be the next best option. Databases such as *ABI INFORM*, *ABIX* (*Australasian Business Intelligence*) and *APAIS* should be searched for this information (see Chapter 4).

A comprehensive website for company information is *Biz@advantage*, a service of WinStar Telebase Inc., (www.bizadvantage.com). The site includes Dun and Bradstreet company information, business and industry searches and worldwide news searches. Searching is free, but for each piece of information retrieved there is a fee. (Note: The websites mentioned here are listed together in Appendix 1.)

A search of individual company web pages also provides quite detailed information. To find the websites of companies, (www.whowhere.com) is a useful resource. Hoover's Company Capsules (www.hoovers.com) contains information on more than 12 000 public and private enterprises in the United States and around the world.

The following resources are also suitable for those seeking information on public companies.

- *DataDisc* is a CD-ROM product of the Australian Stock Exchange. It is a compilation of company reviews of all companies listed on the Stock Exchange. All company information is presented with detailed historical and financial information. There is also a database of delisted companies. Other products published by the Australian Stock Exchange are:
  - *The Statex Investment Service: comparative analysis*, which is produced on a monthly basis and is a comparison of companies' performance in industry groupings;
  - *Stock Exchange Financial and Profitability Study*, an annual comparison of companies' performance against industry norms.
- *AGSM Annual Reports* (Australian Graduate School of Management) is a CD-ROM providing access to the annual reports of the top 500 Australian companies listed on the Australian Stock Exchange. Prior to the CD-ROM format the annual reports were published as microfiche and many libraries hold sets of these microfiche reports.

- *The Annual Report Collection* produced by Connect 4 also covers the top 500 companies listed on the Australian Stock Exchange and includes company prospectuses and merger and acquisition information.

The Australian Stock Exchange website (www.asx.com.au) contains extensive information about public companies and sources of further information. The site has search tools to find companies and provides contact information, an outline of their principal activities and links to more detailed information. Details of public announcements by companies over the past twelve months are provided, as well as information on upcoming company floats.

A web link to world stock exchanges can be found at (www.gsionline.com).

Annual reports of government departments are located in *Commonwealth and State Parliamentary Papers*, which are available in both print and electronic formats at university libraries, the Australian National Library and state libraries.

A major reference point for information on private companies is the Australian Securities and Investment Commission (ASIC). The commission has a website at (www.asic.gov.au) where basic information can be obtained about public and private Australian companies. Searches can be conducted on the name of a company, business or association to obtain details such as company classification, locality of office and a list of any formal company documents lodged with the Commission.

Other well-established sources of company information are the publications of Dun and Bradstreet, and Standard and Poor's. Both companies have websites—Dun and Bradstreet, (www.dnb.com), and Standard and Poor's, (www.compustat.com).

Kompass directories, published as two volumes, are available for an extensive number of countries. One volume covers company information and the other covers products and services. Products are allocated a code at the front of the products and services volume, which then links to tables that indicate the companies that deal in that product and whether, for example, they are an importer or exporter. The company volume lists items such as contact address, the countries the company trades with, any affiliated companies, company assets and turnover. The Kompass website is at (www1.kompass.com).

Fortune 500 is a list of the largest corporations in the USA. A printed version of the top 500 is published in the April–May issues of *Fortune* magazine. Additionally, there is the *Fortune 500* website at (www.fortune.com/fortune/fortune500/).

GOVERNMENT AGENCIES

Government agencies produce substantial amounts of information that can be utilised for research purposes. Major sources of information in Australia include organisations such as the Australian Bureau of Statistics, the Australian Industrial Relations Commission and Austrade. The main federal government website is at (www.australia.gov.au).

Australian Bureau of Statistics (ABS)

The Australian Bureau of Statistics (ABS) is the official compiler of statistics for both the Commonwealth and state governments of Australia. As part of its data collection the ABS undertakes a nationwide census every five years. As in most countries, it is a statutory requirement for householders (and hoteliers) to fill out a census form on 'census night', indicating the number of people—including visitors—in the building, and demographic information such as their age, education, gender, occupation and income. The value of the census data to a manager in either the public or private sectors would be to assist in producing a 'profile' of a geographical area so that the manager has an overall view of the nature of the community being served and potential or existing customers residing in the area.

The range of ABS publications published in both electronic and print formats is extensive. These publications vary in their publication frequency, that is, daily, weekly, monthly, yearly and irregular publications are all available.

ABS data are arranged in broad subject groupings with each group identified by a number from 1 to 9, as shown below. A five-digit code is used to identify printed reports from the ABS. Non-print reports have a ten-digit code. After the main sequence of numbers comes a full stop, followed by a number which indicates whether the data have been collected across Australia or relate to a particular state.

ABS subject groupings:

Subject	*Geographical area*
1 General	0 Australia
2 Census of population and housing	1 New South Wales
3 Demography	2 Victoria
4 Social statistics	3 Queensland
5 National accounts, international trade & finance	4 South Australia
6 Labour statistics and prices	5 Western Australia
7 Agriculture	6 Tasmania
8 Secondary industry and distribution	7 Northern Territory
9 Transport, tourism	8 Aust. Capital Territory
	9 External Territories

Some examples of publications and their code numbers:

- 6356.0 Employer Training Practices, Australia
- 8141.0 Small & Medium Enterprises Business Growth & Performance Survey Australia
- 6201.1 Labour Force, NSW

Australian Bureau of Statistics website: (www.abs.gov.au).

University libraries subscribe to a service called *AUSSTATS: ABS Time Series On-line* that provides access to data collected by the ABS and may only be used for educational and research purposes. The range of data within the time series encompasses: balance of payments figures; company profit information; turnover in retailing; and producer and foreign trade price indexes. The data from the *Time Series* site needs to be downloaded into spreadsheet software such as *Excel* before it can be viewed online. As well as current data, most of the data in the time series extend back fifteen years, with some material extending as far back as forty years.

Australian Industrial Relations Commission

The Australian Industrial Relations Commission website, at (www.airc.gov.au), includes copies of Australian Industrial Awards and Agreements and Commonwealth and state legislation.

Austrade

The Australian Trade Commission (Austrade) helps Australian businesses take advantage of export opportunities. It acts in an advisory role for businesses wishing to expand or enter export markets. The web page *Australian Trade Commission Online* (www.austrade.gov.au) contains details of 4000 Australian companies and their products and services. The database provides keyword searching and is a useful resource for business researchers.

Australian Government Publications

The *Australian Government Publications Register* (www.publications.gov.au) includes links to numerous government agencies and their publication listings.

EDUCATIONAL INSTITUTIONS AND SPECIALIST CENTRES

Universities

This listing is by no means comprehensive, but it aims to identify a sample of the institutional sources that are available, the kinds of research being undertaken and sources of information that these institutions may offer.

- The Australian Graduate School of Management (University of New South Wales and Sydney University) working papers on management and business can be downloaded from (www.agsm.edu.au) (go to 'Information sources')
- The Haas School of Business at the University of California, Berkeley, website (www.haas.berkeley.edu/institutes.html) links to a number of centres and institutes that can be searched. The centres and institutes included are:
  - Clausen Center for International Business and Policy;
  - Fisher Center for Management and Information Technology;
  - Lester Centre for Entrepreneurship and Innovation;
  - Institute for Management Innovation and Organization;
  - Institute for Business and Economics Research; and
  - Institute of Industrial Relations.
- The Harvard Business School website (www.hbs.harvard.edu) includes links to the Division of Research, HBS Publishing and the *Harvard Business Review*.

  Other useful university sites include:
- The *Macquarie University Graduate School of Management* (www.gsm.mq.edu.au) publishes details of research, conferences and news releases;
- The *Monash University-Faculty of Business and Economics Department of Management* provides access to the Leadership Research Unit and the Quality Management Research Unit. Working papers can be found at (www.buseco.monash.edu.au/Depts/Mgt);

- The *University of Technology, Sydney School of Finance and Economics* database of 35 000 working papers in economics and finance at (www.business.uts.edu.au/finance/resources/workingpaper.html).

Specialist centres

The *Australian Technology Park* (ATP) is sponsored by the University of New South Wales, the University of Sydney and the University of Technology, Sydney. A major aim of the facility is to promote the application of world class research to industry and the broader community with a view to encouraging innovative ideas with a technological application. The ATP website is (www.atp.com.au).

CACOM: Centre for Australian Community Organisations and Management at the University of Technology, Sydney has a useful website that can be found at (www.business.uts.edu.au/cacom/links/index.html). This address also provides links to other management resources through the School of Management at UTS.

The MSU-CIBER Michigan State University Center for International Business Education and Research *International Business Resources on the Web* can be found at (http://globaledge.msu.edu/ibrd/ibrd.asp). This site has an excellent list of international news and periodical lists, international trade information and company directories.

The University of Bern website has a link to their *Public Management Competence Center,* which includes working papers at (www.iop.unibe.ch/English). Another useful website is the *Wharton Financial Institutions Center Working Paper Library* at (http://swopec.hhs.se/fiefwp).

Contacting academic researchers

Directories which can be useful for contacting academics and business researchers are listed below. Print sources include:

- the *European Faculty Directory*, an alphabetical and subject classified listing of names and addresses of academic staff at higher learning institutions in eastern and western Europe (London, Gale Research International);
- the *Commonwealth Universities Yearbook*, a directory to the universities of the Commonwealth and the handbook of their association (London, Association of Commonwealth Universities); and
- the *International Handbook of Universities and Other Institutions of Higher Education*, an international directory of names and addresses of universities and their academic staff (Paris, International Association of Universities).

PROFESSIONAL ORGANISATIONS

Information concerning business associations, professional associations, societies, and not-for-profit organisations can be best found through an online search of the Telstra *Yellow* or *White Pages*, at (www.yellowpages.com.au) or (www.whitepages.com.au).

The *Aussie Pages* at (www.aussie.com.au/index.html) includes a business directory with the addresses of over one million Australian businesses and organisations. It can also be used to locate people living in Australia. A printed source for locating associations is the *Directory of Australian Associations* (Brisbane, Qld., Australasia Reference Research Publications).

The *Encyclopedia of Associations* is a CD-ROM with a listing of over 144 000 non-profit organisations worldwide in all subject areas. It includes the publications that have been issued by those organisations, and meetings, conferences and awards.

The Academy of Management is the principal professional and academic association for management research and education in the United States. Three of its publications are:

- *The Academy of Management Journal*;
- *The Academy of Management Review*; and
- *The Academy of Management Executive*.

The *Academy of Management* homepage can be found at (www.aom.pace.edu).

The *Australian and New Zealand Academy of Management* (ANZAM) is the main Australian association for management educators and researchers. It holds an annual conference and produces the *Journal of the Australian and New Zealand Academy of Management*. Details of the association and its journal are available at (www.anzam.uts.edu.au).

The *Australian Institute of Management* (www.aim.com.au) is a professional body that operates on a national level in Australia. It offers professional development activities, training and development programs, and accreditation for managers. The AIM is a member of the Asian Association of Management Organisations (AAMO) and the regional member of the World Council of Management (CIOS).

Another useful address is (www.aipm.com.au), which is the website for the *Australian Institute of Project Management*, a voluntary association for project managers.

MANAGEMENT-RELATED FIELDS

The study of management topics will, in many instances, require a cross-disciplinary approach when seeking resources. Law, psychology, education, sociology and health are some of the main search areas which might be considered. For example, training and development issues could be researched in an education database; communication and teamwork might be explored in a psychology database; and hospital administration might be researched in health-oriented databases. Yearbooks, handbooks and dictionaries in a specialist field are often good places to start searching for secondary information. As well, online databases are a productive source of information and some examples of relevant databases are shown below. These databases are generally available through university libraries.

AustLII—Australasian Legal Information Institute provides free Internet access to Australian legal materials and is the most extensive Internet-based index on Australian law. The majority of Australian legal decisions and legislation are incorporated as full text. The coverage of the database includes Commonwealth, ACT, NSW and SA legislation, as well as the regulations from most federal courts, combined with information on many state courts and tribunals.

Current Contents provides access to the tables of contents and bibliographic data from current issues of more than 7500 leading international scholarly research journals in all subject discipline areas. The file is cumulative for a rolling 52-week period.

ERIC is sponsored by the US Department of Education, Office of Educational Research and Improvement (OERI). To date it is the largest international education database in the world, containing citations to research documents, journal articles, technical reports, descriptions and evaluations of research reports and curricular materials in the field of education.

Expanded Academic Index provides abstracts, tables of contents and some access to full-text articles from academic journals in the arts, humanities, social sciences and science and technology fields.

HealthSTAR is produced by the US National Library of Medicine and the American Hospital Association. It incorporates information on health services areas such as research, technological applications, and personnel and planning in the administration of health facilities and services.

InfoQuick (www.sl.nsw.gov.au/infoquick) indexes articles appearing in the *Sydney Morning Herald* and is published by the State Library of New South Wales.

LEXIS NEXIS includes a large number of specialised libraries covering all major fields of practice in law and has a substantial section on business material. It also provides information from news wire services across the world, such as Agence Presse, the BBC, CNN and Xinhua News Agency. This service includes laws of the United States, Europe, United Kingdom, Australia and New Zealand, as well as international laws.

ARCHIVAL MATERIALS

Archival materials available on the Internet are still developing. Newspaper sites are steadily increasing the amount of archival material they include. They allow browsing at no cost, but charge a fee for acquiring copies of articles. A number of newspaper sites are listed in Appendix 1 (pp. ***).

Two examples of newspaper sites are the *Sydney Morning Herald* at (www.smh.com.au) and the *Washington Post* at (www.washingtonpost.com).

INTERNET-BASED RESOURCES

The following Internet sites are mentioned because of their extensive coverage and the large number of links they offer to other sites. Access privileges to the other links by visitors to these sites may vary.

Libweb Library Servers via WWW provides a series of links to libraries in over seventy countries at (sunsite3.berkeley.edu/Libweb).

Links to business journals can be found at *Business Journals on the Web* (www.brint.com/ISJournal.htm).

Oxford University Press journals in economics and business are found at (www.oup.co.uk/worldbank).

SUMMARY

This chapter has discussed the use of *secondary* or existing sources of data in business research. It makes good sense to use existing information where possible, rather than embarking on new information-collecting exercises which can be expensive and time-consuming. *Primary* data are new data specifically collected in a current research project—the researcher is the primary user. *Secondary* data are data that already exist and which were collected for some other purpose, but which can be used a second time in the current project—the researcher is the *secondary user*. Further analysis of such data is referred to as *secondary analysis*.

In principle, the searching techniques across the electronic databases of various disciplines will be quite similar. As discussed in relation to searching the literature (Chapter 4) the main entry point is a keyword search, which links to the key words in the subject you are exploring. A major issue, however, is that the software used in each database will differ significantly, requiring time to acquire the necessary skill levels for developing an efficient searching technique. It would be advantageous to explore these resources when beginning research studies so that the collection of data itself does not override the key objective of collating and analysing research and applying it to the particular problem at hand. Analysis of secondary data is considered in Chapter 12.

EXERCISES

1 Identify as many internal secondary sources of information relevant to business research that are available in:
   - the organisation in which you are employed;
   - a trade, professional or union organisation with which you are familiar; or
   - an educational organisation.

   Describe each of the sources you identify and their potential use in a business research study.

2 Evaluate each of the secondary sources which you identified in question 1 in terms of the following:
   - The accuracy and reliability of the source. Is the source accurate or based on rough estimates? Is the source biased in any way?
   - The currency of the source. Is it up to date? What time period does it cover?
   - The definition of terms used in the source. What definitions (if any) are used to define items of information in the secondary source?
   - The units of measurement. If the secondary source data are numeric what units of measurement are used? Can they be easily modified for other purposes?

3 Use the Internet to access freely available websites (not restricted sites such as university libraries or internal company websites) and identify sources of information which would assist you to you to prepare a report on:
   - the productivity of auto workers in the USA, Australia, Japan, Canada and Great Britain over the past decade;
   - apparent strengths and weaknesses of the Windows operating system in small business environments;
   - median weekly earnings of full-time workers in Australia, Great Britain, New Zealand and the US;
   - trends in the European trade union movement since the end of the Second World War;
   - companies that offer training programs for middle managers in South Africa, Ireland and New Zealand.

FURTHER READING

For further information concerning secondary data sources, see Cooper and Emory (1995), Chapter 9; Davis and Cosenza (1993), Appendix A: 'A Practitioner's Guide to Secondary Business Information Sources'; Sekaran (1992), Appendix for Chapter 2; or Zikmund (1997), Chapter 7: 'Secondary Data, Global Systems and the Internet'.

CHAPTER 6

Observation

Observation methods are also referred to as 'unobtrusive' methods (Kellehear 1993). They usually involve gathering information about people's behaviour, often without their knowledge. This approach, while it can raise ethical issues in some situations, has advantages over research methods where subjects are aware of the researcher's presence and may therefore modify their behaviour, or where reliance must be placed on subjects' own recall and description of their behaviour, which can be inaccurate or distorted. This chapter draws attention to the importance of *looking* in business research and introduces some of the specific approaches of observation methods. It examines situations in which observation is particularly appropriate and outlines the main steps that should be taken in an observation-based project.

Observation is a neglected technique in business research. While it is rarely possible to base a research project wholly on observation, the technique has a vital role to play, either formally or informally, in most research strategies. It may be the only possible technique to use when researching illicit activity that people may be reluctant to talk about. It is capable of presenting a perspective on a situation that may not be consciously apparent to the individuals involved. Taylor's historic time and motion study of work practices, discussed in Chapter 2, could only have been achieved through the direct observation of people at work. Observation is appropriate when knowledge of the presence of the researcher is likely to lead to unacceptable changes in the subjects' behaviour and when mass patterns of behaviour are of interest.

The technique of *observation* involves *looking*. The results of observation can be recorded and analysed qualitatively or quantitatively. Looking can be done with the naked eye or with the help of sophisticated equipment. Time-lapse photography can be used to photograph an area automatically at set periods, aerial photography can be used to gain a panoramic view of a whole work site. Video recording can also be used. These more sophisticated techniques are considered later in the section, but first the simpler approaches to observation are examined.

Participant observation, where the researcher becomes a participant in the situation being studied, obviously involves observation, but it also involves other forms of research. It is a key technique of qualitative research, so it is dealt with in Chapter 7 rather than in this chapter.

CONTEXTS FOR OBSERVATIONAL RESEARCH

A number of contexts where observation is a necessary part of management research are shown below. These contexts are now discussed in turn.

Contexts for observational research:

- Spatial use of sites
- Workplace behaviour
- Consumer testing
- Complementary research
- Social behaviour

Spatial use of sites

Observation can provide useful information about the spatial use of sites—including workplaces, retail areas, public areas such as roads or urban precincts, and recreational spaces, such as parks, beaches and theme parks. The method can be used to examine how space is used, the level of use of particular areas, traffic flows, and the movement of material and people. In many cases the only way managers can obtain information on these processes is by observation.

A site may be very large, such as a forest or an open cut mine, it might be a large building, or it may be a small and crowded office. Regardless of the total space, understanding how it is used is particularly important in relation to design, layout, safety and capacity. If people tend to crowd spaces such as doorways and photocopiers, then where those entrances and copying facilities are positioned will affect the pattern of use of the site. This can be used as a management tool to influence the pattern of use of a site.

Buildings and open spaces are often designed with either little consideration as to how people will actually use them or on the basis of untested assumptions about how they will be used. In reality, often people do not behave as anticipated—some spaces are under-used while some are over-crowded—or spaces are not designed or equipped for the activities that they are meant to accommodate. Observation is the means by which these aspects of space utilisation can be discovered and understood by researchers.

The movement of people within an area can be recorded for later analysis by using a video camera. Useful insights can also be provided through direct observation of interactions between people. These data can be analysed using a *sociogram* that shows a graphic representation of the amount and direction of interaction among individuals, as shown in Figure 6.1.

FIGURE 6.1

Example of a sociogram

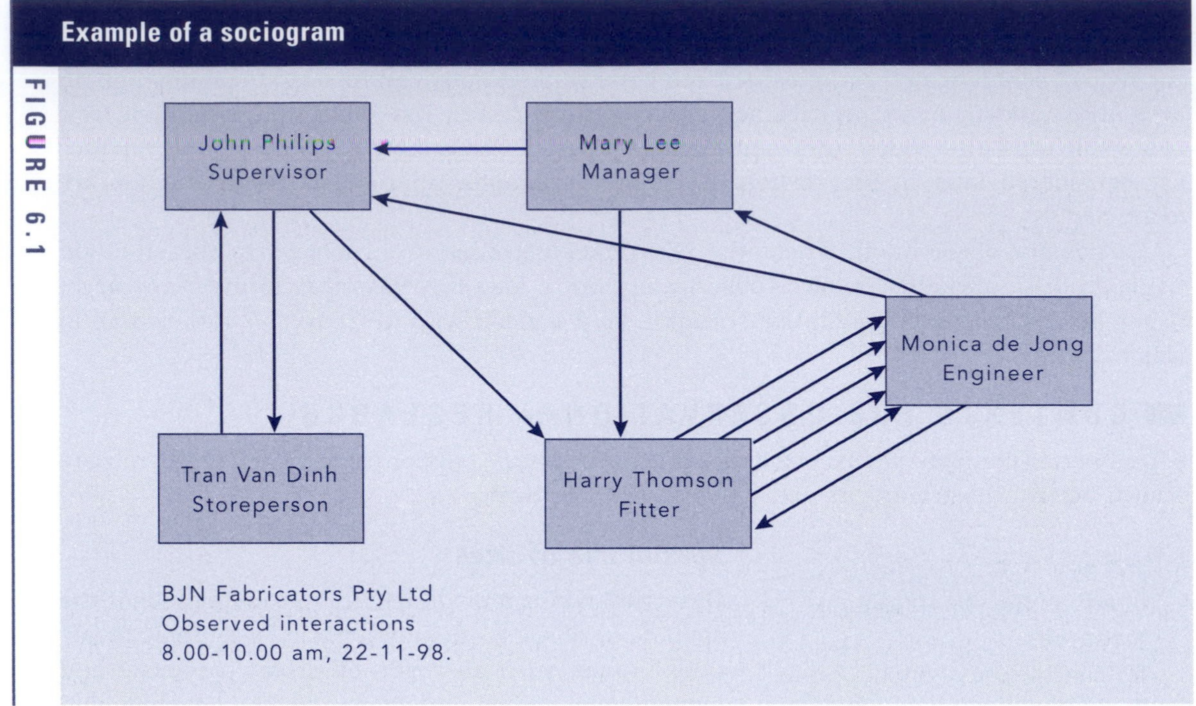

Observation of the movement of materials through a work site is usually carried out through direct tracking or through tagging selected materials and noting their arrival at various sites or departments. This information can later be plotted on a physical map of the site or building for further consideration.

Workplace behaviour

Observation allows a range of workplace behaviours to be examined, but observing behaviour over a long period can be expensive when compared to alternative research methods. It is possible to observe an individual's physical actions, non-verbal behaviours (such as tone of voice and body language) and the time taken to perform tasks, as well as physical distances between people at work (proxemics).

Other forms of observation can provide insights into workplace behaviour. The volume of work completed may be implied from the number of parts used over a period of time in a car assembly process or the volume of turnings found under a lathe. Levels of usage can be determined by wear patterns on carpets, the amount of toner and paper used by a photocopier, and so on.

Observation is likely to be more fruitful than interviews when researching even mildly deviant or potentially deviant behaviour. People are unlikely to tell an interviewer about their untidiness, their lack of adherence to safety rules in the workplace, or their true working hours. Finding out about such things requires observation—sometimes covert observation. This, of course, may raise employee relations issues and ethical issues concerning people's rights to privacy, which were discussed in Chapter 3.

Consumer testing

Consumer testing is another potentially fruitful but under-exploited use of observation, sometimes referred to as 'mystery shopping'. While interviews are the most common means of obtaining information on the quality of the experience offered by, for example, a shopping centre, an additional means is for the researcher to play the role of an *incognito* user/customer/observer. This can be seen as a form of participant observation, as discussed in Chapter 7. Such an observer is required to report on the experience of using facilities or services by means of a checklist of features and thereby observe and evaluate:

- cleanliness;
- information availability;
- information clarity;
- product availability;
- staff availability, courtesy, knowledge.

Again, ethical and employee relations issues may arise in such a study because of the element of deception involved in playing the part of a 'customer'.

Complementary research

Observation can be a necessary complement to interview surveys in order to compensate for variation in sampling rates. For instance, at a typical railway station five interviewers working at a steady rate may be able to interview virtually all users in the off-peak periods, but only manage to interview a small proportion of the users during the busy morning and afternoon period. The final sample would therefore, in this case, over-represent off-peak users and under-represent peak hour users. If these two groups were to have different characteristics it would have a biasing effect on the information obtained, for example, on the balance of views expressed by the users. Counts of the hourly levels of use can provide data to give an appropriate *weight* to the peak hour users. The process of *weighting* of data is described in more detail in Chapter 11.

Social behaviour

Observation has been used in sociological research to develop ideas and theories about social behaviour. Researchers use an interactive and inductive process to build explanations of social behaviour from what they observe. Observation may be used, for example, when seeking to understand an industrial dispute between management and employees in a waterfront setting, or to provide court evidence. Very often, a key feature of such studies is the way the researchers seek to contrast what they have observed with what has apparently been observed by others, particularly those with influence or authority. This includes people such as safety inspectors, insurance assessors, supervisors, union officials, senior management, police, the media and so on. Observational research can challenge existing stereotypical interpretations of events.

ELEMENTS OF OBSERVATIONAL RESEARCH

Zikmund (1991: 199) has proposed a number of key elements that should be observed in the analysis of social behaviour. Naturally, these elements may vary according to the context and the events being observed. Some key elements for observation are shown below.

Some key elements for observation:

The participants	Who are they? What are their interrelationships? How many are there?
The setting	Appearance? Behaviours that the setting might encourage, discourage or permit.
The purpose	What has brought the participants together? What is the official purpose? Are the goals of all the participants compatible?
The social behaviour	What do participants actually do? How do they do it? Stimulus for the behaviour Objective of the behaviour What is the behaviour directed towards? Qualities of behaviour (intensity, appropriateness, etc.) Effects of behaviour (others, responses, etc.)
Frequency and duration	When did the event occur? How long did it last? Does it recur? How frequently does it recur?

Source: Zikmund (1991: 199).

Observation is essentially a simple research method, so there is not a great deal of 'technique' to consider. What is mainly required from the researcher is precision, painstaking attention to detail and patience. The main steps in planning and conducting an observational project are discussed in turn below.

Steps in an observation project:

1. Choose site
2. Choose observation point(s)
3. Choose study time period(s)
4. Decide on continuous observation or sampling
5. Decide on number and length of sampling periods
6. Decide on what to observe
7. Divide site into zones
8. Design a recording sheet
9. Conduct study
10. Analyse data

As with the 'elements of the research process' illustrated in Figure 3.1, it is difficult to produce a list of steps that will cover all eventualities. If the approach is qualitative in nature a number of the tasks discussed here, particularly those concerning counting, may be redundant.

1 Choice of site

In the case of consultancy research, the site or sites to be studied may be fixed. If there is an element of choice, some time should be devoted to inspecting and choosing sites which will offer the appropriate workplace or customer behaviour or characteristics and also provide suitable conditions for observation.

2 Choice of observation point(s)

Choice of an observation point or points within a site is important and needs to be done with care. Some sites can be observed in their entirety from one spot. In other cases a circuit of viewing spots must be devised.

3 Choice of study time period(s)

The choice of study time period is important because of variations in the patterns of use of some sites, such as shopping centres. Variations may be due to the time of the year, day of the week, time of day, weather conditions, or social factors such as public holidays. Designing an observation that covers all time periods may be very demanding in terms of resources, so some form of sampling of time periods will usually be necessary.

4 Continuous observation or sampling?

The question of whether to undertake continuous observation or to sample different time periods is related to the resources available and the nature of the site. The issue is particularly important if one of the aims of the research is to obtain an accurate estimate of the number of visitors to a site. The terminology used to refer to the two approaches is *continuous counts* or *spot counts*. It might be very expensive to place observers at the numerous entrances of a large urban shopping centre for as many as 100 hours in a week in order to count the number of customers. A sampling approach will usually have to be adopted in such cases. Having decided to sample, it is of course necessary to decide how often to do this. This is considered more fully in the next step.

If counting is being undertaken there is also a decision to be made as to whether to count the number of people *entering* the site during specified time periods or the number of people *present* at particular points in time. Counting the number of people present at particular points in time is generally easier, since it may be possible for it to be done by one person regardless of the number of entrances to the site and it can provide information on the spatial use of the site at the same time. This process involves one person making a circuit of the site at specified times and recording the numbers of people present in designated zones.

When qualitative rather than quantitative observation is being undertaken it is more likely that continuous observation will be adopted, since the aim will generally be to observe the dynamics of events and behaviour at the site. However, the question of when to undertake such observation in order to cover all aspects of the use of the site still needs careful consideration.

5 Determine count frequency

Where counts of users are involved, how often should they be undertaken? This depends largely on the rate of change in the level of use of the site. For example, the seven counts shown in Figure 6.2 are clearly insufficient because, if the unbroken line is the pattern of use observed in a research project, but the broken line is the true pattern, the research would have inaccurately represented the actual situation. There is little advice that can be given to overcome this problem, except that it is best to sample frequently at the beginning of a project until the basic patterns of peaks and troughs in usage have been established. After this has been established, it may be possible to sample less often.

6 Decide what to observe

One approach to observing the spatial behaviour of visitors within a facility is to record people's positions directly, as indicated in Figure 6.3. In addition to observing numbers of people and their positions, it is possible to observe and record different types of activity. It is also possible, to a limited extent, to record visitor characteristics. For instance, men and women could be separately identified. It is also possible to distinguish between children and adults, although if more than one observer is involved, care will need to be taken over the dividing line between such categories as child, teenager, young adult, adult and elderly person. It is also possible, if care is taken, to observe the size of groups or parties using a site, especially if they are observed arriving or leaving by an observer positioned in the car park.

In the example of a shopping centre it may also be important to distinguish between employees and shoppers.

FIGURE 6.2 Insufficient usage counts of shopping centre

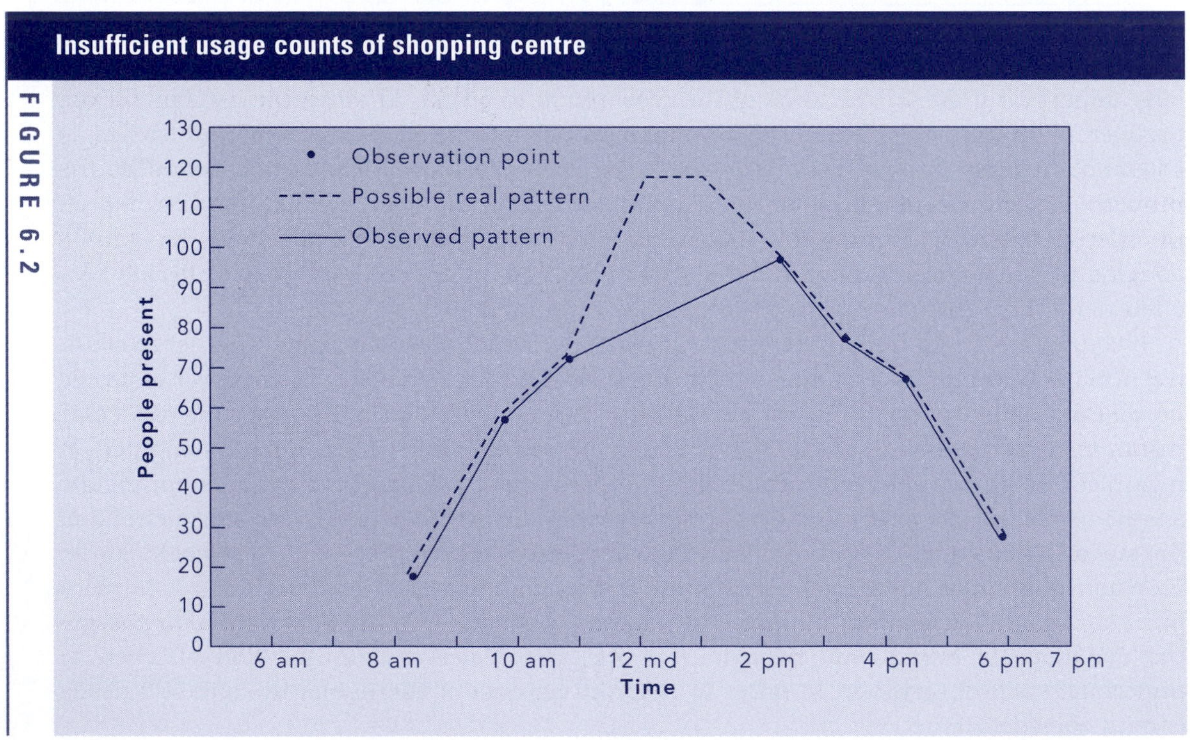

Mapping information directly: division of site into zones

FIGURE 6.3

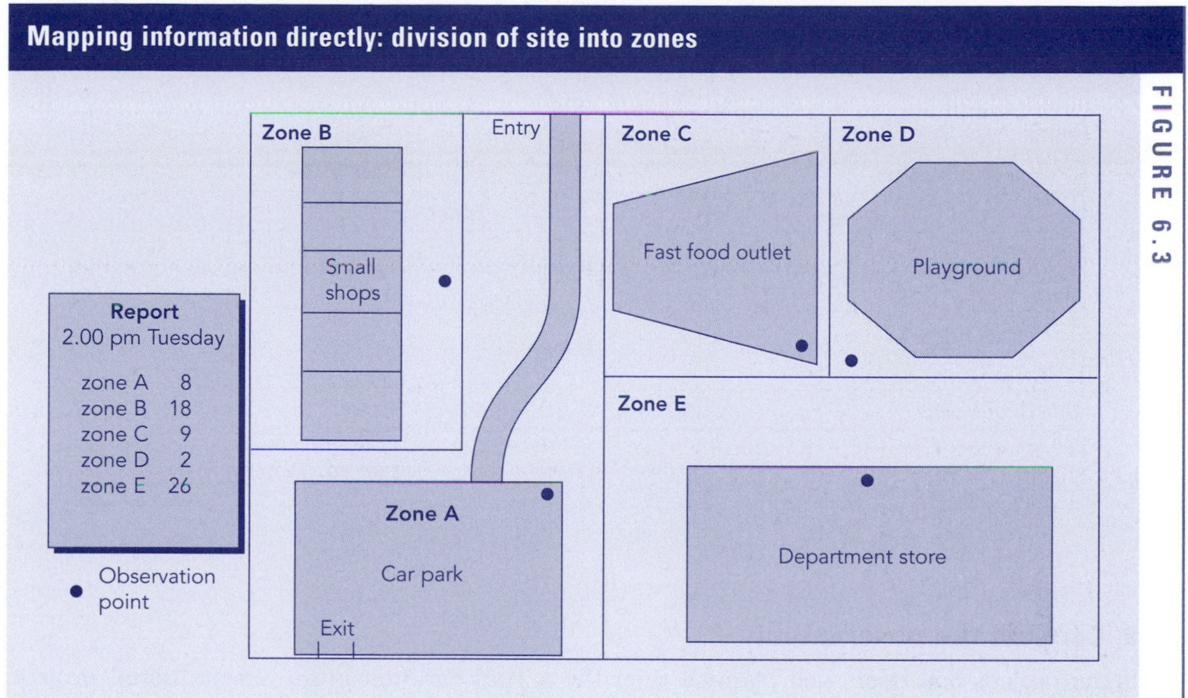

Additional items of information would complicate the recording sheet. Care needs to be taken not to make the data collection so complicated that it becomes difficult for the observers to observe and count, and consequently leads to inaccuracies. This is one of those situations where it is necessary to consider carefully *why* the data are being collected and to avoid getting carried away with data collection for its own sake.

In addition to observing people as they arrive at an entrance, it is also possible to observe visitors' movements through a site. Care must be taken not to give offence by letting visitors become aware that they are being 'followed'; however, if obtained in an appropriate manner, information about the routes taken by visitors can be revealing for management.

7 Division of site into zones

In large sites it is advisable to divide the site into areas or zones and record the numbers of people and their activities within those zones. The zones should be determined primarily by management concerns—for example, the children's playground, the department store, the fast food outlet, parking areas and small shops, as shown in Figure 6.3 for a hypothetical shopping centre. They should also be designed for ease of counting—zones should ideally be such that they can be observed from one spot and should also be clearly demarcated by natural or other features.

8 Design of recording sheet

Figure 6.4 is an example of a counting sheet designed for an area with five zones and the possibility of recording a variety of activities.

FIGURE 6.4

Example of a count recording sheet

Site:			Date:		
Name of observer:			Start time:		
			Zone		
Activity	A	B	C	D	E
Actively shopping					
Eating/drinking					
Playing					
Parking/driving					
Walking around site					
Total					

9 Conduct the observation

If the project has been well planned then the actual conduct of an observational project should be straightforward. The main danger in a large project can be boredom, leading to observational and data-recording inaccuracies. It is therefore advisable to vary the work of those involved with data collection. Where appropriate, data collectors should alternate between behavioural observation and counting, and should switch between sites as well.

10 Analysis of data

How should sample counts be interpreted to obtain an overall estimate of use? The data collected using a form such as that presented in Figure 6.4 are ideal for storage, manipulation and presentation in tabular or graphic form using a spreadsheet program or a statistical analysis program such as *SPSS*. Suppose the observations for one day produced data as shown in Figure 6.5. This could be presented graphically as shown in Figure 6.6, which relates to the whole shopping centre site not to individual zones. Similar graphics could be produced for each zone.

It is estimated that there is an average of 83.5 people in the shopping centre over a ten-hour period, giving a total of 835 *visitor hours*. The number of visitor hours is a valid measure of use in its own right and could be used to compare different sites or to compare the performance of the same site over time. However, ten visitor hours could result from one person visiting the shopping centre and staying all day, two people staying five hours each, ten people staying one hour each or twenty people staying half an hour each. If an estimate is required of the number of *different persons* visiting the shopping centre over the course of the day, additional information concerning the *length of stay* is necessary. If the average user in the example stayed exactly half an hour, then the number of persons would be estimated at twice the number of visitor hours, or 1670 (835 ÷ 0.5); if the average user stayed two hours, the number of users would be 417 (835 ÷ 2). Thus the number of visitors is equal to the number of visitor hours divided by the average length of stay. The length of

FIGURE 6.5

Counts of shopping centre visitor numbers

Time	Actively shopping	Eating/ drinking	Playing	Parking/ driving	Walking around	Total
				Number present		
8.00 a.m.	0	19	2	10	7	38
9.00 a.m.	11	13	0	12	11	47
10.00 a.m.	23	14	3	6	12	58
11.00 a.m.	47	15	3	6	15	86
12.00 noon	57	30	6	22	19	134
1.00 p.m.	64	44	8	22	23	161
2.00 p.m.	42	13	2	5	15	77
3.00 p.m.	36	13	2	4	13	68
4.00 p.m.	28	12	9	5	13	67
5.00 p.m.	49	33	11	16	18	127
6.00 p.m.	0	33	0	11	11	55
Total	357	239	46	119	157	918
Avge no. present	32.5	21.7	4.2	10.8	14.3	83.5

stay could be obtained either by detailed observation of a sample group or by an interview survey.

Details of user characteristics obtained from observation can allow a check on the accuracy of sampling in an interview survey. Such information can be used to weight the results of such surveys so that the final result is a better reflection of the characteristics of the users of the centre. This is similar to the 'time of day' correction discussed above but relates to the personal characteristics of users, rather than their time of use of the facility. For instance, if it was found by observation that three-quarters of the users of a site were women, but only half of the participants in the interview survey were women, the women in the sample could be given a greater weighting at the analysis stage so that their views and attitudes would receive due emphasis. The details of weighting are described more fully in Chapter 11.

TECHNICAL AIDS

A number of technical aids are available for use in some types of observational study. These include:

FIGURE 6.6

Shopping centre usage chart

Shopping centre usage

Walking
Parking
Playing
Eating
Shopping

Total number of persons

200
150
100
50
0

8 am 10 am Noon 2 pm 4 pm 6 pm

Time

Technical aids

- Aerial photography
- Still photography
- Video
- Time-lapse photography
- Automatic counters

Aerial photography

The use of aerial photography is well developed in geography and geology, where a whole subdiscipline of *remote sensing* uses a variety of techniques. It can also be an effective technique in management studies. Where large areas are concerned—such as farmlands, mine sites, airports or major construction sites—or where access is difficult and use of the site is very scattered, aerial photography may be the only way of obtaining estimates of levels and patterns of use. Needless to say, a good quality camera is needed for such work. Slides or digital photographs are generally the best medium because they can easily be projected on to a large screen for the subsequent laborious task of counting.

Still photography

The value of ordinary land-based photography as an adjunct to direct observation should not be overlooked. The level of crowding of a work site, its nature and its atmosphere can all be conveyed to the reader of a report with the aid of photographs. Problems regarding layout or design faults can be conveyed more effectively using visual rather than verbal techniques.

Video

Video can be used to record patterns of site use, but it is more likely to be used for illustrative rather than analytical purposes. Video can provide a useful illustration of before and after situations. It can also be used to illustrate the nature of problems on a site and the effect of measures to ameliorate the problems—for example redesign, changed practices or new equipment.

Time-lapse photography

Time-lapse photography lies somewhere between still photography and video. A time-lapse camera can be set up to automatically take a picture of a scene every designated time period, for example every ten seconds or every minute. The resultant sequence of pictures can then be projected as a film or video to show the speeded-up pattern of use of the area viewed. This technique can be used to show the changing pattern of use of a work site.

Automatic counters

Traffic counters, as used by transport planners—in the form of a black rubber tube laid across a road and attached to a data box—are a common sight. Such devices may be used in some business research contexts, for example in measuring the number of vehicles using a shopping centre car park. Electronic pedestrian counters are also now available which use an electronic beam to count the number of people passing a certain point over a period of time. These devices automate some of the counting processes discussed above, reducing costs or releasing field staff for qualitative observational activity.

'JUST LOOKING'

Finally, we should not forget how important it is to use our eyes even if the research project does not involve systematic observational data collection. Familiarity with a workplace activity or customer behaviour patterns can assist in designing a good research project and aid in interpreting data. Many studies have been simply based on informal, but careful, observation. All useful information is not in the form of numbers. While bearing in mind that observation methods cannot provide evidence concerning such matters as attitudes, expectations, preferences or motivation, careful observation of what is happening in a workplace situation, at a particular facility or type of facility, or among a particular group, can be a more appropriate research approach to use than questionnaires or even informal interviews.

It is important to consider the privacy rights of people who are the subjects of observational research. The ethical responsibilities of the researcher should always be borne in mind.

SUMMARY

Observation methods usually involve gathering information about people's behaviour without their knowledge. *Observation* is appropriate when knowledge of the presence of the researcher is likely to lead to undesirable changes in the subject's behaviour or when mass patterns of behaviour are of interest. The method principally involves *looking*, which can be done with the naked eye or with the help of recording equipment. The results of a researcher's observations can be recorded and analysed qualitatively or quantitatively.

Observation methods are capable of presenting a perspective on a situation that is not apparent to the individuals involved. They are often used in the context of work sites and employee behaviour, consumer testing, social behaviour or as a complementary process to other research methods. Observation is essentially a simple research method, so there is not a great deal of methodology to be considered. However, it is important that the researcher is very precise and patient, and gives great attention to detail in making observations.

TEST QUESTIONS

1. Name five contexts in which observational methods might be used in management research.
2. What is a sociogram?
3. Once an observation site has been designated or selected, decisions have to be made on six aspects of an observational study—what are they?
4. What technical aids are available for observational research?

EXERCISES

1. Select a work site (for example, an office block foyer or a shopping centre) and position yourself in an unobtrusive location where you can see what is going on. Over a period of two hours, record what happens. Write a report on how the site is used, who it is used by, how many people use it, what conflicts there are—if any—between different groups of users and how the design aids or hinders the activity which people engage in on the site.
2. Establish a counting system to record the number of people present at a facility where efficiency might be improved, for example, a marina, petrol station or a gymnasium. Make observations at hourly intervals during the course of a day. Estimate the number of visitor hours at the site for the day.
3. In relation to exercise 1, conduct interviews with three or four visitors each hour and ask them how long they have stayed, or expect to stay, at the site. Establish the average length of stay and, using this information and the data from exercise 1, estimate the number of persons visiting the site in the course of the day.

FURTHER READING

General: Adler and Adler (1994); Cooper and Emory (1995), Chapter 12; Kellehear (1993); and Zikmund (1997), Chapter 10.

Examples of observational studies:

- *Regarding workplace safety* using direct observation and still photography: Flick, Radomsky and Ramani (1999).
- *Customer behaviour* using still photography: Dodd, Clarke and Kirkup (1998).
- *Direct observation* of group decision-making process: Vallaster and Koll (2002).
- *Direct observation/counts* of on-street movement patterns of restaurant customers: Boote and Mathews (1999).
- *Mystery shopping:* Dawson & Hillier (1993); Hudson et al. (2001).

CHAPTER 7

Qualitative methods

This chapter addresses research methods that involve the collection of *qualitative* information rather than numerical data. It discusses the features of qualitative methods and their role in management research and outlines a range of available methods, including in-depth interviews, group interviews, focus groups, participant observation and ethnographic approaches. While it is difficult in many instances to separate data collection from data analysis in qualitative research, the analysis of qualitative data is dealt with separately in Chapter 15.

THE NATURE OF QUALITATIVE METHODS

The term *qualitative* is used to describe research methods and techniques that use and generate qualitative, rather than quantitative, information. As Van Maanen (1983: 9) notes, qualitative methods comprise 'an array of interpretive techniques which seek to describe, decode, translate and otherwise come to terms with the meaning, not the frequency, of certain more or less naturally occurring phenomena in the social world'.

One of the basic assumptions underlying qualitative research, as discussed in Chapter 2, is that reality is socially and subjectively constructed rather than objectively determined. The researcher is seen to be part of the research process and seeks to uncover meanings and understanding of the issues being researched. In general, qualitative methods involve collecting a relatively large amount of 'rich' information about a relatively small number of people or organisations rather than a limited amount of information about a large number of people or organisations. It is, however, possible to envisage qualitative research which deals with relatively large numbers of subjects. For example, a research project on work practices in a factory that involves observation, participation in some of the activities and possibly a small number of informal interviews with workers, could involve information relating to hundreds of people.

Qualitative methods can be used for pragmatic reasons in situations where quantified research is not necessary or possible. But there are also theoretical grounds for their use. Much qualitative research is based on the belief that the people personally involved in a particular situation are best placed to analyse and describe it in their own words, and should be allowed to speak without the intermediary of the researcher—a sort of *cinema verité* or *vox populi* style of research.

Since the researcher is also the front-line data gatherer and recorder, the process of analysis is ongoing. The researcher must constantly be considering what she or he sees as the objectives of the study and drawing interim conclusions. The very act of deciding what to view, what to say and what to record involves choices which will be influenced by the researcher's evolving understanding of the phenomenon being studied. This iterative process results in what Glaser and Strauss (1967) termed *grounded theory*—a concept discussed later in the chapter.

Some advantages of qualitative methods

There are a number of advantages of qualitative research methods compared with quantitative approaches. These advantages arise largely from the basic assumptions and philosophies underlying qualitative research (Easterby-Smith, Thorpe & Lowe 1991; Gummesson 1991; Kelly 1980). The advantages are summarised as follows:

- qualitative methods enable the researcher to understand and explain in detail the personal experiences of individuals;
- qualitative research focuses on people's understanding and interpretations rather than seeking external causes or 'laws' for behaviour;
- qualitative methods allow the researcher to experience research issues from a participant's perspective;
- qualitative research reports are usually presented in a narrative form rather than a statistical form, making them generally more interesting and understandable for readers not trained in statistics;

- qualitative methods are useful in examining personal changes over time;
- qualitative methods tend to focus on human-interest issues that are meaningful to everyday managers.

As noted in Chapters 1 and 2, different research methods are not inherently good or bad. Rather, they are more or less appropriate for the task in hand. The advantages listed here relate to particular types of research with particular purposes. A list of claims can also be made about the merits of various forms of quantitative research, as shown in Chapter 8 in relation to questionnaire surveys.

THE QUALITATIVE RESEARCH PROCESS

Qualitative methods generally require a more flexible approach to overall research design and conduct than quantitative approaches. Most quantitative research tends to be *sequential* in nature. The steps set out in Chapter 3, which in general apply to all forms of research, tend to be particularly distinct and follow a pre-planned sequence in the case of quantitative research. This is inevitable, due to the nature of the core data collection exercise that is generally involved.

Qualitative research involves a more fluid relationship between the various elements of the research—an approach that can be called *recursive*. In this approach, hypothesis formation evolves as the research progresses. Data analysis and collection take place concurrently and writing is also often an evolutionary, ongoing process, rather than a separate process which happens at the end of the project. The two approaches are represented diagrammatically in Figure 7.1. Although the approaches are presented as a contrast between quantitative and qualitative methods, the two approaches can each involve sequential and recursive elements. Thus, it is possible to have an essentially quantitative study that involves a variety of data sources and a number of small-scale studies which build in an iterative way. On the other hand, it is also possible for an

FIGURE 7.1 Sequential and recursive approaches to research

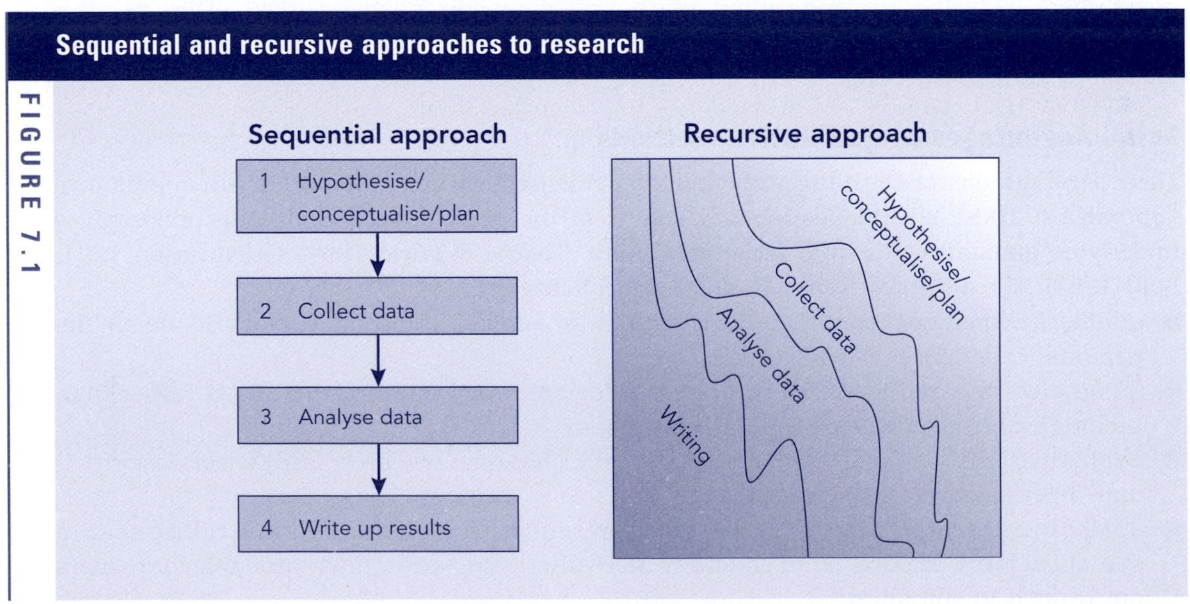

essentially qualitative study to be conducted on a large scale with a single data source—for example, a nationwide study of business leaders, involving fairly standardised in-depth interviews.

A typical qualitative project might involve the following processes:

- collecting empirical materials such as documents, interviews, case histories, personal experience, videos, field notes or press clippings that are the focus of interest;
- searching for key words or phrases from the *text* of empirical materials which are of interest to the researcher;
- coding the key words or phrases (for example, lines, sentences, paragraphs, complete speeches, etc.) according to a preliminary indexing system;
- sorting particular pieces of text and associated ideas using the preliminary indexing system;
- making notes about emerging patterns, relationships and recurring themes that are found, and proposing tentative hypotheses about these patterns;
- on the basis of emerging patterns and relationships, reviewing and extending the preliminary indexing, in accordance with tentative hypotheses; or
- collecting more empirical material if needed and following these steps over again in a recursive fashion.

There is no standard or uniform approach to qualitative analysis. The common thread that binds qualitative analyses together is the shared goal of uncovering the underlying meanings of the phenomena being studied.

THE RANGE OF QUALITATIVE METHODS

The range of qualitative methods available to the researcher, and discussed in this chapter, is shown below.

Qualitative methods: summary:

In-depth interviews

- Usually conducted with a relatively small number of subjects
- Often guided by a checklist rather than a formal questionnaire
- Often tape-recorded and a verbatim transcript prepared
- Take half an hour or more and may extend over several hours; repeat interviews possible.

Group interviews/focus groups

- Similar to in-depth interviews, but conducted with a group
- Interaction between subjects takes place as well as interaction between interviewer and subject.

Participant observation

- Researcher gathers information by being an actual participant along with the subjects being studied
- Researcher may be known by the subjects as a researcher, or may be *incognito.*

Analysis of texts

- Can include print, audio-visual, artefacts.

continues . . .

Ethnography

- Utilises a number of the above techniques, rather than being a single technique—borrowed from anthropology.

Biographical research

- Focuses on individual full or partial life histories
- May involve in-depth interviews but also documentary evidence and subjects' own written accounts.

IN-DEPTH INTERVIEWS

Nature

An in-depth interview is characterised by its length, depth and structure. In-depth interviews tend to be much longer than questionnaire-based interviews, typically taking at least half an hour and often several hours. The method often involves interviewing people more than once. As the name implies, the in-depth interview seeks to probe more deeply than is possible with a typical questionnaire-based interview. Rather than just asking a question, recording a simple answer and moving on, the in-depth interviewer encourages the respondent to talk, asks supplementary questions and asks respondents to explain their answers. The in-depth interview is therefore less structured than a questionnaire-based interview—every interview in a study, although dealing with the same issues, will be different. In a questionnaire-based interview, there is generally little scope for respondents to talk at length on a topic in their own words—or if they do, then the detail is not recorded. In the in-depth interview, the extended comment from respondents is the essence of the method.

Purposes

In-depth interviews tend to be used in three broad situations.

- When the subjects of the research are relatively few in number, so a questionnaire-based, quantitative style of research is inappropriate.
- When the information likely to be obtained from each subject is expected to vary considerably and in complex ways—examples of this include interviews with the management staff of a local council or interviews with the managing directors of major companies in a particular sector, where each interview would be a 'story' in its own right. It would be the unique nature and structure of each of these 'stories' which would be of interest—the question of 'what percentage of respondents said what' would not be relevant.
- When a topic is to be explored as a preliminary stage in planning a larger study, possibly a quantitative study, such as a questionnaire-based survey.

Checklist

Rather than a formal questionnaire, the 'instrument' used in in-depth interviews is often a *checklist* of topics to be raised. For example, a formal questionnaire might include a question: 'Which of the following training or educational activities have you taken part in, in the last ten years?' Answers would involve ticking boxes to record the respondent's involvement with particular activities. The in-depth interview checklist, on the other hand, would probably simply include the words '*training/education*'. The interviewer would shape the question according to the circumstances of a particular interview. For example, if the interviewer is interested in the influence of education on current attitudes to work, in some interviews it may be necessary to ask a specific question, such as: 'What useful skills did you obtain from your formal education?' In other interviews the interviewee might have discussed education in great detail in response to an earlier question: 'How satisfied are you with your current job?' If this is the case, then it is not necessary to ask the separate question about educational influences. Thus in-depth interviews vary from interview to interview; they take on a life of their own. The skill on the part of the interviewer is to ensure that all relevant topics are covered—even though they may be covered in a different order and in different ways in different interviews.

The design of the checklist should nevertheless be as methodical as the design of a formal questionnaire—in particular, the items to be included on the checklist should be based on the conceptual framework for the study and the resultant list of data needs, as discussed in Chapter 3. An example of part of a checklist devised in connection with a study of employee attitudes to training and development is shown in Figure 7.2.

FIGURE 7.2

Example of an in-depth interview checklist

CURRENT TRAINING	Level/type Why? Where? Cost Amount of work Benefits Meaning/importance
TRAINING WOULD LIKE TO DO	Why?
CONSTRAINTS	Home Money Supervisor's attitude Work—time/energy/colleages Qualifications Family roles Being a parent Money/costs Availability of courses
PAST TRAINING/EDUCATION	School TAFE College/university In-service
PERSONALITY	
SKILLS	
CAREER ASPIRATIONS	

A compromise between the formal questionnaire and a minimalist checklist is a 'topic guide' containing key questions, which range over the whole study area and which serve as a 'starter' for discussion of an area. An example is given in Verdurme and Viane (2003).

Interviewing

Conducting a good in-depth interview could be said to require the skills of a good investigative journalist. As Dean and his colleagues put it:

> *Many people feel that a newspaper reporter is a far cry from a social scientist. Yet many of the data of social science today are gathered by interviewing and observation techniques that resemble those of a skilled newspaper man at work on the study of, say, a union strike or a political convention. It makes little sense for us to belittle these less rigorous methods as 'unscientific'. We will do better to study them and the techniques they involve so that we can make better use of them in producing scientific information.*
>
> *(Dean, Eichhorn & Dean, quoted in McCall & Simmons 1969: 1.)*

An important skill in interviewing is to avoid becoming so taken up in the conversational style of the interview that the interviewee is 'led' by the interviewer. The interviewer should avoid agreeing—or disagreeing—with the interviewee or suggesting answers. This is more difficult than it sounds, because in normal conversation we tend to make friendly noises and contribute to the discussion. In the in-depth interview we are torn between the need to maintain a friendly conversational atmosphere and the need not to influence the interviewee's responses.

Some of the carefully planned sequencing of questions built into formal questionnaires must be achieved by the interviewer being very sensitive and quick thinking. For example, having discovered that the respondent does not go to professional conferences, the interviewer should *not* say, 'Is this because it is too expensive?' Rather, the interviewee should be asked something like 'Why is that?'. If the interviewee does not mention cost, but cost is of particular interest in the study, then a question such as, 'What about registration costs?' might be asked, but only *after* the interviewee has given his or her own reasons for not attending conferences.

Whyte (1982) lists a form of hierarchy in interviewer responses that vary in their degree of intervention in the interview. Whyte also sees this as the interviewer exercising varying degrees of control over the interview. Beginning with the least intrusive style of intervention, Whyte's list is outlined below.

Whyte's hierarchy of interviewer responses:

1. 'Uh-huh'
   A non-verbal response which merely indicates that the interviewer is still listening and interested.
2. 'That's interesting'
   Encourages the subject to keep talking or expand on the current topic.
3. Reflection
   Repeating the last statement as a question—eg 'So you don't think you need further training?'

4 Probe
Inviting explanations of statements—eg 'Why don't you think you need further training?'

5 Backtracking
Remembering something the subject said earlier and inviting further information—eg 'Let's go back to what you were saying about your university days.'

6 New topic
Initiating a new topic—eg 'Can we talk about other sorts of training—what about computer literacy?'

It should be noted that, except for the sixth of these responses, the interviewer is essentially drawing on what the subject has already said and is inviting him or her to expand on it.

An important skill in interviewing of this sort is not to be afraid of silence. Some questions puzzle respondents and they need time to think. The interviewer does not have to fill the space with noise under the guise of 'helping' the interviewee. The interviewee should be allowed time to ponder. The initiative can be left with the respondent to ask for an explanation if a question is unclear. While it is pleasant to engender a conversational atmosphere in these situations, the in-depth interview is in fact different from a conversation. The interviewer is meant to listen and encourage the respondent to talk—not to engage in debate.

Recording

Tape recording of in-depth interviews is common, although in some cases it might be felt that such a procedure could inhibit respondents. If tape recording is not possible then notes must be taken, at the time or immediately afterwards. There can be great value in producing complete verbatim (word-for-word) transcripts of interviews. This is a laborious process—one hour of interview can take as much as six hours to transcribe. Such transcripts can, however, be used to analyse the results of interviews in a more methodical and complete manner than is possible with notes.

Example

An example of the use of in-depth interviews is given in Case Study Example 7.1, which explores potentially conflicting 'discourse', or sets of beliefs and attitudes, within a single company. Since the research involves a case study of a single company and the topic is a complex one, the in-depth interview approach, aided by documentary evidence, was considered appropriate.

CASE STUDY EXAMPLE 7.1

In-depth interviews/Case study: discursive tension in a travel agency

Source: Ian Palmer and Richard Dunford 2002, Managing discursive tension: the co-existence of individualist and collaborative discourses in Flight Centre. *Journal of Management Studies*. 39(8), 1045-70.
Methods/approaches: In-depth interviews; case study; qualitative; *Nvivo*
Topic: Organisational culture

This paper reports on a case study of a single successful international travel agency with almost 500 outlets in Australia, the UK, USA, New Zealand, Canada and South Africa. The study is concerned with two contrasting 'discourses'—ways of thinking and communicating about the business—within the organisation and how they manage to co-exist.

The idea of 'multiple discourses' within organisations was drawn from the literature and it was decided to explore the existence of such discourses within Flight Centre. The study involved two data sources: 1. Written documents, including annual reports, newspaper reports and internal documents such as operational manuals, and 2. Interviews with 19 Flight Centre staff. The interviews, which were tape recorded and transcribed, and analysed using the *Nvivo* software package (see Chapter 15), provide the main basis for the analysis. It was during the coding of the interview data for analysis that two particular discourses emerged: a discourse of 'competitive individualism' and a discourse of 'collaborative teamwork'. These were clearly potentially conflicting and so became the focus of the researchers' interest.

The existence of each of the two discourses is demonstrated through the identification of themes from interview transcripts largely illustrated through quotations. For example, competitive individualism is demonstrated by: the 'flat' organisational structure of the company, with the basic unit being a group of five or six agency shops identified as a 'village'; formalised systems for recognising individual sales success; and sales-driven commission. Collaborative teamwork is demonstrated by interdependency between sales staff, and cooperation and interdependency of shops and 'villages'.

While the existence of the two discourses sometimes comes into conflict, Palmer and Dunford conclude that, generally, the staff are able to accommodate both in a state of 'discursive co-existence'. It is concluded that the success of Flight Centre in a highly competitive market is due to its ability to foster and take advantage of both discourses.

GROUP INTERVIEWS AND FOCUS GROUPS

Nature

Interviewing groups of people together rather than individually is becoming an increasingly popular form of qualitative research. This approach often sees the interviewer become the *facilitator* of a discussion rather than an interviewer as such. The aim of the process is much the same as in an in-depth interview, but in this case the 'subjects' interact with each other as well as with the researcher.

Purposes

The technique can be used:

- when a particular group is important to a study but is so small in number that members of the group would not be adequately represented in a general sample survey—for example, members of minority ethnic groups or people with disabilities;
- when the interaction/discussion process itself is of interest—for example, when testing reactions to a proposed new product or when investigating how people form political opinions; or
- as an alternative to the in-depth interview when it may not be practical to arrange a single interview per subject, but people are willing to be interviewed as a group.

It has been argued by some that focus groups are being inappropriately used, particularly when views and opinions emerging from focus group sessions have been interpreted as being quantitatively representative of a wider population. This is clearly inappropriate if a representative sample of participants is not involved, but it is also the case that the interaction which takes place in focus groups' discussion can result in participants' expressed views changing, making the method unsuitable for assessing individual attitudes (Bristol & Fern 2003).

Methods

A focus group usually comprises between five and twelve participants. They may be chosen from a 'panel' of people who make themselves available to market researchers for this sort of exercise. They may also be chosen because they are members of a particular group of interest to the research—for instance, they may be local residents in a particular area, members of a union, managers at a certain level or users of a particular computer software package. The members of the group may or may not be known to one another.

The usual procedure is to tape record the discussion and for the researcher to produce a summary from the recording.

Many of the same considerations apply here as in the in-depth interview situation: the process is informal, but the interviewer, or 'facilitator', still has a role in guiding the discussion and ensuring that all aspects of the topic are covered. In addition, in the group interview the interviewer has the task of ensuring that everyone in the group has their say and that one or two vociferous members of the group do not dominate the discussion.

PARTICIPANT OBSERVATION

Nature

In participant observation the researcher becomes a direct participant in the social process being studied. An early example of the use of this method in business was the study by Roy (1952), who worked as an employee of a large company in a machine shop. His work provided important insights into employees' motives in manipulating a piecework incentive scheme and the ways in which this manipulation was achieved.

Purposes

In much social research there are elements of 'participant observation'; however, traditionally the participant observation process has involved considerably more interaction between the researcher and the people being researched than is usual in other forms of research. In many cases some sort of participant observation is the only way of researching particular phenomena—for instance, it would be difficult to study what really happens on a shop floor in some organisational subcultures by using a questionnaire and clipboard. Where complex and detailed information is required on group dynamics or interpersonal relationships, becoming part of the group is the most effective study approach.

Methods

Participant observation raises a number of practical challenges. For example, in some cases actually gaining admittance to the social setting of interest may be a problem, particularly when close-knit groups are involved. Having gained admittance to the setting, the question arises as to whether to pose as a 'typical' member of the group, whether to adopt a plausible 'disguise' (eg a 'journalist' or 'writer'), or whether to admit to being a researcher. The question of the researcher's relationship with informants also raises ethical questions, which were discussed in Chapter 3.

Selection of informants is an issue to be addressed by the participant observer in the same way that sampling must be considered by the survey researcher. The most friendly and talkative members of the study group may give a biased picture of the views and behaviour of the group. In addition, there are practical problems regarding how to record information. When the researcher's identity has not been revealed, the taking of notes or the use of a tape recorder may be impossible. Even when the researcher has been identified as such or has a plausible 'identity', the use of such devices may interfere with the sort of natural relationship that the researcher is trying to establish.

Recording of information can present particular problems if the researcher is *incognito* or simply wishes to avoid introducing the distancing and inhibitions that the presence of a notebook may entail. The taking of regular and detailed notes is, however, the basic data recording method. This may be supplemented by photographs and even video and tape recordings in some instances.

ANALYSIS OF TEXTS

Analysis of texts can include not just written or printed documents but also such phenomena as film and video, broadcasts and the Internet. Such analysis overlaps with literature reviews on the one hand and observation on the other. While the approach is discussed in this chapter on qualitative methods, texts can also be analysed quantitatively. As indicated in Chapter 2, when texts are analysed qualitatively the process is sometimes referred to as *hermeneutics*, originally the study of the meaning of religious texts. When the research is quantitative it is sometimes referred to as *content analysis*. The analysis process is therefore similar to the analysis of in-depth interview transcripts as discussed in Chapter 15.

While textual analysis is not common in business research, examples do exist, including:

CASE STUDY EXAMPLE 7.2

Participant observation: Work and family time

Source: Leslie A. Perlow, 1998, Boundary control: the social ordering of work and family time in a high-tech corporation. *Administrative Science Quarterly*, 43(2), 328–357.
Methods/approaches: Participant observation, in-depth interviews
Topic: Balancing work and family time

Of the four types of participant observation (complete observer, observer as participant, participant as observer, complete participant) this study is an example of the second: the researcher studied the 17 members of a software team of a large company during a nine-month period in which they were developing a new product. The researcher did not become a member of the team engaged in software work, but observed them closely for an average of four days a week, attending work meetings, taking coffee and lunch with them and attending work-based social functions. In addition she conducted in-depth interviews, lasting 1-2 hours each, with all team members, five colleagues outside of the team and 12 spouses in their homes. The topic was the maintenance of the boundary between work and family life. Three questions were posed: 1. How is boundary control maintained by managers? 2. How do employees respond to these controls? 3. How do spouses respond to these controls?

The recursive nature of qualitative research is indicated in the following quotation:

> . . . I developed empirically grounded sets of *categories* related to work demands (how these demands are made, the implications on individuals' lives outside of work, the consequences for individuals not responding etc.). In doing so, I followed an iterative process, fitting *observations* to *categories*. As new observations arose, I continually made choices as to whether to retain, revise, or discard particular categories or category sets. Periodic analysis *throughout the data collection process* helped sharpen questions, focus interviews and observations, and ground evolving theory. (Perlow, 1998: 336, emphasis added)

In the case of question 1, on the methods used by managers to exert control over staff, Perlow identifies three techniques: *imposing demands* (by formal requests, meetings, etc.), *monitoring* (standing over, observing), and *modelling* (demonstrating requirements through their own behaviour). In regard to question 2 and 3, employees' and spouses' response to management's demands, employees and spouses are divided into 'acceptors' and 'resisters'. A table is presented, listing each of the team members and spouse, where applicable, and their status as acceptor or resister.

The various forms which the of demand and control techniques take and employees' and spouses' reactions to them are discussed in turn, with quotations from interviews used as illustrations.

- Okazaki and Rivas's (2003) content analysis of website marketing by Japanese multinationals in different countries—see Case Study Example 7.2.
- Carty's (1997) qualitative study of Nike's portrayal of women in its advertising—see Case Study Example 9.1.

ETHNOGRAPHY

The *ethnographic* style of research is not one technique but an approach which draws on a variety of techniques. It sometimes combines a number of the methods discussed above. Generally, it seeks to see the world through the eyes of those being researched, allowing them to speak for themselves, often through extensive direct quotations. Sometimes the aim is to debunk conventional 'common sense' views of social and work situations, sexual and ethnic stereotypes and so on. Researchers seek to immerse themselves in the workplace setting and become part of the group in which they are interested. This is done in order to provide understanding of the meaning and importance that members of the group impart to their own behaviour and the behaviour of others.

BIOGRAPHICAL RESEARCH

Biographical research covers a range of research methods which involve researching all or a substantial part of individuals' or groups of individuals' lives. The most common example of such research is the conventional biography or autobiography, but the biographical approach includes a number of research approaches and outputs other than a full biography. Detailed guidance on the conduct of biographical research is not given in this book, but a brief overview of the field is given here and sources of further information in the Further Reading section.

Biographical methods:
- Biography
- Autobiography
- Oral history
- Memory work
- Personal domain histories

Biography/Autobiography

There are many published accounts of lives of business leaders which, while often read for entertainment, also provide insight into how business and business leaders operate. Perhaps the most well known is the autobiography of Lee Iacocca (1984), the CEO of Chrysler during a turbulent period. In the case of Walt Disney, there is an enormous literature bank in which the biography of Walt Disney himself and the story of the corporation are intertwined (eg Bryman 1996; Foglesong 2001; Project on Disney 1995). In Australia, *The Rise and Fall of Alan Bond* and the *Rise and Rise of Kerry Packer*, both by Paul Barry (1990, 1993), are notable examples of business biographies.

Oral history

Oral history involves tape recording eyewitness accounts of events and typically storing the tapes and/or a transcription of them in an archive as a source for research. While such accounts range more widely than the interviewees' own lives, they are nevertheless personal accounts. An example is Parker's (1988) study of a British mining community during the miners' strikes of the 1980s—the book includes accounts by miners, Coal Board employees, police and community members.

Memory work

Memory work is a structured way of eliciting subjects' memories of events; it can be seen as a focus group aided by individual writing. Participants are asked to write a short account of an experience related to the research topic—for example bullying at the workplace or successful selling. The written accounts are read aloud in focus group settings and discussed, and may be followed up with further writing and/or interviewing.

Personal domain histories

In the 1980s, a technique termed 'personal leisure histories' was developed by Hedges (1986) to study the ways in which significant changes in life circumstances (marriage, birth of a child, change of job, health issues, etc.) impacted on patterns of leisure participation. While no known example exists, it seems clear that such a technique might be used to focus on other domains of life of interest to the business researcher, notably career. Hence the use of the term personal *domain* histories.

GROUNDED THEORY AND QUALITATIVE RESEARCH

An important philosophical perspective in the analysis of qualitative data is the concept of *grounded theory* developed by two sociologists, Barney Glaser and Anselm Strauss (1967). Their approach has been especially influential in European management research studies.

Grounded theory is concerned with the generation of theory from research, as opposed to research that tests existing theory. In this paradigm, theories and models should be *grounded* in real empirical observations rather than being governed by traditional methodologies and theories. As Jones (1987: 25) notes, 'research should be used to generate grounded theory which "fits" and "works" because it is derived from the concepts and categories used by social actors themselves to interpret and organise their worlds'.

In the generation of grounded theory the researcher approaches the data with no preformed notions in mind, instead seeking to uncover patterns and contradictions through intuition and feelings. To achieve this the researcher needs to be very familiar with the data, the subjects and the cultural context of the research. The process is a complex and personal one, as described in Strauss (1987) and Strauss and Corbin (1994).

Although a detailed review of grounded theory is outside the scope of this book, researchers interested in these approaches should acquaint themselves with the underlying philosophy as a guide to understanding the research work of others. Easterby-Smith, Thorpe and Lowe (1991: 104–13) provide a summary of qualitative analysis procedures using a grounded theory approach.

MANAGEMENT CONTEXTS FOR THE USE OF QUALITATIVE METHODS

Qualitative methods can be a useful research approach in most management contexts. They are most widely used in research involving corporate culture, power relationships and consumer decision-making. In these areas, the researcher's understanding of *meanings* within the domain of human behaviour is usually essential to achieving research goals. The examples outlined below illustrate the importance of this understanding in relation to corporate culture and consumer decision-making.

Corporate culture

In relation to corporate culture, Schein (1985) has described his experiences as a consultant when he was asked to develop appropriate methods for improving conflicting relationships and decision-making among senior managers in a corporation. After a period of observing the largely negative behaviours among the managers, Schein made a series of recommendations designed to resolve this argumentation and conflict. His recommendations were politely received but made no change to the situation in the company. Following an intensive study of the corporate culture using an ethnographic approach, Schein discovered the underlying *meaning* of conflict within the organisation—conflict was the means through which truth was uncovered and all managers were expected to fight for ideas in this management arena. Conflict was therefore valued in the corporate culture (Schein 1985: 12-13). It was only through the information gained by his qualitative research that Schein was able to develop strategies to bring about changes in the managers' behaviours and relationships.

Consumer decision-making

An example involving the understanding of consumer decision-making is provided by the 1970s case study, Sunshine Machine Tools (SMT), a Queensland importing business. SMT found that their Adelaide agent had far higher sales than did their outlets in other Australian cities. Following the advice of a management consultant, the marketing manager and the consultant spent a week in the back office of the Adelaide outlet, listening and noting the sales approach used by the Adelaide agent. They hoped to document his selling approach for use by their agents in other states. To their surprise they found that he had very little conversation with customers. Customers usually came in and selected their needs from the expansive display shelves, paid and left. It was then decided to interview a number of customers as to why they used the Adelaide agency. It was discovered that the main street frontage, clear signage, a clean well-lit shop and the large number of items on display were the main reasons for their patronage. The customers were all tradespeople who knew what they wanted and wanted to obtain it quickly and conveniently. This was the *meaning* of the Adelaide store for them. It was then recognised that the traditional shop fronts in other cities were small and poorly lit, had a counter with tools stored behind it and were usually in an industrial back street. These factors were what was inhibiting sales. A year later, changes made to the shops in other states saw a significant improvement in SMT sales.

Qualitative methods provide *alternative* perspectives for researching management issues rather than competing with more traditional quantitative methods. They are complementary to quantitative methods and seek to uncover a different understanding of the common problems that interest management researchers. Gummesson suggests that, unless researchers have access to these underlying meanings, their research findings will be meaningless, no matter how sophisticated their research design and quantitative analysis. Without the insights provided by qualitative approaches the old computer adage, 'garbage in, garbage out' may well apply to much management research (Gummesson 1991: 11–12).

SUMMARY

This chapter introduced the role of qualitative approaches in business research. One of the basic assumptions of qualitative research is that reality is socially and subjectively constructed rather than objectively determined. In this perspective researchers are seen as part of the research process seeking to uncover meanings and gain an understanding of the issues they are researching. In general, qualitative research involves the collection of a large amount of 'rich' information concerning relatively few people in an organisation rather than collecting more limited information from a large number of people or organisations.

Qualitative methods generally require a more flexible approach to overall research design and conduct than quantitative approaches. Most quantitative research tends to be sequential in nature; however, qualitative research involves a more fluid relationship between the various elements of the research—an approach that can be called *recursive*. In this approach, hypothesis formation evolves as the research progresses. Data analysis and collection take place concurrently and writing is also often an evolutionary process, rather than a separate process which happens at the end of the project. There is no standard or uniform approach to qualitative research. The common thread that binds qualitative research together is the shared goal of uncovering the underlying meanings of the phenomena being studied.

There is a range of qualitative methods available to the researcher, including in-depth interviews, group interviews, focus groups, participant observation and ethnographic methods. An in-depth interview is characterised by its length, depth and structure. The method often involves interviewing people more than once and seeks to probe more deeply than it is possible to probe with a questionnaire-based interview. Rather than just asking a question, recording a simple answer and moving on, the in-depth interviewer encourages the respondent to talk, asks supplementary questions and asks respondents to explain their answers.

Group interviews and focus groups are becoming an increasingly popular form of qualitative research. In this approach the interviewer becomes the facilitator of a discussion rather than an interviewer as such. The aim of the process is much the same as in an in-depth interview, but in this case the 'subjects' interact with each other as well as with the researcher. Group interviews are often used when a small group is important in a study, when the interaction and discussion process itself is of interest, or as an alternative to the in-depth interview. In participant observation the researcher becomes a participant in the social process being studied. In many cases participant observation is the only way of researching particular phenomena. Where complex and detailed information is required on group dynamics or interpersonal relationships, participant observation is the most effective way of studying the group. Ethnographic methods describe a range of techniques and generally combine a number of the methods discussed above. Ethnographic researchers seek to immerse themselves in the workplace setting and provide understanding of the meanings and importance that members of the group attach to their own behaviour and the behaviour of others.

TEST QUESTIONS

1 What are the advantages of qualitative methods?
2 What is the difference between a sequential and recursive research process?
3 What is often used instead of a questionnaire in in-depth interviews?
4 What are the six types of intervention in Whyte's hierarchy of interview responses?
5 In what contexts might a focus group or group interview be used?
6 What is **a.** ethnography, **b.** grounded theory?
7 Name three types of biographical research and outline their defining characteristics.

EXERCISES

1 Senior management in a large organisation is concerned that there may be a decline in the effectiveness of security staff arising from an apparent increase in their workplace social activities over the past year. This has been evidenced by a number of theatre parties, strong attendance at farewells, birthday cakes at morning tea and so on. However, management is unsure if there really is a problem. Suggest a qualitative investigation into this issue to determine whether there is a problem for management.
2 Qualitative research conducted by SMT Inc. in their Adelaide store was described in this chapter. As part of the project, customers were interviewed as to why they used the store. Design a checklist or an in-depth interview with an SMT customer (see Figure 7.2) concerning their patronage. Use this checklist as a guide to format.
3 In his 1985 study, Schein came to understand the underlying meaning of conflict within an organisation using an ethnographic approach. Describe a combination of qualitative methods that a researcher could use to better understand the organisational climate in a high school.
4 The conduct of an in-depth interview can be a very difficult task since it involves sensitive two-way communication between the interviewer and respondent. Outline some of the problems that could arise in an interview that might hinder data collection.

FURTHER READING

- *General overviews of qualitative research*: Berg (1995); Denzin and Lincoln (1994); Higgs (1997); Mason (1996); Maxwell (1996); Miles & Huberman (1994); Kellehear, (1993); Robson and Foster (1989); Silverman (1997); Tesch (1990).
- *Qualitative methods and management*: Gummesson (1991); Easterby-Smith, Thorpe and Lowe (1993), Chapter 5; Morgan and Smircich (1980).
- *Interview techniques*: Dunne (1995); Hart (1991); Healey and Rawlinson (1994); Kvale (1996); Seidman (1991).

- *Focus group techniques*: Jankowicz (1991), Chapter 11; Greenbaum (1998, 2000); Krueger (1994); Morgan (1988); Stewart and Shamdasani (1990); Templeton (1994); Vaughn, Schumm and Sinagub (1996).
- *Biographical methods*: Atkinson (1998); Bertaux (1981); Roberts (2002); personal domain histories: Hedges (1986); memory work: Small and Onyx (2001); Willig (2001), Chapter 8; Zuber-Skerritt (1996), Chapter 5.
- *Participant observation*: Jorgensen (1989); Spradley (1980); Perlow (1988)—Case Study Example 7.2.
- *Ethnographic methods*: Fetterman (1989), Hammersley and Atkinson (1995); Schwartzman (1993); Spradley (1979).
- *Grounded theory* in the qualitative analysis of organisational behaviour: Turner (1987).

Examples of use of qualitative methods:

- *In-depth interviews*—discursive tension in a travel agency: Palmer & Dunford (2002)—Case Study Example 7.1.
- *Focus groups and in-depth interviews*—in assessing benefits of telework in Australia: Whitehouse, Diamond and Lafferty (2002).
- *Focus groups using 'topic guide' questions*—in a study of consumers' attitudes to genetically modified foods in Europe: Verdune and Viane (2003).
- *Focus groups*—in a study of objectives of small/medium enterprise owner-occupiers in Australia: Newby, Watson and Woodliff (2003).
- *Oral history*—British miners during the strikes of the 1980s: Parker (1988).
- Biography: Barry (1990, 1993); Iacocca (1984), Bryman (1995); Foglesong (2001); Project on Disney (1995).

CHAPTER 8

Questionnaire surveys

This chapter presents an overview of different types of questionnaire survey and describes issues to be considered in their design. The nature and merits of questionnaire surveys and the difference between interviewer-completion and respondent-completion are first discussed, followed by examination of the basic characteristics of eight types of questionnaire survey. This is followed by an overview of questionnaire design, notes on the conduct of pilot surveys and discussions of validity issues in questionnaire surveys and questionnaire-based interviewing. Finally, the chapter considers the coding of questionnaire data for computer analysis.

THE NATURE OF QUESTIONNAIRE SURVEYS

Questionnaire surveys involve the gathering of information from individuals using a formally designed schedule of questions called a *questionnaire* or *interview schedule*. This is arguably the most commonly used technique in management research. It should be noted that the term *survey* does not refer to the questionnaire but to the whole process of conducting the data collection.

Questionnaire surveys usually involve only a proportion, or *sample*, of the population that the researcher is interested in. For example, political opinion polls commonly use samples of only a few thousand people to represent millions of voters (see Figure 11.2). Procedures for choosing such samples, deciding the sample size and the implications of relying on a sample to represent a population are discussed in Chapter 11.

Questionnaire surveys rely on information from respondents—self-reported data, as discussed in Chapter 2. What respondents say depends on their own powers of recall, their honesty and the questions included in the questionnaire. There has been very little research on the validity or accuracy of questionnaire data, but some research has suggested that respondents tend to exaggerate some things and downplay others. There is some reason to believe that interviewees are affected by the desire to be helpful and friendly. Respondents may tend to exaggerate their interest in and involvement with such worthy pastimes as physical exercise or education but downplay the amount of alcohol they drink or the amount they spend on gambling. Because of this, the researcher and the user of research results should always bear in mind the nature and source of the data and try to avoid falling into the trap of believing that, because information is presented in numerical form and is based on large numbers, it represents an immutable 'truth'.

Questionnaire surveys usually involve substantial numbers of *subjects* (the people or organisations being surveyed), ranging from perhaps fifty or sixty to many thousands. This, together with the complexity of some forms of quantitative analysis, means that computers are invariably used to analyse the results. The practical implications of this for questionnaire design are discussed below in the section on *coding*, while the actual process of computer analysis of results is covered in Chapter 13.

MERITS OF THE QUESTIONNAIRE SURVEY METHOD

In contrast to the qualitative methods discussed in Chapter 7, questionnaire surveys usually involve quantification—the presentation of results in numerical form. This has implications for the way data are collected, analysed and interpreted. Each research method has its merits and appropriate uses; questionnaire surveys are useful when the research questions indicate the need for relatively structured data and when data are required from samples representative of a defined wider population.

Merits of questionnaire surveys:

Quantified data for decision-making

Questionnaire surveys are an ideal means of providing quantified information for organisations that rely on quantified information for aspects of their decision-making.

continues . . .

Transparency
While absolute 'objectivity' is impossible, questionnaire methods provide a 'transparent' set of research procedures. How information has been collected and how it has been analysed is clear for all to see. Indeed, data from surveys can be re-analysed by others if they wish to extend the research or provide an alternative interpretation.

Succinct presentation
Quantification can provide relatively complex information in a succinct, easily understood form.

Comparability
Methods such as longitudinal surveys and annually repeated surveys provide the opportunity to study change over time, using comparable methodology.

Capturing complexity
Questionnaires can be an effective means of gathering a wide range of complex information on individuals or organisations on a comparable basis.

INTERVIEWER-COMPLETION VERSUS RESPONDENT-COMPLETION

Questionnaire surveys can take one of two forms: they can be *interviewer-completed* or *respondent-completed*. When it is interviewer-completed, the questionnaire provides the *script for an interview*. An interviewer reads the questions out to the respondent and records the respondent's answers on the questionnaire. This may be done in face-to-face situations or by telephone. When the questionnaire is respondent-completed, respondents read and fill out the questionnaires for themselves. The questionnaire may be handed to the respondent by a field worker, mailed or emailed. The two approaches have advantages and disadvantages, as shown in Figure 8.1.

FIGURE 8.1 **Interviewer-completion vs. respondent-completion**

	Interviewer-completion	Respondent-completion
Advantages	More accuracy Higher response rates Fuller and more complete answers Design can be less 'user-friendly'	Cheaper Quicker Relatively anonymous
Disadvantages	Higher cost Less anonymity Exaggerated desire to please interviewer	Patchy response Incomplete response Risk of frivolous responses More care needed in layout and presentation

The interviewer-completion method is more expensive in terms of interviewers' time (which usually has to be paid for), but the use of an interviewer generally ensures a more accurate and complete response.

Respondent-completion can be cheaper and quicker, but it often results in low response rates. This can introduce bias into the results because people who choose not to respond or are unable to respond, perhaps because of language or literacy difficulties, may differ from those who do respond. When designing a questionnaire for respondent completion, greater care must be paid to layout and presentation, since it will be read and completed by 'untrained' people. In terms of design, respondent-completed questionnaires should consist primarily of 'closed' questions, that is, questions that can be answered by ticking boxes. 'Open-ended' questions, which involve respondents writing out their answers, should be used sparingly, since they invariably achieve only a low response. For example, in a face-to-face interview respondents will often give expansive answers to questions such as 'Do you have any comments to make on the overall management of this service?' They will not as readily make the effort to write down such answers in a respondent-completed questionnaire.

There may be cases when respondent-completion is preferred or is the only practicable approach. When the people to be surveyed are widely scattered geographically, making face-to-face interviews impossibly expensive, a mail survey becomes an obvious choice. A mail survey may also be appropriate when sensitive matters are involved, in which case respondents might prefer the anonymity of the respondent-completed questionnaire. Some of the issues connected with respondent-completed questionnaires are discussed more fully in the section on mail surveys.

TYPES OF QUESTIONNAIRE SURVEY

Questionnaire surveys can be divided into the following types:

Types of questionnaire survey:

- *household surveys* in which people are selected on the basis of where they live and are interviewed in their home;
- *street/quota intercept surveys* in which respondents are selected by stopping them in the street, in shopping malls, etc;
- *telephone surveys* in which interviews are conducted by telephone;
- *mail surveys* in which questionnaires are sent and returned by mail;
- *e-surveys*—a special case of the mail survey, using email or the Internet;
- *customer/visitor on-site intercept surveys* in which users or customers of a facility are surveyed on-site;
- *captive group surveys* in which members of groups such as IT users, members of a club or groups in an organisation are surveyed; or
- *organisation surveys* in which members of an organisation (or organisations) are surveyed.

Some of the basic characteristics of each type of survey are summarised in Figure 8.2, and further discussed on the following pages.

FIGURE 8.2

Types of questionnaire survey: characteristics

Type of questionnaire survey	Respondent- or interviewer-completion	Cost	Possible length of questionnaire	Nature of sample	Response rate
Household	either	expensive	long	community	high
Street	interviewer	medium	short	community	medium
Telephone	interviewer	medium	short	subscribers	high
Mail	respondent	cheap	varies	specialist	low
E-survey	respondent	cheap	varies	specialist	low-medium
Customer/visitor	either	medium	medium	customer/visitor	high
Captive	respondent	cheap	medium	specialist	high
Organisation	either	comparatively cheap	varies	specialist	high

The household questionnaire survey

A household survey involves people being selected for interview on the basis of their place of residence and interviewed there, either face-to-face or contacted by mail or telephone. The latter two types of survey are sufficiently distinct to be discussed in their own right, so in this section we discuss only those surveys where there is a face-to-face element in the process. A great deal of quantified data in the field of social research derives from household, or community, questionnaire surveys. While academics draw on the data extensively, government and commercial organisations commission the majority of such surveys for policy development or marketing purposes. The advantage of household surveys is that they are generally representative of a defined community—such as a neighbourhood, a local government area, a state or a country. The samples selected tend to include all age groups above a certain minimum and all occupational groups. Household surveys therefore provide information on the community as a whole.

Household questionnaire surveys are normally interviewer-completed, but it is possible for questionnaires to be left at the respondent's home for respondent-completion and collection at a later date. This is the practice, for example, in the national population census carried out every five years by the Australian Bureau of Statistics and comparable national statistical agencies in other countries. After collecting the completed questionnaires, the field worker then has the responsibility of checking that they have been fully completed and possibly conducting an interview in those situations where respondents have been unable to fill in the questionnaire. This may be because the respondents have been too busy, have forgotten, have lost the questionnaire, have literacy or language problems, or because of infirmity.

Since it is home-based, this type of survey can involve quite lengthy questionnaires and interviews. It can be difficult to conduct a lengthy interview in the street, at a service outlet or over the telephone, but with the home-based interview it is usually possible to pursue issues at greater length. An interview of three-quarters of an hour in duration is not out of the question and twenty to thirty minutes is quite common.

A variation on the household interview/questionnaire is a combination of interviewer-completed and respondent-completed elements. This often happens with market surveys. In such surveys, the interviewer conducts an interview with one member of the household about the household—how many people live there, whether the dwelling is owned or rented, perhaps information on ownership of consumer products, or anything to do with the household as a whole. Then an individual questionnaire is left for each member of the household to complete, concerning their own behaviour, buying patterns, etc. The interviewer calls back later to collect these individual questionnaires.

The potential length of interviews, the problems of contacting representative samples and, on occasions, the wide geographical spread of the study area, mean that household surveys are usually the most expensive to conduct per interview. Costs of $40 or $50 per interview are typical, depending on the amount of analysis included in the price. When samples of several thousand people are involved the costs can therefore be substantial.

Omnibus surveys

Omnibus surveys are single surveys conducted by a market research or survey organisation for several clients who each contribute their own particular questions to the questionnaire. In an omnibus survey the main cost of the survey, which lies in sampling and contacting respondents, is shared by a number of clients. In addition, the cost of collecting fairly standard demographic and socioeconomic information—such as age, gender, family structure, occupation and income—is shared among the clients. The ABS *General Social Survey* and the ACNielsen *Market Monitor* are examples of such surveys conducted regularly in Australia.

Street/quota intercept surveys

The street survey involves a relatively short questionnaire and is conducted, as the name implies, on the street, in squares or in shopping malls where a cross-section of the community might be found. This can also be called an 'intercept' survey, but this term is also used for other types of customer survey, as discussed below.

Stopping people in such environments for an interview places certain limitations on the interview process. First, an interview conducted on the street generally cannot last as long as one held at someone's home, especially when the interviewee is in a hurry. Of course, some household interviews can be very short because the interviewee is in a hurry or is a reluctant respondent, and some street interviews can be lengthy because the respondent has plenty of time—but as a general rule the street interview will be shorter. Both in the home and street interview situation potential respondents often ask, 'How long will it take?' before committing themselves to an interview. In the home-based situation a reply of 'Fifteen to twenty minutes' is generally acceptable, but in the street situation anything more than five minutes is likely to lead to a marked reduction in the number of people prepared to cooperate. The range of topics, issues or activities that can be covered is therefore restricted and this must be taken into account in designing the questionnaire.

The second limitation of the street survey is the problem of contacting a representative sample of the population. Certain types of people might not frequent shopping areas at all, or only infrequently—for instance, people who are housebound for various reasons or people who do not habitually do the household shopping. Such individuals might be of particular importance in some research and their omission might significantly compromise the results. There is little that can be done to overcome this limitation, except by adopting a different survey method. The other side of this coin is that certain groups will be over-represented—notably full-time home and child carers and retired individuals in suburban shopping areas, or office workers in business areas. It might also be the case that certain areas are frequented more by young people than older people, or by more men than women, so any sample would be, strictly speaking, representative of the users of the area, but not of the population as a whole.

Quota sampling

The means used to overcome the problem of unrepresentative samples, at least in part, is the process of *quota sampling*, in which the interviewer is given a 'quota' of different types of people—different ages, gender, occupations, etc.—to interview. The proportions in each category are determined by reference to the population census or other appropriate information sources. If the sample is still not representative when the survey is completed, further adjustments can be achieved through the process of 'weighting', which is discussed in Chapter 11.

The telephone survey

The telephone survey is particularly popular with political pollsters because of its speed and the ease with which a widespread sample of the community can be contacted. It is used extensively in market and academic research for the same reasons.

An obvious limitation of the technique is that it excludes non-telephone subscribers—generally low-income groups and some mobile sections of the population. Now that telephones can be found in virtually all homes in developed countries, this is not as serious a problem as it was in the past. However, a newly emerging issue is that some people, mainly young people, may rely entirely on mobile phones, which are not publicly listed, and do not have access to a landline. Thus the *White Pages* listings may become less and less representative of the community in future. In the case of fairly simple surveys like political opinion polls, in which the researcher has access to previous survey results using both telephone and face-to-face interviews, this problem can be overcome by the use of a correction factor. For instance, it might be known that non-telephone subscribers always add x per cent to the Labor vote. In certain kinds of market research the absence of the poorer parts of the community from the survey may be unimportant because they do not form a significant part of the market, but it can be a significant limitation for some public policy and academic research.

Length of interview can be a limitation with regard to telephone surveys, but not as serious a limitation as for street interviews. Telephone interviews of ten or fifteen minutes are usually acceptable.

The technique has its own unique set of problems in relation to sampling. Generally, the numbers to be called are selected at random from the telephone directory—many market research companies have equipment that will automatically dial random telephone numbers as required (computer-aided telephone interviewing—CATI). It is necessary for this type of interviewing to be done in the evening and at weekends if those who have paid jobs are to be included.

A further limitation of the telephone interview is that respondents cannot be shown display items such as lists. Surveys that involve long checklists are therefore not easily conducted by telephone.

It can be argued that telephones have an advantage over face-to-face interviews in that respondents may feel that they are more anonymous and therefore may be more forthcoming in their opinions. But it could also be argued that the face-to-face interview has other advantages in terms of eye contact and body language, which enable the skilled interviewer to conduct a better interview than is possible over the telephone.

The main advantage of the telephone survey is that it is quick and relatively cheap to conduct. A further advantage is that arrangements can be made for the interviewer to key answers directly into a computer, another feature of CATI, thus dispensing with the printed questionnaire. This speeds up the analysis process considerably and cuts down the possibility of error in transcribing results from questionnaire to computer. It explains how the results of overnight political opinion polls can be published in newspapers the next morning.

The mail survey

There are certain situations where the postal method is the only practical survey technique to use. The most common example is where members or customers of some national organisation are to be surveyed. The costs of conducting face-to-face interviews with even a sample of such a group would be substantial. A mail survey has the advantage that a large sample can be surveyed at low cost. In the case of a membership organisation, there may be advantages in surveying the whole membership, even though this may not be necessary in statistical terms. It can be very helpful for the internal politics of the organisation for all members to be given the opportunity to participate in the survey and to 'have their say'.

The problem of response rates

The most notorious problem of postal surveys is low response rates. Typically, only 25 or 30 per cent of people who are sent a questionnaire bother to reply. Surveys with only 30 per cent response rates are regularly reported in the literature, but questions must be raised as to their validity when 70 per cent of the target sample is not represented.

What affects the response rate? Seven different factors can be identified, as shown below. These factors and ways of dealing with them are discussed more fully in Appendix 2 (p. 329).

Factors affecting mail survey responses:

1. The interest of the respondent in the survey topic
2. The length of the questionnaire
3. Questionnaire design, presentation and complexity
4. The style, content and authorship of the accompanying letter
5. The provision of a reply-paid envelope
6. Rewards for responding
7. The number and timing of reminders and follow-ups

Of particular importance is understanding the pattern of response in mail surveys and the need, where possible, to send reminders. An early flood of replies can lead to optimism that a good response rate will be achieved, but the flow of responses can quickly decline if non-respondents are not sent reminders. Figure 8.3 indicates a typical pattern of response for a survey sent to urban residents concerning an environmental matter; it shows how the initial response rate quickly declines, but responds to reminders. Without reminders it is likely that this particular survey would have received a response rate of about 35 per cent, but as a result of two reminders 74 per cent was achieved.

E-surveys

Standard 'hard copy' mail has been the traditional medium for mail surveys and is still popular, but email and the Internet are rising rapidly in popularity. Email can be used simply to transmit a letter of request and an attached copy of a questionnaire to potential respondents, thus saving in postage costs. Respondents then print out the attached questionnaire, fill it out and mail it back to the researcher. Alternatively, the questionnaire can be completed using a word processor and emailed back to the researcher.

FIGURE 8.3

Mail survey response pattern

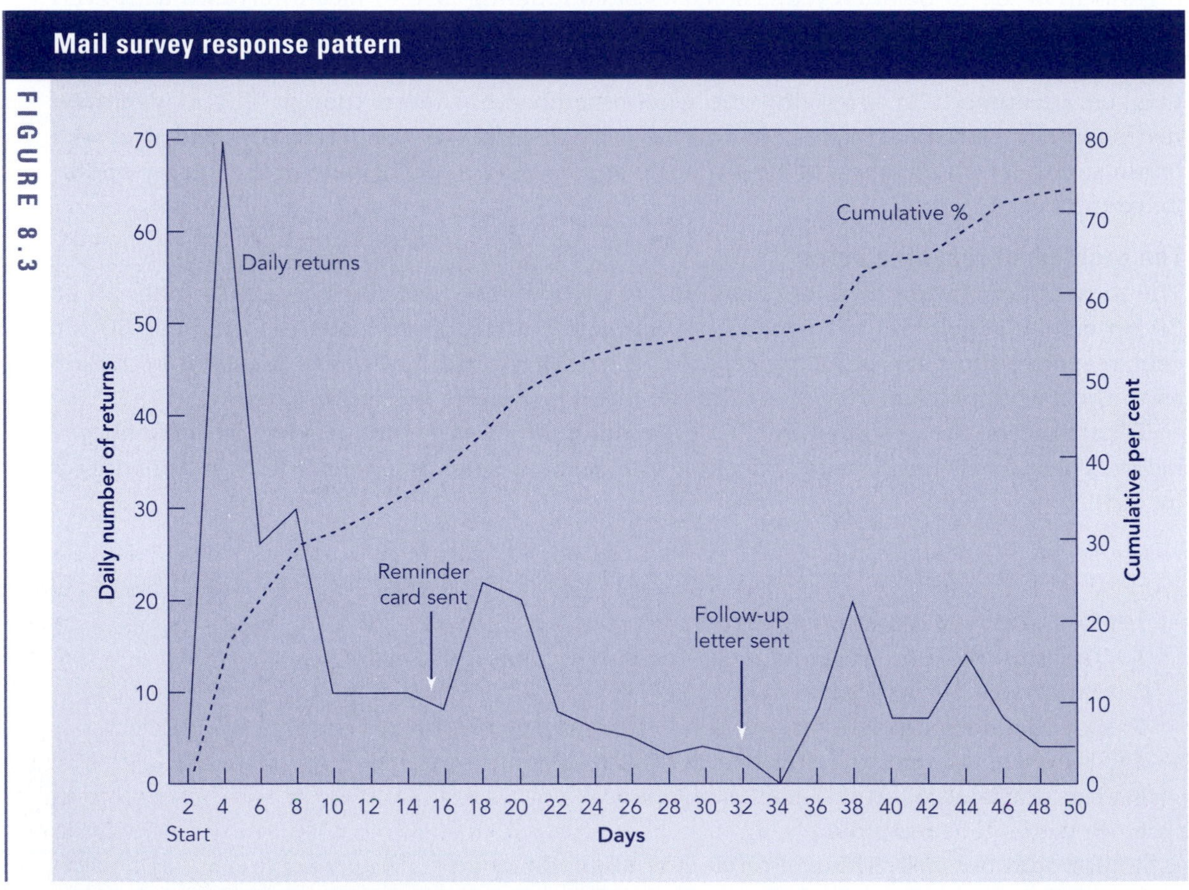

Source: School of Leisure, Sport & Tourism, University of Technology, Sydney, unpublished data.

A fully electronic survey involves the respondent logging into a specified Internet site and completing the questionnaire online. This has the advantage to the researcher that the data are delivered in electronic form and can be instantly analysed using appropriate software. Commercial organisations offer e-survey services in which the customer specifies the questions to be included and can download the results on demand. Such online surveys can also simplify completion for the respondent when 'filter' questions are involved, which mean that parts of the questionnaire are irrelevant to some users. One of the most well known e-surveys in Australia is the 'e-tax' service, which allows taxpayers to complete their income tax return online.

The disadvantage of the e-survey is that it is confined to those with access to the Internet and, while the sending of reminders is cheap, the problem of low response may still be a problem for some surveys.

Customer/visitor on-site intercept surveys

A survey which takes place at a site or facility, and includes the users of the site or facility, may be referred to as a *customer, visitor, on-site, user* or *intercept* survey. In this chapter, *customer survey* is used to cover all these situations. This type of survey is particularly suitable for studying customers of service industries such as transport, hospitality or the retail sector.

Customer surveys can be conducted using interviewer-completion or respondent-completion methods. Unless carefully supervised, respondent-completion methods can lead to a poor standard in the completion of questionnaires and a low response level. As with all low response levels, this can be a source of serious bias, in that those who reply may be unrepresentative of the customers or users as a whole.

The usual respondent-completion survey involves handing visitors a questionnaire on their arrival at the site and collecting them on their departure, or conducting the whole procedure upon departure. When respondent completion is thought to be desirable or necessary, sufficient staff should be employed to collect completed questionnaires as people leave the site, to provide replacements for questionnaires which have been mislaid, and to assist in completing questionnaires, including completion by interview if necessary.

Conducting customer surveys by interview is generally preferable to respondent-completion for the reasons discussed above. The use of interviewers obviously has a cost disadvantage but, depending on the length of the interview, costs per interview are generally relatively low. Typically a customer survey interview will take five minutes or less. Given the need to check through questionnaires, the gaps in visitor traffic and the need for interviewers to take breaks, it is reasonable to expect interviewers in such situations to complete about six interviews in an hour. Such estimates of interview rates are necessary when considering budgets and timetables.

The survey methods considered so far have been fairly multipurpose, that is, they could be used for market research for a range of products or services, by public agencies for a variety of policy-oriented purposes, or for academic research. Customer surveys are more specific. While academics may wish to conduct customer surveys as a convenient way of gathering data on a particular activity, the more usual use of such surveys is for policy, planning or management purposes.

Captive group surveys

The 'captive group' survey refers to a situation where the subjects of the survey comprise the membership of some group where access can be negotiated *en bloc*. Such groups include adult education groups, clubs of various kinds and groups in an organisation. In these cases cooperation is requested or required by the person in charge.

A room full of cooperative people can provide a number of respondent-completed questionnaires very quickly. Respondent-completion is less problematic in 'captive' situations than in less controlled situations because it is possible to take the group through the questionnaire question by question and therefore ensure good standards of completion. Interview methods can also be used with captive groups, although this is not as cost-effective as respondent-completed questionnaires.

The research advantage of a captive group is that access to members of the group is usually facilitated and members of the group are gathered together in one place at one time. Such groups have unique characteristics. It is important to be aware of the criteria for membership of the group and to compare these with the needs of the research. In some cases an apparent match can be misleading. For example, a sample of engineers from one company will not represent all engineers, and the membership of a retired people's club does not include all types of retired people; for example, it excludes 'non-joiners' and the housebound.

Organisation surveys

Organisation surveys can take a variety of forms including telephone surveys, mail-outs or captive group surveys, as discussed above. They can be interviewer-completed or respondent-completed. The form of survey used in an organisation will depend on the purpose of the research and the characteristics of the organisation, including its culture, structure, diversity and size. In each case the advantages and disadvantages associated with each of these forms will need to be taken into account.

In choosing a sample it needs to be recognised that senior staff can usually provide more reliable information concerning the operation of their administrative units than junior staff, but senior staff may be unable to describe the experiences and perceptions of lower level employees. The location of respondents in an organisation has a number of advantages—response rates are usually higher in organisation surveys than external surveys, follow-up is easier if further information is needed, and costs are usually lower.

QUESTIONNAIRE DESIGN

Research problems and information requirements

When designing questionnaires it is important to take it slowly and carefully and also to remember why the research is being done. People often go too quickly into 'questionnaire design mode' and begin listing all the things 'it would be interesting to ask'. In many organisations a draft questionnaire is circulated for comment and everyone in the organisation joins in. The process begins to resemble Christmas tree decorating—nobody must be left out and everybody must be allowed to contribute their favourite bauble. This is not the way to proceed.

The decision to conduct a questionnaire survey should itself be the culmination of a careful process of thought and discussion, involving consideration of all possible techniques, as discussed in Chapter 2. The concepts and variables involved and the relationships being investigated—possibly in the form of hypotheses, theories, models or evaluative frameworks—should be clear and should guide the questionnaire design process, as illustrated in Figure 8.4. It is not advisable to *begin* with a list of questions to be included in the questionnaire. The starting point should be an examination of the management, planning, policy or theoretical questions to be addressed, followed by the drawing up of a list of information required to address the problems, as discussed in Chapter 3. Questions should only be included in the questionnaire if they relate to the information needs listed in element 5 of the research process (as shown in Figure 3.1). This means that every question included must be linked back to the research questions.

Questionnaire design process

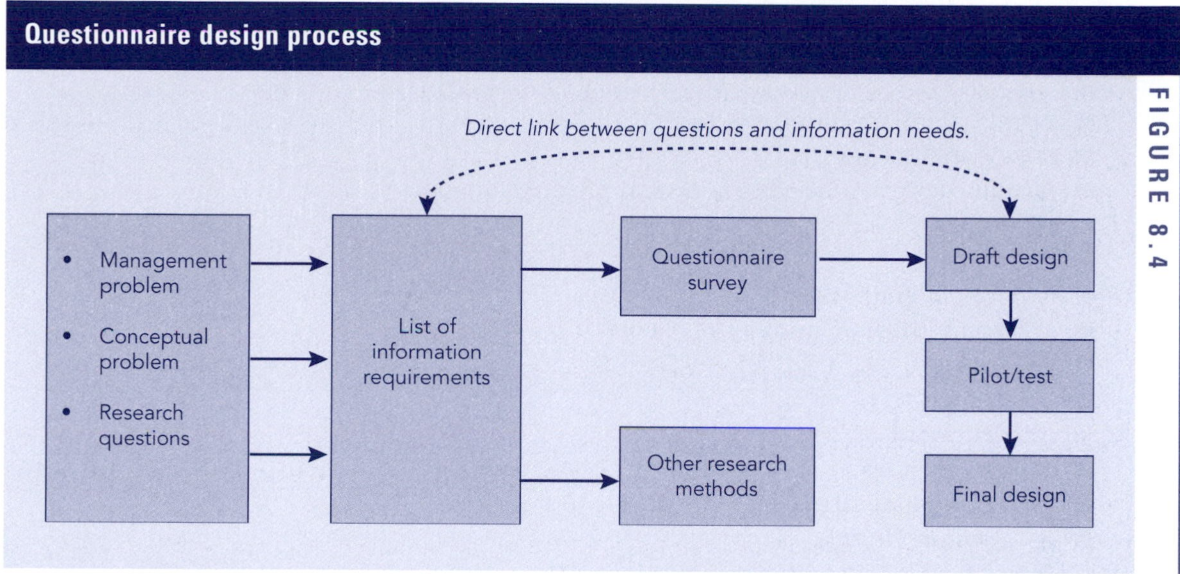

FIGURE 8.4

When designing a questionnaire, the researcher should seek out as much previous research on the topic or related topics as possible. More specifically, if it is decided that the study should have points of comparison with other studies, then data will need to be collected in a similar fashion to those studies. Questionnaires from previous studies then become part of the input into the questionnaire design process.

Types of information

The information to be gathered about people from questionnaire surveys can generally be divided into three groups.

Types of information:

- Respondent characteristics — Who?
- Activities and behaviour — What?
- Attitudes and motivations — Why?

Some of the common characteristics of individuals and organisations that are addressed in questionnaire surveys are set out overleaf. The type of information collected on activities/behaviour and on attitudes/opinions varies according to the topic of the research.

Some characteristics of individuals and organisations:

Individuals:

- Gender
- Age
- Status in an organisation
- Economic status
- Occupation and social class (respondent and/or 'head of household')
- Previous employment history
- Income (respondent and/or household)
- Education or qualifications
- Marital or family status
- Household type and family size
- Life cycle
- Ethnic group or country of birth
- Residential location
- Mobility—driver's licence, access to private transport

Organisations:

- Number of employees
- Turnover, sales or number of clients
- Products
- Capital
- Annual profit
- Number of sites
- Organisational structure
- Establishment date

Open-ended and pre-coded questions

An *open-ended* question is one where the interviewer asks a question without any prompting in regard to the range of answers to be expected, and writes down the respondent's reply verbatim. In a self-completed questionnaire a line or space is left for the respondent to write their own answer. There is no prior list of answers.

A *closed* or *pre-coded* question is one where the interviewer offers the respondent a range of answers to choose from, either verbally or from a show card. In the case of a self-completed questionnaire, a range of answers is set out in the questionnaire and the respondent is asked to tick the appropriate boxes. Figure 8.5 gives an example of the two approaches.

A third possibility in an interviewer-administered survey is a combination of the two approaches. The question is asked in an open-ended manner, but the interviewer's questionnaire schedule includes a pre-coded list where the answer is recorded. If respondents answer 'other', it is usual to write in details of what the 'other' is.

The advantage of the open-ended question is that the respondent's answer is not

Open-ended vs. pre-coded questions: examples

FIGURE 8.5

Open-ended	Pre-coded/closed
What is the main constraint on your ability to study?	Which of the following items is the main constraint on your ability to study? (show card if interviewer-completed) A My job ☐1 B Timetabling ☐2 C Childcare ☐3 D Spouse/partner ☐4 E Money ☐5 F Energy ☐6 G Other ________ ☐7 Card shown to respondent: A My job B Timetabling C Childcare D Spouse/partner E Money F Energy G Other ________

influenced unduly by the interviewer or the questionnaire, and the verbatim replies from respondents can provide a rich source of varied material which might have been untapped by categories on a pre-coded list.

Open-ended questions have two major disadvantages. Firstly, classification of verbatim answers for computer analysis is laborious and may result in a final set of categories which is of no more value than a well-constructed *a priori* list. Secondly, in the case of self-completed questionnaires, response rates to open-ended questions can be very low—people are often too lazy or too busy to write out full-length answers. When to use open-ended or closed questions is therefore a matter of judgement.

Wording of questions

When wording the questions for a questionnaire there are a number of principles which the researcher should observe, namely:

- avoid jargon;
- simplify wherever possible;
- avoid ambiguity;
- avoid leading questions; and
- ask only one question at a time (avoid multi-purpose questions).

Examples of good and bad practice in question wording are given in Figure 8.6.

Some attitude/opinion measurement techniques:

- Open-ended or direct questions
- Checklist
- Ranking
- Likert scales
- Attitude statements
- Semantic differential

Measuring attitudes and opinions

The measurement of attitudes and opinions is one of the more complex aspects of questionnaire design. A range of techniques exists to

FIGURE 8.6

Examples of good and bad question wording

Principle	Bad example	Improved version
Use simple language	What is your frequency of utilisation of retail travel outlets for corporate travel?	How often do you use travel agents for business trips?
Avoid ambiguity	Do you use computer software very often?	Which computer software have you used in the last four weeks? (present list)
Avoid leading questions	Are you against the opening of the new mine?	What is your opinion on the opening of the new mine? Are you for it, against it or not concerned?
Ask just one question at a time	Do you use the company fitness centre, and if so what do you think of its facilities?	1. Do you use the company fitness centre? Yes/No 2. What do you think of the facilities in the company fitness centre?

explore people's attitudes and opinions. Some examples of the use of these formats are given in Figure 8.7.

Open-ended direct questions and checklists

The first two formats, open-ended direct questions and checklists, are straightforward, but the other formats require comment.

Ranking

Asking respondents to rank items in order of importance is a relatively straightforward process, provided that the list is not too long. Having to rank more than five or six items could test respondents' patience. The responses can be quantified in the analysis—for example, by considering the average rank for each item.

Likert scales

Scaling techniques are sometimes known as 'Likert scales', named after the psychologist who developed methods for their use and analysis. In this technique, respondents are asked to indicate their agreement or disagreement with a proposition or the importance they attach to a factor, using a standard set of responses. The responses can be quantified as discussed below.

Attitude statements

Attitude statements are a means of exploring respondents' attitudes towards a wide range of possibly complex issues, including questions of a philosophical or political nature. Respondents are shown a series of statements and asked to indicate, using a scale, the extent to which they agree or disagree with them.

Responses to both Likert scale questions and attitude statements can be scored, as indicated by the numerals beside the answer boxes in Figure 8.7. For example, 'Agree strongly' could be given a score of 1, 'Agree' a score of 2, and so on. Scores can subsequently be averaged across a number of respondents. For example, a group of people who mostly

FIGURE 8.7

Attitude/opinion question formats

a Open-ended/direct:

What attracted you to apply for this training course?

____

____

b Checklist:

Which of the items on the card was the most important to you in applying for this training course?

A Good reputation
B Easy access
C Curriculum
D Management pays fees
E Easy parking

c Ranking:

Please rank the following items in terms of their importance to you in choosing a training course. Rank them 1 for the most important to 5 for the least important.

	Rank
A Good reputation	___
B Easy access	___
C Curriculum	___
D Management pays fees	___
E Easy parking	___

d Likert scales:

How important was each of the following items in your decision to choose this training course?

	Very important	Quite important	Not very important	Not at all important
A Good reputation	☐ 1	☐ 2	☐ 3	☐ 4
B Easy access	☐ 1	☐ 2	☐ 3	☐ 4
C Curriculum	☐ 1	☐ 2	☐ 3	☐ 4
D Management pays fees	☐ 1	☐ 2	☐ 3	☐ 4
E Easy parking	☐ 1	☐ 2	☐ 3	☐ 4

e Attitude statements:

Please read the statements below and indicate your level of agreement or disagreement with them by ticking the appropriate box.

	Agree strongly	Agree	No opinion	Disagree	Disagree strongly
The learning experience is more important than the qualification in education	☐ 1	☐ 2	☐ 3	☐ 4	☐ 5
Graduate course fees are too high	☐ 1	☐ 2	☐ 3	☐ 4	☐ 5

f Semantic differential:

Please look at the list below and tick the line to indicate where you think this training course falls in relation to each factor listed.

Difficult	|___|___|___|___|	Easy
Irrelevant	|___|___|___|___|	Relevant
Professional	|___|___|___|___|	Unprofessional
Dull	|___|___|___|___|	Interesting

'Agree' or 'Agree strongly' with a statement would produce an average score between 1 and 2, whereas a group who mostly 'Disagree' or 'Disagree strongly' would produce a low score between 4 and 5. Such scores enable the strength of agreement with different statements to be compared, as well as allowing comparison of the opinions of different groups of people.

Semantic differential

The semantic differential method involves offering respondents *pairs* of contrasting descriptors and asking them to indicate how the concept being studied relates to the descriptors. This technique is suitable for a respondent-completion questionnaire, since the respondent is required to place a tick on each line. It would be difficult to replicate this exactly in an interview situation with no visual prompts, such as in a telephone survey. The effect would be to reduce the possible answers to three: close to one end or the other and 'in the middle'. The choice of pairs of words used in a semantic differential list should arise from the research context and underlying theory.

A further development of this approach is the *repertory grid* technique, in which pairs of words—called *personal constructs*—are developed by the respondent to provide insights into how the respondent understands and manages his or her world (Kelly 1955). This technique is not explored here; however, further explanation and references to its use in management contexts are provided in Easterby-Smith, Thorpe and Lowe (1993: 84–7).

Scales generally

By design or accident, some scaling systems, often based on Likert scales or semantic differential but also including a variety of other measures, come to be used more widely than in single research projects. One of the most well-known and widely used in social research is the Myers-Briggs Type Indicator used to assess personality types (Murray 1990). The principle behind such scales is that each researcher who wishes to measure a particular phenomenon should not have to 'reinvent the wheel' by developing a new scale, but can draw on an existing scale, which has been tested and found to measure the phenomenon satisfactorily. Bruner and Hensel (1992) provide details of no less than 588 scales used in the field of marketing.

Ordering of questions

It is important that a questionnaire, or an interview based on a questionnaire, flows in a logical and comfortable manner. A number of principles should be borne in mind.

Ordering of questions:

1. Start with easy questions
2. Start with 'relevant' questions
3. Leave sensitive questions until later

Layout

A questionnaire must be laid out and printed in such a way that the person who needs to read it—whether interviewer or respondent—can follow all the instructions easily and answer all the questions that he or she is meant to answer.

In the case of respondent-completion questionnaires, extra care must be taken because it can be very difficult to rectify faults 'in the field'. Clarity of layout and the overall impression given by the questionnaire can be all-important in obtaining a good response.

Mail surveys, in which the researcher does not have direct contact with the respondent, are the most demanding to prepare. A professionally laid out, typeset and printed questionnaire will pay dividends in terms of response rate and accuracy and completeness of response. In so far as the length of a questionnaire can affect the response rate in a postal survey, a typeset format can reduce the number of pages considerably.

The use of coloured paper can make a mail questionnaire stand out from other paper on a busy person's desk. There is some evidence to suggest that the use of warm colours, such as yellow or peach, will achieve a higher response rate than cold colours such as blue or green. Avoid dark colours that make the questionnaire hard to read.

Even when interviewers are used there are advantages in keeping the questionnaire as compact as possible for ease of handling. A two-column format—relatively easily achieved with modern word processing packages—is worth exploring.

Filters

Layout becomes particularly important when a questionnaire contains *filters*. These arise when the necessity for respondents to answer certain questions depends on their answer to a prior question. Examples are shown in Figure 8.8.

Introductory remarks

The introductory remarks used in a questionnaire survey, which explain the purpose of the survey and ask for the respondent's assistance, need careful consideration.

In the case of a postal survey, this material is included in the covering letter. In the case of other forms of self-completion questionnaire, a note is advisable unless the field workers handing out the questionnaires have sufficient time to provide the necessary introduction and explanation. In the case of interviewer-administered questionnaires, the remarks can be printed on the top of each questionnaire or can be included in the interviewers' written instructions.

Filtering: examples

FIGURE 8.8

1 a Have you worked for this company before?

Yes ☐ 1
No ☐ 2

b If YES: How long ago did you work here? —— years

Alternative layout

1 Have you worked at this company before?

Yes ☐ 1 Go to question 2
No ☐ 2 Go to question 3

2 How long ago did you work here? —— years

Interviewers are unlikely to approach potential interviewees and actually read from a script. When seeking cooperation from a potential interviewee it is usually necessary to maintain eye contact, so the interviewer must know in advance what they want to say. In the case of household surveys, potential interviewees may require a considerable amount of information and proof of identity from the interviewer before agreeing to be interviewed. In the case of site and street interviews, respondents are generally more interested in knowing how long the interview will take and what sorts of questions they will be asked. In this case only minimal opening remarks are necessary, such as, 'Excuse me, we are conducting a survey of employees in this department. Would you mind answering a few questions?'

It is usually necessary for interviewers to indicate what organisation they represent. An identity badge can reinforce this. Market research or consultancy companies have the advantage of being able to instruct interviewers to indicate that they represent the research company only and not the client. This ensures that unbiased opinions are obtained, although it can raise ethical considerations concerning the respondent's right to know what organisation will be using the information gathered.

Opening remarks can reassure the respondent about confidentiality. In the case of site surveys, in which names and addresses are not collected, confidentiality is easy to maintain. In the case of household and some postal surveys, respondents can be identified. One way of ensuring that confidentiality is maintained is to arrange for names and addresses to be kept separate from the actual questionnaires, and for questionnaires to include only an identifying number.

CONDUCTING A PILOT SURVEY

Pilot surveys are small-scale 'trial runs' of a larger survey. Pilot surveys relate particularly to questionnaire surveys, but can relate to trying out any type of research procedure. It is always advisable to carry out one or more pilot surveys before embarking on the main data collection exercise. The purposes of pilot surveys are summarised in the list below. Clearly the pilot can be used to test out all aspects of the survey, not just question wording.

Pilot survey purposes:

1. Testing questionnaire wording
2. Testing question sequencing
3. Testing questionnaire layout
4. Gaining familiarity with respondents
5. Testing fieldwork arrangements (if required)
6. Training and testing fieldworkers (if required)
7. Estimating response rate
8. Estimating interview or questionnaire completion time
9. Testing analysis procedures

Item 4, 'Gaining familiarity with respondents', refers to the role of the pilot survey in alerting the researcher to any characteristics, idiosyncrasies or sensitivities of the respondent group with which they are not familiar. Such matters can affect the design and conduct of the main survey. Items 7 and 8, concerning the response rate and length of interview, can be important in providing information to 'fine tune' the survey process. For example, it may be necessary to shorten the questionnaire or vary the planned number of field staff so that the project keeps on schedule and within budget.

In principle, at least some of the pilot interviews should be carried out by the researcher in charge or by experienced interviewers. The interviewers will be required to report back on the pilot survey experience and contribute to discussions on any revisions to the questionnaire or fieldwork arrangements that might be made. The debriefing session following the pilot survey is very important and should take place as soon as possible after the completion of the exercise, so that the details are fresh in the interviewers' minds.

VALIDITY OF QUESTIONNAIRE SURVEYS

Questionnaires are designed to gather information from individuals about their characteristics, behaviours and attitudes. The interview situation is not always conducive to careful, thoughtful responses. Respondents may tend to exaggerate answers to some questions and understate answers to other questions. They may also have problems in recalling some information accurately. Respondents may tend to give answers that they believe will please the interviewer. Thus the validity of questionnaire-based data—the extent to which they accurately reflect what they are meant to reflect—is a constant source of concern. To some extent the researcher must simply live with these limitations of the survey method and hope that they are not too significant or that some of them cancel each other out. However, there are some measures which can be taken to check on the presence of this type of problem.

Testing validity:

- Include 'dummy' categories
- Ask the same question twice
- Repeat interviews

One approach is to include 'dummy' categories in some questions. For example, in a survey of public sector managers in the early 1980s, respondents were asked to indicate from a list what government reports they had heard of and had read. Included in the list was one plausible but non-existent title. A significant proportion of respondents indicated that they had heard of the report and a small proportion claimed to have read it. Such a response does not necessarily mean that respondents were lying—they may simply have been confused about the titles of particular reports. This provides cautionary information to the researcher on the degree of error in responses to such questions, since it suggests that responses to the genuine titles may also include a measure of inaccuracy.

Another approach is to include two or more questions in different parts of the questionnaire that essentially ask the same thing. An early question could ask respondents to rank a list of office furniture suppliers in order of preference, while later in the questionnaire, in the context of asking some detailed questions, respondents could be asked to indicate their favourite supplier. The responses could then be tested for consistency.

One reason for this may be that the interview experience itself may cause respondents to change their opinion by causing them to think something through in detail that they might previously have only considered superficially. Similar questions at the beginning and end of the interview may detect this.

In an Australian survey which included questions concerning a proposed casino development, Grichting and Caltabiano (1986) asked at the beginning of the interview 'What do you think about the casino coming to Townsville? Are you for it or against it?'. At the end of the interview they asked, 'Taking everything you have said into consideration, what do you think now about the casino coming to Townsville? Are you for it or against it?' The researchers found that about 16 per cent of respondents changed their attitude toward the casino during the course of the interview.

In a British study, O'Brien and Ford (1988) found that in repeat interviews with the same sample a few months apart, substantial changes occurred in respondents' socioeconomic classification, based on respondents' own description of their occupation, suggesting that even *factual* survey data must be treated with caution.

There is a wide and varied range of issues to which the researcher needs to be constantly alert in relation to the validity of questionnaire surveys. These include different interpretations of the meanings of questions by respondents, fixed response sets in long questionnaires, question order biases, and exaggeration and understatement in interview responses. To some extent, practices such as the inclusion of dummy categories, repeat questions and repeated interviews can alert the researcher to validity problems. However, the researcher's careful attention to the research process and questionnaire design, including the careful conduct of a pilot survey, is probably the best form of protection against these potential research errors.

QUESTIONNAIRE-BASED INTERVIEWING

The general approach to interviewing using a questionnaire is that the interviewer should be instructed to stick precisely to the wording on the questionnaire. If the respondent does not understand the question it should simply be repeated exactly as before. If the respondent still does not understand then the interviewer should move on to the next question. Adoption of this procedure highlights the importance of question wording and the testing of such wording in one or more pilot surveys.

The above procedure is clearly important in relation to attitude questions. Any word of explanation or elaboration could influence, and therefore bias, the response. It may be less important in relation to factual questions—a word of explanation from the interviewer may be acceptable if it results in obtaining accurate information. It is important to convey these rules and the reasons for them to interviewers in training sessions and through written instructions.

CODING OF QUESTIONNAIRE RESPONSES

Most questionnaire data are analysed by computer. This means that the information in the questionnaire must be coded, that is, converted into numerical codes and organised in a systematic *machine-readable* manner. Different procedures apply to pre-coded and open-ended questions, as discussed below.

Pre-coded questions

The principle for coding of pre-coded questions should be clear from the examples shown in Figure 8.5. The *code* is the number against the answer. Generally, only one answer is possible, so only one code is recorded as the answer to the question.

Where the answer is a number already, there is no need to code the answer because the computer can handle the numerical answer. For example, 'How many days have you been absent from work because of sickness in the last three months?'

As noted earlier, scaled answers to Likert scales and attitude statements readily lend themselves to coding. These scores enable the strength of agreement with different statements to be compared, as well as allowing comparison of the opinions of different groups.

Open-ended questions

In the case of completely open-ended questions, quite an elaborate procedure must be followed to devise a coding system. The answers to open-ended questions can of course be simply copied from the questionnaires and presented in a report in their 'raw' form. If this is all that is required from the open-ended questions then there is no point in spending the considerable labour necessary to code the information for computer analysis. The computer will merely reproduce what can be more easily achieved manually.

Computer analysis comes into its own if it is intended to analyse the results in more detail by comparing the opinions of two or more subgroups. If such comparisons are to be made it will be difficult to do so with fifty or sixty different answers to compare, especially if many of the answers are only given by one or two respondents. The aim then is to devise a coding system that groups the answers into a manageable number of categories.

If a large sample is involved, it is advisable to select a representative subsample of the responses and write out the answers, noting the number of occurrences of each answer. Individual codes should then be given for the most frequent answers and the others should be grouped into meaningful categories—determination of what constitutes a 'meaningful category' is a matter of judgement. The aim is not to leave too many answers in the 'other' category. An example is shown in Figure 8.9.

Recording coded information

Computer analysis is conducted using the coded information from a questionnaire. This is best illustrated by the example of a completed questionnaire shown in Figure 8.10.

The questionnaire is set out for self-completion by the respondent, so it is made fairly simple by providing boxes to be ticked. The codes for the answers are discretely printed beside the boxes. An 'office use' column is provided into which the coded information is transferred, ready for keying into the computer. This layout might be different for an interviewer-completed questionnaire, as discussed in the section on layout.

In the 'office use' column, *spaces* are provided into which the codes from the answers can be written. The 'variable names' in the office column—*qno*, *crse*, etc. are required to facilitate computer data entry.

- Questionnaire number (qno) in the 'office use' column is an identifier so that a link can be made between data in the computer and actual questionnaires—the example questionnaire is number 001.
- Question 1 has only one space, because only one answer/code can be given.
- Question 2 requires four spaces because respondents can tick up to four boxes.
- Question 3 requires five spaces because five ranks must be recorded.
- Question 4 asks for an actual number and this will be transferred into the computer without coding.

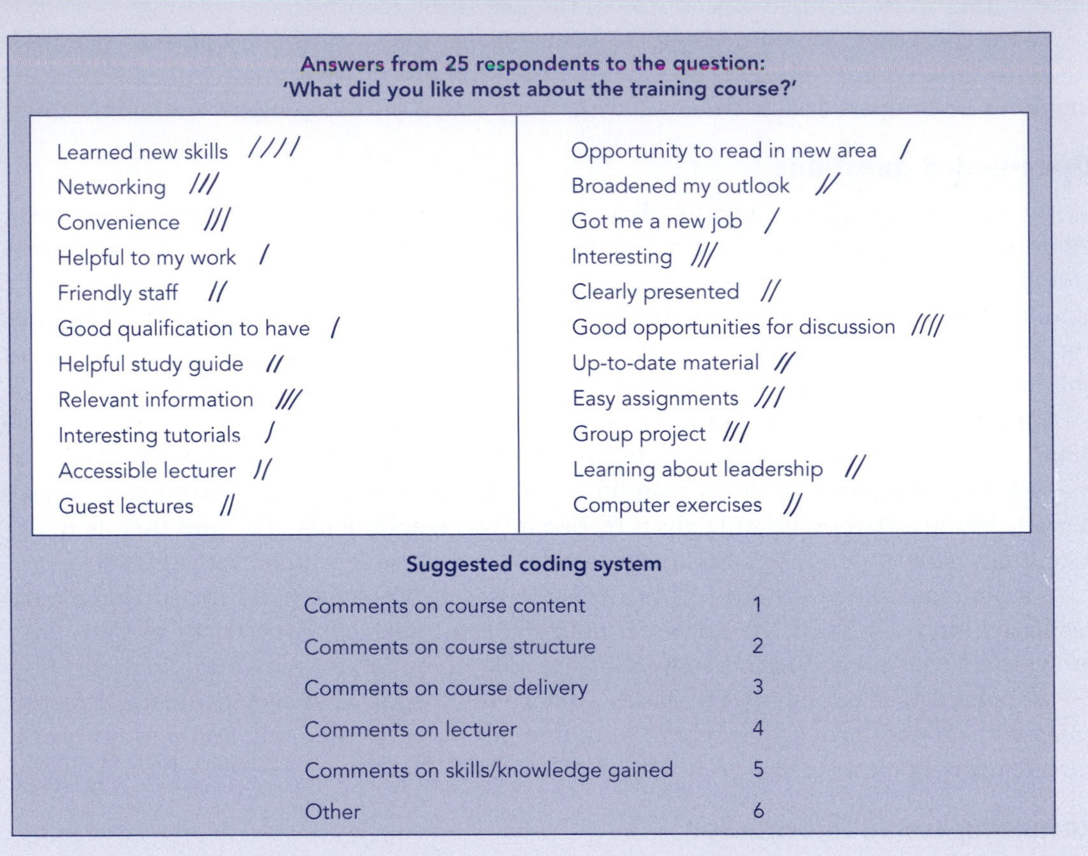

FIGURE 8.9

Coding open-ended questions: example

Answers from 25 respondents to the question: 'What did you like most about the training course?'

Learned new skills ////	Opportunity to read in new area /
Networking ///	Broadened my outlook //
Convenience ///	Got me a new job /
Helpful to my work /	Interesting ///
Friendly staff //	Clearly presented //
Good qualification to have /	Good opportunities for discussion ////
Helpful study guide //	Up-to-date material //
Relevant information ///	Easy assignments ///
Interesting tutorials /	Group project ///
Accessible lecturer //	Learning about leadership //
Guest lectures //	Computer exercises //

Suggested coding system

Comments on course content	1
Comments on course structure	2
Comments on course delivery	3
Comments on lecturer	4
Comments on skills/knowledge gained	5
Other	6

- Question 5 consists of three Likert scale items, so three spaces are provided.
- Question 6 is an open-ended question. It is envisaged that some respondents might give more than one answer, so spaces have been reserved for three answers, although only one has been given in the example. The answers have a coding system devised (as discussed above) as follows:
  - Comments on course content 1
  - Comments on course structure 2
  - Comments on course delivery 3
  - Comments on lecturer 4
  - Comments on skills/knowledge gained 5
  - Other 6

The data from this particular completed questionnaire in Figure 8.10 become a single row of numbers, as shown in the first row of Figure 8.11, which shows how data from five completed questionnaires would appear. The analysis of this data set by computer is discussed in Chapter 13.

Completed questionnaire

FIGURE 8.10

MANAGEMENT TRAINEE SURVEY 2004 — Office Use: 001 qno

1 Which training course are you attending?

		Office Use
People Skills	☐ 1	
Global Business	☑ 2	
Strategic Management	☐ 3	
Other	☐ 4	2 crse

2 What staff development services have you used in the last six months?

		Office Use
Career planning	☑ 1	1 cp
Mentoring clinic	☑ 1	1 ment
Computer training	☐ 1	0 comp
Performance appraisal	☐ 1	0 pa

3 Please rank the items below in terms of their importance to you in choosing a training course, from 1 for the most important down to 5 for the least important.

	Rank	Office Use
a Good reputation	1	1 rep
b Easy access	4	4 access
c Curriculum	2	2 curr
d Management pays fees	3	3 fees
e Easy parking	5	5 park

4 How much have you spent on books for the training course? $ 100 — Office Use: 100 cost

5 Please indicate the importance of the following to you in studying.

	Very important	Important	Not at all important	Office Use
Good textbook	☑ 3	☐ 2	☐ 1	3 text
Knowledgeable lecturer	☑ 3	☐ 2	☐ 1	3 lect
Easy assignments	☐ 3	☐ 2	☑ 1	1 assgn

6 Do you have any suggestions for improving the training course?

Less theory

Office Use: 1 sug 1; ___ sug 2; ___ sug 3

FIGURE 8.11

Data from five completed questionnaires

	Question Number																	
	qno	1	2				3					4	5			6		
	1	2	1	1	0	0	1	4	2	3	5	100	3	3	1	1		
	2	2	1	1	1	0	1	4	2	3	5	50	2	3	1	2	1	
DATA:	3	3	1	0	0	0	2	5	1	3	4	250	2	2	2	3	4	
	4	4	0	0	0	0	2	3	1	4	5	25	3	2	2	1	2	4
	5	3	1	0	0	1	1	4	3	2	5	55	3	3	1			

Based on questionnaire in Figure 8.10. The first row represents the answers given in Figure 8.10. Subsequent rows relate to a further five completed questionnaires.

SUMMARY

This chapter discussed different types of questionnaire surveys and issues to be considered in their design and application. *Questionnaire surveys* involve the gathering of information from individuals using a formally designed schedule of questions called a *questionnaire* or *interview schedule*. Surveys are useful when the research questions indicate the need for relatively structured data and when data are required from samples representative of a defined wider population. They usually involve substantial numbers of *subjects* (the people or organisations being surveyed), ranging from fifty or sixty to many thousands. This, together with the complexity of some forms of quantitative analysis, means that computers are invariably used to analyse the results of questionnaire surveys.

Questionnaire surveys can take one of two forms. They can be *interviewer-completed* or *respondent-completed*. When it is *interviewer-completed*, a questionnaire provides the *script* for the interview. An interviewer reads the questions out to the respondent and records the respondent's answers on the questionnaire. When the questionnaire is *respondent-completed*, respondents read and fill out the questionnaires for themselves. The interviewer-completion method is more expensive in terms of interviewers' time, but the use of an interviewer usually ensures a more accurate and complete response. Respondent completion can be cheaper and quicker, but often results in low response rates.

Questionnaire surveys used in management research can be divided into a number of different types: *household surveys*, in which people are selected on the basis of where they live and are interviewed in their home; *street surveys*, in which respondents are selected by stopping them in the street or in shopping malls; *telephone surveys*, in which interviews are conducted by telephone; *mail surveys*, in which questionnaires are sent and returned by mail; *customer surveys*, in which users or customers of a facility are surveyed on site; *captive group surveys*, in which members of groups are surveyed; and *organisation surveys*, in which members of an organisation (or organisations) are surveyed.

Questionnaire design is of paramount importance for researchers using questionnaire surveys. The decision to conduct a questionnaire survey should itself be the culmination of a careful process of thought and discussion involving consideration of all possible data collection techniques. The concepts and variables involved and the relationships being investigated—possibly in the form of hypotheses, theories, models or evaluative frameworks—should be clear and should guide the questionnaire design process. The starting point should be an examination of the management, planning, policy or theoretical questions to be addressed, followed by the drawing up of a list of information items required to address the problems. Questions should only be included in the questionnaire if they relate to the information needs of the research process. Every question included in the questionnaire must be linked back to the research questions or hypotheses.

It is important that a *pilot survey* is conducted before embarking on the main data collection exercise using a questionnaire survey. The *pilot survey* can be used to test questionnaire wording, sequencing and layout, to increase the researcher's familiarity with respondents and to test fieldwork arrangements. It is also useful for training and testing fieldworkers in order to estimate the response rate and interview or questionnaire completion time. The pilot can be used to test all aspects of the survey, not just question wording.

Finally, the use of questionnaire surveys requires that careful attention be paid to the *validity* of the data gathered using the survey method. There are many issues to which the researcher needs to be aware of in relation to the validity of questionnaire surveys. To some extent, practices such as the inclusion of dummy categories, repeat questions and repeated interviews can alert the researcher to validity problems. The researcher's careful attention to the research process and questionnaire design is essential to minimise these potential validity problems.

The chapter concludes with an introduction to the coding of questionnaire responses, which is followed up in Chapter 13, Survey analysis.

TEST QUESTIONS

1 What are the advantages of the questionnaire method?
2 What is the difference between a questionnaire and a survey?
3 The chapter lists eight different types of questionnaire survey—what are they?
4 Name a limitation of each of the eight survey types.
5 What is an omnibus survey?
6 What measures can be taken to increase the response rate in a mail survey?
7 What alternative types of question exist to gather information on attitudes and opinions?
8 What is a filter question?
9 What are the purposes of running a pilot survey?
10 How can the validity of a questionnaire be tested?

EXERCISES

1 Prepare a questionnaire concerning the transport difficulties of employees getting to and from work. The questionnaire should be designed for mailing to employees by internal

company mail. It should contain six different question types, similar to those shown in Figure 8.7.

2 Test the questionnaire on five people and observe any difficulties or misunderstandings they experience when completing the questionnaire. Modify the questionnaire in light of these difficulties.

3 Prepare a covering letter for the questionnaire providing:
   - **a** the reason for conducting the survey
   - **b** a request for assistance in completing the survey
   - **c** a statement concerning the confidentiality of survey responses and results
   - **d** details of where further information concerning the background to the survey can be obtained.

   You should give attention to the quality of your covering letter in relation to presentational style and grammar.

4 Provide ten people with the covering letter and the modified questionnaire. Collect the completed questionnaires. After developing a coding system, code the responses on a data sheet similar to the one shown in Figure 8.11.

FURTHER READING

Survey research generally: Alreck and Settle (1995); Babbie (1990); Backstrom and Hursh-Cesar (1981); Bainbridge (1989); Fowler (1993); Rea and Parker (1992).

Questionnaire design, interviewing and attitude measurement in general: Berdie, Anderson and Niebuhr (1986); Hague (1993); Lees-Haley (1980); Oppenheim (1992); Tanur (1991); Foddy (1993).

Questionnaire design and the use of surveys in business and management contexts: Gay and Diehl (1992: 243–54); Hutton (1990); Kervin (1992: 301–44); Kraut (1996); Sekaran (1992: 200–15) and Zikmund (1991: 296–325).

Telephone survey methods: Frey (1989) and Lavrakas (1993).

CHAPTER 9

The case study method

A *case* is a single *example* of some phenomenon of interest. A *case study* is therefore a study focused on a single example, such as a single organisation, or part of an organisation, for example a work unit or workplace, or a product or an event. Reliance on a single example is, therefore, the characteristic which distinguishes the *case study method* from other research methods, which are generally based on a number—sometimes a large number—of cases. A research project using the case study method may involve more than one case, with comparisons between them being a feature of the research, but each case will be separately identifiable and subject to individual description and analysis, typically involving comparable types of data.

DEFINING THE CASE STUDY METHOD

The case study *research method* should be distinguished from other uses of cases. The most well known use is in the law, where legal cases are important in setting precedents. Cases are also used in medicine and can become the basis of teaching, particularly in the area of psychology. Oliver Sacks's (1985) *The Man who Mistook his Wife for a Hat* is one of the more celebrated examples of clinical cases being used to bring medical issues to a wider public. Case studies are widely used for teaching purposes, particularly in business, the most well known being the Harvard Business School cases (Harvard Business School, nd). The Case Study Examples in this book are teaching cases used to illustrate the various research methods.

The fact that research projects using the case study method typically involve only one or a few cases suggests some similarity with qualitative research methods and in some texts the case study method is subsumed under 'qualitative methods' (eg Finn, et al. 2000: 81) but, as Robert Stake (1994: 236) points out in his book on the case study method: 'Some case studies are qualitative studies, some are not'. And as Yin (1994: 14) states: '. . . the case study strategy should not be confused with "qualitative research" . . . case studies can include, and even be limited to, quantitative evidence'.

One type of qualitative research is, however, invariably also a case study, namely participant observation (Jorgensen 1989: 19). Often, however, a case study involves a variety of quantitative and qualitative data about the case, which may be collected and analysed using a number of methods. In fact, the use of a variety of types of data and types of analysis can be said to be a key feature of the case study method.

Robert Yin (1994: 13) discusses the case study method in relation to other research approaches, including experiments, surveys and histories, and concludes that the case study can be defined as an empirical inquiry that:

- investigates a contemporary phenomenon within its real-life context; when
- the boundaries between phenomenon and context are not clearly evident; and
- relies on multiple sources of evidence, with data needing to converge in a triangulating fashion.

To some extent all social research is a case study at some level, since all research is geographically and temporally unique. Thus, for example, a survey of 500 employees of a single company can be seen as a case study of the company and even a nationwide opinion survey of, say, 20 000 people in Australia carried out in 2004, could be seen, in one sense, as a case study of the opinion of the population of one affluent country in the early twenty-first century. To be seen as case studies in the full sense, however, these studies would need to involve more than just a survey; they would require additional information on the company and its environment and history, on the social and demographic characteristics of the country and perhaps on factors which were likely to influence opinion now and in the past. Thus, the sheer variety of data and types of data analysis would offer a 'rich' description of the *case*—the company or the country and its people.

The case study method can be particularly useful in business research since the focus of research in this setting is often the workings of organisations, or parts of an organisation. Since an organisation is complex, generally with a large number of stakeholders and with numerous internal and external factors at work, a study of one or a limited number of organisations, in-depth and 'in the round', will often be a suitable research approach.

This chapter considers in turn: the purposes of case studies; the merits of the case study method; types of case study; data collection; and data analysis. Examples of case study research in the business environment are then presented.

PURPOSES

Some commentators (for example, Zikmund 1997: 108) have implied that the case study method is used only for 'exploratory' purposes but, while it can certainly be used for such a purpose, as Robert Yin (1994: 3) asserts: 'case studies are far from being only an exploratory strategy'. They can be the basis of substantive research projects in their own right.

Because, in case study research, only one or a few cases are examined, the method does not seek to produce findings which are generally or universally representative. Thus a case study of an organisation does not conclude: 'This explains the behaviour of organisation X, therefore it will explain or predict the behaviour of the 50 000 similar organisations in similar situations or a significant proportion of them'. However, if research has *no* implications beyond the particular case at a particular time and place, there would be little point in conducting it. Case study conclusions can, however, present general propositions relating to theory and policy issues and to possibilities, so they might be in the form: 'This explains the behaviour of organisation X, which is contrary to theoretical expectations, suggesting the possible need for some modification to the theory', or 'This explains the behaviour of organisation X, suggesting that other types of organisation might be examined to see whether the explanation applies more widely'. Thus, while case study research may not result in generalisations about a population, it can have valid things to say in relation to theory in the case of explanatory research and in relation to policy in the case of evaluative research. A number of scenarios can be envisaged in regard to theory and policy, as indicated in Figure 9.1.

In the case of explanatory research a case study can be used to confirm an existing theory or raise doubts about it. This might occur in situations where a theoretical proposition has never been tested empirically or where it has not been tested in a particular environment. For example, much of the management research literature emanates from the United States and has not been tested in other countries. If the theory is found to be non-applicable in a case study situation, this does not necessarily 'disprove' the theory, but can raise doubts as to its universality. In the case of policy-related evaluative research it is quite likely that the effectiveness of a policy will not have been evaluated in its current form. For example, while the impact of changes in occupational health and safety regulations could be examined by use of aggregate statistics on workplace accidents, it could also be examined by means of a case study of the experience of one or more companies, particularly if the results of the statistical analysis were unclear or indicated an apparent lack of impact.

Where there are competing theories or theoretical perspectives, especially if there is empirical evidence supporting both, a case study might be used to explore the reasons for the apparent impasse. This might be done by bringing to bear a much wider range of data than has hitherto been done, or it might be achieved by means of contrasting cases. Again, case studies are unlikely to be definitive, but may point in certain theoretical or empirical directions. Clearly a similar approach could be followed in evaluative research. To continue the occupational health and safety example: the effect of differing occupational health and

FIGURE 9.1

Scenarios for case study research

Explanatory research	Testing a single existing theory	Case study *confirms* applicability of theory in at least one setting or, alternatively, *raises doubts* as to applicability of theory and suggests modification or alternatives.
	Testing alternative/competing theories	Case study demonstrates that one theory works better than the other in a particular situation, or that neither works.
	Develop theory where none exists	The task of the case study is to suggest *possible* theory.
Evaluative research	Testing effectiveness of a single policy	Case study *confirms* effectiveness of the policy in at least one setting or, alternatively, *raises doubts* as to effectiveness of the policy and possibly suggests modification or alternatives.
	Testing alternative/competing policies	Case study demonstrates that one policy is more effective than the other in a particular situation, or that neither works.
	Establish need for policy measures	The case study outlines the current problems and their likely causes and suggests the need for policy action.

safety regulations in two jurisdictions could be examined by case studies in the two jurisdictions.

Where no known relevant theoretical framework exists to address a topic, or those that purport to do so are seen as inadequate, one possible task of the case study can be to develop new theoretical propositions or insights, which are consistent with the case study data and which might be further tested by additional empirical study. The corresponding situation in evaluative research is where no policies exist and research is undertaken to establish whether there is a need for a policy. In occupational health and safety a case study of the history of accidents in a single place of employment could be undertaken, or the cases could be individual accidents, with their causes, effects and outcomes being the object of the research.

MERITS OF THE CASE STUDY APPROACH

The particular merits of the case study method can be summarised as follows:

- The ability to place people, organisations, events and experiences in their social and historical context.
- Ability to treat the subject of study as a whole, rather than abstracting a limited set of pre-selected features.
- Multiple methods—triangulation—are implicit and seen as a strength.
- The single, or limited number of, cases offer a manageable data collection task when resources are limited.
- Flexibility in data collection strategy allows researchers to adapt their research strategy as the research proceeds.
- There is no need to generalise to a defined wider population.

TYPES OF CASE STUDY

Burns (1994: 314–17) identifies six types of case study as follows:

- *Historical case studies* 'trace the development of an organisation/system over time', drawing primarily on documentary sources and, obviously, using historical methods.
- *Observational case studies*—distinguished by being based primarily on visual observation.
- *Oral history*—study of a past event or experience with reliance based on 'eyewitness' accounts, typically using in-depth interviews.
- *Situational analysis*—relate to a particular recent event and typically include interviews with individuals involved in, or eyewitness to, the event, but also documentary evidence.
- *Clinical case study*—unusual in business research, but could arise in research related to workers' health or accidents and customer liability.
- *Multi case studies*—where more than one case is involved. This could apply to any of the above.

A case can range from a single individual or organisation, or part of an organisation, to a whole country or empire, from a short-term event to an historical era, and from a single product to a whole industry sector. Figure 9.2 provides a list of types of case study with examples from the research literature and an indication of the research methods used. It illustrates the variety of topics, research issues and data collection and analysis methods used in business case study research.

It is also possible for one or more case studies to form part of a wider research or investigative project. For example, in investigating possible sites for the location of a business, a company might commission case studies of a number of locations. Such case studies would generally involve the collection of comparable data on each potential site, which would then be entered into some comparative evaluation process. But the initial case studies would be relatively self-contained 'portraits' of the locality and may include qualitative and quantitative data.

DESIGN OF CASE STUDIES

While the case study method offers flexibility, it does not absolve the researcher from undertaking the usual initial preparatory steps—specifying research questions, reviewing the literature, establishing a theoretical framework and determining data needs and sources—as discussed in Chapter 3. As in any research, it is important to plan to avoid the problem of having collected a lot of data and not knowing what to do with it. While the method offers flexibility in the research strategy, this is rarely unlimited. For example, in some circumstances it may be possible to interview people or ask them for data a number of times as new issues emerge in the course of the research, but in other circumstances this may not be appropriate.

In addition to the general guidance on the planning of research projects set out in Chapter 3, three specific issues are discussed here: defining the unit of analysis, selection of cases and data gathering.

Defining the unit of analysis

While it might be a somewhat obvious point to make: it is necessary to be clear about the *unit of analysis* in case study research. For example, if the unit of analysis—the case—is a

FIGURE 9.2

Types of case study

Type of case	Particular case	References	Data collection/analysis			
			Quant/ qual	Data collection/sources	Data sources	Analysis methods
One person	CEO—Success/failure of a CEO—Autobiography of CEO of Chrysler	Iacocca (1984)	Qual	Biographical, historical sources	Primary & Secondary: documents & Personal recall	Historical, narrative, qualitative
	CEOs—Multiple examples of leadership success/failure	Ward (2003)—see Case Study Example 9.3	Qual	Biographical In-depth interviews	Secondary: documents	Historical, narrative, qualitative
	Entrepreneur—Biography of Alan Bond, failed Australian entrepreneur	Barry (1990)	Qual	Biographical	Secondary: documents	Historical, narrative, qualitative
	Entrepreneur—Biography of Kerry Packer, successful Australian entrepreneur	Barry (1993)	Qual	Biographical	Secondary: documents	Historical, narrative, qualitative
	Recent graduate—The experiences of business graduate 'Jason' in the transition from university to the world of work	Perrone & Vickers (2003)	Qual	In-depth interviews	Primary	Qualitative
Part of an organisation	Hospital pharmacy department—Functioning and image of a pharmacy department within a hospital	Paul (1996)	Quant	In-depth interviews Participant obs. Observation	Primary & Secondary	Qualitative
One organisation	One multinational company—Ethical issues and Nike Corp's Third World labour practices	Goldman & Papson (1998); Katz (1994); Hummels & Timmer (2004); Shaw (1999)	Qual		Secondary: documents	Qualitative
	One multinational company—Success story of Walt Disney Corporation	Foglesong (2001); Project on Disney (1995); Lainsbury (2000)	Qual	Documentary, secondary sources; media reports	Secondary	Historical, narrative, qualitative
	One multi-branch national company—Competing corporate cultures within one company—An Australian travel agency	Palmer & Dunford (2002)—See Case Study Example 7.1	Qual	In-depth interviews	Primary	Qualitative

Type of case	Particular case	References	Data collection/analysis			
			Quant/ qual	Data collection/sources	Data sources	Analysis methods
	One multinational company—Nike, advertising and gender	Carty (1997)—see Case Study Example 9.1	Qual	Content analysis of advertising	Secondary plus company's ads	Qualitative: content analysis
One industry sector	National industry sector—Contribution of the Hong King manufacturing sector to GDP	Mahadevan (2004) —see Case Study Example 9.2	Quant	Official statistics	Secondary	Quantitative; regression analysis
	Regional industries—Regional clustering to promote industry: Defence & media (SA); Multiple industry clusters (Qld); Wine industry (NSW)	Enright & Roberts (2001)	Both	Literature Official statistics	Secondary	Case study
One product	Sony Walkman—Explaining the success and longevity of the Sony Walkman	Sanderson & Uzumeri (1995)	Both	Documents Interviews	Secondary and primary	Trend analysis
One industry	Automotive industry—Issues facing Australia's automotive industry	Conlon & Perkins (2001)	Both	Multiple sources	Secondary and primary	Case study
One country	Singapore—Competitive advantage through networking in Singapore	Venard and Tsai (1998)	Both	Multiple sources	Secondary	Case study
One event	Major sporting event 1. Economic impact of the Olympic Games 2. Economic impact of a Grand Prix	1. Preuss (2000) 2. Burns et al. (1986)	1. Quant 2. Quant	1. Secondary sources 2. Surveys	1. Secondary 2. Primary	1. Quantitative 2. Quantitative
	Economic crisis—The Great Crash of 1929	Keynes (1973)	Both	Documentary	Secondary	Historical

department within a large organisation, it is important to keep the analysis at the departmental level. Thus, for example, the policies and practices of the parent organisation are inevitably relevant, but they are 'given' influences on the department, the research is not *about* the parent organisation. Conversely, data about the staff of the department will form part of the research, but only insofar as they contribute to an understanding of the operation of the department as a unit.

Selecting the case(s)

Of key importance in the case study method is the selection of the case or cases. This is comparable to sampling in a quantitative study. Four types of case selection can be considered.

- *Purposive:* where multiple cases are involved, the selection of cases is likely to be purposive—for example, in selecting a range of firms of similar or different sizes, in the same or different industries, in comparable or contrasting geographical locations or of similar or contrasting levels of profitability.
- *Illustrative:* often the case(s) will be deliberately chosen to increase the likelihood of illustrating a particular proposition—for example, if the research is concerned with leadership success, then *successful* organisations with high profile leaders may be deliberately chosen.
- *Typical/Atypical:* the case may be chosen because it is believed to be typical of the phenomenon being studied, or it may be deliberately chosen as an extreme or atypical case. Thus, a study examining the secrets of success in a particular industry might well select the *most* successful company for study.
- *Pragmatic:* in some cases the selection of cases may be pragmatic—for example, when the researcher has ready access to a company, possibly because he or she is an employee of it.

Whatever the rationale for the selection of a case or cases, it should be clearly articulated in the research report, and the implications of the selection discussed.

Data gathering

A case study project generally uses a number of data sources and data gathering techniques, including: the use of documentary evidence; secondary data analysis; in-depth interviews; questionnaire surveys; observation; and participant observation. The process of selecting data sources and collection techniques is the same as in any other research process, as discussed in Chapter 3. In that chapter, the idea that different data sources might be used in the same project to address different research questions or aspects of research questions is illustrated. In particular, it is noted that all data collection should be linked to the research questions, even in cases where the research questions are being modified as the research progresses.

When a number of disparate data types and sources are involved, two other issues should be born in mind:

- *consistency of the unit of analysis*—if, for example, staffing and financial data are involved, it is important that the data relate to the same organisational unit;
- *temporal consistency*—ideally all data should relate to the same time period. This is because organisational change can result in alterations to the size, composition and functions of units of analysis over time.

ANALYSIS

To the extent that the design of the case study, or parts of it, resembles that of more formalised research projects, with fixed research questions and corresponding data collection and analysis procedures, the analysis process will tend to be deductive in nature and designed to address the questions posed in advance. But a case study can involve qualitative methods with a recursive, more inductive format, as discussed in Chapter 7. Indeed, the flexibility of the whole case study approach suggests a more inductive approach. Thus, the discovery in the course of the research of a previously unknown source of information might lead the researcher to ask the question, 'Can this data add something to the research?'. While the new data source might help in addressing the existing research questions in unanticipated ways, it could also suggest additional, new research questions.

Three main methods of analysis are outlined by both Burns (1995: 324–5) and Yin (1994: 106–18):

- *pattern matching*—relating the features of the case to what might be expected from some existing theory;
- *explanation building*—often an iterative process whereby a logical/causal explanation of what is discovered is developed by to-and-fro referencing between theory, explanation and data;
- *time series analysis*—explanations are developed on the basis of observing change over time.

In fact, all forms of analysis are possible within the context of a case study, as Figure 9.2 suggests. It is the pulling together of the results of different sorts of analyses to form coherent conclusions which presents the challenge.

The use of multiple data sources suggests that *triangulation*, as discussed in Chapter 2, is common in case study research. While different data sets may address different research questions or hypotheses, often different data sets will provide information on the same question—as illustrated in Figure 9.3. Sometimes the different data sets will point to the same conclusion, sometimes they will be contradictory. The task of the researcher is to come to a conclusion, even if the conclusion is that no firm conclusion is possible!

CASE STUDIES IN PRACTICE

Four case study examples are presented to conclude the chapter. The purpose of the brief discussion here is to illustrate the variety of business-related case study research. The case study examples provide a little more detail on each study, but the reader can, of course, follow up the original references for the full report on the research (most of which is available electronically via libraries). The four examples cover, in turn, a combination of secondary data, textual and qualitative analysis; secondary data subject to quantitative analysis; multiple case studies using mostly the biographical method; and historical narrative.

Secondary data/Textual/Qualitative

Case Study Example 9.1 summarises research by Victoria Carty on a single aspect of the behaviour of a single company, the sports apparel multinational Nike. As the Case Study

FIGURE 9.3 Triangulation

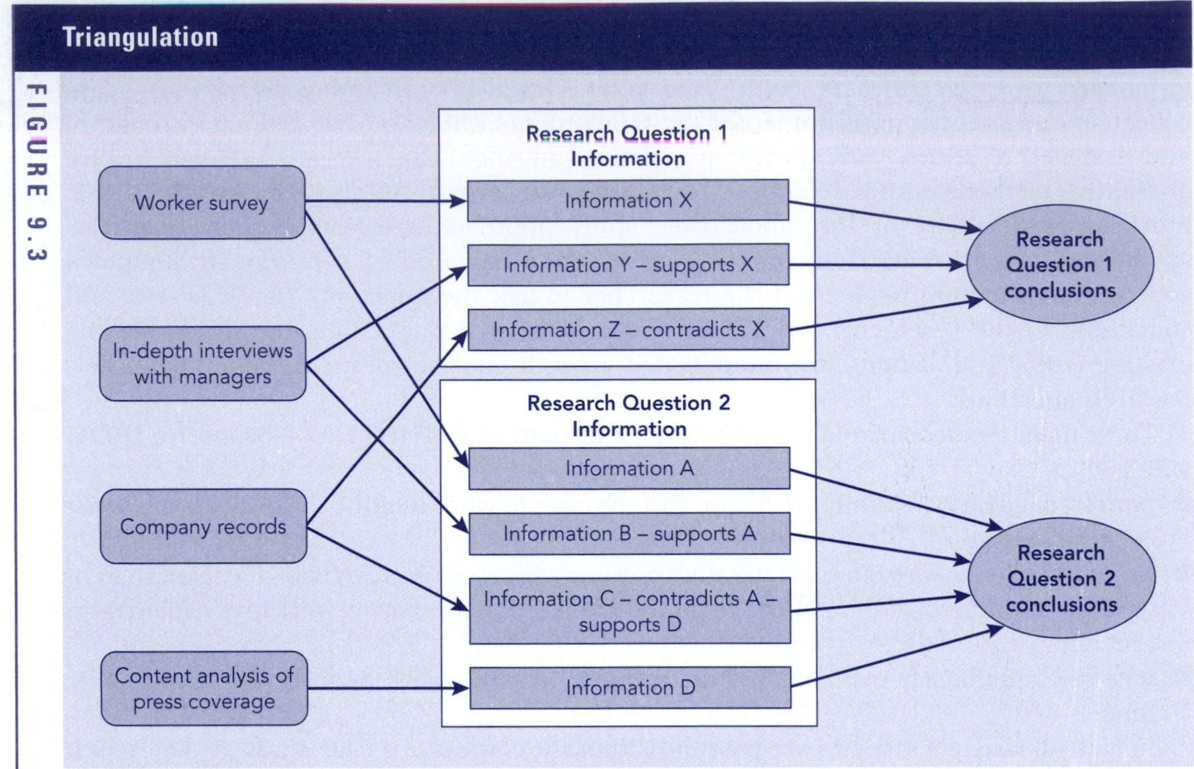

Example suggests, Nike has been subject to considerable research and commentary as perhaps the most high profile of those companies that outsource their manufacturing to Third World, cheap labour countries and therefore have been the particular focus of criticisms from antiglobalisation activists (Klein 1999). This study, however, focuses on a particular aspect of this ethical issue, namely whether Nike's rhetoric about treating women as respected customers is followed through in its management practices. The study uses a number of data sources but in particular illustrates the use of content analysis of print, poster and television advertising as a research method. It has some similarities to Case Study Example 14.1, which refers to a content analysis of corporate websites.

While conclusions from case studies can, strictly speaking, apply only to the 'case' involved in the study, they would be of limited use if they did not at least raise the possibility of wider implications. Here the implication is that Nike may not be unique among multinational companies in its exploitative approach to women.

Secondary data/Quantitative

Case Study Example 9.2 illustrates a totally different type of case study, this time dealing with a whole economic sector in a national economy—the manufacturing sector in Hong Kong. It is highly quantitative, being an econometric study, using multiple regression analysis (see Chapter 14). The data used are not primary but secondary, drawn from official, published government sources over a 14-year period. The aims of the study are quite technical, being one of a number of case studies in a book which explores alternative

CASE STUDY EXAMPLE 9.1

Case study/Secondary/Textual: Nike, advertising and women

Source: Victoria Carty, 1997, Ideologies and forms of domination in the organization of the global production and consumption of goods in the emerging postmodern era: a case study of Nike Corporation and the implications for gender. *Gender, Work and Organization*, 4(4), 189–201.
Methods/approaches: Case study; secondary sources and textual analysis (TV and print advertising)
Topic: Nike Corporation's advertising and marketing in relation to women.

This study draws on a number of information sources and theoretical perspectives to explore and critique the *modus operandi* of sports shoe manufacturer Nike, particularly in regard to its treatment of women. The main information sources are existing accounts of the development of Nike from the academic and popular literature and examples of Nike advertising on television and in print.

Theoretical perspectives include: theories of globalisation and postmodernism; and the concept of 'global commodity chains', which geographically trace manufactured products from the point of consumption to the point of manufacturer. The thesis of the study is that Nike's advertising, aimed at Western women consumers, projects an image of the independent woman, while their manufacturing practices exploit Third World women, who make up the majority of its manufacturing labour employed at low wages and in poor conditions in its own factories and those of its subcontractors.

The research seeks to demonstrate the validity of well-established theoretical frameworks which are critical of the role of multinational global corporations, particularly in the production of fashion products where the costs of manufacturing are heavily outweighed by the costs of marketing and the retail mark-up. Thus, using a case study of a single firm, the study seeks to 'illustrate the interdependencies between production and consumption, or economics and culture, as organised in the global economy'.

ways of assessing factor productivity, ie the relative contribution of labour and capital in an economy. The Hong Kong case study demonstrates one such approach.

Multiple case studies/Biographical

Case Study Example 9.3 is concerned with the question of whether different leadership styles are required depending on the stage an organisation is at in its life cycle. It demonstrates the use of multiple case studies. In fact, the number of examples drawn on places it at the boundary of the case study approach since, for some of the leaders referred to in the study, only a limited amount of information is presented. However, since each corporate leader is presented as a unique character leading a specific company, the spirit of the case study method is maintained.

CASE STUDY EXAMPLE 9.2

Case study/Quantitative/Secondary data: manufacturing in Hong Kong

Renuka Mahadevan 2004, Case study: Hong Kong's manufacturing sector. Section 4.3 of *The Economics of Productivity in Asia and Australia.* Edward Elgar, Cheltenham, UK, pp. 80–88.
Approaches/methods: Case study, quantitative, secondary data
Topic: Industrial productivity

This book contains a number of case studies of industry sectors in Australia, Hong Kong, Malaysia, South Korea and Singapore, all highly quantitative, using economic modelling and drawing on secondary data. This case study consists of five sections.

1. A review of the literature to demonstrate that most studies of productivity in Hong Kong have been of the economy as a whole and few have looked at individual sectors, such as manufacturing or services.
2. Secondary data, presented descriptively to indicate trends in, and sectoral and industry contributions to, GDP over the period 1983 to 1999.
3. Data sources: data were obtained for the Hong Kong manufacturing sector for the period 1983–1999 from such official sources as the *Annual Survey of Industrial Production* and the *Monthly Digest of Statistics.*
4. Models used: a 'production function' is put forward in the form of an equation relating the dependent variable *value added* (contribution to GDP) to the independent variables: capital stock and number of workers employed.
5. Empirical results and analysis: results of the regression analysis which indicate the relative share of labour and capital in adding value to the Hong Kong GDP are presented, discussed and compared with findings from other studies.

This is an example of the case study method, drawing on secondary data and using highly quantitative methods to produce a neat, focused study.

The historical narrative

Case Study Example 9.4 presents a history of events over a ten-year period, during which the Euro Disney theme park and resort, north of Paris, was conceived, planned, developed and opened, up to its third year of operation, when it made its first profit following a series of losses. Based on participant observation, interviews and secondary sources, the study covers a wide range of development, design, marketing and financial issues.

Multiple case studies: the leadership life cycle

Andrew Ward, 2003, *The Leadership Lifecycle: Matching Leaders to Evolving Organizations.* Palgrave MacMillan, Basingstoke, UK.
Methods/approaches: Case studies, biography
Topic: Leadership

The thesis put forward here is that different styles of leadership are required for different stages in an organisation's life cycle, as follows:

Stage in organisation's life cycle	Leadership style
Creation	The Creator
Growth	The Accelerator
Maturity	The Sustainer
Turnaround	The Transformer
Decline	The Terminator

Of course not all organisations experience decline: if the Transformer is successful in achieving turnaround, then the organisation begins another cycle and avoids decline.

Having outlined the above theory, the author presents five chapters dealing with each of the leadership types and providing short case studies of CEOs, outlining how they succeeded in performing the appropriate role, and sometimes subsequently failed when required to perform other roles. Thus the case studies include:

Creators:	Anita Roddick (The Body Shop); Sam Walton (Wal-Mart)
Accelerators:	John Chambers (Cisco Systems)
Sustainers:	Douglas Daft (Coca-Cola); Marsha Johnson Evans (Girl Scouts)
Transformer:	Steve Jobs (Apple—return in 1997); Philippe Bourguignon (Club Med)
Terminators:	Jeff Hawkins & Donna Dubinsky (Palm Pilot)

Having explored the life cycle ideas cross-sectionally, Ward pursues them longitudinally with two company case studies, Walt Disney and Marks and Spencer. Here the life cycle stages of the company and the changing roles and 'leadership life cycle' capabilities of their CEOs over the years are explored.

Throughout, the data sources used include published sources, including magazines and biographies.

CASE STUDY EXAMPLE 9.4

Case study/Historical: Euro Disney

Andrew Lainsbury 2000, *Once upon an American Dream: The Story of Euro Disneyland*. University of Kansas Press, Lawrence, KS.
Methods/approaches: Participant observation, In-depth interviews, secondary sources, historical
Topic: Theme park investment/development/ management

This book-length case study is based on the experiences of the author, a graduate in American studies, in a year spent working as a general hand (and a period playing Prince Charming) in the Euro Disney theme park and resort, north of Paris. Opened in 1992 amid much publicity and controversy over its appropriateness and viability in a European context, the development had a chequered history in its early years.

The book has five main chapters, dealing with:

1 the development of the idea of a European Disneyland and the political activity of selecting and securing a site;
2 the design, or 'imagineering', of the project;
3 marketing of the project;
4 the financial struggles of the early years; and
5 the global Disney operation.

The book is written in a popular, narrative style, but is underpinned by extensive endnotes and references. The historical accounts draw mostly on press coverage which, given the high profile of the Walt Disney Company, was extensive. Use is also made of the considerable body of literature on Disney, which comprises a mixture of popular and academic books, and papers in journals in such fields as cultural, media and American studies (University of California, Berkeley, Library, nd).

Numerous themes emerge in each of the chapters. Thus Chapter 1 provides an insight into the common phenomenon of countries and communities competing to attract industry and jobs, the financial and other 'deals' that are struck to attract enterprises, and the 'Not in My Back Yard' (NIMBY) politics of communities living in the immediate neighbourhood of proposed projects. In France, the Disney project led to the establishment of the 'Association for the Protection of People Concerned by the Euro Disney Development'. Chapter 1 also discusses the clash of cultures between 'old Europe' and 'new America', an increasingly salient issue in an era of globalisation.

Much of Chapter 2 is design-orientated rather than business-orientated, but the 'vertical integration' practice of the Walt Disney Company in developing not only the theme park but also the ancillary hotels and golf courses—which it failed to do in the original Disneyland in California—is outlined. Chapter 3 outlines the complex strategy for marketing the project, both before and after its opening.

The development made substantial losses in its early years and Chapter 4 documents the various measures taken to 'rescue' the project by improving income and attendance, cutting costs and reorganising its finances. This resulted in the achievement of the park's first profits in

1995. The final chapter briefly examines the international development of Disney theme parks and the growth of competitors.

While the book does not present 'hard' research data, it uses a variety of perspectives, issues and data sources to explore the saga of Euro Disney and therefore presents a valid case study of a major transnational investment project.

SUMMARY

This chapter provided a broad overview of the case study as an approach to research. It considers the purposes and merits of the case study method, types of case study, and their design and analysis. Case study research is distinguished by its reliance on a single 'case' or a few contrasting 'cases', and the use of a variety of data sources and types, including quantitative and qualitative data, and consequently a variety of types of analysis. Because of this, the chapter cannot be seen as self-contained—all the other chapters dealing with specific forms of data collection and analysis are relevant to the case study method. A case can be a single individual, organisation or community, or part of an organisation or community, a single product or a single workplace. While the results of case study research cannot be generalised to a wider population, they can be used to explore theoretical issues, in the case of explanatory research, and policy issues in the case of evaluative research. The chapter concludes by examining four contrasting case studies from the business studies literature.

TEST QUESTIONS

1 What are the characteristics which distinguish case study research?
2 If case study research cannot generalise to a wider population, what can it do?
3 Contrast the role of case study research in explanatory and evaluative research.
4 Burns lists six types of case study: what are they?
5 Four different types of case selection are outlined in the chapter: what are they?
6 Why is case study research likely to involve triangulation?

EXERCISES

1 Read and critically evaluate, from a methodological perspective, the original report of one of the case study examples presented in this chapter.
2 At the end of the section on types of case study, it is noted that case studies might well be used in a search process for the location of a site for a business. Select a type of retail or service business and conduct a case study of two possible locations for such a business—for example, two main streets as locations for a bistro restaurant. Time will restrict the amount of data you can collect, but you should note: the types of data you are able to collect on each site; data which might be collected, given time; the way in

which ideas for additional types of data emerge; the sources and data collection methods used or likely to be used; and the way in which each type of information might affect the location decision.

3 A number of multinational companies have attracted media and research attention over the years, often of a critical nature. Examples are Nike (as discussed in Case Study Example 9.1) because of its employment practices, McDonald's because of the nutritional value of its food, and media companies because of their tendency to gain monopoly status in some markets. Select one such company and, using Internet and library sources, produce a case study of its recent research coverage and media coverage, noting both the comments of the critics and the responses of the company.

4 Select a consumer product or service of interest and conduct a case study of its development over the last 10–20 years, with a view to anticipating likely future scenarios for the product. A variety of information sources might be used, including trade and business publications, data from statistical agencies, such as the Australian Bureau of Statistics, company websites, direct observation and interviews with consumers and retailers/producers.

5 Interview one person concerning their consumption habits with regard to one class of products or services—for example, entertainment, clothes, groceries, alcohol, transport. Explore the subject's motivations and rationale for choice of brands. As this is a case study, we might expect to draw on more than one source of information for the study: so examine the advertising of a selection of the subject's preferred and rejected brands to see whether this throws light on the type of consumer the subject is.

FURTHER READING

The most commonly referred to text on case study research is Robert Yin's (1994, 2003a) *Case Study Research*. His *Applications of Case Study Research* provides actual case study research projects, including a number from the management/business sector (Yin 2003b). Robert Stake's (1995) book, *The Art of Case Study Research*, is more discursive and is orientated particularly towards the education sector. Rose (1991) provides a short introduction and reviews the approach of a number of British industrial case studies. Burns (1994: 312–331) and Craig Smith (1991) provide brief overviews.

CHAPTER 10

Experimental research

The experimental approach is closely associated with the positivist paradigm, discussed in Chapter 2. The approach is consistent with the classic 'scientific' model of testing hypotheses and establishing cause and effect relationships. While experimental research formed part of the foundation of the field, in the form of the 'Hawthorne' experiments referred to in Chapter 1, and is common in the consumer component of marketing research, it is comparatively rare in other areas of contemporary business research. Experiments involve research in a controlled environment. Some places where business is conducted might be thought to offer such conditions, but experiments also require the researcher to be able to vary the conditions of the environment for research purposes and this presents problems when people—employees or customers—are involved, and when the costs of varying aspects of the environment can be high. Experimentation for research purposes in business environments is therefore rare and most experimental work in the field is either 'quasi-experimental', in that it does not fully meet the conditions for a true experiment, or it is conducted in an artificial environment abstracted from the 'real' world.

Experimental design is of paramount importance in experimental research and *threats to the validity* of experimental and quasi-experimental research approaches are among the issues discussed in this chapter.

PRINCIPLES OF EXPERIMENTAL RESEARCH

As noted in Chapter 2, experimental methods are usually associated with natural science and laboratories. However, it is possible to conduct some experiments in organisational and management contexts. The essence of the experiment is that, ideally, the researcher controls all the relevant variables in the experiment. Selected variables are manipulated while others are held constant and the effects on subjects are measured. Knowledge progresses on the basis that, in a controlled experimental situation, any change in A (effect) must have been brought about by a change in B (cause), because everything except A and B was deliberately held constant.

In management settings the researcher does not have the degree of control that is available in a scientific laboratory. Nevertheless, in some areas, such as organisational behaviour and product testing, experimental approaches may be used. Examples of some of these include variations in production-line settings, and experiments in management situations in relation to workplace hours or office design. The research tools available to the researcher in experimental research are much the same as for non-experimental approaches—observation, use of secondary data and questionnaire surveys—and the overall approach is explanatory or evaluative.

Variables, treatment and control

In an experimental study the researcher is concerned with a *dependent variable*, an *independent variable* and a number of *control variables*. There may be one or more of each of these variables.

The *dependent variable* is some kind of measurable outcome of the experiment. Communication satisfaction, productivity, number of sick days, employee morale or organisational commitment could all be dependent variables. There is a clear advantage if the dependent variable is easily measured; for example, sick days are much easier to measure than employee morale.

The *independent variable* or *treatment variable* represents a quality or characteristic that is varied or manipulated during the experiment. Some examples of independent variables are: quality of feedback to employees, training methods, remuneration, standard of office equipment, availability of information and work hours. The independent or treatment variable is manipulated during the experiment to examine its effect on the dependent variable. The process of manipulation is the treatment received by the participants in the study. The group of participants receiving the treatment is referred to as the *treatment* or *experimental* group.

In order to control for the possible effects of other variables on the outcome of the experiment, the researcher often uses a *control* group that is not subject to the treatment. The idea of control relates to the researcher's efforts to remove the influence of extraneous variables that might influence the outcome of the experiment. Some of these variables might include gender, age, job category or years with the company. The attributes of the control group are matched with the attributes of the experimental or treatment group so that the two groups are as similar as possible. This can be done by random assignment of individuals to groups. The researcher can then be sure that any changes in the dependent variable are caused only by the independent variable (or treatment) and not by some other variable.

EXPERIMENTAL DESIGN

Experimental research designs can be represented symbolically to provide greater understanding and to clarify the methods used (Campbell & Stanley 1972). An example of a *true experimental design* is shown in Figure 10.1. It represents the classic design for experimental research.

In the figure each line of Rs, Xs and Os represents a group involved in the experiment. In this case there are two groups: a treatment group and a control group. The left-to-right placement of the symbols indicates the sequence of events that takes place for each group.

The Rs indicate that the subjects in the experiment have been randomly assigned to each group. Random assignment ensures that the two groups are as closely matched as possible in relation to extraneous variables that could affect the outcome of the experiment. X represents the experimental treatment that is only received by the first group.

The Os represent a pre-test (O_1) and a post-test (O_2) given to both groups. The pre-test and post-test concern the subjects' performance on the dependent variable. The pre-test is used to confirm that the treatment and control groups are in fact equivalent before the treatment is applied to the treatment group. The post-test measures the performance of the two groups after the treatment.

If the two groups are essentially the same on the pre-test, then the post-test scores on the dependent variable indicate the comparative effectiveness of the treatment received by the treatment group compared with the control group. The statistical significance of the differences in the post-test scores can be determined using a t-test or an analysis of variance. These procedures are described in Chapter 14.

An example of a research study involving a true experimental design could be a study of the effect of sales commission paid to employees on the sales achieved. An Australian bank has been concerned with the level of staff enthusiasm for selling retirement investment plans to its customers. One salaried staff member in each of its 850 branches has the responsibility for selling the plans. Although the bank is very conservative, management is persuaded by a consulting firm to support an experimental research project that investigates the effect of paying salaried employees a 0.5 per cent commission on sales. It is decided to test the following hypothesis:

Bank employees who are paid a commission for selling retirement investment plans will achieve higher sales than employees who are not paid a commission.

Pre-test–post-test control group design

Treatment group [R] O_1 X O_2

Control group [R] O_1 O_2

Key: [R] = random selection of subjects

O_1 = observation 1

O_2 = observation 2

X = experimental treatment

FIGURE 10.1

The experiment is to be conducted over one month. The 850 employees are randomly assigned (R) to two groups: a treatment group and a control group. Each group has 425 members. Group members are unlikely to contact each other, as they live in different towns. Sales for each member of the two groups for the preceding month (dependent variable) are recorded (pre-test O_1). Each member of the treatment group is sent a letter from the human resources branch of the bank informing them that they will be paid a 0.5 per cent commission on sales (independent variable) for a one-month trial period (treatment X). This money is paid to them at the end of the trial. Members of the control group do not receive this letter or any additional money.

Sales for each member of the two groups are recorded at the end of the trial period (post-test O_2). It is noted that the treatment group and the control group had equivalent sales in the month preceding the trial (pre-test), indicating their equivalency on the dependent variable. It is found that the commission group has significantly (see Chapter 14) higher sales than the non-commission group. The hypothesis is supported by these findings. The results of the experimental research are presented in a report to management for a policy decision.

VALIDITY

Validity refers to the extent to which the information collected in a research study truly reflects the phenomenon being studied. We are concerned with issues of validity because they determine the confidence that researchers and managers can have in the outcomes of a study. However, there is often a trade-off to be made between research validity and practicality. In the practical world of business research it is often difficult to control all the extraneous variables which might affect the validity of a study. It is important that researchers be aware of threats to validity and that they make appropriate judgements in the design of the study to take these threats into account. Validity is of special concern in experimental research since it is often claimed to be the only research method that can truly test hypotheses concerning cause and effect relationships. Threats to the validity of experimental research fall into two main groups—*internal* and *external* threats (Campbell & Stanley 1972: 5).

Internal validity

Internal validity concerns the likelihood that any changes in the dependent variable can only be attributed to manipulation of the independent variable and not to some other variable. When this is the case, a study is said to have high internal validity. If it is possible to provide an alternative explanation for the results of the study, the study has low internal validity. The following factors are important threats to the internal validity of a study.

History

History becomes a concern when external events affect the outcome of a study. For example, in the banking study discussed above, a public crisis of confidence in the bank during the period of the study or a policy statement by government on superannuation and retirement pensions would adversely affect the experimental outcomes. The longer a study lasts, the more likely it is that history will become a problem.

Maturation

Maturation refers to changes that can occur in the subjects of the study over a period of time. Such changes might include ageing, fatigue and acquisition of skills or experience over time. For example, bank employees might become accustomed to the commission incentive after two weeks and stop trying to sell more.

Testing

Testing effects can be attributed to changes in subjects that arise from the influence of the testing process itself. For example, it is possible that a pre-test can sensitise or bias a subject's behaviour and result in an improved performance on the post-test which is not due to the payment of commission alone. One way to overcome this threat is to use a different post-test to the pre-test.

Instrumentation

Instrumentation refers to inconsistency or unreliability in the measuring instruments or observation procedures during a study. For example, observers may be inconsistent in what they record during a study, or a post-test may be much more difficult than a pre-test.

Selection

Selection problems arise from one group in an experiment being different to another group. For example, one group might be brighter, more experienced or more receptive to change than another group. In other words, 'people factors' can cause a bias in the study. The purpose of random assignment of subjects to groups is to avoid this threat as far as possible. It remains a problem where existing groups are used for the treatment and control groups (see, for example, the static group design discussed below).

Mortality

Mortality refers to the attrition of subjects from a study. The longer a study proceeds, the more likely it is that mortality will become a problem, especially if the subjects who drop out share a common characteristic with the entire group. In the banking study above, subjects who are thinking of leaving because of lack of incentives in a banking career may be more likely to drop out of the control group than the treatment group.

External validity

External validity refers to the degree to which the findings of a research study can be generalised to other settings and situations. When conducting an experiment a researcher hopes that the findings can be applied at a later time to other groups of people in other geographical locations. The following factors may threaten the external validity of a study.

Reactive effects of testing

The artificial effects of pre-testing may sensitise the subjects to the treatment. Without a pre-test, different outcomes may result from the experiment than would occur in practice. For example, if a study of attitude change was to begin with a pre-testing of attitudes, participants might become sensitised to the attitudes in question and therefore show more attitude change as the result of the experimental treatment. In the banking example given above, the sending of a letter to the treatment group may also have caused subjects to try harder than would be expected, in addition to the commission incentive. In a real world situation employees would not receive such a letter from human resources.

Reactive effects of selection

If the samples drawn for a study are dissimilar to the general population, it becomes difficult to generalise findings from the sample to the broader population. For example, the findings of a study involving only urban dwellers may not be applicable in rural settings. It is desirable to use samples which are representative of the broadest population possible. One widespread selection practice in management research is to use university students as subjects. This practice poses a significant external validity threat to many studies if results are extended to the commercial world.

Reactive effects of experimental setting

The arrangements for an experiment or the experience of participating in the experiment may limit the generalisability of the findings to other settings. For example, in the bank commission experiment the treatment was tested in a particular setting with particular staff at a given time. This setting may not be generalisable to any other situation, for example commission sales in an insurance company in Canada.

Reactive effects can also occur when subjects know that they are participating in an experiment. This effect was demonstrated many years ago in the Hawthorne plant of the Western Electric Company in the USA, as discussed in Chapter 1. A part of this study investigated the relationship between productivity and the brightness of lighting in the factory. As expected, productivity increased when illumination was increased. However, when brightness was decreased productivity also rose. It was concluded that it was the additional attention the workers were receiving, rather than lighting, which was affecting production. This type of experimental participatory effect has become known as the *Hawthorne effect*.

Field experiments vs. laboratory experiments

There is a trade-off between field experiments and laboratory experiments in relation to external and internal validity. In general, field experiments undertaken in natural organisational settings have greater external validity than laboratory-based experiments. On the other hand, laboratory-based experiments tend to have greater internal reliability than field experiments. There is more control of extraneous variables in a laboratory-based experiment. The decision as to which experimental approach to take in a research project is a difficult one. The decision should only be made after careful examination of the threats to internal and external validity described above, and consideration of the objectives of the research. Time and cost may also be important. In practice, opportunities for laboratory experiments in management research are very limited.

QUASI-EXPERIMENTAL DESIGNS

It is often difficult to conduct true experimental research in contemporary organisational settings. As a result, a number of compromise designs are frequently used in management research. These are known as *quasi-experimental* (or *pre-experimental*) research designs. Three common quasi-experimental designs are shown in Figure 10.2. They are used where time, cost and practicality are important considerations, but there is often a loss of validity

Quasi-experimental research design

One-shot design	X O_1
One group pre-test–post-test design	O_1 X O_2
Static group design	
Treatment group	X O_1
Control group	O_1

For key see Figure 10.1

FIGURE 10.2

associated with each design. They are: the one-shot design; the one group pre-test–post-test design and the static group design.

One-shot design

The one-shot design is the simplest quasi-experimental design. It involves only one group, one treatment and one measurement or post-test, and is the weakest of all experimental designs. It does not measure any cause–effect relationship, since there is no comparison with a control group and no measure of how the dependent variable might have changed due to the treatment. This design suffers from all the potential sources of invalidity.

An example of a project using the one-shot design is the introduction of a new computer software package in a data-processing department followed by a survey of employee satisfaction after one year of operation.

One group pre-test–post-test design

The one group pre-test–post-test design permits a comparison of pre- and post-treatment results. The effect of the treatment can be obtained by measuring the difference between the pre- and post-tests, but there is no control group. Testing and instrumentation effects may decrease internal validity. If the experiment is conducted over a period of time, then maturation, mortality and history may also impact on the results. This quasi-experimental design is used quite frequently in business research.

An example of this design might involve employees undertaking a training course (treatment X) to prevent the occurrence of repetitive strain injury. The employees would take a pre-test (O_1) to measure their knowledge before the training course and a post-test (O_2) to measure their knowledge after the course.

The static group design

In the static group design, two groups are chosen—an experimental group and a control group. The groups are not randomly chosen and may already exist intact. The effects of the treatment are determined by studying the difference between the post-test scores of the experimental group and the control group. Selection bias and mortality pose a threat to the internal validity of this design. The introduction of a control group can lessen the threats to validity of testing, instrumentation and, to some degree, history.

In an experiment of this type, employees who have undertaken an employer-sponsored fitness program (treatment X) could be tested for cardiovascular fitness after six months (O_1). A similar group of employees who have not undertaken the program would also be tested for fitness (O_1).

EXPERIMENTAL RESEARCH DECISIONS

The researcher and manager are faced with a range of choices in choosing a research design to suit their management needs. The research designs listed above represent only some of the available approaches to experimental and quasi-experimental business research. Readers are advised to examine other available approaches. Some of these approaches are described in more specialist or detailed texts such as Gay and Diehl (1992: 381–453), Zikmund (1997: 286–328) and Campbell and Stanley (1972).

Davis and Cosenza (1993: 143–4) note that when choosing a research design it is important to recognise that 'there is no one single, correct design for a research problem'. There is no design that will clearly answer all managers' questions. Most research designs are a compromise between information needs, cost, timing, practicality, internal politics, and environmental and strategic goals. Davis and Cosenza also note that it is important to use a research design that will provide answers to the research problem. All too often research that 'seemed a good idea at the time' is conducted without asking the question, 'Will the outcomes of this research clearly answer the research problem?' Obviously there is little purpose in using well-established surveys to provide answers that are of no use to management planning or decision-making.

As an aid to decision-making, Davis and Cosenza list a set of six design questions, which should be asked by researchers and managers to ensure that appropriate information is gathered for management decision-making purposes. Management questions concerning research design are:

1 Which design will best answer the research question?
2 Will the design produce information that is timely and cost-effective for management decision-making?
3 Does the design adequately control for the major sources of error inherent in the research process?
4 How does the design explicitly control the major threats to internal and external validity?
5 Has the researcher clearly thought through the details of the research design so that major modifications and/or unanticipated cost overruns are avoided after the project is initiated?
6 Why is the design chosen by the researcher the best one to address management's problem?

Source: Davis & Cosenza (1993: 144).

Case Study Example 10.1 presents a synopsis of an experiment conducted in a management context. It illustrates how experiments can be used in situations where the costs are relatively low and the outcomes are relatively trivial for the subjects—although they may be significant in aggregate to management.

Experiment: Bottoms Up! Consumer behaviour and packaging

Source: Brian Wansink and Koert van Ittersum 2003, Bottoms up! The influence of elongation on pouring and consumption volume. *Journal of Consumer Research*, 30(4), 455–463.
Methods/approaches: Experimental methods
Topic: Consumer behaviour

We are all familiar with excessive packaging in products like cosmetics and confectionary, and imagine that considerable thought—and expense—must go into the design of such packaging. But to what extent does the shape of packaging influence our consumption behaviour?

Brian Wansink of the University of Illinois and Koert van Ittersum of the Georgia Institute of Technology explored this issue using *experimental* methods relating to the consumption of beverages. Children aged 12–17 at a six-week health and fitness camp in New Hampshire were randomly given two differently shaped glasses when entering the cafeteria line for breakfast. Although the capacity of both glasses was the same, one was short and wide, with a height of 10.6 cm, while the other was tall and slender, with a height of 18.9 cm. The 97 children who selected one of the available juices were stopped on leaving the line and asked how many ounces they thought they had poured and how thirsty they felt (from 1 = not very thirsty to 9 = very thirsty). While these questions were being asked their glasses were weighed. As shown in the table below, it was found that, on average, those with the tall, slender glass poured less than those with the short, wide glass; and they overestimated the amount the former had poured, while those with the short, wide glass underestimated the amount they had poured. A similar experiment was conducted with adults attending a weekend camp on jazz improvisation, producing similar results, as shown in the table.

		Tall, slender glass	Short, wide glass
		Amount poured, oz.	
Children	Actual	5.5	9.7
	Perceived	7.5	7.0
Adults	Actual	5.7	6.9
	Perceived	7.1	5.8

A further experiment was conducted with 41 bartenders, who were asked in their places of work to pour standard 1.5 oz spirit drinks without the aid of a measure, with half the sample given a tall, slender, 12-oz 'highball' glass and half given a short, wide 12-oz tumbler. The bartenders given the short, wide tumblers poured significantly more than the 1.5 oz requested and more than those given the tall, slender glasses. This was true for both experienced and less experienced bartenders.

The implications of these results are discussed in relation to the hospitality industry seeking to decrease costs by minimising portion size without decreasing customer satisfaction and those concerned with health and diet wishing to find ways of assisting people to control their calorific intakes.

The experimental method was possible because, in the case of the first two experiments, the researchers were able to control aspects of the environment in which they were interested and in a semi-public setting were able to intervene in an acceptable way to gather the data required. In the case of the bartenders the experiment was set up as a sort of game or test of skills.

SUMMARY

Experimental methods are closely associated with the *positivist paradigm*, and from this perspective they are seen to provide the most valid insights into business research problems. The experimental approach is consistent with the classic 'scientific' model of testing hypotheses and establishing cause-and-effect relationships. The essence of the experiment is that the researcher ideally controls all the relevant variables in the experiment. Selected variables are manipulated, while others are held constant and the effects on subjects are measured. Although *experimental methods* are usually associated with natural science and laboratories, it is possible to conduct some experiments in management contexts in areas such as organisational behaviour, production line settings and product testing.

In an experimental study the researcher is concerned with a *dependent variable*, an *independent variable* and a number of *control variables*. There may be one or more of each of these variables that are of interest. The *dependent variable* is a measurable outcome of the experiment. The *independent variable* or *treatment variable* represents a quality or characteristic that is varied or manipulated during the experiment. This manipulation is carried out in order to determine its effect on the dependent variable. The process of manipulation is the *treatment* received by the participants in the study. The group of participants receiving the treatment is referred to as the *treatment* or *experimental* group.

In order to control for the possible effects of other variables on the outcome of the experiment, the researcher often uses a *control* group that is not subject to the *treatment* to control for these effects. The idea of control relates to the researcher's efforts to remove the influence of extraneous variables that might influence the outcome of the experiment. The attributes of the control group are matched with the attributes of the experimental or *treatment* group so that the two groups are as similar as possible. This can be done by random assignment of individuals to groups. The researcher can then be sure that any changes in the dependent variable are caused only by the *independent* variable (or *treatment*) and not by some other variable.

Experimental design is an important aspect of research that utilises experimental methods. The *pre-test–post-test control group design* (Figure 10.1) is a *true experimental design*. In this experimental model subjects are randomly assigned to the treatment and control groups and pre-test and post-test measures are conducted on both groups. In many business research contexts it is not possible to use a true experimental design and *quasi-experimental designs*, such as the *one-shot design*, *one group pre-test–post-test design* and the *static group design*, are utilised.

The *validity of experiments* refers to the extent to which the information collected in a research study truly reflects the phenomenon being studied. Validity issues determine the confidence researchers and managers can have in the outcomes of a study. Threats to the validity of experimental research fall into two main groups—*internal* and *external*. *Internal* validity concerns issues such as *history*, *maturation*, *testing*, *instrumentation*, *selection* and *mortality*. External validity concerns issues such as the *reactive effects of testing*, *selection* and *experimental setting*. There is often a trade-off to be made between research validity and practicality. In business research it is often difficult to control all the extraneous variables which might affect the validity of a research study. It is important that the researcher is aware of threats to validity and makes appropriate judgements in the design of the study to take into account these threats.

TEST QUESTIONS

1 Define: *dependent variable*, *independent variable* and *control variable*.
2 Outline the difference between a *true experimental* design and any one of the three types of *quasi-experimental* designs discussed in the chapter.
3 What is *internal validity* and what are the threats to it in experimental research?
4 What is *external validity* and what are the threats to it in experimental research?

EXERCISES

1 Outline a true experimental research design to test the hypothesis that users of new word processing software who undertake a two-day training course in use of the software will be more productive than users who do not take the course. Discuss likely threats to the internal and external validity of the experiment.
2 Repeat exercise 1 using a quasi-experimental one group pre-test–post-test design. Discuss likely threats to the internal and external validity of the experiment.

FURTHER READING

The classic work on experimental design for research is Campbell and Stanley (1972). See also Grunow (1995).

Experimental research methods in business and management contexts: Cooper and Emory (1995), Chapter 13; Gay and Diehl (1992), Chapter 10; Gill and Johnson (1997), Chapters 4 and 5; and Zikmund (1997), Chapter 10.

Experimenter effects in research: Rosenthal (1966).

CHAPTER 11

Sampling and its implications

The idea of sampling

This chapter provides an introduction to the principles of sampling. It addresses the concept of sampling and discusses the relationship between samples and populations. The chapter discusses representativeness and random sampling and then considers sample sizes and their consequences in terms of confidence intervals and weighting.

In most survey research and some observational research it is necessary to sample a proportion of the people or organisations that are the focus of the research. It is not usually possible to interview everyone because of costs, and there is often little research advantage to be gained. In general, the only time that the entire population of Australia is interviewed is every five years, when the Australian Bureau of Statistics conducts the Australian Population Census—the cost of collecting and analysing such a large quantity of data runs into tens of millions of dollars.

In many research situations it is virtually impossible to conduct face-to-face interviews with all the people or organisations being studied. The usual procedure is to interview a sample—a proportion—of the group we are interested in.

SAMPLES AND POPULATIONS

The total category of subjects that is the focus of attention in a particular research project is known as the *population*. A *sample* is selected from the population. The use of the term 'population' makes sense when dealing with communities of people, for instance 'the adult population of Australia'. However, in the research context the term also applies in other instances. For example, the employees of a company constitute the population of the employees of the company; and the users of a particular service are the population of users.

The term 'population' can also be applied to non-human phenomena. For example, if a study of the roadworthiness of Australian trucks found that there were 10 000 trucks in all, out of which 100 were to be selected for testing, then the 10 000 trucks would be referred to as the *population of trucks*. The 100 trucks selected for study would be the *sample*. Similarly, it is possible to consider all the manufacturing companies in Australia as the *population of manufacturing companies*, and the companies selected for a study of the characteristics of manufacturing companies as the sample. In some texts the word *universe* is used instead of population.

If a sample is to be selected for study, two questions arise:

1. What procedures must be followed to ensure that the sample is representative of the population from which it is drawn?
2. How large should the sample be?

These two questions are related since, in general, the larger the sample, the more chance it has of being representative of the population. But there are other, arguably more important, factors to be taken into consideration to ensure representativeness.

RANDOM SAMPLING

Introduction

A sample that is not representative of the population is described as *biased*. The whole process of sample selection must be aimed at *minimising bias* in the sample. The process of *random sampling* aims to provide a representative sample and to reduce bias. It is not the most helpful term since it implies that the process is not methodical. This is far from the case—random does not mean 'haphazard'. The strict definition of random sampling is: 'a selection process which ensures that all members of the population have an equal chance of inclusion in the sample'.

For example, if a sample of 1000 people is to be selected from a population of 10 000, then every member of the population must have a one in ten chance of being selected. In practice, most sampling methods involving human beings can only approximate this rule. The problems of achieving random sampling vary with the type of survey or research being conducted.

Random sampling in household surveys

The problem of achieving a random selection can be examined in the case of a household survey of the adult residents of a country. If the adult population of the country is 10 million and we wish to interview 1000, then every member of the adult population should have a one in 10 000 chance of being included in the sample. How can this be achieved? Ideally, there should be a complete list of all the country's adults—their names should be written on slips of paper and placed in a revolving drum, as in a Lotto draw, and 1000 names should be drawn out. Each time a choice is made everyone has a one in 10 million chance of selection. Since this happens 1000 times, each person has a total 1000 in 10 million, or one in 10 000, chance of selection.

This is a very laborious process. A close approximation would be to forget the slips of paper and the drum and choose every 10 000th name on the list of 10 million. To ensure that this is a random sample, the starting point of this procedure should be a random point between 1 and 10 000. *Tables of random numbers* are available for this purpose. Strictly speaking, the whole sample should be chosen using random numbers, since this would approximate most closely the *names in a drum* procedure.

However, a list of the population being studied rarely exists. The nearest thing to it would be the electoral rolls of all the electorates in the country. Electoral rolls are fairly comprehensive because adults are required by law to register, but they are not perfect. Highly mobile and homeless people are often not included, and many people who live in shared accommodation are omitted. The physical task of selecting the names from such a list would be immense, but there is another disadvantage with this approach. If every 10 000th voter on the registers were selected, the sample would be scattered throughout the country. The cost of visiting every one of those selected for a face-to-face interview would be very high.

Organisations conducting national surveys compromise by employing *multi-stage* sampling and *clustered* sampling. Multi-stage means that sampling is not done directly, but by stages. For example, if the country had four states or regions, a proposed sample of 2000 would be subdivided in the same proportions as the populations of the regions, as shown in Figure 11.1.

Within each region, local government areas would then be divided into 'country' and 'urban' areas. Four urban and two rural areas would be selected at random with the intention of selecting appropriate subsamples of perhaps 25, 40 or 50 from each area. These subsamples could be selected from electoral rolls, or streets could be selected and individuals contacted by calling on every fifth house in the street. In any one street interviewers might be instructed to interview ten or fifteen people. By interviewing 'clusters'

FIGURE 11.1

Multi-stage sampling

Region	Population		Sample	
	Millions	%	Number	%
A	4.0	40.0	800	40.0
B	2.5	25.0	500	25.0
C	2.0	20.0	400	20.0
D	1.5	15.0	300	15.0
Total	10.0	100.0	2000	100.0

of people in this way, costs are minimised. Care must be taken not to reduce the number of clusters too much, since in that case the full range of population and area types would not be included (Keller & Warrack 1991).

Random sampling in site/visitor/intercept surveys

Conditions at work sites or retail or service facilities vary enormously depending on the type and size of the enterprise, the day of the week, the time of day or the weather. Therefore this discussion can only be presented in general terms.

To ensure randomness and therefore representativeness it is necessary for interviewers to adhere to strict rules. Site interviewers operate in two ways. The interviewer can be stationary and the respondents mobile—for instance, when the interviewer is located near the entrance to a workplace and interviews people as they enter or leave. Alternatively, the user may be stationary and the interviewer mobile—for instance, when interviewing employees at their workstations in a manufacturing plant or a public sector organisation department.

In the case of stationary interviewers, the instructions they should follow would be something like:

- When one interview is complete, check through the questionnaire for completeness and legibility.
- When you are ready with a new questionnaire stop the next person to enter the gate or entrance.
- Stick strictly to this rule and do not select interviewees on any other basis.

The important thing is that interviewers should not avoid certain types of user by picking and choosing whom to interview. There should be some rule, such as interviewing every fifth person to come through the door or gate, but since users enter at a varying rate and interviews vary in length, this is rarely possible.

In the case of stationary users and a mobile interviewer, the interviewer should be given a certain route to follow on the site and be instructed to interview every second, third or tenth person they pass, depending on the needs of the research project.

When interviewers are used in a research project, the success of the process will depend on the training given to the interviewers. This could involve observation of them on-site to ensure that they are following the rules.

As indicated in Chapter 8, sampling in site surveys or customer surveys leads inevitably to a variation in the proportion of customers interviewed at different times of the day. In places where customers tend to stay for long periods—as in the case of a work site—this may not matter. However, in places where people stay for shorter periods and where the type of customer may vary during the course of the day or week, the sample will probably be unrepresentative, that is, biased. This bias can be corrected with weighting, as discussed below.

When surveys involve the handing out of questionnaires for self-completion, unless field staff are available to encourage their completion and return, respondents will be self-selected. Busy receptionists can rarely be relied upon to do a thorough job in handing out and collecting questionnaires, unless the survey is a priority of the management and therefore closely supervised. A significant proportion of the population will usually fail to return the questionnaire, but it is unlikely that this self-selection process will be a random one. For example, people who have difficulties in reading or writing, or people who are in a hurry are less likely to return their questionnaires. People with 'something to say', whether positive or negative, are more likely to return their questionnaires than people who are apathetic or content with the service or management. This can give a misleading impression of the proportion of customers who have strong opinions and introduce serious bias into the sample. This sort of 'uncontrolled' survey should therefore be avoided if at all possible.

Quota sampling

Although the technique of quota sampling can be used in a number of situations, it is most commonly used in street surveys. The street survey is usually seen as a means of contacting a representative sample of the community, but in fact it can also be seen as a sort of 'site survey'; the site being a shopping area. As such, a street survey which involves a random sample of the users of the street would be representative of the users of the shopping area rather than of the community as a whole. For example, a suburban shopping centre would have a high proportion of retired people and full-time home and child carers.

If the aim is to obtain a representative sample of the whole community, interviewers are given *quotas* of people of different types to contact, the quotas being based on information about the community which is available from the census. For example, if the census indicates that 12 per cent of the population is retired then interviewers would be required to include twelve retired people in every 100 interviewed. Once interviewers have filled their quota in certain age and gender groups they are required to become more selective in whom they approach in order to fill the gaps in their quotas. The quota method can only be used when background information on the target population is known. If this information is not known, strict adherence to random sampling procedures must be relied upon.

In research involving the employees of organisations, the distribution of the target population is often known from the organisation's human resources database. The selection of quotas to provide a representative sample from senior management, computer staff, supervisors, clerical staff and so on, is easily accomplished.

Random sampling and mail surveys

The initial list of people to whom the questionnaire is sent in a postal survey may be the whole population or a sample. If a sample is selected it can be done completely randomly because the mailing list for the whole population is usually available.

The *respondents* to a postal survey form a sample, but this is a self-selected sample rather than a random sample. This introduces sources of bias similar to those in the uncontrolled self-completion site surveys discussed above. There is little that can be done about this except to make every effort to achieve a high response rate. In some cases information may be available on the population which can be used to weight the sample to correct for certain sources of bias. For example, in the case of a national survey, the sample can be weighted to correct for any geographical bias in the response rate because the geographical distribution of the population is known. If, for example, the survey is of an occupational association and the proportion of members in various grades is known from records, then this can be used for weighting purposes. Postal surveys ultimately suffer from an unknown and uncorrectable element of bias caused by non-response. All surveys experience non-response, but the problem is greater with postal surveys because the level of non-response is relatively higher.

SAMPLE SIZE

Introduction

There is a popular misconception that the size of a sample should be decided on the basis of its relationship to the size of the population, that is, a sample should be 5 per cent or 10 per cent of the population. This is generally not so. What is important is the *absolute size* of the sample, regardless of the size of the population. For example, a sample size of 1000 is equally valid, provided proper sampling procedures have been followed, regardless of whether it is a sample of the Australian adult population (14 million), the residents of Sydney (population 4 million), the residents of Canberra (population 300 000), or the employees of a multinational company (population, say, 10 000). This is illustrated in Figure 11.2, which presents the results of recent political opinion polls in the USA and

FIGURE 11.2

Opinion polls and sample size

USA—NBC News/*Wall Street Journal* poll, 17–19 Sept., 2004		
Registered voters	156 million	
Voting intentions, registered voters:		**Confidence intervals**
Bush/Cheney	48%	±3.1%
Kerry/Edwards	45%	±3.1%
Nader/Camejo	2%	±0.9%
None/other	1%	±0.6%
Not sure	4%	±1.2%
Sample size	1006	
Source: (www.pollingreport.com)—accessed Dec. 2, 2004		
Australia—Newspoll/*The Australian* poll, 13–15 August 2004		
Voting population	13 million	
Voting intentions, primary vote:		**Confidence intervals**
Liberal/National coalition	39%	±3.0%
Labor	42%	±3.0%
Democrats	1%	±0.6%
Greens	6%	±1.4%
One Nation	1%	±0.6%
Other	11%	±1.9%
Sample size	1047*	
Source: (www.newspoll.com.au)—accessed August 2004 *Actual sample size: 1145 but 7% 'uncommitted' and 3% 'refused' excluded		

Australia. Despite the much larger population the sample size used in the American opinion poll is actually smaller than that used in the Australian poll. The 'confidence intervals', which are explained below, are similar.

It is worth repeating that it is the *absolute* size of the sample that is important, *not* its size relative to the population. This is true except when the population itself is small, as discussed later.

On what criteria therefore should a sample size be determined? The criteria are basically fourfold, as shown below.

Determinants of sample size:

- The required level of precision in the results
- The level of detail in the proposed analysis
- The available budget

The idea of the level of precision can be explained as follows. The question is, *To what extent do the findings from a sample precisely reflect this characteristic or opinion in the population as a whole?*

For example, if a survey was designed to investigate sick leave and it was found that 50 per cent of a sample of 500 employed adults took sick leave in the previous year, how sure can we be that this finding, that is, this 'statistic', is true of the population of employed adults as a whole? How sure can we be, despite all efforts taken to choose a representative sample, that the sample is not unrepresentative, and that the real percentage of sick leave in the population is in fact, say, 70 per cent or 30 per cent per annum?

If the true value in the population is around 50 per cent, the chances of drawing a random sample in which no one had been on sick leave would be remote—almost impossible one might say. On the other hand, the chances of coming up with 48 or 49 or 51 or 52 per cent would be fairly high. The chances of coming up with a figure around 70 or 30 per cent would be somewhere in between.

Confidence intervals

Statisticians have examined the likely pattern of distribution of all possible samples of various sizes drawn from different sized populations. They have established that the *sample* value of a statistic (when a sample is randomly drawn) has a certain probability of being within a certain range either side of the *real population* value of the statistic. That range is plus or minus twice the *standard error* of the statistic. The size of the standard error depends on the size of the sample and is unrelated to the size of the population. A randomly drawn sample has a 95 per cent chance of producing a statistic value that is within two standard errors of the true population value so, conversely, there is a 95 per cent chance that the true population value lies within two standard errors of the sample value. This means that if a hundred samples of the same size were drawn, in 95 cases we would expect the statistic to be within two standard errors of the population value. In five cases we would expect it to be outside the range. Since we do not generally know the population value, we have to rely on this theoretical statement of probability about the likely accuracy of our finding—we have a 95 per cent chance of being approximately right and a 5 per cent chance of being wrong.

This two standard error range is referred to as the *95 per cent confidence interval* of a statistic. The relationship between standard errors and level of probability is a property of the *normal curve*—a bell-shaped curve with certain mathematical properties that we are not able to pursue here. The idea of a normal distribution curve and 95 per cent confidence intervals is illustrated in Figure 11.3. The general idea of probabilities related to the properties of certain types of *distribution* is pursued in more detail in Chapter 14.

Tables have been drawn up by statisticians that show the confidence intervals for various statistics for various sample sizes, as shown in Figure 11.4. Down the side of the table are various sample sizes, ranging from 50 to 10 000. Across the top of the table are the percentages one might find from a survey—for example 20 per cent of a certain population play tennis. The table shows 20 *and* 80 because if it is found that 20 per cent of the sample play tennis, then clearly 80 per cent *do not* play tennis. Any conclusion about the accuracy of the finding of 20 per cent also applies to the finding of 80 per cent. In the body of the table are the *confidence intervals.*

Suppose we have a sample size of 500 and we find that 30 per cent of the sample have a certain characteristic—they have been away on sick leave in the previous year (so 70 per cent have *not* been on sick leave). Reading from the table, for a sample size of 500 we find that a finding of 30 per cent (and 70 per cent) is subject to a confidence interval of plus or

The normal distribution curve and confidence intervals

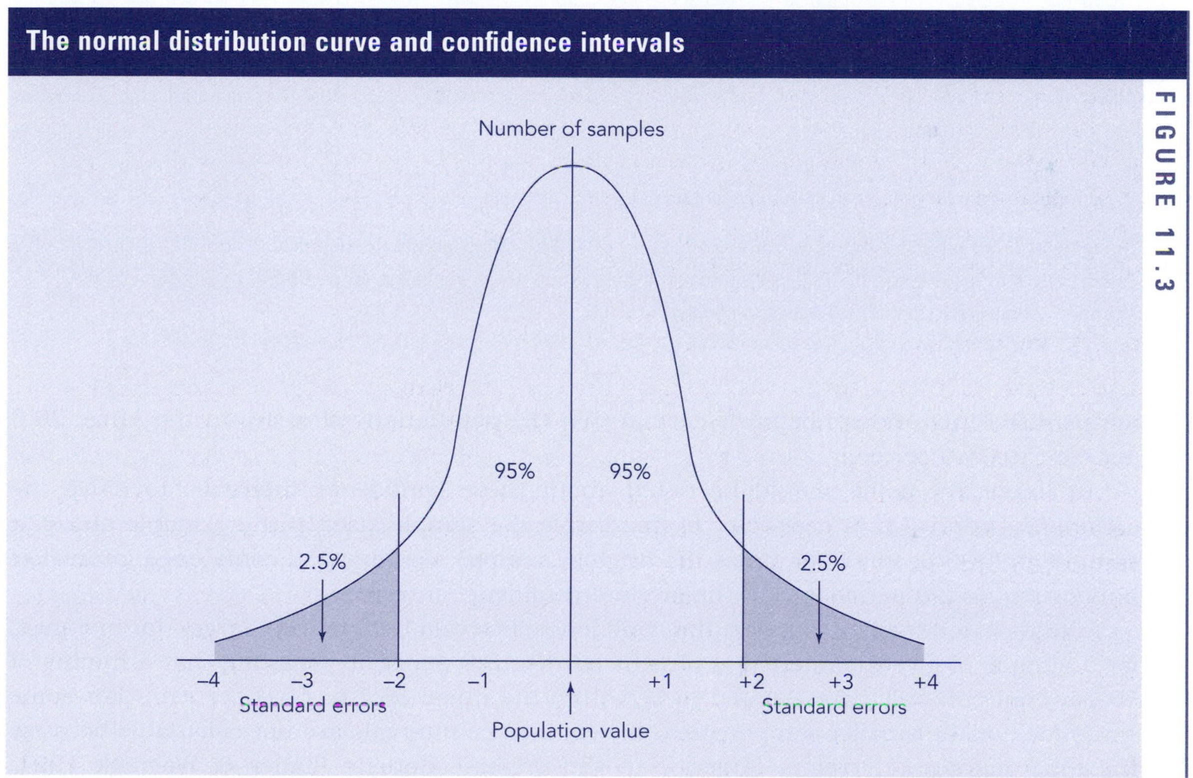

FIGURE 11.3

FIGURE 11.4

Confidence intervals related to sample size

Sample size	Percentages found from sample ('results')							
	50%	40 or 60%	30 or 70%	20 or 80%	10 or 90%	5 or 95%	2 or 98%	1 or 99%
	Confidence intervals (+ %)							
50	±13.9	±13.6	±12.7	±11.1	±8.3	*	*	*
80	±11.0	±10.7	±10.0	±8.8	±6.6	*	*	*
100	±9.8	±9.6	±9.0	±7.8	±5.9	±4.3	*	*
150	±8.0	±7.8	±7.3	±6.4	±4.8	±3.5	*	*
200	±6.9	±6.8	±6.3	±5.5	±4.2	±3.0	±1.9	*
250	±6.2	±6.1	±5.7	±5.0	±3.7	±2.7	±1.7	*
300	±5.7	±5.5	±5.2	±4.5	±3.4	±2.5	±1.6	*
400	±4.9	±4.8	±4.5	±3.9	±2.9	±2.1	±1.4	±1.0
500	±4.4	±4.3	±4.0	±3.5	±2.6	±1.9	±1.2	±0.9
750	±3.6	±3.5	±3.3	±2.9	±2.1	±1.6	±1.0	±0.7
1000	±3.1	±3.0	±2.8	±2.5	±1.9	±1.3	±0.9	±0.6
2000	±2.2	±2.1	±2.0	±1.7	±1.3	±1.0	±0.6	±0.4
4000	±1.5	±1.5	±1.4	±1.2	±0.9	±0.7	±0.4	±0.3
10 000	±1.0	±1.0	±0.9	±0.8	±0.6	±0.4	±0.3	±0.2

* confidence interval greater than the percentage

Interpretation of table: for example, for a sample size of 400 a finding of 30% is subject to a confidence interval of ±4.5 (that is to say, we can be 95% certain that the population value lies in the range 25.5% to 34.5%). For the formula to calculate confidence intervals see Appendix 5.

minus 4.0. Thus, we can be fairly certain that the population value lies in the range 26.0 per cent to 34.0 per cent.

An important point should be noted about these confidence intervals: to halve the confidence interval it is necessary to quadruple the sample size. In the example above, a sample of 2000 people (four times the original sample) would give a confidence interval of plus or minus 2.0 per cent (half the original confidence interval).

Note that, for smaller samples, the confidence intervals become very large—for instance, for a sample of fifty the interval is plus or minus 13.9 per cent, meaning that a finding of 50 per cent can only be estimated to be within the range 36.1 to 63.9 per cent. For some statistics, for the smaller sample sizes, the confidence intervals are not calculable because the total margin of error is larger than the original statistic (Keller & Warrack 1991:

205–25). It should be noted that these confidence intervals apply only for samples that have been drawn using random sampling methods; other methods, such as multi-stage sampling, tend to produce larger confidence intervals.

The implications of the first criterion for deciding sample size now become clear. A sample size of, say, 1000 would give a confidence interval for a finding of 50 per cent of plus or minus 3.1 per cent. If that margin of error was not considered acceptable then a larger sample size would be necessary. Whether or not it is considered acceptable depends on the uses to which the data will be put and is related to the type of analysis to be done, as discussed below. An alternative way of considering the relationships between sample size and confidence interval is presented in Figure 11.5. This presents, in the body of the table, the necessary sample size to achieve a given confidence interval.

Level of detail of analysis

The confidence intervals in Figures 11.4 and 11.5 illustrate the second criterion concerning the choice of sample size, which is that the necessary sample size depends on the type of analysis to be undertaken. If many detailed comparisons are to be made, especially concerning small proportions of the population, then too small a sample size will tend to preclude meaningful analysis.

For instance, suppose a survey is conducted with a sample of 200 and it is found that 20 per cent of respondents used personal computers (PCs) and 30 per cent used Macintosh computers (Macs). The 20 per cent is subject to a margin of error of plus or minus 5.5 per

Necessary sample sizes to achieve given confidence intervals

FIGURE 11.5

	Percentages found from samples ('results')						
Conf. Interval	50%	40 or 60%	30 or 70%	20 or 80%	10 or 90%	5 or 95%	1 or 99%
	Necessary sample size						
±1%	9600	9216	8064	6144	3456	1824	380
±2%	2400	2304	2016	1536	864	456	*
±3%	1067	1024	896	683	384	203	*
±4%	600	576	504	384	216	114	*
±5%	384	369	323	246	138	73	*
±6%	267	256	224	171	96	*	*
±7%	196	188	165	125	71	*	*
±8%	150	144	126	96	53	*	*
±9%	119	114	100	76	43	*	*
±10%	96	92	81	61	35	*	*

cent, and the 30 per cent is subject to a margin of plus or minus 6.3 per cent. Thus it is estimated that the proportions using the two types of computers are as follows:

PCs 14.5–25.5 per cent Macs 23.7–36.3 per cent

The confidence intervals overlap, so we cannot conclude that there is any 'significant' difference in the popularity of the two computers, despite a 10 per cent difference given by the survey. This is likely to be very limiting in any analysis. With a sample of 500 the confidence intervals are 3.5 per cent and 4.0 per cent respectively, giving estimates as follows:

PCs 16.5–23.5 per cent Macs 26.0–34.0 per cent

In this case the confidence intervals do not overlap and we can be fairly certain that Macs are more popular than the PCs.

The detail of the analysis, the extent of subdivision of the sample into subsamples, and the acceptable level of precision will therefore determine the necessary size of the sample. By and large this has nothing to do with the overall size of the original population, although there is a likelihood that the larger the population the greater its diversity and therefore the greater the need for subdivision into subsamples during analysis.

Budget

It could be positively wasteful to expend resources on a large sample when it can be shown to be unnecessary. For example, a sample of 10 000 gives estimates of statistics with a maximum confidence interval of ±1 per cent. Such a survey could cost as much as $400 000 to conduct. To halve that confidence interval to ±0.5 per cent would mean quadrupling the sample size to 40 000 at an additional cost of $1 200 000. There can be very few situations where such expenditure would be justified for such a small return.

The limiting factor in determining sample size will ultimately be the resources available. Even if the available budget limits the sample size severely it may be decided to go ahead and risk the possibility of an unrepresentative sample. If the sample is small, however, the detail of the analysis will need to be limited. If resources are so limited that the validity of quantitative research is questionable, it may be sensible to consider qualitative research that may be more feasible. Alternatively, the proposed research could be seen as a 'pilot' study with an emphasis on methodology, preparatory to a more adequately resourced full-scale project.

Reporting size of sampling errors

How should the issue of sample size and confidence intervals be reported in the research report? In some scientific research, complex statistical tests are considered necessary when reporting statistical results from surveys. Requirements are less rigorous in a lot of business research, especially in the reporting of applied research. The researcher should be aware of the limitations imposed by the sample size and avoid making comparisons that the data cannot support. An appendix can be included indicating the size of the sampling errors (see Appendix 3 for a possible format), but a great deal of statistical jargon is not generally required. The lay reader expects the researcher to do a good job, and expert readers should be given enough information to check the analysis in the report for themselves. In academic journals the rules are somewhat different and there is an expectation that statistical tests should be 'up front'. It is not proposed to pursue the question of statistical tests further here. As noted in Chapter 14, an array of standard tests is available using computer packages such as *SPSS*, once data have been prepared for computer analysis.

Small populations

The above discussion of sample size assumes that the population is large—in fact, the statistical formulae used to calculate the confidence intervals are based on the assumption that the population is infinite. The relationship between the size of confidence intervals and the size of the population becomes noticeable when the population size falls below about 50 000, as shown in Figure 11.6. The table presents sample sizes necessary to produce

FIGURE 11.6

Sample size and population size

Population size	Minimum sample sizes for confidence interval of ±5% and ±1% on a sample finding of 50%	
	±5%	±1%
Infinite*	384	9,602
10 000 000	384	9,593
5 000 000	384	9,584
1 000 000	384	9,511
500 000	384	9,422
100 000	383	8,761
50 000	381	8,056
25 000	378	6,938
20 000	377	6,488
10 000	370	4,899
5000	357	3,288
2000	322	1,655
1000	278	906
500	217	475
200	132	196
100	80	99
50	44	50

* as in Figures 11.4 and 11.5 and formula in Appendix 5

95 per cent confidence intervals of ±5 per cent and ±1 per cent for a sample finding of 50 per cent for different population sizes. Only the sample sizes for a 50 per cent finding are presented since, as shown in Figures 11.4 and 11.5, the 50 per cent finding is the most demanding in terms of sample size: for a given sample size, the confidence intervals for other findings—for example 30/70 per cent—is always smaller. The table first indicates the sample size for an infinite population and it can be seen that the sample sizes are the same as indicated for a ±5 per cent or ±1 per cent confidence interval in the first column of Figure 11.5. The details of the formula relating confidence intervals to population size can be found in Krejcie and Morgan (1970).

WEIGHTING

Situations where weighting of survey or count data may be required have been indicated in previous sections. The principles involved in weighting are discussed below. In Chapter 13 the procedures for implementing weighting using the *SPSS* software package are outlined. The data shown in Figure 11.7 refer to customer satisfaction interviews conducted at a hypothetical fast food outlet.

In the sample of 45 interviews, the number of interviews is spread fairly equally through the day, whereas more than half of the actual customers visit the outlet around the middle of the day (this information probably having been obtained by observation and counts or from cash register records). This can be a source of bias in the sample, since the midday customers may differ from the others in their characteristics or opinions, and they will be underrepresented in the sample. The aim of weighting is to produce a weighted sample with a distribution similar to that of the population of customers.

One approach is to 'gross up' the sample numbers to reflect the actual numbers—for example, the 9.00–11.00 a.m. group is weighted by 25/10 = 2.5, the 11.00–1.00 p.m. group is weighted by 240/12 = 20 and so on, as shown in Figure 11.8.

The weighting factors can be fed into the computer for the weighting to be done automatically—this is discussed in Chapter 12. The initial weighting factors are equal to the customer number divided by the sample number for that time period. The weighted sample therefore is made to resemble the overall customer numbers. It should be noted, however,

FIGURE 11.7

Interview and usage data

Time	Interviews		All users	
	Number	%	Number (counts)	%
9.00–11.00 a.m.	10	22.2	25	5.7
11.01 a.m.–1.00 p.m.	12	26.7	240	55.2
1.01–3.00 p.m.	11	24.4	110	25.3
3.01–5.00 p.m.	12	26.7	60	2.7
Total	45	100.0	435	100.0

Weighting

	A	B	C	D
Time	**Number of interviews**	**Number of users**	**Weighting factors**	**Weighted sample no.**
Source:	**Survey**	**Counts**	**B/A**	**C x A**
9.00–11.00 a.m.	10	25	2.5	25
11.01 a.m.–1.00 p.m.	12	240	20.0	240
1.01–3.00 p.m.	11	110	10.0	110
3.01–5.00 p.m.	12	60	5.0	60
Total	45	435		435

FIGURE 11.8

that the sample size remains 45 not 435. If statistical tests are to be carried out, it would be advisable to divide the weighting factors by 435/45 (or multiply by 45/435) to bring the weighted sample total back to 45.

In this example the basis of the weighting relates to the pattern of visits to the fast food outlet over the course of the day, which happened to be information that was available in relation to this particular type of survey. Any other relevant data available on the population could be used. If age structure is available, then age groups rather than time periods could be used.

SAMPLING FOR QUALITATIVE RESEARCH

As discussed in Chapter 7, qualitative research often makes no claim to representativeness and, by definition, does not involve statistical calculation demanding prescribed levels of precision. Generally, therefore, the considerations outlined above are not relevant to qualitative research. However, in some cases a degree of representativeness is claimed. For example, in Case Study Example 9.1, Palmer and Dunford conduct 19 qualitative interviews with a sample of employees of a travel agency. In describing their methods, they indicate that the interviewees included the CEO and six other members of the top management team and a 'vertical cross-section slice of the organisation in a particular region in Australia and included a regional leader, five store managers, five consultants within these stores and one person associated with fitting out Flight Centre stores . . . In all, ten men and nine women were interviewed' (Palmer & Dunford 2002: 1052). While they do not make any explicit statement about representativeness, the implication is that this group of interviewees is generally representative of the range of the company's employees, at least in Australia.

Often, therefore, the qualitative researcher will *purposively* select a group of subjects according to one or more key variables. While the variety of subjects may be necessary to explore the effects of the key variables, it may also be used to support a claim for a degree of representativeness. However, in reporting results, it is necessary to avoid falling into the trap of claiming, or implying, quantitative representativeness. Thus, for example, although Palmer and Dunford's interviewees were split roughly 50:50 between men and women, any gender-related findings would be unrepresentative of the company as a whole if the work-force as a whole were split, say, 20:80 between men and women.

SUMMARY

This chapter introduced the principles of sampling and the implications of these principles for business research. In most survey research and some observational research it is not possible to survey everyone because of costs, and there is often little research advantage to be gained, so a *sample* of the people or organisations to be studied is selected. The total category of subjects which is the focus in a particular research project is known as the *population*. The employees of a company constitute the population of the employees of the company, and the customers of a particular service are the population of customers.

A sample is selected *from* the population. The larger the sample the more chance it has of being *representative* of the population. A sample that is not representative of the population is described as *biased*. The process of *random sampling* seeks to provide a representative sample and to minimise bias. In the process of random sampling all members of the population have an *equal chance* of inclusion in the sample although, in practice, most sampling methods involving human beings can only approximate this rule. The problems of achieving random sampling vary with the type of survey or research being conducted, so *household surveys*, *site surveys*, *street surveys* and *mail surveys* all present characteristic challenges in the selection of random samples.

The issue of the appropriate *sample size* to provide a representative sample of a population is an important one. There is a popular misconception that the size of a sample should be decided on the basis of its relationship to the size of the population, for example, that a sample should be 5 per cent or 10 per cent of the population. This is not the case. Except when the population itself is small, it is the *absolute* size of the sample which is important, regardless of the size of the population.

There are three criteria for determining sample size: the *level of precision of results*, the *level of detail in the proposed analysis* and the *budget*. The *level of precision of results* concerns the degree to which the researcher wants the findings from the sample to precisely reflect this characteristic in the whole population. When a sample is randomly drawn, the sample value of a statistic has a certain probability of being within a particular range either side of the real population value of the statistic. Tables have been drawn up by statisticians that show the *confidence intervals* for various statistics for various sample sizes—the acceptability of confidence intervals of different sizes will therefore influence the sample size required for a study.

The sample size required for a study also depends on the level of detail in the proposed analysis. If many detailed comparisons are to be made, especially concerning small proportions of the population, then a small sample size may not allow meaningful analysis. The level of detail of the analysis will therefore influence the size of the sample selected.

The available budget for a study also determines the sample size. Resources available will ultimately be the limiting factor in determining sample size. Even if the available budget limits the sample size severely, it may be decided to go ahead and risk the possibility of an unrepresentative sample, but in such a situation the study might be presented as a 'pilot' or 'exploratory' study and the detail of the analysis will need to be limited.

When certain characteristics of the population are known (for example, the age structure and gender split), the process of *weighting* can be used to correct any unrepresentativeness in the sample.

TEST QUESTIONS

1 Define *random sampling.*
2 How can random sampling be achieved in a site/visitor/intercept survey where the site has multiple, unticketed entrances and exits.
3 What is quota sampling?
4 What determines the size of the sample in a given research project?
5 What is a confidence interval?
6 What is 'weighting' and why is it used?

EXERCISES

1 Examine either a published research report or a journal article related to an empirical study and identify the procedures used to ensure a random sample.
2 Using the report discussed in exercise 1, produce confidence intervals for a range of percentage statistics occurring in the report.
3 In the example comparing PC users and Mac users given in this chapter, what would the confidence intervals be if the sample size was 4000?
4 Examine the results from a national management survey and produce confidence intervals for a number of the key findings.
5 Examine the results of recent political opinion polls via the Internet, eg for USA at (www.usatoday.com/news/politicselections/pollsindex.htm); (www.pollingreport.com); for Australia at (www.newspoll.com.au). Check what the pollsters say about sample size and sampling error and assess the implications for the closeness of the likely election results.

FURTHER READING

Introduction to sampling and sampling distributions: Keller and Warrack (1991), Chapter 6.
General introduction to reading quantitative research: Williams (1986).
Issues of sampling: Williams (1986) Chapter 4.
Sampling for qualitative research: Miles and Huberman (1994: 27-34).
Sampling in the context of mail surveys: Dillman (2000), Chapter 5.
Sampling and the statistical implications of sampling are covered in most general statistics textbooks.

data
analysis
PART
3

CHAPTER 12

Analysing secondary data

This chapter builds on Chapter 5, which reviews sources of secondary data. The potential for the analysis of such data is enormous. Arguably the bulk of business research is, in fact, based on analysis of secondary data, particularly financial data. At its most basic level, all organisations use data to monitor performance, such as trends in sales, revenue, costs and profit. Drawing a boundary between such routine compilation of basic data and research is difficult. Quite sophisticated use of financial data is enshrined in managerial accounting practices and it is not possible to cover that field of activity in one short chapter in a general text such as this. Here, therefore, we concentrate on less routine uses of internal, organisational data and on data drawn from outside sources.

INTERNAL DATA

Trend analysis

Some products or services display a seasonal pattern, with data on sales produced on a weekly, monthly or quarterly basis. In such situations, the fluctuating sales data make it difficult to analyse long-term trends. Column A in Figure 12.1 shows a series of quarterly sales figures, portrayed graphically by the zig-zag line in Figure 12.2. Each quarterly figure reflects two factors: seasonal variation and longer-term trends. The fluctuations could be avoided by aggregating the data and analysing it on an annual basis, but this would mean that a full set of data would only be analysed at twelve-monthly intervals. One way of examining the longer-term trend without the distraction of the seasonal variation is to produce a 'smoothed' trend series by calculating a 'moving average'. The moving average, shown in column B in Figure 12.1, consists of the average of the previous four quarters' figures. For example:

- the moving average for Oct-Dec 1999 is the average of the four figures for 1999;
- the moving average for Jan-Mar 2000 is the average of the figures from Apr-Jun 1999 to Jan-Mar 2000.

The calculations can be done very easily with a spreadsheet program. The effect is to present a 'smoothed' trend series, as shown graphically in Figure 12.2.

FIGURE 12.1

Quarterly sales and moving average, 1999–2003

Year	Quarter	A. Sales revenue, $million	B. Moving average
1999	Jan–Mar	1.1	–
	Apr–Jun	2.5	–
	Jul–Sept	4.5	–
	Oct–Dec	3.3	2.9
2000	Jan–Mar	1.3	2.9
	Apr–Jun	2.8	3.0
	Jul–Sept	4.9	3.1
	Oct–Dec	3.9	3.2
2001	Jan–Mar	1.6	3.3
	Apr–Jun	3.0	3.4
	Jul–Sept	5.5	3.5
	Oct–Dec	4.3	3.6
2002	Jan–Mar	1.8	3.7
	Apr–Jun	3.0	3.7
	Jul–Sept	5.2	3.6
	Oct–Dec	3.1	3.3
2003	Jan–Mar	1.7	3.3
	Apr–Jun	2.8	3.2
	Jul–Sept	4.8	3.1
	Oct–Dec	3.0	3.1

FIGURE 12.2

Trend/moving average

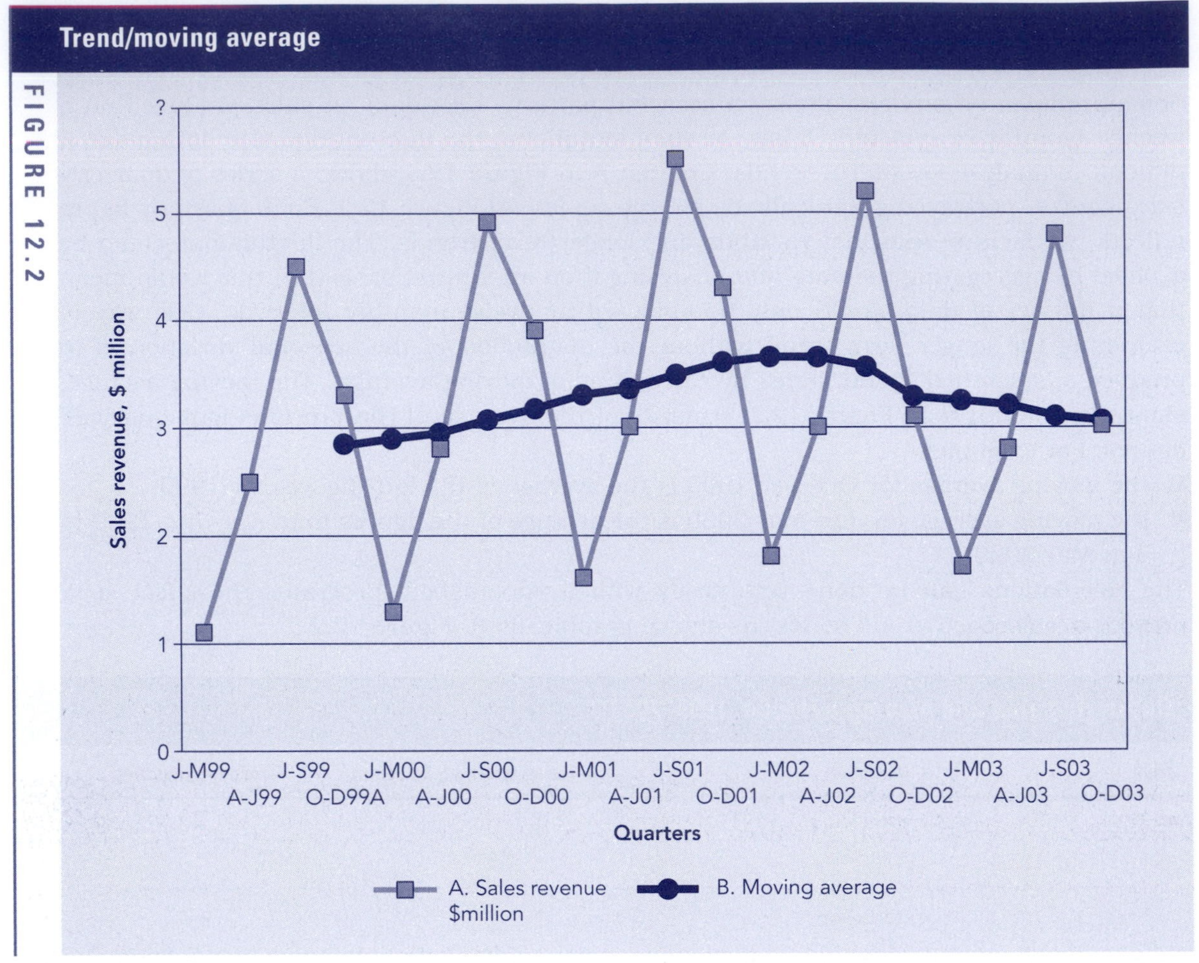

Catchment area analysis

Service outlets have *catchment areas*—a term borrowed from geography referring to the area from which water drains into a river system. In the business context catchment area—or market area—refers to the area from which a business draws its customers. Different types of service outlets have different sizes of catchment area. For example, a specialist fashion outlet will have a larger catchment area than a newspaper shop. Since a few customers may travel exceptionally long distances to use an outlet, thus skewing the apparent size of the catchment area, it is customary to use an arbitrary cut-off point to define the area; for example, a catchment area could be defined as the area from which the nearest 80 per cent of customers travel.

Knowing something about the size and characteristics of the population living in a catchment area can be useful for a variety of purposes:

1 comparing the information with information on the number and characteristics of actual customers (perhaps drawn from a survey) in order to appraise the extent to which the potential market is being reached;

2 making decisions about which local media to use in advertising;
3 making decisions on the likely viability of potential new outlets in other areas, given knowledge of the typical catchment area size and level of patronage from a given population.

Information on the population of areas just beyond the catchment area might also be used when considering whether marketing activity might be implemented to extend the catchment area.

A catchment area may be identified on the basis of customer records if the outlet is the sort which routinely records customers' addresses. If such records are not available it may be necessary to conduct a customer survey, in which case the data would be 'primary' rather than 'secondary'. Some retailers use an 'in-between' method—for example, by asking cash customers their postcode or suburb at the time of purchase and recording this on the sales record.

Figure 12.3 presents an example of analysis of customer information which might be used to define a catchment area. A catchment area can be defined as an irregular shape but in this case it would appear that a circular area of radius 4 km would be appropriate.

Compiling information on the population of a catchment area is discussed in the next section on 'external sources'.

Employee data

The project by Glebbeek and Bax (2004) summarised in Case Study Example 5.1 shows how readily available aggregated employee records can be used for research purposes. Four

FIGURE 12.3

Catchment/market area

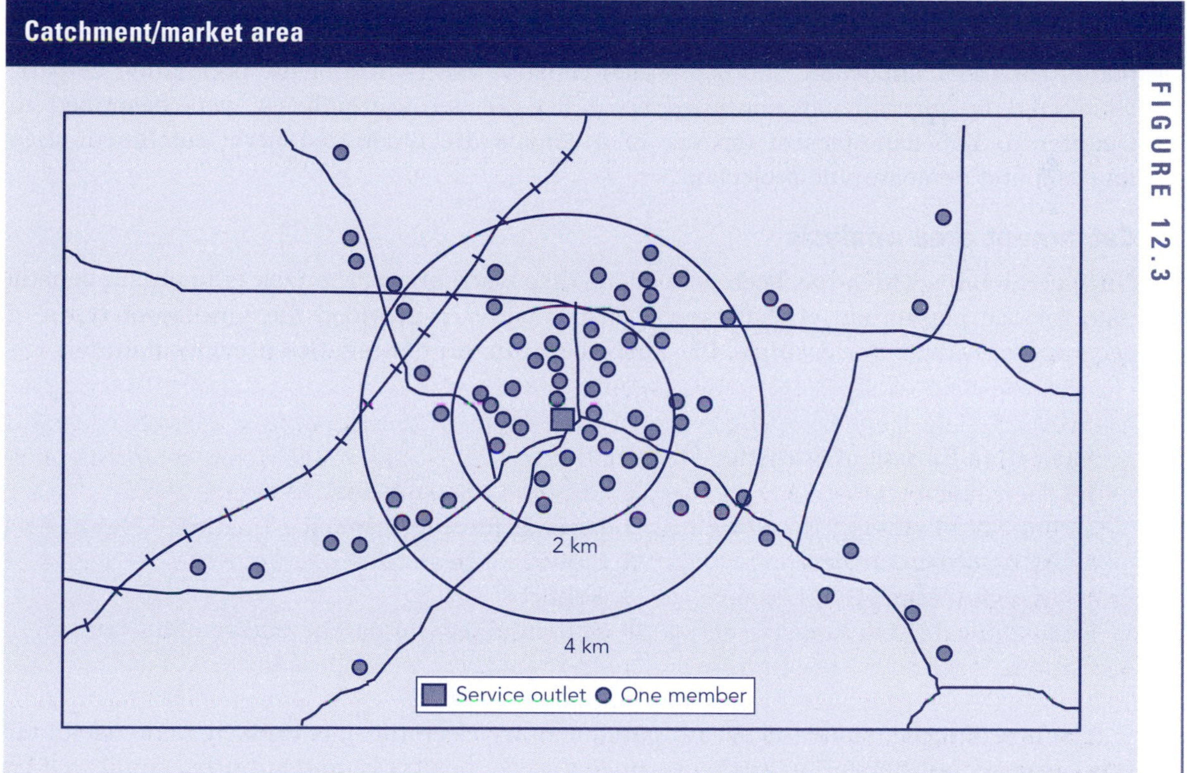

years' worth of data on employee turnover and absentee rates from 100 branch offices of a Dutch job agency were analysed, together with data on the sales performance of each branch, to demonstrate statistically the relationship between these variables.

Data-mining

Data-mining is the process by which organisations analyse large computerised databases for management purposes. Such databases could refer to current and former customers or clients, suppliers and processes. Banks, for example, hold considerable amounts of information on individual customers often stretching over a number of years. Even when the relationship is less personal, as in the case of retailers, information on individuals is stored as a result of credit transactions and loyalty schemes. Groups of customers with similar purchasing patterns can be identified and targeted for particular promotions. Customers who are lost to the competition—for example, bank customers who transfer their custom to another bank—can be analysed as a group to determine whether they have common characteristics so that 'at risk' customers can be identified in advance and given special attention to reduce the risk of losing their custom. Hormozi and Giles (2004) point out that data-mining is also used for fraud detection—for example, by flagging suspicious credit card transactions. While the idea of data-mining is a simple one, in practice it is a highly technical process, given the substantial amount of data involved—in some cases millions of customers each with hundreds or thousands of transactions. It is therefore not possible to pursue the topic in detail here, but sources of information are identified in the Further Reading section.

EXTERNAL DATA SOURCES

A wide range of external data sources was discussed in Chapter 5; here we concentrate on one of the most important, the population census. The nature of the population census, conducted by virtually all countries on a five- or ten-yearly basis, was described in Chapter 5. Two examples of the use of a census are illustrated here: catchment area analysis and demographic projection.

Catchment area analysis

Once a catchment area has been defined, as discussed above, the task is to obtain census data for the population of that area. Census data are provided for a range of types of geographical areas. For example, the Australian Bureau of Statistics provides data for:

Australian Bureau of Statistics statistical areas:

1. The whole country
2. Individual states
3. ABS Statistical Divisions
4. ABS Statistical Subdivisions
5. Statistical Local Areas
6. Census Collection Districts
7. Local government areas
8. Individual postcodes
9. Suburbs
10. State and federal parliamentary electorates

The last of these, state and federal parliamentary electorates, is unlikely to be useful for this purpose, but items 7-9, local government areas, postcodes and suburbs, could well be a close approximation to a catchment area for some business outlets. The first six area types in the list form a hierarchy of areas for which ABS produces data, and definitions and maps of the areas are available from the ABS in hard copy and via its website. Figure 12.4 shows how the system works from state level down to one area in New South Wales, in central Sydney. The smallest areas are Census Collection Districts (CCDs), which form the basis on which the census data are physically collected, and generally contain a population of 200-300. Figure 12.4 shows that the Inner Sydney Statistical Local Area (SLA) contains 19 CCDs. Using ABS maps it is possible to identify the statistical areas, including CCDs, which match the outlet's catchment area as closely as possible. A computerised package for the Australian census—CDATA—will select the areas within a specified distance of a user-identified geographical location and produce population data for the area.

For any of the areas discussed above, including individual CCDs, a substantial range of information is available, as shown in Figure 12.5. This listing refers only to the resident

FIGURE 12.4

Australian Bureau of Statistics statistical areas

States in Australia	Statistical Divisions in NSW	Statistical Subdivisions in Sydney Statistical Division	Statistical Local Areas in Inner Sydney Statistical Subdivision	CCDs in Inner Sydney SLA*
New South Wales	Sydney	Inner Sydney	Sydney—Inner	1400101
Victoria	Hunter	Eastern Suburbs	Botany Bay	1400102
Queensland	Illawarra	St George–Sutherland	Leichhardt	1400103
South Australia	Richmond–Tweed	Canterbury–Bankstown	Marrickville	1400104
Western Australia	Mid-North Coast	Fairfield–Liverpool	South Sydney	1400105
Tasmania	Northern	Outer South Western	Sydney–Remainder	1400106
Northern Territory	North Western	Sydney		1400107
Aust. Capital Territory	Central West	Inner Western Sydney		1400108
Other Territories	South Eastern	Central Western Sydney		1400109
	Murrumbidgee	Outer Western Sydney		1400110
	Murray	Blacktown		1400111
	Far West	Lower Northern Sydney		1400112
	Off-Shore etc.	Central Northern		1400113
		Sydney		1400114
		Northern Beaches		1400115
		Gosford–Wyong		1400116
				1400117
				1400118
				1400119

*CCD = Census Collection District SLA = Statistical Local Area

FIGURE 12.5

Census data available

Resident population

- Number of males/females
- Number/proportion in 5-year age-groups (and single years for under 20s)
- Numbers of people:
  - with different religions
  - born in Australia and other countries
  - speaking different languages
  - with parents born in Australia and other countries
- Numbers of families/households:
  - of different sizes
  - with different numbers of dependent children
  - which are single-parent families
  - with various numbers of vehicles
- Numbers of people:
  - who left school at various ages
  - with different educational/technical qualifications
  - in different occupational groups
  - unemployed
  - living in different types of dwelling

population, but some data are also available on the working population, that is people who work in an area but live elsewhere. The choice of data to use will vary according to the type of product and availability of customer data for comparison purposes.

Demographic projection

Much has been made in recent years of the ageing of the population in Western countries. For companies taking the long-term view, this can be a highly significant phenomenon. Census organisations, such as the Australian Bureau of Statistics, regularly publish projections of future population levels and age structures (ABS 2002a) and these can be used to anticipate shifts in markets, enabling organisations to plan their responses.

Figure 12.6 shows the ABS population projections for Australia for the period 2006-2021. The ABS publishes three sets of projections, based on different assumptions about immigration and migration, birth rates and death rates; here the middle projection is used. The projections were published in 2002, based on the 2001 census, so the 2006 data as well as the 2021 data are projections. It can be seen that there is expected to be little growth among the younger age groups but substantial growth among the older age groups, due to the phenomenon of the 'baby-boomer' generation, born between 1946 and the 1960s.

Figure 12.7 shows how information on population projections can be used to provide estimates of future demand in a given market. The data relate to cinema attendance and are drawn from another ABS data source: its five-yearly survey of *Attendance at Cultural Venues and Events* (ABS 2002b). Cinema attendances fluctuate from year to year, according to a variety of factors, including film-makers' ability to produce blockbusters, but this exercise seeks to estimate the underlying effects of demographic change.

FIGURE 12.6

Australian population projections by age, 2006-2021

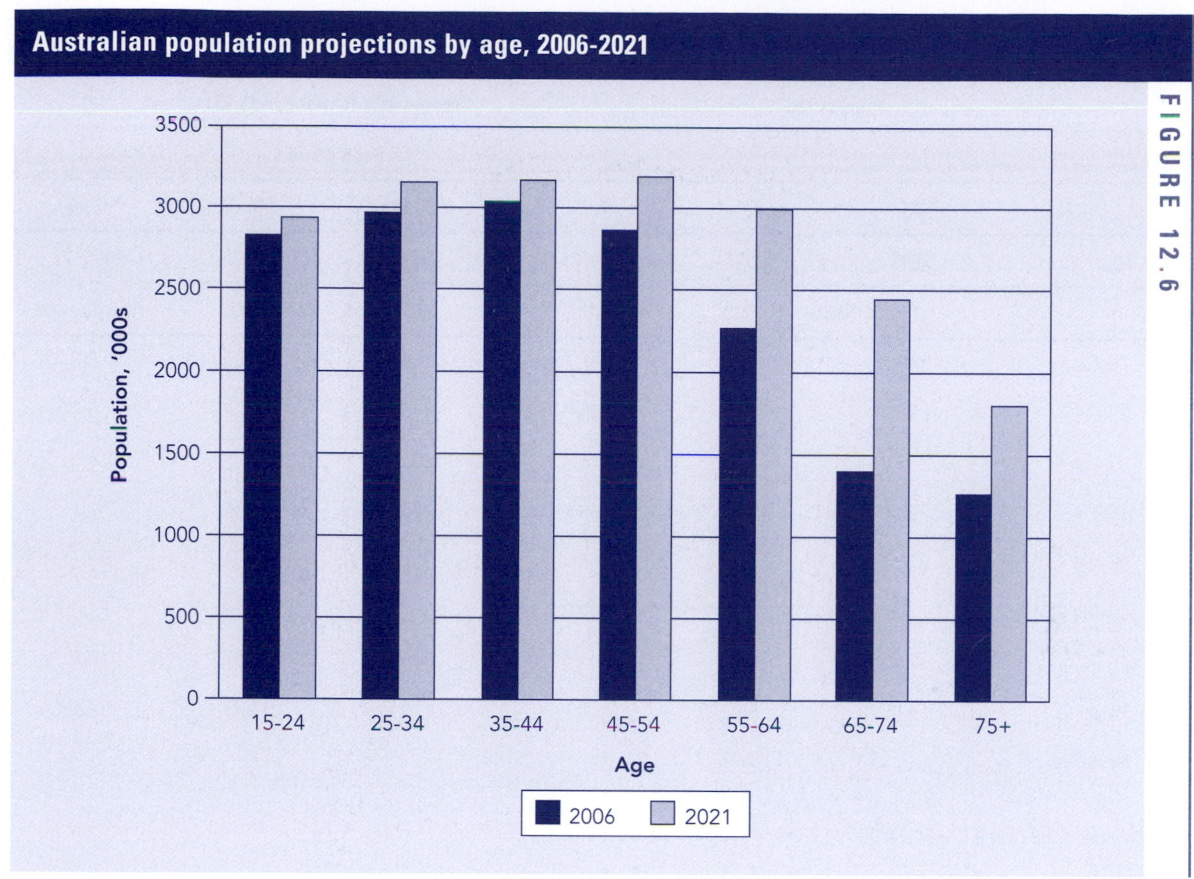

Source: ABS (2002a: 71)

Columns A and B of the table show the 2006 and 2021 population data. The latest available data on cinema attendances are shown in column C and it can be seen that attendance levels decline with age. Applying these percentage attendance rates to the population data gives estimates of attendances in 2006 and 2021. It can be seen that, whereas the population as a whole is expected to grow by 18.5 per cent, attendances at the cinema can be expected to grow by only 14 per cent. Moreover, while young people will continue to dominate cinema audiences, the bulk of the growth in attendance will come from those aged 55 and over. Of course, many other factors may affect cinema attendances in the intervening years: this is not, therefore a forecast, but simply an estimate of the likely effects of demographic trends on demand.

COMPANY ADVERTISING AND PRESS COVERAGE

In Carty's (1997) study of the advertising practices of Nike Corporation, as summarised in Case Study Example 9.1, she uses existing accounts of Nike's activities in the literature and the media to compile a case study of the company and its practices and pronouncements. In one sense the material analysed could be seen as *primary* data—in the way that historians or cultural studies analysts use such material—but in another sense, given that

FIGURE 12.7

Projecting cinema attendances, Australia, 2006–2021

	Population		Cinema attendances, age 15+			
				Projection		
	A*	B*	C**	D(CxA)	E(CxB)	F(E–D)
Age	2006	2021	2002	2006	2021	2006–21
	'000s		%***	'000s	'000s	% increase
15–24	2824	2932	92.1	2601	2700	3.8
25–34	2963	3151	81.0	2400	2552	6.3
35–44	3037	3167	76.7	2329	2429	4.3
45–54	2863	3192	69.9	2001	2231	11.5
55–64	2264	2992	56.7	1284	1696	32.2
65–74	1400	2442	44.2	619	1079	74.4
75+	1260	1801	31.1	391	558	42.9
Total	16 611	19 677		11 625	13 247	14.0
Increase		8.5%				

Sources: **ABS* (2002a); ***ABS* (2002b); *** % attending at least once in a year

the accounts were initially used to inform the public as part of current affairs coverage, it might be seen as *secondary* data.

THE LITERATURE: META-ANALYSIS

Meta-analysis is the process by which the findings of a comparatively large number of research projects on the same topic are reanalysed and reassessed: it can be seen as the equivalent of a quantified literature. Typically, the results of the studies reviewed are expressed in the form of a common statistic, such as a correlation coefficient or average score on a Likert-type scale. The meta-analysis then examines the variations in the values of the statistic in the various studies, whether the findings are similar or different, and if the latter, seeking explanations. Thorsteinson (2003), for example, examined 38 studies of the job attitudes of full-time and part-time workers, noting the possible implications of the issue for productivity, with increased levels of part-time working in Western economies. The 38 studies had combined samples of more than 51,000. While most of the studies included a 'job satisfaction' score, they varied in the number and types of other job attitude measures used, the gender of the samples and whether they were professional or non-professional. Overall, Thorsteinson concluded that the studies revealed no significant difference between full-time and part-time workers in regard to job satisfaction, organisational commitment, intention to leave and particular facets of the job.

Because of differences in sample size between studies and other differences in study design, achieving valid comparisons in meta-analysis can be a quite technical process and computer programs have been developed to assist in keeping track of study details and aiding with statistical processing and presentation (Beaubien 2003).

SUMMARY

This chapter builds on Chapter 5, which outlined the range of secondary data sources for business research, and considers ways in which such data might be analysed. This is demonstrated by examples, first, using data generated internally in an organisation, and second, data available from outside the organisation. Examples of use of internal data include: examination of trends over time in phenomena such as sales, particularly when data vary on a seasonal basis; the use of customer information to establish the catchment or market area of a service outlet; the use of employee records to examine the relationship between employee turnover and performance; and data-mining. Data-mining, in which organisations analyse computerised database information held on customers for marketing, customer risk analysis and fraud detection, is briefly reviewed. In the case of externally available data, two examples are given of the use of population census data: first, the examination of the characteristics of a catchment area population, and second, projection of future demand for a product or service using population projections. Use of company advertising and media coverage as data sources are also examined. Finally, meta-analysis—the reanalysis of the findings of comparatively large numbers of research projects on the same topic—is considered.

TEST QUESTIONS

1. Name three types of internal secondary data which might be used in business research.
2. What is a moving average?
3. What is a catchment area and how is knowledge of it useful in management?
4. What is data-mining?
5. Name one use of population census data in business research.
6. What is meta-analysis?

EXERCISES

1. Enter the data in column A of Figure 12.1 into a spreadsheet and replicate column B of Figure 12.1 and the diagram in Figure 12.2.
2. Assume that you have been asked to compare two areas for the siting of a new retail outlet aimed mainly at young people aged 18–29. The areas are two postcodes in contrasting parts of the city/area where you live. You should select the two areas for this exercise. Download data on the age structure of the two areas from the Australian Bureau of Statistics website (www.abs.gov.au) or similar in another country and indicate which will be the best location for the outlet.

3 Figure 12.7 presents a projection of cinema attendance for Australia in 2021. Using the same population projection data produce a similar projection for another of the activities in ABS (2002b) or another activity for which you can obtain age-related participation data.

FURTHER READING

Data-mining: General: Berry and Linoff (2004); Adriaans and Zantinge (1996); uses in banking and retailing: Hormozi and Giles (2004); Pyle (2003) and associated website: (www.modelandmine.com).

Meta-analysis: general: Glass *et al.* (1981); examples of studies: Brewer and Shapard (2004) on employee burnout; Daniel *et al.* (2004) on slack resources and firm performance; Garcia-Quevedo (2004) on public subsidies and business R&D complementarity; Thorsteinson (2003) on job attitudes of full-time and part-time workers; review of *Comprehensive Meta-Analysis* software package: Beaubien (2003).

CHAPTER 13

Survey analysis

This chapter introduces procedures for analysing questionnaire data from surveys. Survey research data is ideally suited to computer analysis because of the considerable amount of sorting of data, coding and statistical calculations which is typically involved in a survey-based management research project. The most widely used software for the analysis of survey data is the *Statistical Package for the Social Sciences* (*SPSS*). The chapter is organised around step-by-step procedures for using *SPSS for Windows* (Version 12) software. It is envisaged that the reader will have access to a computer with *SPSS for Windows* software available on it, so that the various procedures can be tried out in practice.

In this chapter four main analysis procedures are described:

- **Frequencies**, which involves counts and percentages of categories for individual variables;
- **Crosstabs**, which concerns the crosstabulation of two or more variables;
- **Means**, which involves obtaining means or averages of appropriate variables; and
- **Graphics**, which concerns the production of graphs and charts.

Further analysis procedures are covered in Chapter 14. The areas discussed here and in Chapter 14 are shown in Figure13.1.

FIGURE 13.1 Survey analysis overview

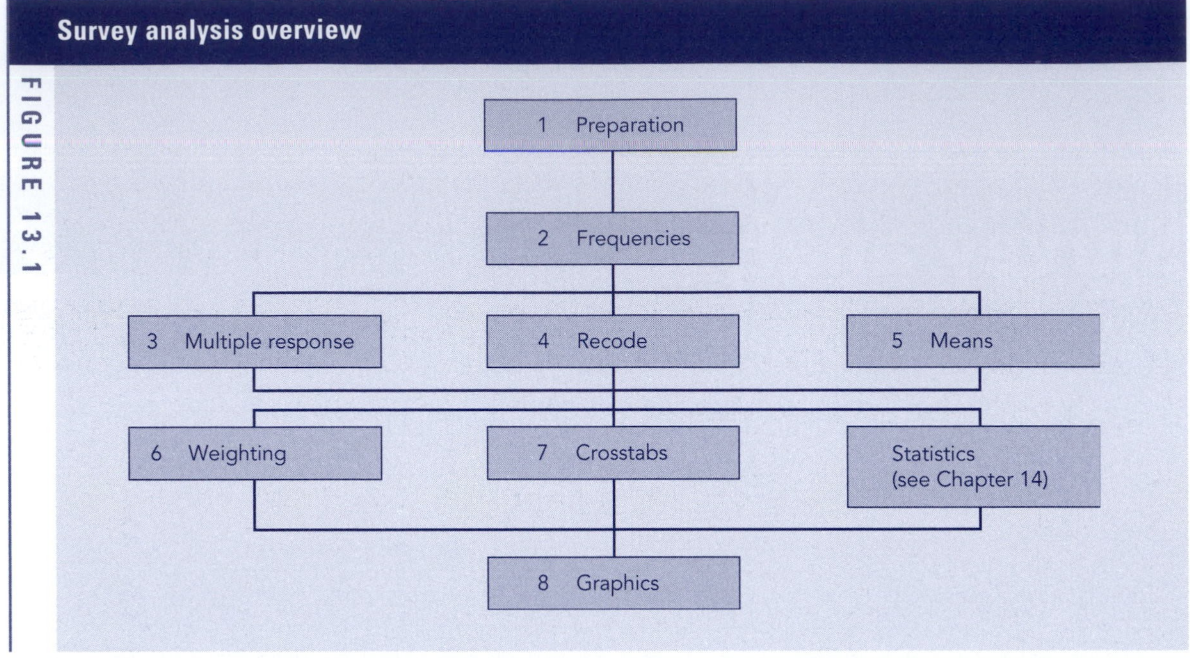

Although this chapter deals principally with the analysis of data from questionnaire surveys, *SPSS* can be used to analyse data from other sources as well. And it can be used in the analysis of numerical data and non-numerical data. Any data which are organised on the basis of *cases*, and a common range of *variables* for each case, can be analysed using the *SPSS* package (*cases* and *variables* are defined below). In this chapter and Chapters 15 and 16 text appearing in bold indicates options etc which appear on the screen.

INTRODUCTION TO SPSS

General

This chapter provides an introduction to the basics of *SPSS*. Further statistical analysis features of the package are outlined in Chapter 14. Additional capabilities of *SPSS* can be explored using *SPSS User Guides* held in most university libraries. Alternatively, *SPSS* has a step-by-step **Tutorial** facility and a **Statistics Coach** available under the *SPSS* **Help** menu. The *SPSS* homepage at (www.spss.com) can provide useful information on *SPSS* products and assistance. Further training in *SPSS* and other survey packages is available through universities, commercial computer training organisations and the *SPSS* company itself, located in major centres around the world.

The chapter does not deal with procedures for logging into a computer, file handling, or the installation of the *SPSS* software.

In higher education institutions *SPSS*, as with other computer packages, is often made available in computer laboratories on licence. A student version of *SPSS* is available which is less expensive than the full version described here, but it is restricted in the number of variables and procedures that it can handle. Versions of *SPSS* are also available for Macintosh computers and for mainframe computers. *SPSS* is one of the most commonly used statistical analysis packages; others include *Minitab*, *BMDP* (Biomedical Data package), *SAS* (Statistical Analysis System) and *Turbostats*.

Starting up

To start an *SPSS* session on a computer, activate the *SPSS* program by double clicking the mouse on the *SPSS* icon (or selecting *SPSS* from **Start** and **Programs**). You are presented with a blank **SPSS Variable View** window as shown in Figure 13.2 and a blank **SPSS Data View** window, as shown in Figure 13.3. These two windows provide the basis for *SPSS*

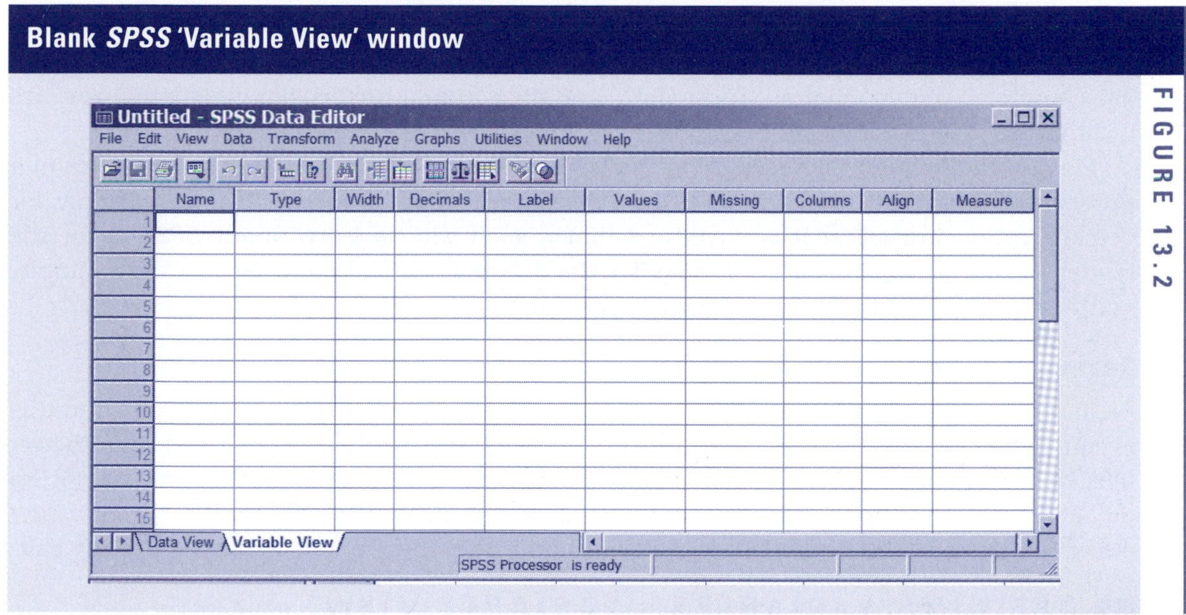

FIGURE 13.2 Blank *SPSS* 'Variable View' window

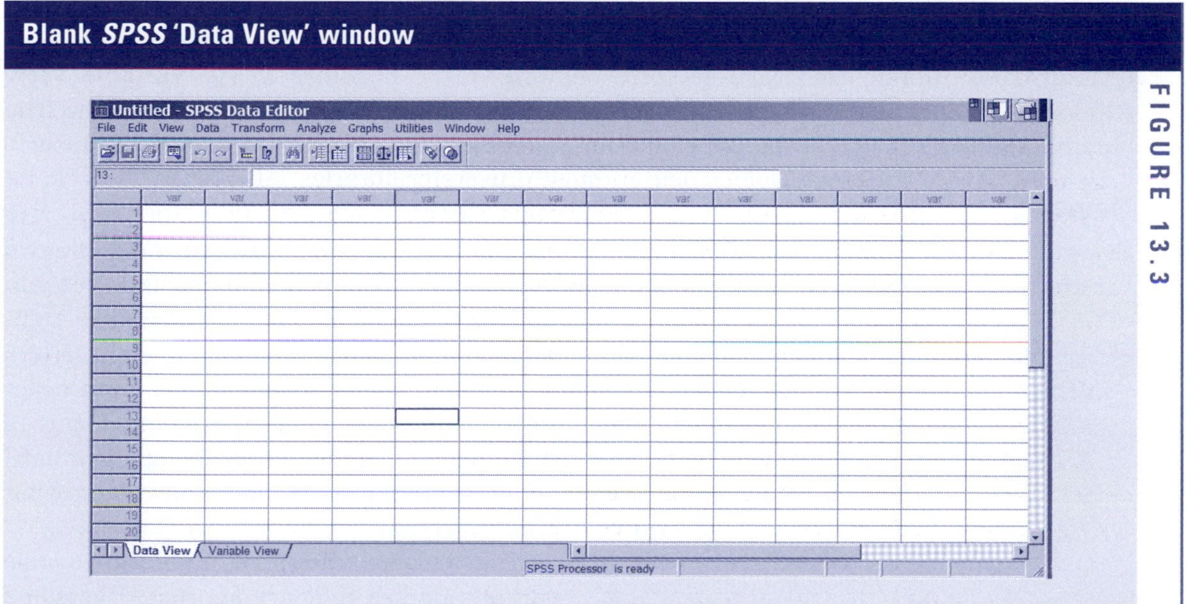

FIGURE 13.3 Blank *SPSS* 'Data View' window

analysis. You can toggle between the two windows using the tabs at the bottom of the screen. Switch to the 'Variable view' window to start.

Before analysis can begin:

- information about the questionnaire to be analysed must be entered into the **Variable View** window;
- data from the completed questionnaire must be entered in the **Data View** window.

These two processes form the basis for the outline of *SPSS* presented below.

Example data

The use of *SPSS* is demonstrated by using the example Training Survey questionnaire presented in Chapter 8 and Figure 8.10 (p. 165). Figure 8.11 (p. 166) presents data from five completed questionnaires. These data, and data from a further ten questionnaires, are used in the discussion below.

Most of the chapter is presented in the form of a short manual outlining the basics of a number of analytical procedures, using hypothetical data from the Training Survey for demonstration purposes. It is suggested that a good way to learn about *SPSS* is for the reader to run a live session of *SPSS*, enter the information and data used in the example, and replicate the procedures and results presented.

Saving your work

As in any computer work, it is of course wise to *save* your work to disk periodically and this is equally true of working with *SPSS*. In the same way that word processing and spreadsheet files have standard suffixes (eg .doc and .xls respectively for Microsoft Word and Excel), so do *SPSS* files. An *SPSS* datafile has the suffix **.sav**. A suitable filename for the example data set which will be used in the following discussion would therefore be **Training Survey.sav**.

DEFINING VARIABLES: 'VARIABLE VIEW'

The 'Office Use' column of Figure 8.10 is annotated with *variable names* for each item of information; these are reproduced in Figure 13.4, together with the an additional nine items of information about each variable corresponding to the headings in the **Variable View** window. This constitutes the information to be entered into the **Variable View** window. The variable name and each of the additional nine items of data are discussed in turn below.

Name

Every item of information, or *variable*, on the questionnaire is given a unique name (no two variables should have the same name). Variable names are typed into the first column in the window, as shown in Figure 13.5. A variable name can have up to eight letters or numbers with no spaces, and must begin with a letter. It is not permitted to use any of the variable names shown on the left, because *SPSS* already uses these names for other purposes.

Variable names disallowed by *SPSS*:

ALL	GT	OR
AND	LE	TO
BY	LT	WITH
EQ	NE	
GE	NOT	

The practice adopted here is to use variable names that are shortened versions

FIGURE 13.4 Variable names, labels and values

Question No.*	Name**	Type	Width**	Decimal places	Label	Values	Missing	Columns	Alignment	Measure/ Data type
–	qno	Numeric	4	0	Questionnaire number	None	None	4	Right	Scale
1	crse	Numeric	1	0	Course enrolled in	1 People Skills 2 Global Business 3 Strategic Management 4 Other	None	4	Right	Nominal
2	cp	Numeric	1	0	Used career planning/last 6 months	1 Yes 0 No	None	4	Right	Nominal
	ment	Numeric	1	0	Used mentoring/last 6 months	as above	None	4	Right	Nominal
	comp	Numeric	1	0	Used computer training/last 6 months	as above	None	4	Right	Nominal
	pa	Numeric	1	0	Used perf. appraisal/last 6 months	as above	None	4	Right	Nominal
3	rep	Numeric	1	0	Good reputation (rank importance)	None	None	4	Right	Ordinal
	access	Numeric	1	0	Easy access (rank importance)	None	None	4	Right	Ordinal
	curr	Numeric	1	0	Curriculum (rank importance)	None	None	4	Right	Ordinal
	fees	Numeric	1	0	Fees paid (rank importance)	None	None	4	Right	Ordinal
	park	Numeric	1	0	Easy parking (rank importance)	None	None	4	Right	Ordinal
4	cost	Numeric	4	0	Cost of books	None	None	4	Right	Scale
5	text	Numeric	1	0	Good textbook—importance	3 Very important 2 Important 1 Not at all important	None	4	Right	Scale
	lect	Numeric	1	0	Knowledgeable lecturer—importance	as above	None	4	Right	Scale
	assg	Numeric	1	0	Easy assignments—importance	as above	None	4		Scale
6	sug1	Numeric	1	0	Suggestions for improving course—1	1 Course content*** 2 Course structure 3 Delivery 4 Lecturer 5 Skills/ knowledge 6 Other	None	4	Right	Nominal
	sug2	Numeric	1	0	Suggestions for improving course—2	as above	None	4	Right	Nominal
	sug3	Numeric	1	0	Suggestions for improving course—3	as above	None	4	Right	Nominal

* From Figure 8.10 ** max. no. of characters *** See Figure 8.9 for derivation of coding system

FIGURE 13.5

Completed 'Variable View' window

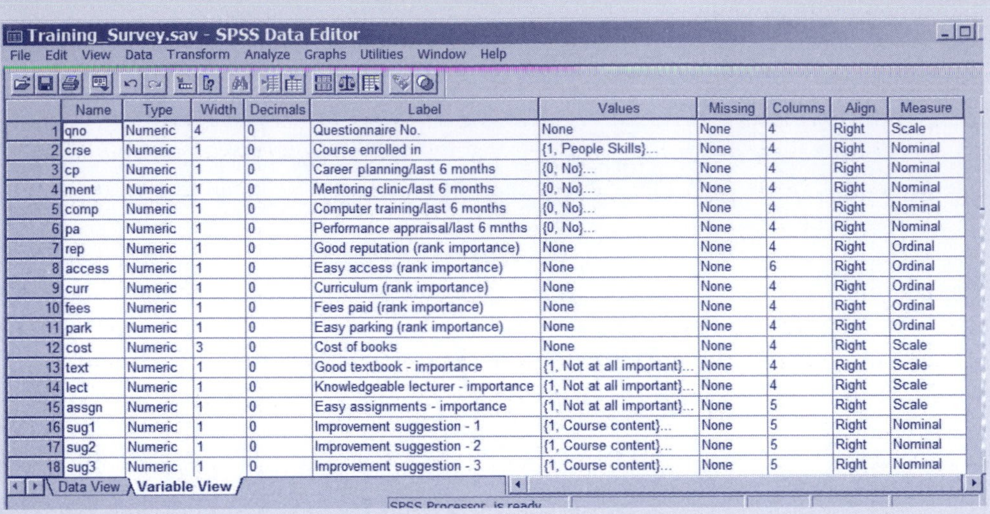

Training_Survey.sav - SPSS Data Editor

File Edit View Data Transform Analyze Graphs Utilities Window Help

	Name	Type	Width	Decimals	Label	Values	Missing	Columns	Align	Measure
1	qno	Numeric	4	0	Questionnaire No.	None	None	4	Right	Scale
2	crse	Numeric	1	0	Course enrolled in	{1, People Skills}...	None	4	Right	Nominal
3	cp	Numeric	1	0	Career planning/last 6 months	{0, No}...	None	4	Right	Nominal
4	ment	Numeric	1	0	Mentoring clinic/last 6 months	{0, No}...	None	4	Right	Nominal
5	comp	Numeric	1	0	Computer training/last 6 months	{0, No}...	None	4	Right	Nominal
6	pa	Numeric	1	0	Performance appraisal/last 6 mnths	{0, No}...	None	4	Right	Nominal
7	rep	Numeric	1	0	Good reputation (rank importance)	None	None	4	Right	Ordinal
8	access	Numeric	1	0	Easy access (rank importance)	None	None	6	Right	Ordinal
9	curr	Numeric	1	0	Curriculum (rank importance)	None	None	4	Right	Ordinal
10	fees	Numeric	1	0	Fees paid (rank importance)	None	None	4	Right	Ordinal
11	park	Numeric	1	0	Easy parking (rank importance)	None	None	4	Right	Ordinal
12	cost	Numeric	3	0	Cost of books	None	None	4	Right	Scale
13	text	Numeric	1	0	Good textbook - importance	{1, Not at all important}...	None	4	Right	Scale
14	lect	Numeric	1	0	Knowledgeable lecturer - importance	{1, Not at all important}...	None	4	Right	Scale
15	assgn	Numeric	1	0	Easy assignments - importance	{1, Not at all important}...	None	5	Right	Scale
16	sug1	Numeric	1	0	Improvement suggestion - 1	{1, Course content}...	None	5	Right	Nominal
17	sug2	Numeric	1	0	Improvement suggestion - 2	{1, Course content}...	None	5	Right	Nominal
18	sug3	Numeric	1	0	Improvement suggestion - 3	{1, Course content}...	None	5	Right	Nominal

Data View | Variable View

SPSS Processor is ready

of how the item might be described. For example, *crse* is used for 'course' and *ment* for 'mentoring clinic'. An alternative method of naming variables is to use a generalised name such as *var* for variable, so a questionnaire with five variables would have the variable names *var1*, *var2*, *var3*, *var4* and *var5*. In fact, *SPSS* has a system of default variable names already set up in this form, which can be used instead of customised variable names. A further alternative is to use question numbers for variable names or part of variable names—for example, q1, q2a, q2b, and so on. Whatever method is used, it is strongly recommended that a blank questionnaire that has been annotated with variable names be prepared for reference during the analysis process.

Type

SPSS requires the user to specify the variable *type*. All the variables in the Management Training Survey questionnaire are *numeric*, that is, they can only be numbers. A number of other possibilities exist, including *string*, which means text comprising any combination of letters and numbers, and *date*. A string variable might be used for textual information about, for example, an individual respondent's home location, such as a city or suburb, or the brand of a product used. However, coding of variables such as these saves time in data entry.

Width

Width specifies the maximum number of characters for a variable. In the Management Training Survey, all except two variables are single digit. The width of variable *qno* will depend on the size of the sample—here a width of four digits is specified, indicating a maximum sample size of 9999. The *cost* variable width has been put at three digits, suggesting maximum individual annual expenditure on books of $999—which should accommodate all respondents!

Decimals

This column specifies the number of decimal places included in a data item. None of the data in the example includes decimal places, so all entries are zero.

Label

The *variable label* is a longer version of the variable name that explains more fully what the variable name represents—for example, the variable name *crse* has a variable label *Training Course Attended.* The variable label is optional but, if provided, it is automatically included in any presentation of results.

Values

The *values* column contains information on each value which a variable can take and what each stands for. This is optional and is not required for numerical variables such as the questionnaire number *qno* and *cost.* The variable *crse*, for example, has the following values and value labels:

1 People Skills
2 Global Business
3 Strategic Management
4 Other

These are entered into the Variable View window by clicking on the shaded three dots to the right of the cell—a dialog box is presented in which each value and value label can be entered, followed by clicking 'add' and clicking 'OK' when complete. Where the same values/value labels apply to multiple variables, as in *cp, ment . . . pa,* the values/value label cell can be copied and pasted.

Variables based on question 3 consist of ranks from 1 to 5—they have therefore been specified as having no value labels. In fact, they could be given labels as follows: 1 = 'First', 2 = 'Second', 3 = 'Third', 4 = 'Fourth', 5 = 'Fifth'. The values/labels for the open-ended question 6 were derived as shown in Figure 8.9 (p. 164).

Missing

If a respondent does not answer a question in a questionnaire, the data entry space may be left blank, or a 'No answer' or 'Not applicable' code may be provided. In the analysis, as discussed later in the chapter, *SPSS* automatically treats a blank in the data as a *system missing value.* But 'No answer' and 'Not applicable' codes can be provided by the researcher and specified as *user missing values.* The implications are that *SPSS* excludes missing values when it is calculating means and percentages. In the Training Survey data set, the phenomenon of missing values becomes apparent in the case of variables *sug1, sug2* and *sug3,* since some respondents offer no suggestions at all, many offer only one and very few offer three, so there are usually numerous blanks in the data. It would be possible for non-use of services in question 2 to be left as a blank, giving rise to missing values, but in this case non-use has been coded as a zero. The *missing value* phenomenon is not pursued in great detail in this chapter but is apparent in a number of the outputs from *SPSS.*

Columns

The number of columns or digits per variable is a presentational matter concerning the layout of the **Data View** screen discussed below. A variable can be *displayed* with any number of columns regardless of the specified *width* of the underlying variable. In the Management Training Survey example, four columns are specified enabling all variables to be seen at once, on a typical computer screen.

Align

Align refers to the left/right alignment of the data in the **Data View** window and is also presentational. As in a spreadsheet, numerical data are easier to read if aligned to the right, while text is more suitably aligned to the left.

Measure

Data can be divided into three data types: *nominal*, *ordinal* and *scale*.

- *Nominal data* are made up of non-numerical *categories*, such as the course names in question 1 and 'Yes/No' in question 2 of the example questionnaire. While numerical codes are used for computer analysis, they have no numerical meaning. For example, code 2 is not 'half' of code 4—the codes could equally well be A and B or X and Y. It does not make sense, therefore, to calculate, for example, an average or mean of such codes.
- *Ordinal data* reflect a *ranking*, as in question 3 of the example questionnaire; the 1, 2, 3 in this question represent the *order of importance*, but rank 3 cannot be interpreted as being '3 times as high' as rank 1. It is, however, possible to calculate an average or mean rank—for example, to speak of an 'average ranking'.
- *Scale data* are fully numerical—as in question 4 of the example questionnaire. Numerical information, such as a person's age or expenditure, or a company's turnover, are *scale* data. In this case an answer of 4 *is* twice as high as an answer of 2 and averages or means are clearly appropriate.

The data type of a variable affects the range of statistical analysis which can be performed using the variable and the appropriate graphical presentation, as discussed in Chapter 14.

For the example questionnaire:

- *qno* is identified as a **scale** variable, although it will not be used in statistical analysis;
- variables *crse* and *sug1*, *sug2*, *sug3* from questions 2 and 6 are **nominal**;
- variables *rep* to *park* from question 3 are **ordinal**;
- the question 4 variable, *cost* is a **scale** variable;
- question 5 variables are 'Likert-style' variables, specified as **scale** variables for the reasons discussed below.

Variables arising from *Attitude/Likert variables* have been used extensively in psychological and market research and have come to be seen almost as **scale** variables when, strictly speaking, they are just ordinal. Means are an appropriate form of analysis when using such variables. The scores of 1 to 3 in question 5 in the example questionnaire can be treated as numerical indicators of the level of importance respondents attach to textbooks, the lecturer and ease of assignments. The means can be interpreted as average 'scores' on importance. It is possible to add scores in some circumstances.

DATA ENTRY

The actual data from a completed questionnaire survey can now be entered in the **Data View** window. Each line of data is called a *case* and corresponds to one completed questionnaire. Data from completed questionnaires, as shown for five questionnaires in Figure 8.10 (p. 165), can now be keyed in. The data from 15 sample questionnaires then appears as shown in Figure 13.6.

SURVEY ANALYSIS

Types of research and approaches to analysis

In Chapter 1 it was noted that research can be either descriptive, explanatory or evaluative. These types of research and their relationship to survey analysis using *SPSS* are discussed in turn below.

Descriptive research

Descriptive research usually involves the presentation of information in a fairly simple form. Of the *SPSS* procedures described in this chapter, the two most appropriate for descriptive research are **Frequencies** and **Means**. **Frequencies** presents counts and percentages for each variable. **Means** provides averages for numerical variables. **Frequencies** and **Means** are used if the aim of the research is simply 'finding out'.

Explanatory research

Presenting descriptive data does not *explain* anything. To explain the patterns in data we must consider the question of causality and how data analysis can address the issue of whether A is caused by B. *SPSS* lends itself particularly to establishing the *associations* between variables and their strength and size. The particular procedures that are appropriate for this are **Crosstabs** and **Regression**. The latter is discussed further in Chapter 14.

FIGURE 13.6 Data from fifteen questionnaires

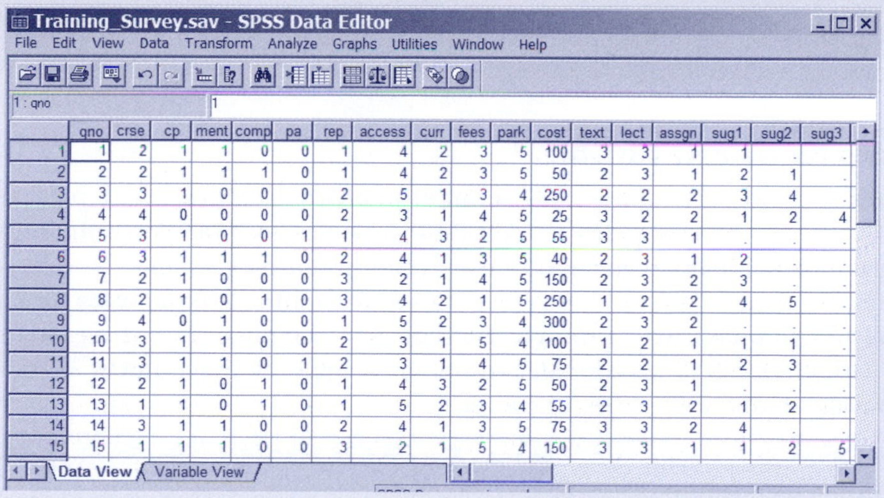

Training_Survey.sav - SPSS Data Editor

File Edit View Data Transform Analyze Graphs Utilities Window Help

1 : qno 1

	qno	crse	cp	ment	comp	pa	rep	access	curr	fees	park	cost	text	lect	assgn	sug1	sug2	sug3
1	1	2	1	1	0	0	1	4	2	3	5	100	3	3	1	1	.	.
2	2	2	1	1	1	0	1	4	2	3	5	50	2	3	1	2	1	.
3	3	3	1	0	0	0	2	5	1	3	4	250	2	2	2	3	4	.
4	4	4	0	0	0	0	2	3	1	4	5	25	3	2	2	1	2	4
5	5	3	1	0	0	1	1	4	3	2	5	55	3	3	1	.	.	.
6	6	3	1	1	1	0	2	4	1	3	5	40	2	3	1	2	.	.
7	7	2	1	0	0	0	3	2	1	4	5	150	2	3	2	3	.	.
8	8	2	1	0	1	0	3	4	2	1	5	250	1	2	2	4	5	.
9	9	4	0	1	0	0	1	5	2	3	4	300	2	3	2	.	.	.
10	10	3	1	1	0	0	2	3	1	5	4	100	1	2	1	1	1	.
11	11	3	1	1	0	1	2	3	1	4	5	75	2	2	1	2	3	.
12	12	2	1	0	1	0	1	4	3	2	5	50	2	3	1	.	.	.
13	13	1	1	0	1	0	1	5	2	3	4	55	2	3	2	1	2	.
14	14	3	1	1	0	0	2	4	1	3	5	75	3	3	2	4	.	.
15	15	1	1	1	0	0	3	2	1	5	4	150	3	3	1	1	2	5

Data View / Variable View

Evaluative research

Evaluative research basically involves comparisons. Are the survey findings higher or lower than some external benchmark? External benchmarks may take the form of established performance standards, comparisons with previous years' figures or comparisons with similar programs elsewhere. The analysis called for is therefore relatively simple and generally descriptive in nature. This kind of analysis is easily facilitated by *SPSS*.

Starting up

The data may already be on-screen if you have just completed typing in your data. If not, you need to open the data file, which can happen in one of two ways:

1 At start-up *SPSS* presents a dialog box which lists data files recently used from which the file of interest may be selected. Clicking on **More files ...** enables the user to browse the computer disks to locate the required file.

2 Select **File** from the menu bar.
- Select **Open**
- In the **Open File** dialog box, select **Files of Type** *SPSS (*.sav)* and then select the data file from the folder or disk drive where it was saved, for example, *Training Survey.sav*.

Basic analysis procedures used in most business/management research are examined in turn below:

Basic analyses:

- Frequencies for a single variable
- Frequencies for multiple variables
- Missing values
- Checking for errors
- Multiple response
- Recoding
- Means
- Attitude/Likert scales
- Presenting results
- Crosstabulation
- Weighting
- Graphics

Frequencies for a single variable

Frequencies is the simplest form of descriptive analysis. The procedure produces counts and percentages for the categories of individual variables—for instance, the numbers and percentages of respondents registered in each training course (*crse*).

It is advisable to begin the analysis of a data set by running **Frequencies** for one variable so that the program can read through the data and establish that there are no serious problems with the data. For example, to obtain a table of the number of management trainees enrolled in different types of course:

- Select **Analyze** from the menu bar, then **Descriptive Statistics**, then **Frequencies**. This opens the **Frequencies** dialog box.

- In the **Frequencies** dialog box select the variable of interest—*crse*—by highlighting it and then clicking on the **right arrow** box. This will transfer the variable *crse* to the **Variable(s)** box for analysis. Make sure that **Display frequency tables** in the dialog box is ticked.

- Select **OK** and the results will appear in the **Output1 SPSS Viewer** (referred to as the **Output** window below), as shown in Figure 13.7.

NB. The list of variables in the **Frequencies** dialog box can be in the form of variable *names* or the longer *variable labels*. You can change from one format to the other via **Edit, Options, Variable Lists.** Other changes to the format of output tables can also be made here.

The **Output** window presents two tables. The first, **Statistics**, indicates the number of 'valid cases' on which the analysis is based—in this case 15. The second table is headed *Course enrolled in* and shows:

- *Frequency* is a count of the numbers of respondents attending each course;
- *Percent* converts frequency numbers into percentages;
- *Valid Percent* is explained below under 'Missing values'; and
- *Cumulative Percent* adds percentages cumulatively, which may be useful for a variable like *expenditure* or *income*, but is not particularly useful for the variable *crse*.

Saving the output file to disk

- Select **File** from the menu bar, then select **Save**.

- In the **Save As** dialog box replace the default file name with a file name of your choice, for example, *trainee1.spo*, and save in an appropriate folder or disk.

SPSS output: frequencies, single variable

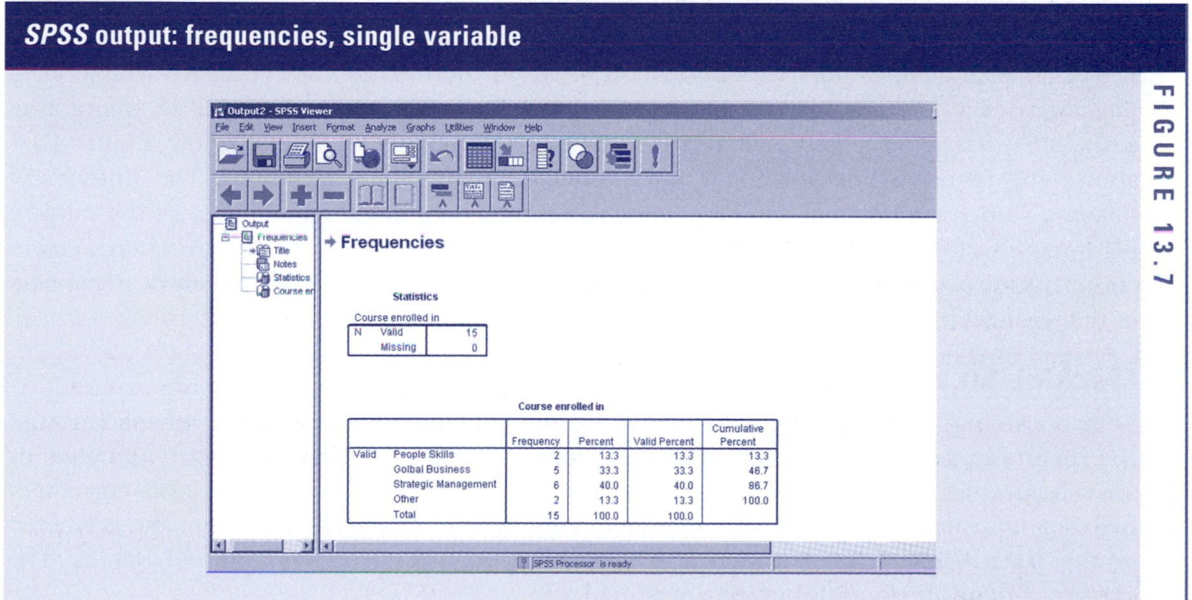

FIGURE 13.7

NB1. The format of the output shown in Figure 13.7 is not suitable for inclusion in a word processed research report. It must be saved as an html file *(*.htm)* or a text file *(*.txt)* using the **SPSS Export** command, which is found by selecting **File** on the menu bar. These html and text files can then be read by a word processing program for inclusion in a report. Alternatively, the output can be printed out and re-typed, or cut and pasted, for inclusion in tables as discussed in 'presenting results' below.

NB2. Results from any additional analyses are added to the bottom of results already in the **Output** window. It is possible to scroll up and down this output file and delete and edit sections as required. As with data files, you should save the output file frequently to avoid losing material in case of a computer failure.

Frequencies for multiple variables

If the single variable table has worked satisfactorily, frequency tables for all the variables can be obtained by the same procedure as above, but this time selecting all the variables in the dialog box (except *qno*). This runs frequency tables for all variables and is a common initial instruction in survey analysis. It is a good way of obtaining an overview of the results and checking that there are no incorrect values accidentally entered in the data file.

NB3. For reasons of space the output from this exercise is not reproduced here, but if the reader runs the procedure it will be seen that a considerable amount of output is produced. Dealing with this is discussed under 'Presenting results' below. Ways in which output from questions 2 and 6 can be better presented are discussed under 'Multiple response' below.

Missing values

As discussed above, blanks in the data are treated as *system missing values* and the researcher can specify *user missing values* for such things as 'no answer' or 'not applicable'. No *user missing values* are included in the Training Survey questionnaire, but cases of *system missing values* do arise in question 6. When there is no answer for a variable for a particular case—that is, when it has been left blank when entering data—*SPSS* treats it as a *system missing value* and indicates it as a full stop in the *Data View* window. Figure 13.8 shows the results from running **Frequencies** for *sug1*, *sug2* and *sug3*. The number of missing values is shown in the *Frequency* column next to the label *Missing*. In the *Percent* column, missing values are included in the overall percentage, but in the *Valid Percent* column they are excluded. In any particular situation, the question of which of these sets of percentages to use is a matter of judgement.

Checking for errors

After obtaining the **Frequencies** print-out for all variables it is necessary to check through the results to see if there are any errors. Errors can be in the form of a non-valid code or an unexpected missing value. The error must be traced in the data file and corrected, perhaps by reference back to the original questionnaire. The data must then be corrected in the **Data View** window and the **Frequencies** table for that variable run again. The corrected data file should then be saved to disk.

FIGURE 13.8

SPSS output: frequencies with system missing values

Statistics

		SUG1 Improvement suggestion—1	SUG2 Improvement Suggestion—2	SUG3 Improvement Suggestion—3
N	Value	12	8	2
	Missing	3	7	13

SUG1 Improvement suggestion—1

		Frequency	Percent	Valid Percent	Cumulative Percent
Valid	Course content	5	33.3	41.7	41.7
	Course structure	3	22.0	25.0	66.7
	Delivery/organisation	2	13.3	16.7	83.3
	Lecturer	2	13.3	16.7	100.0
	Total	12	80.0	100.0	
Missing	System	3	20.0		
Total		15	100.0		

SUG2 Improvement suggestion—2

		Frequency	Percent	Valid Percent	Cumulative Percent
Valid	Course content	2	13.3	25.0	25.0
	Course structure	3	20.0	37.5	62.5
	Delivery/organisation	1	6.7	12.5	75.0
	Lecturer	1	6.7	12.5	87.5
	Skills/knowledge	1	6.7	12.5	100.0
	Total	8	53.3	100.0	
Missing	System	7	56.7		
Total		15	100.0		

SUG2 Improvement suggestion—3

		Frequency	Percent	Valid Percent	Cumulative Percent
Valid	Lecturer	1	6.7	50.0	50.0
	Skills/knowledge	1	6.7	50.0	100.0
	Total	2	13.3	100.0	
Missing	System	13	86.7		
Total		15	100.0		

Multiple response

Note that questions 2 and 6 in Figure 8.10 are *multiple response* questions, since respondents can provide more than one answer to the question.

Question 2 is a *multiple response, dichotomous (two values only)* variable, because each answer category is essentially a yes/no variable. One respondent could tick all four boxes, so each of the four responses needs to be a separate variable. **Frequencies** produces four separate tables of results.

Question 6 is a *multiple response, categories* variable. Three variables are assigned, *sug1*, *sug2* and *sug3*, so that up to three answers can be recorded. Not all respondents will give three answers, as demonstrated above. Some may give more than three answers, in which case it would not be possible to record the fourth or any subsequent answers. If more than a handful of respondents record more than three answers, a fourth variable (*sug4*) should be added. The decision as to how many answers should be anticipated depends on prior examination of the survey returns. **Frequencies** produces three separate tables of results, as demonstrated above.

SPSS can combine multiple response variables into one frequencies table. To prepare a multiple response frequencies table it is first necessary to define a *multiple response set*. Two procedures are required, one for the *dichotomous* type and one for the *categories* type.

Multiple response—categories type

In the case of question 6, variables *sug1, sug2 and sug3*, a multiple response set can be defined as follows:

- Select **Analyze** from the menu bar, then **Multiple Response**.
- Select **Define Sets** to open the **Define Multiple Response Sets** dialog box.
- Define the multiple response set by highlighting *sug1, sug2* and *sug3* in the **Set Definition** box and clicking on the right arrow box to transfer the selected variables to the **Variables in Set** box.
- Select the **Categories** button and enter the range of values used to define the categories of this set, in this case: 1 through 6—at this stage the dialog box should appear as in Figure 13.9.
- Enter a suitable **Name** for the multiple response set, in this case *suggest,* and a Variable **Label**, in this case *Suggestions for Improving Training.*
- Click **Add** and the new multiple response variable, *$suggest* appears in the **Multiple Response Sets** box.
- **Close** the **Define Multiple Response Sets** dialog box.

A multiple response set has now been defined. It is now possible to prepare a frequencies table for the variable *$suggest* as follows.

Define Multiple Response Sets dialog box

FIGURE 13.9

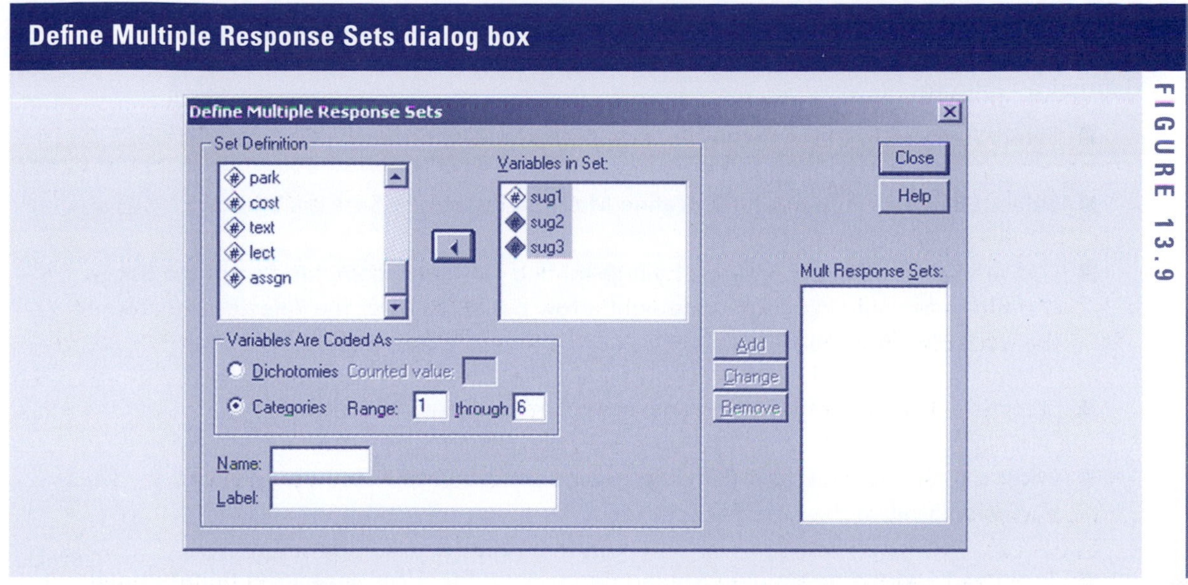

- Select **Analyze** from the menu bar, then **Multiple Response,** then **Frequencies**.
- In the **Frequencies** dialog box move *$suggest* into the right hand box
- Click **OK** to generate a Multiple Response output file as shown in Figure 13.10.

The output shows two sets of percentages—one relating to the number of valid cases (12) and one to the total number of responses (22). The choice of which to use is a matter of judgement, depending on the purpose of the analysis.

SPSS output: Multiple Response—categories

FIGURE 13.10

Group $suggest Suggestions for Improving Training

Category label	Code	Count	Pct of responses	Pct of cases
Course content	1	7	31.8	58.3
Course structure	2	6	27.3	50.0
Delivery/organisation	3	3	13.6	25.0
Lecturer	4	4	18.2	33.3
Skills/knowledge	5	2	9.1	16.7
		22	100.0	183.3

3 missing cases 12 valid cases

Multiple response—dichotomous type

In the case of question 2 variables, *cp, ment, comp* and *pa*, a multiple response set can be defined as follows:

- Select **Analyze** from the menu bar, then **Multiple Response**.
- Select **Define Sets** to open the **Define Multiple Response Sets** dialog box.
- Define the multiple response set by highlighting *cp, ment, comp* and *pa* in the **Set Definition** box and clicking on the right arrow box to transfer the selected variables to the **Variables in Set** box.
- Select the **Dichotomous** button and enter 1 in the **Counted values** box.
- Enter a suitable **Name** for the multiple response set, in this case *services,* and a **Variable Label**, in this case *Services used.*
- Click **Add** and the new multiple response variable, *$services* appears in the **Multiple Response Sets** box.
- **Close** the **Define Multiple Response Sets** dialog box.

A multiple response table for *$services* can now be produced in the same way as for the categories type outlined above. This produces a table as shown in Figure 13.11.

Recoding

As the name implies, **Recode** is a procedure that can be used to change the codes of variables. This applies particularly to numerical variables, such as *cost* in the Training Survey questionnaire. This is a numerical variable that is not 'pre-coded'—the actual expenditure was recorded on the questionnaire rather than a categorical code. The advantage of not having the variable pre-coded is that it is possible to be flexible about what groupings are required. It is also possible, as shown below, to use procedures such as **Means** to find an average cost. This is generally not possible with pre-coded variables.

FIGURE 13.11

***SPSS* output: Multiple Response—dichotomous**

Group $service Services used (Value tabulated = 1)

Dichotomy label	Name	Count	Pct of Responses	Pct of Cases
Career planning/last 6 months	cp	13	46.4	92.9
Mentoring clinic/last 6 months	ment	8	28.6	57.1
Computer training/last 6 months	comp	5	17.9	35.7
Performance appraisal/last 6 months	pa	2	7.1	14.3
Total responses		**28**	**100.0**	**200.0**

1 missing cases; 14 valid cases

However, because *cost* is not pre-coded, the **Frequencies** output lists every single level of expenditure given by respondents. This can become unmanageable, especially in large surveys with hundreds of respondents, and can make a procedure such as **crosstabulation** particularly difficult.

A *Recoded* and grouped version of the expenditure variable can be produced using the following *SPSS* procedure.

- Select **Transform** from the menu bar, then **Recode**, then **Into Different Variables**. The **Recode into Different Variables** dialog box will appear.
- Select *cost* and click the **right arrow** to move it into the **Numeric Variable->Output Variable** box.
- Enter the name and label for the new recoded variable, *costr*, and label *Cost Recoded*, in the **Output Variable** box, then click **Change**—see Figure 13.12.
- To specify the groups for *costr*, select **Old and New Values**, then the **Recode into Different Variables: Old and New Values** dialog box will appear.
- To recode the first range of values, *0-50*, select **Range** and enter the values *1* and *50* in the highlighted spaces.
- In the **New Value** box click on the **Value** button and enter the recoded value *1* into the highlighted space.
- Click on **Add** in the **Old->New** box and the recode equation will appear.
- Repeat these steps to recode the values *51-100*, *101-200*, and *201 thru highest* into *2*, *3* and *4* respectively: the dialog box will appear as shown in Figure 13.13.
- Click on **Continue** to return to the **Recode into Different Variables** dialog box.
- Click on **OK** to complete the recoding procedure. The recoded variable, *costr*, will now appear in the ***SPSS* Data View** window as an extra column and in the lists of variables.
- *Value labels* can be added to the recoded variable via the **View Variables** window.
- The file should be saved (**Ctrl + S**) to save the recoded variable for use in later analyses.
- Produce frequencies table for *costr* in the usual way, resulting in a table as shown in Figure 13.14.

FIGURE 13.12 ***SPSS* Recode dialog box**

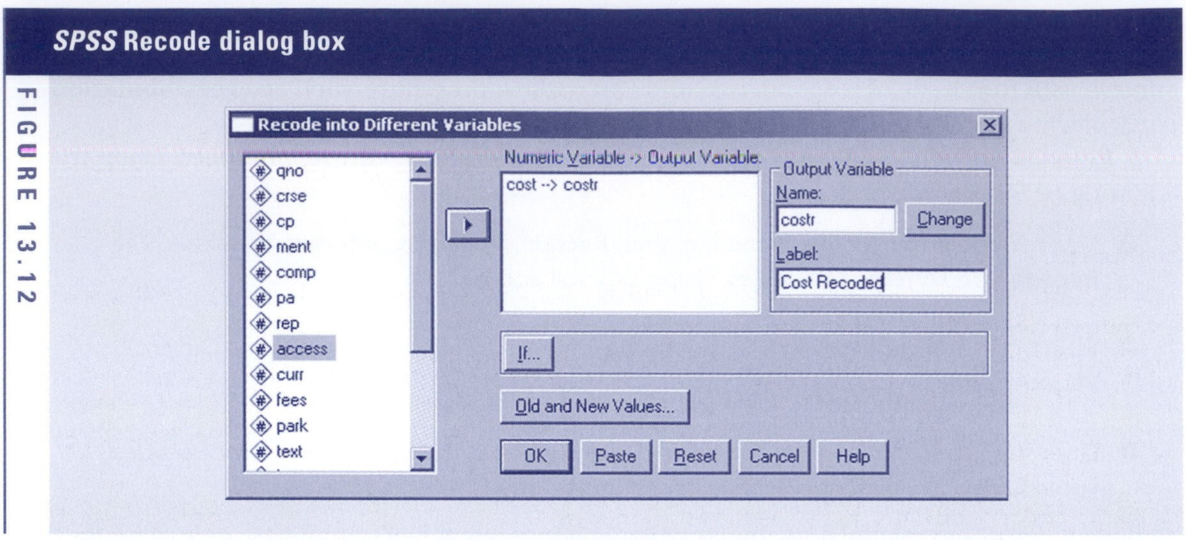

FIGURE 13.13 ***SPSS* 'Recode into Different Variables; Old and New Values' dialog box**

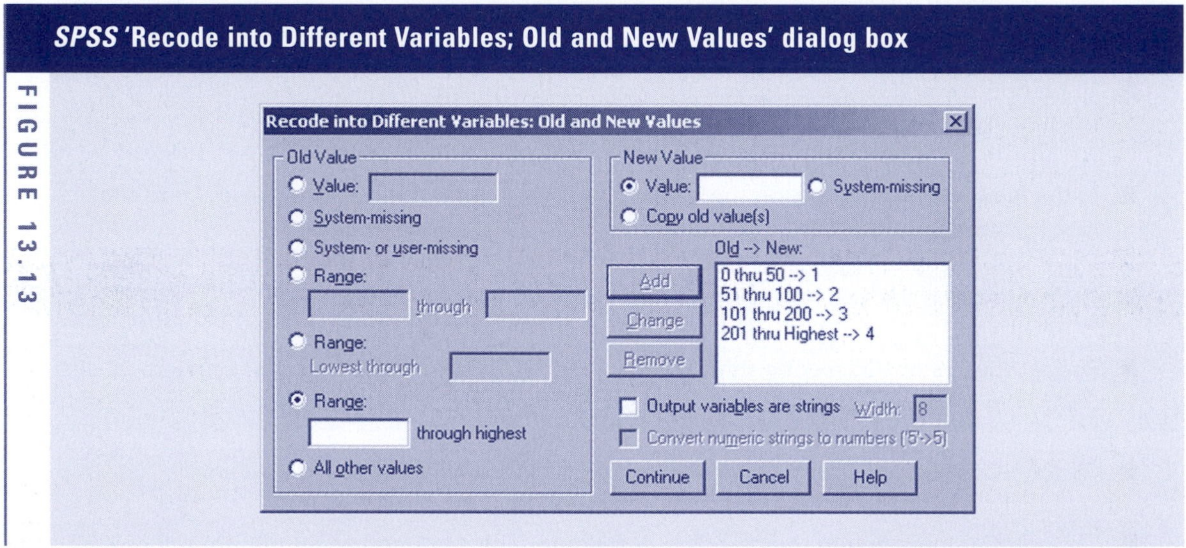

FIGURE 13.14 ***SPSS* output: recode of cost**

		Frequency	Percent	Value Percent	Cumulative Percent
Valid	Up to $50	4	26.7	26.7	26.7
	$51–100	6	40.0	40.0	66.7
	$101–200	2	13.3	13.3	80.0
	4.00	3	20.0	20.0	
Total		15	100.0	100.0	

Means

A *mean* is the same as an average. It is often useful to be able to produce means in the analysis of a survey, for instance mean ages, incomes or time spent. Means can only be produced for numerical data (scale and ordinal). Means *should not* be produced for coded variables where the codes represent qualitative categories and not quantities, that is, where the variables type is *nominal*.

Simple means

The simplest method of finding the mean value for a variable using *SPSS* is by adding it to a **Frequencies** table, as follows:

- Select **Analyze** from the menu bar, then **Descriptives Statistics**, then **Frequencies**.
- Select *cost* and transfer to the **Variable(s)** box.
- Select **Statistics** and then **Mean**, then **Continue**
- Click on **OK** button to produce a **Frequencies** table in the usual way—in addition to the **Frequencies** table the mean of $115 will be given as shown in Figure 13.15.

NB. Depending on the options chosen, other statistics such as minimum and maximum values, and standard deviations, can also be produced by this procedure.

FIGURE 13.15 ***SPSS* output: mean book costs**

COST Cost of books

N	Valid	15
	Missing	0
Mean		115.0

Comparing means

It is also possible to compare means across a range of categories of a selected variable, or groups of respondents. For example, the average cost of books can be found for respondents on each of the training courses available. This can be achieved by the following procedure:

- Select **Analyze** from the menu bar, then **Compare Means**, then **Means**.
- In the **Means** dialog box highlight the variable *cost* and move it into the **Dependent List**.
- Move *crse* into the **Independent List** box.

- Click on **OK** and the means of *cost* for each category of *crse* will appear as output, as Figure 13.16.

NB. Note that this analysis moves into the area of *explanation*, since it reveals that different courses lead to different levels of expenditure.

FIGURE 13.16

***SPSS* output: compare means—mean book costs by courses**

COST Cost of books

CRSE Course enrolled in	**Mean**	**N**	**Std. Deviaiton**
People Skills	102.00	2	67.175
Global Business	120.00	5	83.666
Strategic Management	99.17	6	76.643
Other	162.50	2	194.454
Total	115.00	15	87.076

Attitude/Likert scales

Means are an appropriate form of analysis when using attitude statements or 'Likert'-type scales. The values 1 to 3 in the question 5 variables, *text, lect, assg* can be treated as numerical indicators of the level of importance respondents attach to textbooks, the lecturer and ease of assignments.

For example, running the **Means** procedure for these three variables produces:

- *text* (good textbook): Mean score: 2.2
- *lect* (knowledgeable lecturer) Mean score: 2.7
- *assgn* (easy assignments) Mean score: 1.5

The means can be interpreted as *scores* on *importance*. In the example a knowledgeable lecturer is seen as the most important, followed by the textbook and then ease of assignments, which is seen as not so important. Further discussion of such scales and how they might be presented is included below.

Presenting the results: statistical summaries

The layout of the tables produced by *SPSS* contains more detail than is necessary for most reports. It is recommended that a *Statistical summary* be prepared for inclusion in any report, rather than include a copy of the *SPSS* printout. The summary must be prepared with a word processor, either by typing it out afresh or editing the saved *SPSS* output file. The output from a **Frequencies** analysis for all variables could be summarised as shown in Figure 13.17.

It should be noted in Figure 13.17 that:

- the results from multiple response variables are presented in single tables;

Statistical summary

FIGURE 13.17

Statistical Summary: Management Training Survey 2003

Sample size	15
Training course attended	**%**
People Skills	13.3
Global Business	33.3
Strategic Management	40.0
Other	13.3
Staff development services used in the last six months	**%**
Career planning	86.7
Mentoring clinic	53.3
Computer training	33.3
Performance appraisal	13.3
Importance of factors in choosing a training course	
	Average Rank
Good reputation	1.8
Easy access	3.7
Curriculum	1.6
Management pays fees	3.2
Easy parking	4.7
Cost of books for the training course	**%**
$0–50	26.7
$51–100	40.0
$100–200	13.3
Over $200	20.0
Average cost	$115

Importance of factors in studying

	Very important %	Important %	Not important %	Mean score*
Good textbook	33.3	53.3	13.3	2.2
Knowledgeable lecturer	66.7	33.3	0.0	2.7
Easy assignments	0.0	46.7	53.3	1.5

*3 = very important, 2 = important, 1 = not important

Suggestions for improving the training course

	%
Comments on course contents	58.3
Comments on course structure	50.0
Comments on course delivery	25.0
Comments on lecturer	33.3
Comments on skills learned	16.7

- the average cost and the scores for the attitude variables come from the **Means** procedure discussed above; and
- it is generally not necessary to include actual frequency counts as well as percentages in reports, as long as the sample size is indicated, so that, if needed, readers of the table could work out the raw numbers for themselves.

Crosstabulation

Crosstabs is probably the most commonly used *SPSS* command after **Frequencies** and **Means**. The **Crosstabs** procedure compares two or more variables by forming a two-way table, with the categories of each variable forming the vertical and horizontal sides of the table. An example of a crosstabulation table comparing the variables *crse* (Training Course Attended) and *comp* (Computer Training) is shown in Figure 13.18.

The following *SPSS* **Crosstabs** procedure was used to prepare this table.

- Select **Analyze** from the menu bar, then **Descriptive Statistics,** then **Crosstabs**.

- In the **Crosstabs** dialog box move *crse* into the **Row(s)** box and move *comp* into the **Column(s)** box.

- Click on the **OK** button and the required crosstabulation table will appear in the **Output** window, as shown in Figure 13.18.

This crosstabs analysis marks a move from purely descriptive to explanatory analysis. For example, examination of the crosstabulation table suggests that people who attended the Strategic Management training course were less likely to have taken a Computer Training course (in the ratio 5:1) than people who attended the other two courses (ratios of 1:1 and 2:3). Of course this simple observation would need further investigation before any firm conclusions could be drawn.

Use of the optional **Statistics** and **Cells** buttons in the **Crosstabs** dialog box allows the production of more informative crosstabulation tables showing percentage breakdowns in each cell, the observed and expected counts in each cell and the correlations between variables. Figure 13.19 shows the same table with *row percentages*.

FIGURE 13.18

***SPSS* output: Crosstabulation**

CRSE Course enrolled in * COMP Computer training/last 6 months Crosstabulation

Count		**COMP Computer training/last 6 monhths**		**Total**
		No	**Yes**	
CRSE Course enrolled in	People Skills	1	1	2
	Global Business	2	3	5
	Strategic Management	5	1	6
	Other	2	0	2
Total		10	5	15

SPSS output: Crosstabs with row percentages

CRSE Course enrolled in *COMP Computer training/last 6 months Crosstabulation

% within CRSE Course enrolled in		COMP Computer training/last 6 months		Total
		No	Yes	
CRSE Course enrolled in	People Skills	50.0%	50.0%	100.0%
	Global Business	40.0%	60.0%	100.0%
	Strategic Management	83.3%	16.7%	100.0%
	Other	100.0%		100.0%
Total		66.7%	33.3%	100.0%

FIGURE 13.19

Weighting

The weighting of data to correct for biased samples was discussed in Chapter 11. The simplest way of introducing a weighting factor into an *SPSS* analysis is to add the factor to the data file as an additional variable. For example, the 'weighting' variable might be called *wt* and the weights entered into the data file like any other item of data. Weighted frequency and crosstabulation tables can then be produced using the weighting procedure.

Suppose in the Training Survey it was known from the course records that the sample of 15, to be representative, should have been as shown in Figure 13.20.

To perform the weighting a new variable, *wf*, is added to the *SPSS* file via the *Variable View* and the Weighting Factors shown in Figure 13.20 are entered into the data file via the **Data View**. Thus, for example, for the two attendees at the 'People Skills' course, a value of 2.5 is entered for the new variable *wf*. The *SPSS Weighting* procedure is then conducted as follows:

- Select **Data** from the menu bar, then select **Weight Cases**.
- In the **Weight Cases** dialog box select **Weight case by** and move the *wt* variable to the **Frequency Variable** box.
- Clicking **OK** and a **Weight On** sign will now appear in the information bar along the bottom of the **Data View** window.
- If any procedure is now run, the results will be weighted. Figure 13.21 shows the *Frequencies* for *crse* now with the correct, weighted, sample distribution.
- Weighting can be turned *off* in the **Weight Cases** dialog box by selecting **Do not weight cases.**

Weighting may or may not make a difference to the rest of the results. In this case it does. For example, running **Means** for the cost of books produces a mean expenditure level of $112.91, compared with the former unweighted value of $115, reflecting the fact that

FIGURE 13.20

Sample weighting

Course	Actual N	Correct N	Weighting factor
	A	B	(B/A)
People Skills	2	5	2.50
Global Business	5	3	0.60
Strategic Management	6	5	0.83
Other	2	2	1.00
Total	15	15	

FIGURE 13.21

***SPSS* output: Weighted frequencies table**

CRSE Course enrolled in		Frequency	Percent	Valid Percent	Cumulative Percent
Valid	People Skills	5	33.4	33.4	33.4
	Global Business	3	20.0	20.0	53.4
	Strategic Management	5	33.2	33.2	86.6
	Other	2	13.4	13.4	100.0
	Total	15	100.0	100.0	

the 'People Skills' attendees, who were weighted heavily, spend less on books than do the others, which was shown in Figure 13.16.

Graphics

Graphical presentation of data is generally considered to be an aid to communication. Most people can see trends and patterns more easily in graphic form. The following graphics are the most common formats:

- bar graph (or histogram);
- stacked bar graph;
- pie chart; and
- line graph.

Most software packages will produce the four formats from any one set of data, but all formats are not equally appropriate for all types of data. The most suitable type of graphic depends on the type of data or level of measurement involved. As discussed under Data Entry above, data can be nominal, ordinal or scale data.

Types of graphs

The three data types lend themselves to different graphical treatment. The relationships between these types of data and permitted graphical types are summarised in Figure 13.22.

- The *bar graph* or *histogram* is perhaps the most commonly used in management research. Since it deals with categories, any numerical or ratio variable must first be divided into groups as was done in the *recoding* of the *cost* variable above.
- *Stacked bar graphs* can include information on two or more variables rather than one. They are the graphical equivalent of crosstabulation.
- The *pie chart* is just that—it divides something into sections like a pie. The categories making up the pie chart must therefore add up to some sort of meaningful total, often the total sample or 100 per cent.
- The *line graph* is the most constrained in its usage and is used more generally in research in quantified fields such as economics and operations management. The line graph relates two scale variables and the scales on both axes are generally continuous scale numbers. Examples are shown in Chapter 14, p. 281.

Graphics can be produced by *SPSS* in the following way:

- Select the **Graphs** option from the menu bar, then select the kind of graphic to be produced from the **Graphs** menu.
- Specify the variables required in the relevant dialog box. Click on the **OK** button.
- The graphic is presented in the *SPSS* **Output** window.

Some examples of graphics output from *SPSS* are shown in Figure 13.23. The data in the Training Survey do not lend themselves very readily to presentation in line graph form, so this is illustrated in Chapter 14, where more quantified data are introduced.

THE ANALYSIS PROCESS

The above is only a brief introduction to the mechanics of survey data analysis. While *SPSS* is capable of much more sophisticated analyses, mastery of the procedures presented here can provide a sound basis for more ambitious programs of analysis.

Data types and graphics

Data type	Characteristics	Example questions in Figure 8.10	Mean/average possible?	Types of graphic		
				Bar gragh	Pie chart	Line graph
Nominal	Qualitative categories	1, 2, 6	No	Yes	Yes	No
Ordinal	Ranks/Likert-type scale	3, 5	Yes	Yes	Yes	No
Ratio	Numerical	4	Yes	Yes (grouped)	Yes (grouped)	Yes

FIGURE 13.22

FIGURE 13.23

SPSS output: graphs

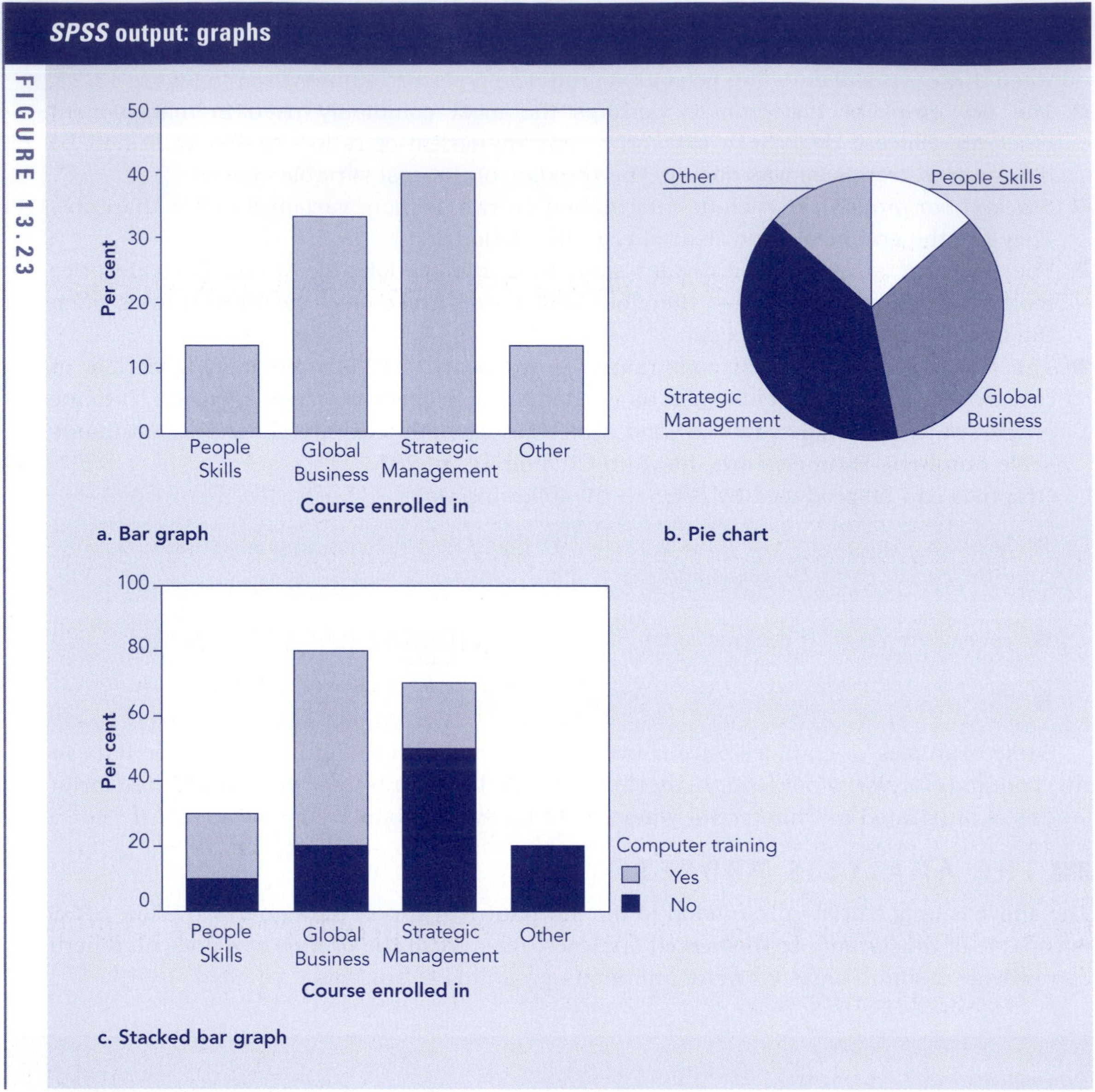

SUMMARY

This chapter introduced procedures for analysing questionnaire survey data. Survey data is ideally suited to computer-based analysis because of the large amount of data consolidation and analysis that is typically involved in the analysis of a survey. Consequently, this chapter detailed procedures for using the *Statistical Package for the Social Sciences* (*SPSS*). Before *SPSS* analysis can proceed, an *SPSS* data file needs to be prepared from the survey data. This involves the *naming* and *labelling* of variables, management of *multiple response* questions, data entry and saving the *SPSS* data file to disk.

Four main *SPSS* analysis procedures are outlined in the chapter, namely *Frequencies, Crosstabs, Means* and *Graphs*. These analyses involve a number of procedures, including selection and definition of the desired analysis by the researcher, management of *missing values, recoding* variables, *weighting* selected variables and saving the results of the analysis to an *SPSS* output file. Mastery of these procedures should equip the researcher to conduct a typical questionnaire survey analysis which does not require statistical tests—the latter are dealt with in Chapter 14.

EXERCISES

The exercises all relate to the Training Survey data shown in Figure 13.6 (p. 233).

1 Replicate the Training Survey *SPSS* data file used in this chapter and save it with the file name *exercise.sav*.

2 Prepare a breakdown of the categories of each variable in the *exercise.sav* file using the *SPSS* **Frequencies** procedure. Examine the output for each variable to find any values that were entered in error on the data file. If you find any errors, correct the *exercise.sav* file and again run the **Frequencies** procedure to check for errors.

3 Use the **Multiple Response** procedure to prepare a frequencies table for the Staff Development services used in the last six months as outlined in question 2. Include variable labels and value labels as appropriate.

4 Use the **Crosstabs** procedure to prepare a crosstabulation table for question 1, *Training Course Attending* with question 3c *Curriculum*. What can you conclude about the importance of curriculum in choosing a course and attendance at the Strategic Management training course?

5 Use the **Graphs** procedure to prepare a bar graph concerning the importance of management paying fees (question 3d) in choosing a training course. Prepare a pie chart concerning the importance of easy access (question 3b) in choosing a training course.

FURTHER READING

Use of SPSS in social research: Babbie and Halley (1995); Francis (1996); Gerber and Voelkl (1997); Coakes and Steed (1997) or Green, Salkind and Akey (1997); George and Mallery (1995).

CHAPTER 14

Statistical analysis

This chapter provides an introduction to statistics, building on the outline of sampling theory in Chapter 11 and the introduction to the *SPSS* package in Chapter 13. The chapter is introductory and is not intended to be a complete course in statistics. There are many textbooks covering the same ground as covered here, but in more detail and more depth, and reference to some of these is given in the Further Reading section. After dealing with some general concepts related to the statistical method, the chapter covers: the Chi-square test; the t-test; analysis of variance; correlation; linear and multiple regression and multi-variate analysis. In each case the *SPSS* procedures for carrying out the tests are described.

THE STATISTICS APPROACH

Before examining particular statistical tests, some preliminary concepts and ideas should be discussed.

Statistical concepts and ideas:

- Measures of central tendency and dispersion
- The idea of probabilistic statements
- The normal distribution
- Probabilistic statement formats
- Significance
- The null hypothesis
- Dependent and independent variables

Measures of central tendency and dispersion

Raw data collected in a research project are often difficult to organise. Consequently, researchers usually consolidate their data into a summary that enables them to gain further insights into trends and patterns in the data and provides the basis for further statistical comparisons between variables. In a research report this summary is typically located under the heading 'descriptive statistics' and is presented in terms of two indexes or measures—*central tendency* and *dispersion.*

Central tendency describes how the scores on a variable tend to cluster about the centre of their distribution. It describes what scores on a variable are like 'on average'. Three indexes of central tendency are the *mean, mode* and *median.*

- The *mean* is the sum of scores in a distribution divided by the number of cases.
- The *mode* is the most frequent score in a distribution.
- The *median* is the mid-point or mid-score in a distribution.

The mean is the most important index of central tendency and is frequently used in the statistical tests discussed below.

Dispersion describes how the scores on a variable are dispersed across the measurement scale. Three indexes of dispersion are *range, variance* and *standard deviation.*

- The *range* is the highest score in a distribution minus the lowest score in the same distribution.
- The *variance* is the mean of the squared deviation scores around the mean of a distribution.
- The *standard deviation* is the square root of the variance.

Variance is one of the most important measures of dispersion and its use in statistical tests is discussed further below under 'Variance'. In a table of descriptive statistics it is usual to report the means and standard deviations for a set of variables.

Probabilistic statements

In general, inferential statistics seeks to make *probabilistic* statements about a population on the basis of information available from a sample drawn from that population. The statements are probabilistic because its is not possible to be absolutely sure that any sample is truly representative of the population from which it has been drawn. It is only possible to estimate the *probability* that results obtained from a sample are true of the population. Such statements can be descriptive, comparative or relational.

- *descriptive*: 10 per cent of managers use Macs.
- *comparative*: 10 per cent of managers use Macs and 90 per cent use PCs.
- *relational*: people with high incomes use Macs more than people with low incomes.

If these statements are based on data from samples, they cannot be made without qualification. The sample may indicate these findings, but it is not certain that they apply precisely to the population from which the sample is drawn, because there is always an element of doubt about any sample. Inferential statistics modifies the above example statements to forms such as the following:

- We can be 95 per cent confident that the proportion of managers who use Macs is between 9 per cent and 11 per cent.
- The proportion of PC users is *significantly* higher than the proportion of Mac users (at the 95 per cent level of probability).
- There is a positive relationship between level of income and use of Mac computers (at the 95 per cent level of probability).

The basis of probabilistic statements: the normal distribution

Descriptive statements and *confidence intervals* were discussed in general terms in Chapter 11 in relation to sample size. The probability or confidence interval statement is based on the *theoretical* idea of drawing repeated samples of the same size from the same population. The sample drawn in any one piece of research is only one of a large number of *possible* samples which *might* have been drawn. If a large number of samples *could* be drawn such an exercise would produce a variety of results, some very unrepresentative of the population, but most, assuming random sampling procedures are used, tending to produce results close to the true population values. Statistical theory, which we are unable to explore in detail here, is able to quantify this tendency. It is possible to say that, in 95 or 99 out of 100 such samples, the values found from the sample will fall within a certain range either side of the true population value—hence the idea of confidence intervals.

The theory relates to the bell-shaped normal distribution which would result if repeated samples were drawn and the values of a statistic plotted (for example the proportion who use Macs), as shown in Figure 14.1. The population value of a statistic (such as a percentage or average) lies at the centre of the distribution and the value of the statistic found from a sample in a particular research project is just one among the many sample possibilities. This is the basis of the *normal curve*, which was discussed in Chapter 11 and illustrated in Figure 11.3 (p. 203).

This idea of levels of probability about the accuracy of sample findings based on the theoretical possibility of drawing many samples is common to most of the statistical procedures examined in this chapter.

Probabilistic statement formats

It is customary in social research to use probability levels of 95 per cent or 99 per cent and occasionally 90 per cent or 99.9 per cent. As probability estimates these can be interpreted exactly as in everyday language. For example, when we say '90 per cent certain', '50:50' or 'nine times out of ten' we are making probabilistic statements. If a finding is significant (see below) at the '99 per cent level', we are saying that we believe there is a 99 per cent chance that what we have found is true of the population. It follows, then, that there is a 1 per cent

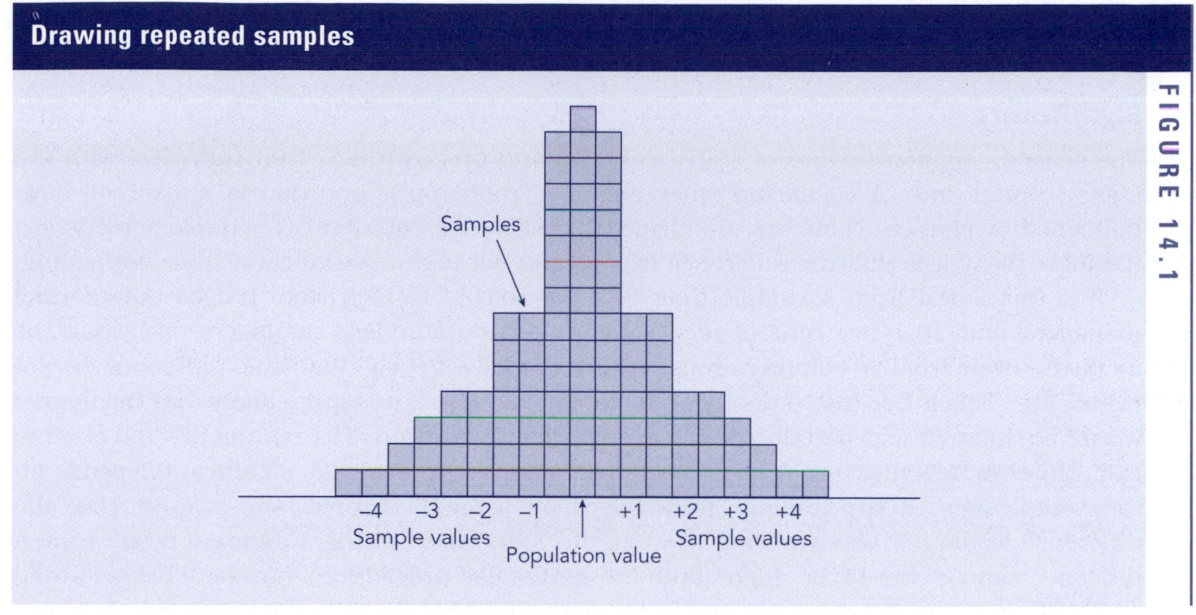

FIGURE 14.1

chance that what we have found is not true. If we say that something is significant at the 95 per cent level, we are less confident, that is, there is a 5 per cent chance that what we have found is not true. Thus the phrase 'highly significant' is sometimes used in relation to findings at the 99 per cent level and 'significant' for the 95 per cent level.

In some cases, instead of the computer-generated results of statistical tests using these conventional cut-off points, they calculate the *exact probability*. For example, it might be found that a result is significant at the 96.5 per cent level or the 82.5 per cent level. It is then left up to the researcher to judge whether such levels are acceptable.

Sometimes the result is expressed as 1 per cent and sometimes as 99 per cent, or 5 per cent rather than 95 per cent. A further variation is to express the probability as a proportion rather than a percentage—for example 0.05 rather than 5 per cent or 0.01 rather than 1 per cent. Similarly, the exact calculations may be expressed as proportions, for example, 0.035 rather than 3.5 per cent or 96.5 per cent. In the following table, therefore, the three forms are equivalent:

5%	95%	0.05
1%	99%	0.01
0.1%	99.9%	0.001
3.5%	96.5%	0.035
7.5%	92.5%	0.075

In computer printouts from *SPSS*, if the probability is below .0005 the probability may appear as .000 because it is printed only to three decimal places.

In some research reports and computer printouts, results which are significant at the 5 per cent level are indicated by * and those significant at the 1 per cent level are indicated by **.

Significance

The second common feature of statistical tests and procedures is that they deal with the idea of *significance*. A *significant* difference or relationship is one that is unlikely to have happened by chance. Therefore, the bigger the difference between two sample percentages the more likely it is that the difference is 'real' and not just a statistical chance happening.

If it was found from a sample that 10.2 per cent of women were judged outstanding managers and 10.1 per cent of men were judged outstanding managers, we would be inclined—even from a common sense point of view—to say that the difference is not significant. This is because if another sample were selected, it is quite likely that the figures would be different and perhaps even the opposite way around. The results are 'too close to call'. However, whether or not such a small difference is *statistically* significant depends on the sample size. If the findings were based on a small sample, say around 100, the difference would not be significant, that is, the chances of getting a different result from a different sample would be high (and the statistical procedures outlined below would establish this). But if the sample was large—say, around 1000—then the difference between 10.1 and 10.2 per cent might turn out to be statistically significant. If the result is based on such a large sample we can be much more confident that it is 'real' and could be reproduced if another sample of similar size were drawn.

Statistical theory enables us to quantify and assess significance—to determine what sizes of differences are significant for what sizes of sample.

Statistical significance should not, however, be confused with *social*, *theoretical* or *managerial* significance. If the above finding about men's and women's management ability was based on a sample of 10 000 it would certainly be *statistically* significant, but this does not make the difference significant in any *social* sense. For all practical purposes, on the basis of such findings we would say that the proportion of men and women who are judged as outstanding managers is the same. This is a very important point to bear in mind when reading research results based on statistics—large samples can produce many statistically significant findings, but that does not necessarily make them significant in any other way.

The null hypothesis

Another common feature of the statistical method is the concept of the *null hypothesis*, which was discussed earlier in Chapter 3. It is based around the idea of setting up two mutually incompatible hypotheses, so that only one can be true. For example, *either* more managers use PCs than use Macs, *or* the number of managers who use PCs is less than or equal to the number who use Macs. If one proposition is true then the other must be untrue. The null hypothesis usually proposes that there is *no difference* between two observed values or that there is *no relationship* between two variables. There are therefore two possibilities:

H_0 – Null hypothesis: there is *no* difference or relationship.
H_1 – Alternative hypothesis: there *is* a difference or relationship.

Usually it is the *alternative* hypothesis, H_1, that the researcher is interested in, but statistical theory explores the implications of the null hypothesis.

The use of the null hypothesis idea can be illustrated by example. Suppose that in a study of computer user patterns surveying a sample of 1000 managers, part of the study focuses on the levels of use of *Excel* and *Lotus* spreadsheet programs. The null hypothesis would be that the usage levels are the same.

H_0 – Excel and Lotus usage levels are the same.
H_1 – Excel and Lotus usage levels are different.

Suppose it is found that 120 respondents (12 per cent) use *Excel* and 120 respondents (12 per cent) use *Lotus*. Clearly there is no difference between the two figures—they are consistent with the null hypothesis. The null hypothesis is accepted and the alternative hypothesis is rejected. In terms of the approaches discussed in Chapter 1, this is very much a *deductive* approach—the hypothesis is set up in advance of the analysis, possibly within a theoretical framework.

But suppose the number of people using *Excel* was found to be 121 (12.1 per cent) and the number of people using *Lotus* was found to be 120 (12.0 per cent). Should we reject the null hypothesis and accept the alternative, that *Excel* and *Lotus* usage levels are different? From what we know of samples, clearly not, this would be 'too close to call'. Such a small difference between the two figures is still consistent with the null hypothesis. So how big would the difference have to be before we would reject the null hypothesis? A difference of 5, 10 or 15 users? This is where statistical theory is able to provide a test of what is an acceptable difference. Case Study Example 14.1 illustrates the use of hypotheses and two of the statistical procedures covered in this chapter. The rest of this chapter is concerned with various ways to test the relationship between sample findings and the null hypothesis for different situations.

Dependent and independent variables

The terms *dependent variable* and *independent variable* are frequently used in statistical analysis. The concept of dependent and independent variables was discussed earlier in Chapter 10 in relation to experimental research designs. If there is a relationship between a dependent and an independent variable, the implication is that changes in the former are caused by changes in the latter. The independent variable influences the dependent variable. For example, if it is suggested that the amount of money spent on textbooks is related to income level then the amount of money spent is the dependent variable and income level is the independent variable. Even though a certain level of income does not *cause* people to spend money on textbooks, it makes more sense to suggest that level of income facilitates or constrains spending on textbooks than to suggest that spending on textbooks facilitates or constrains level of income. It makes sense to talk of spending on textbooks being *dependent* on income. One variable can be dependent on a number of independent variables, as illustrated in Figure 14.2. For example, it may be hypothesised that textbook spending is dependent on income, occupation *and* age.

CASE STUDY EXAMPLE 14.1

Content analysis: beyond the net—culture and advertising

Source: Shintaro Okazaki and Javier Alonson Rivas, 2003, Beyond the net: cultural values reflected in Japanese multinationals' web communication strategies. *Journal of International Consumer Marketing*, 16(1), 47–70.
Methods/approaches: Content analysis; hypothesis-testing; quantitative; chi-square; ANOVA
Topic: Culture orientation of advertising

This study begins with the observation that 'individualism' and 'collectivism' remain important distinguishing features of contemporary cultures and this has implications for the conduct of business in a globalised environment. Of the three countries represented in the study: the USA is seen as the most individualist; Japan the most collectivist; and Spain one of the more collectivist of the Western countries. It is further noted that advertising often tends to run counter to national cultures (the 'cultural paradox' theory), since consumers are often 'attracted by not what they have, but what they lack'. The question then arises as to how multinational companies (MNCs) project themselves in different parts of the world. In particular Okazaki and Rivas set out to examine how this is reflected in Japanese MNCs' websites directed at different markets. They put forward five *hypotheses*. In summary, they are:

H_1: Websites for the Japanese market would reflect more individualist than collectivist values.
H_2: Websites for the Spanish market would reflect more individualist than collectivist values.
H_3: Websites for the US market would reflect more collectivist than individualist values.
H_4: Websites for the Japanese market would reflect more individualist values than those for the Spanish and US markets.
H_5: Websites for the Spanish market would reflect more individualist values than those for the US market.

Fifty of the largest Japanese companies were selected which had foreign investments in at least five countries and had websites in Japan, USA and Spain. A 'typical product' and its associated website were selected for each company, giving 150 websites for study. Ten 'cultural values', reflecting 'individualism' and ten reflecting 'collectivism' were identified from the literature.

The *content analysis* involved identifying the dominant cultural value reflected in three types of cue from each website: overall, verbal and non-verbal. It was found that the average number of 'individualist' values identified per site was: 2.16 for sites directed at Japan, 2.08 for Spain and 1.94 for USA. This seemed to confirm hypotheses 1 and 2 but not hypothesis 3. Analysis of variance confirmed that websites for all three markets reflected a similar level of individualist values, thus not lending support for hypotheses 4 and 5. The 'cultural paradox' theory is therefore generally supported, particularly with regard to websites directed at Japan.

The existence of the Internet facilitates an international study at minimal cost, with scope for further replication. The study presents a simple example of hypothesis-testing using statistical techniques.

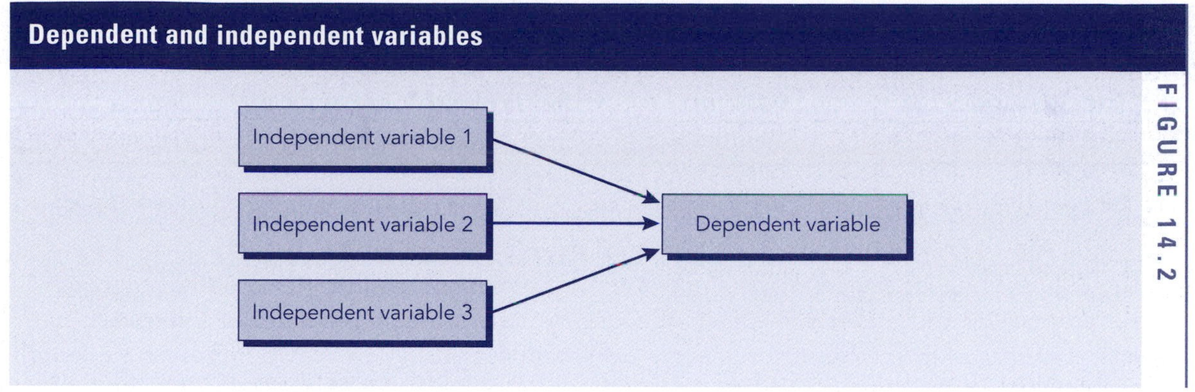

Dependent and independent variables

FIGURE 14.2

WHAT TESTS?

The idea of levels of measurement or types of data was introduced in Chapter 13; nominal, ordinal and ratio data were discussed in the section on 'Measure' (p. 232). The higher the level of measurement, the greater the range of analysis that can be carried out on the data. It is possible to calculate means and averages for ordinal and ratio measures, but not for nominal data. Consequently, different statistical tests are associated with different levels of measurement. The rest of this chapter sets out different statistical tests to be used in various situations as summarised in Figure 14.3. The tests all relate to comparisons between variables and relationships between variables. The type of test to be used depends on the format of the data, the level of measurement and the number of variables involved.

In the following pages some fictitious data are used to illustrate the various tests. The data arise from a questionnaire survey similar to that used in Chapters 8 and 13, but with a sample size of 50 and the addition of a number of variables including age, gender, income and use of information resources. A list of the variables used and the data set is included in Appendix 4 (p. 332). As in Chapter 13, the example analyses have been created using *SPSS for Windows*, Version 12. Readers will find it useful to actually enter the data shown in Appendix 4 into the *SPPS Data Editor* window so that the procedures can be practised while reading the chapter. The data entry process was described in Chapter 13.

CHI-SQUARE TEST

Introduction

The *Chi-square test* (symbol: χ^2, based on the Greek letter χ and pronounced 'ky' to rhyme with 'sky') can be used in a number of situations, but its use is demonstrated here in relation to the crosstabulation of two *nominal* variables. When examining crosstabulation tables it is possible to use 'common sense' and an underlying knowledge of the size of confidence intervals to make an approximate judgement as to whether there is any sort of relationship between the two variables involved in the table. However, unless the pattern is very clear it can be difficult to judge whether the overall differences are *significant*. The Chi-square test is designed to achieve this.

Figure 14.4 shows an example of the output from a crosstabulation and a Chi-square test. The example chosen relates to the type of course enrolled in (*crse*) and gender (*gender*). The interpretation of the results is discussed below.

FIGURE 14.3

Types of data and type of statistical test

Task	Data format	No. of variables	Types of variable*	Test
Relationship between two variables	Crosstabulation of frequencies	2	Nominal	Chi-square
Difference between two means—paired	Means—whole sample	2	Scale or ordinal	t-test—paired
Difference between two means—independent samples	Means—two subgroups	2	1 scale or ordinal (means) 2 nominal (with 2 groups only)	t-test—independent samples
Relationship between two variables	Means—3 or more subgroups	2	1 scale or ordinal (means) 2 nominal (3 or more groups)	One-way analysis of variance
Relationship between three or more variables	Means—crosstabulated	3+	1 scale or ordinal (means) 2 two or more nominal	Factorial analysis of variance
Relationship between two variables	Individual measures	2	Scale or ordinal (2)	Correlation
Linear relationship between two variables	Individual measures	2	Scale or ordinal (2)	Linear regression
Linear relationship between three or more variables	Individual measures	3+	Three or more scale or ordinal variables	Multiple regression
Relationships between large numbers of variables	Individual measures	many	Large numbers of scale or ordinal variables	Factor analysis; cluster analysis

The following procedure was used to produce the tables shown in Figure 14.4:

- From the menu bar select **Analyze**, then **Descriptive Statistics**, then **Crosstabs**.
- In the **Crosstabs** dialog box move the variable *crse* to the **Row(s)** box and *gender* and to the **Column(s)** box.
- Select **Statistics**, then **Chi-square** and then click on **Continue**.
- Select **Cells**, then select **Observed** and **Expected**, then click on **Continue**.
- Click **OK** in the **Crosstabs** to complete the procedure. The Crosstabs table and accompanying Chi-square test will be produced in the **Output** window.

Null hypothesis

The null hypothesis for this test is that there is no difference in course enrolment patterns between male and female respondents. That is:

FIGURE 14.4

SPSS output: Chi-square test

Course * Gender Crosstabulation

			Gender		
			Male	Female	Total
Course	People Skills	Count	9	4	13
		Expected Count	6.5	6.5	13.0
	Global Business	Count	9	5	14
		Expected Count	7.0	7.0	14.0
	Strategic Management	Count	7	16	23
		Expected Count	11.5	11.5	23.0
Total		Count	25	25	50
		Expected Count	25.0	25.0	50.0

Chi-Square Tests

	Value	df	Asymp. Sig. (2-sided)
Pearson Chi-Square	6.588(a)	2	.037
Likelihood Ratio	6.750	2	.034
Linear-by-Linear Association	5.649	1	.017
No. of Valid Cases	50		

a 0 cells (.0%) have expected count less than 5. The minimum expected count is 6.50.

H_0 – there is *no* relationship between course enrolment pattern and gender in the population.
H_1 – there *is* a relationship between course enrolment pattern and gender in the population.

The cells of the table include counts and also *expected counts*, sometimes referred to as expected frequencies, or expected values. These are the counts that would be expected if the null hypothesis were *true*, that is, if there was no difference between males and females in their pattern of course enrolment. In this case we have an equal number of men and women in the sample, so the expected values show a 50:50 split for each of the three types of course.

Note that the proposition being tested can therefore be expressed in three ways, as shown in Figure 14.5.

The value of Chi-square

Chi-square is a statistic based on the sum of the differences between the counts (or *observed* values) and the *expected* counts. The greater the aggregate difference between the observed and the expected values, the greater the value of Chi-square. However, if you simply add the differences between the observed and expected values in the table you will find that the positives cancel out the negatives, giving zero. Chi-square is therefore based on the sum of the *squared* values of the differences. For readers who are mathematically inclined, the formula for Chi-square is shown in Appendix 5 (p. 336). Fortunately, the *SPSS*

FIGURE 14.5

Alternative expressions of hypotheses

Option 1	Option 2	Option 3
Null hypothesis (H_0): there is *no* relationship between course enrolment pattern and gender in the population	Male and female enrolment patterns in the population are the same	Observed and expected values are not significantly different
Alternative hypothesis (H_1): there *is* a relationship between course enrolment pattern and gender in the population	Male and female enrolment patterns in the population are different	Observed and expected values are significantly different

package calculates the value of Chi-square for us, so it is not necessary to know the details of the formula. It is sufficient to understand that Chi-square is a statistical measure of the difference between the observed and expected values in the table.

In the example in Figure 14.4, the value of Chi-square is 6.588. We are using the 'Pearson' value, devised by the statistician Pearson—the other values (*Likelihood Ratio* and *Linear-by-Linear Association*) do not concern us here. How should this be interpreted? We have noted that the greater the difference between the observed and expected values the greater the value of Chi-square. Our null hypothesis is that there is *no* difference between the two sets of values. There can be some *minor* differences between two sets of values and the null hypothesis can still be accepted. If the split between males and females in the People Skills course was 6:7, or if the split between males and females in the Global Business course was, say 8:6, the null hypothesis could still be accepted. But just how big do the differences have to be before we reject the null hypothesis and conclude that there *is* a difference between male and female enrolment patterns?

For a given size of table (in this case three cells by two), statisticians have been able to calculate the likelihood of obtaining various values of Chi-square when the null hypothesis is true. As with the normal distribution discussed in Chapter 11, this is based on the theoretical possibility of drawing lots of samples of the same size. This distribution is shown in Figure 14.6. It shows that, for a given table size, if the null hypothesis is true (that is, if men's and women's observed and expected values are the same) then *some* differences in observed and expected values can be expected from most samples drawn, so a range of values of Chi-square can be expected. Most values of Chi-square would be fairly small. Larger values would occur, but they are unlikely. As with the normal distribution curve discussed in Chapter 11, it is customary to adopt either a 5 per cent or 1 per cent cut-off to decide what is considered to be 'unlikely'. Five per cent is used in the ensuing discussions. Therefore, any value of Chi-square above the 5 per cent point is considered unlikely and *inconsistent* with the null hypothesis. Thus, if the value of Chi-square is *above* the 5 per cent point, so the probability is in the 0–4.99 per cent range, we can *reject* the null hypothesis; if it is *below* the 5 per cent point, so the probability is in the 5–100 range, we *accept* the null hypothesis.

In Figure 14.4 the *SPSS* output tells us where the particular value of Chi-square lies in

Distribution of chi-square when null hypothesis is true

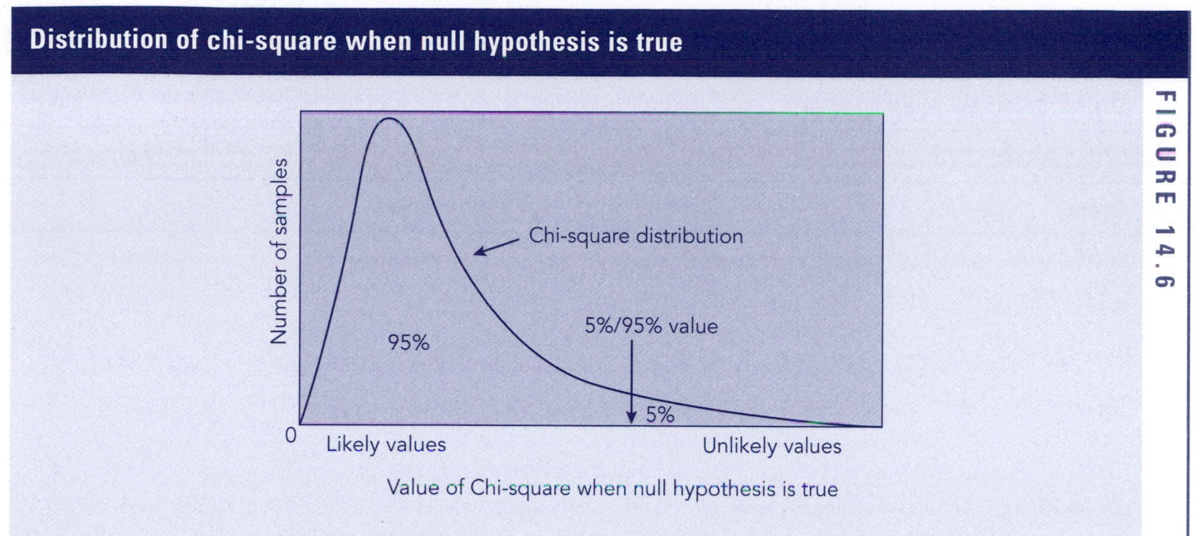

FIGURE 14.6

terms of probability. The 'significance' column (*Asymp. Sig. (2-sided)*) gives a value of 0.037 or 3.7 per cent. Our value of Chi-square is therefore an unlikely one, so we reject the null hypothesis and conclude that there *is* a significant difference between the male and female enrolment pattern.

Degrees of freedom

The values of Chi-square depend on the table size, which is indirectly measured by the *degrees of freedom*. Degrees of freedom are calculated by the number of rows less one, multiplied by the number of columns less one. So, for the table in Figure 14.4 the 'degrees of freedom' are:

$$(2 - 1) \times (3 - 1) = 1 \times 2 = 2.$$

This is shown in the *SPSS* output under '*df*'.

Expected counts rule

One rule for the application of Chi-square is that there should not be more than one-fifth of the cells of the table with 'expected counts' of less than five, and none with an expected frequency of less than one. The *SPSS* output (Figure 14.4) indicates whether such cells exist—in the example the minimum expected count is 6.5, so there is no problem. In cases where there is a problem, grouping of some of the values by recoding can be used to reduce the number of cells and thus increase the expected frequencies.

Presentation of results

How should the results of statistical tests such as Chi-square be reported? One approach is to include the results of the test in a table in the report, as in Figure 14.7. The commentary could then merely say: 'The relationship between enrolment patterns and gender was significant at the 5 per cent level'. Another approach is to include the test results in the text, for example: 'The relationship between enrolment patterns and gender

FIGURE 14.7

Presentation of Chi-square test results

Table A: Course enrolment by gender

	Male	**Female**	**Total**
Course		**% enrolled**	
People Skills	36.0	16.0	26.0
Global Business	36.0	20.0	28.0
Strategic Management	28.0	64.0	46.0
Total	100.0	100.0	100.0
Sample size	25	25	50

X^2 = 6.59, df 2, significant at the 5% level

was significant at the 5 per cent level (χ^2 = 6.6, 2 DF)'. A third approach, which makes the statistics less intrusive, is to include a note in the report or paper indicating that all tests were conducted at the 5 per cent level, and possibly that test values are included in the tables, are listed in an appendix or even excluded altogether for non-technical audiences. A fourth approach is to use the * and ** approach as discussed above under '*Statement formats*'.

COMPARING TWO MEANS: THE T-TEST

Introduction

So far we have dealt only with research findings expressed as proportions or percentages, either singly or in crosstabulations. However, many research results are in the form of averages—for example, the average age of a group of participants in an activity, the average salary of managers from different industries, or the average score of a group on a Likert scale. In statistical terminology an average is referred to as a *mean*. As indicated in Chapter 13 when discussing data types, means can be calculated for ordinal and ratio variables, but not for nominal variables.

The simplest form of analysis of means is to compare two means to see whether they are significantly different. For example, we might want to test whether the average age of the Mac users in a sample is significantly different from that of the PC users. The null hypothesis is expressed as follows:

H_0 – Null hypothesis: there is *no* difference between the means.
H_1 – Alternative hypothesis: there *is* a difference between the means.

In this situation, a statistic referred to as 't' is calculated rather than Chi-square. This statistic is based on a formula involving the sample size and the comparison between the two means (see Appendix 5). If there is *no difference* between two means in the population (H_0) then, for a given sample size, t has a known *distribution* of likely values (see Figure 14.8).

Chi-square and t distributions

FIGURE 14.8

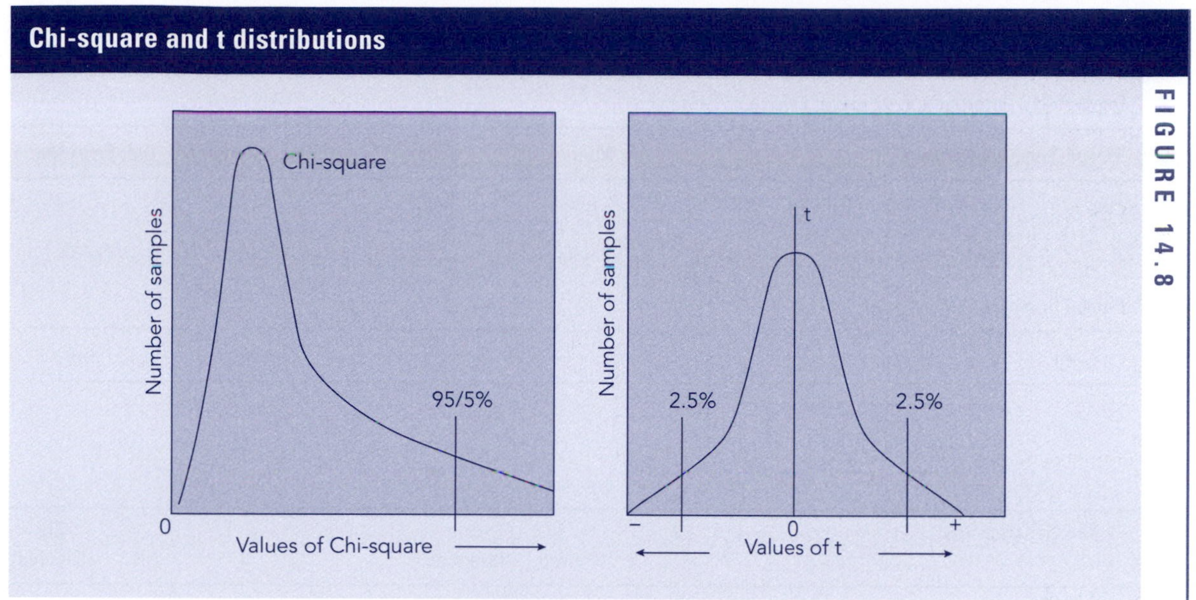

High values are rare, so if the value from a sample is high, that is, in the top 5 per cent of values for that sample size, then we reject H_0 and accept H_1, concluding that there *is* a significant difference at the 5 per cent level of probability.

There are two situations in which we might want to compare means:

- When comparing the means of two variables that apply to everyone in the sample—for example, comparing the average amount of money spent on professional journals with the average amount spent on conference travel (for everybody in the sample). This is known as a *paired samples* test.
- When comparing the means of one variable for two subgroups in the sample—for example, comparing the average age of the men in the sample with the average age of the women. The sample is divided into two subgroups, men and women; this is known as a *group* or *independent samples* test.

Paired samples test

Figure 14.9 gives two examples of the paired samples t-test. The output that appears in the *Output* window provides a range of statistics, some of which do not concern us here. Example 1 compares the frequency of *Internet use* with the frequency of *reading the Financial Review*. The members of the sample use the Internet 25.48 times per year on average and read the *Financial Review* 37.00 times per year on average. The value of t is –1.286, and its (2-tailed) significance is 0.205 or 20.05 per cent. The result is consistent with the null hypothesis (0.205 is much higher than 0.05), so we accept that there is *no significant difference* between the frequency of Internet use and the frequency of reading the *Financial Review*. The second example compares the frequency of *Internet use* (mean 25.48) with the frequency of *library use* (mean 9.92). In this case the value of t is 4.047 and its significance level is 0.000, which is below 0.05, so we reject the null hypothesis and conclude that there is a significant difference between the frequency of Internet use and the frequency of library use.

FIGURE 14.9

SPSS output: Comparing means: t-test—paired samples

Example 1—Internet use vs reads *Financial Review*

Paired Samples Statistics		Mean	N	Std. Deviation	Std. Error Mean
Pair 1	Times used Internet in last year	25.48	50	19.771	2.796
	Times read Fin. Review in last year	37.00	50	61.079	8.638

Paired Samples Correlations		N	Correlation	Sig.
Pair 1	Times used Internet in last year & Times read Fin. Review in last year	50	.044	.761

Paired Samples Test		Paired Differences					t	df	Sig. (2-tailed)
		Mean	Std. Deviation	Std. Error Mean	95% Confidence Interval of the Difference				
					Lower	Upper			
Pair 1	Times used Internet in last year & Times read Fin. Review in last year	–11.52	63.365	8.961	–29.53	6.49	–1.286	49	.205

Example 2—Internet use vs library use

Paired Samples Statistics		Mean	N	Std. Deviation	Std. Error Mean
Pair 1	Times used Internet in last year	25.48	50	19.771	2.796
	Times used library in last year	9.92	50	11.789	1.667

Paired Samples Correlations		N	Correlation	Sig.
Pair 1	Times used Internet in last year & Times used library in last year	50	–.449	.001

Paired Samples T-Test		Paired Differences					t	df	Sig. (2-tailed)
		Mean	Std. Deviation	Std. Error Mean	95% Confidence Interval of the Difference				
					Lower	Upper			
Pair 1	Times used Internet in last year—Times used library in last year	15.56	27.186	3.845	7.83	23.29	4.047	49	.000

The t-test output from *SPSS* refers to the column headed *Sig. (2-tailed)*. This is because, unlike Chi-square, the test involves both ends of the distribution. As shown in Figure 14.8, the value of t can be negative or positive. The interpretation is, however, the same. The output also provides a table of *Paired Samples Correlations*. Correlations are discussed later in this chapter.

The following *SPSS* procedure was used to produce the first paired sample t-test shown in Figure 14.9.

- Select **Analyze** from the menu bar, then **Compare Means**, then **Paired Samples T-Test.**

- Select the two variables—*int* and *finrev*. The two variables appear in the **Current Selections** box.

- Move the variables to the **Paired Variables** box.

- Click on **OK** to produce the **Paired Samples T-Test** tables in the **Output** window.

Independent samples test

Figure 14.10 compares levels of expenditure on textbooks (*cost*) by male and female management trainees (*gender*). For males, average expenditure is $142.44, and for females it is $96.52. In this case t has a value of 1.547 and a significance level of 0.130. Since 0.130 is above 0.05, which is consistent with the null hypothesis, we accept that there is *no significant difference* between the two expenditure figures.

One important aspect of reading an **Independent Samples Test** table is the need to check for equality of variances between the two independent samples. If in **Levene's Test for Equality of Variances** (the column with the heading 'Sig.'), p is greater than 0.05, then use the **Equal Variances Assumed** t-test. If p is 0.05 or less, then use the **Equal Variances Not Assumed** test.

In this example equal variances were not assumed since p was 0.011, and the Sig. (2-tailed) value used was therefore 0.130. There is a discussion on the concept of variance later in the chapter.

The following *SPSS* procedure was used to produce the independent sample t-test shown in Figure 14.10.

- Select **Analyze** from the menu bar, then **Compare Means** then **Independent-Samples T-Test**

- Select the *dependent* variable: *cost (Dollars spent on texts)* and move it to the **Test Variable(s)** box.

- Select the *independent* or *grouping* variable *gender*, and transfer it to the **Grouping Variables** box. This variable will be used to define the two groups being compared: *male* and *female*.

- Click on **Define Groups** to open the **Define Groups** dialog box.

- Enter the values 1 and 2 (for male and female) into **Group 1** and **Group 2** respectively.

- Select **Continue**, then click on **OK** to produce the **Independent-Samples T-Test** tables in the **Output** window.

FIGURE 14.10

***SPSS* output: Comparing means: t-test—independent samples**

Group Statistics

	Gender	N	Mean	Std. Deviation	Std. Error Mean
Dollars spent on texts	Male	25	142.44	127.282	25.456
	Female	25	96.52	76.243	15.249

Independent Samples Test

		Levene's Test for Equality of Variances		t-test for Equality of Means						
		F	Sig.	t	df	Sig. (2-tailed)	Mean Difference	Std. Error Difference	95% Confidence Interval of the Mean	
									Lower	Upper
Dollars spent on texts	Equal variances assumed	7.054	.011	1.547	48	.128	45.92	29.674	–13.744	105.584
	Equal variances not assumed			1.547	39.258	.130	45.92	29.674	–14.089	105.929

COMPARING MORE THAN TWO MEANS: ONE-WAY ANALYSIS OF VARIANCE (ANOVA)

The t-test was used to examine differences between two means at a time. *Analysis of variance* (ANOVA) is used to compare differences between *more than two* means at a time. This procedure begins to resemble a frequencies table, but with *means* appearing in the cells of the table instead of sample numbers, as shown in Figure 14.11. The table of means shown in Figure 14.11 was prepared using the *SPSS* procedure outlined in the section on *Means* in Chapter 13.

In the following example we will seek to determine whether the mean course expenditures on textbooks for the different groups of training course members (*crse*) are statistically different from the overall mean (*cost*), that is, whether expenditure is related to type of

Comparing a range of means

Expenditure on books by course attended

Course	Mean	N	Std. Deviation
People Skills	124.69	13	86.518
Global Business	152.36	14	140.048
Strategic Management	96.52	23	91.025
Total	119.48	50	106.396

FIGURE 14.11

training course attended. An ANOVA procedure will be used to provide the answer to this question.

Null hypothesis

The null hypothesis is expressed as follows:

H_0 – Null hypothesis: each of the group means is equal to the overall mean.
H_1 – Alternative hypothesis: there is a difference between the groups means and the overall mean.

How different must the group means be from the overall mean before we reject this hypothesis? Before answering this question an understanding of the idea of *variance* is necessary.

Variance

Whether or not the means are in effect from *one* population (with *one* mean) or from *different* sub-populations (with different means) depends not only on the differences between the means, but also on how much they are spread out—their spread or *variance*. Figure 14.12 shows four examples of three means, with the associated *spread* of cases around each mean. In example A the means are well-spaced and there is very little overlap in the cases, whereas in example C the means are closer together and there is considerable overlap. In example B the means are spaced as in A, but the spread (variance) around the means is greater and so overlap is considerable. Example D presents the greatest case of overlap. We might expect to find that for example A there *is* a significant difference between the means, while for example D there is not. Examples B and C raise doubts because of the overlaps. (Note that a visual presentation of this type of information, although in a different format, can be obtained using the *Boxplot* feature within the *Graphics* procedure of *SPSS*.)

The spread of sample values is referred to as the variance and can be measured by adding up the differences between the scores of individual observations/cases and the mean score. The formula for calculating *variance* is shown in Appendix 5 (p. 336).

Whether or not subgroup means are significantly different from the overall mean depends on:

FIGURE 14.12 Comparing means and variance

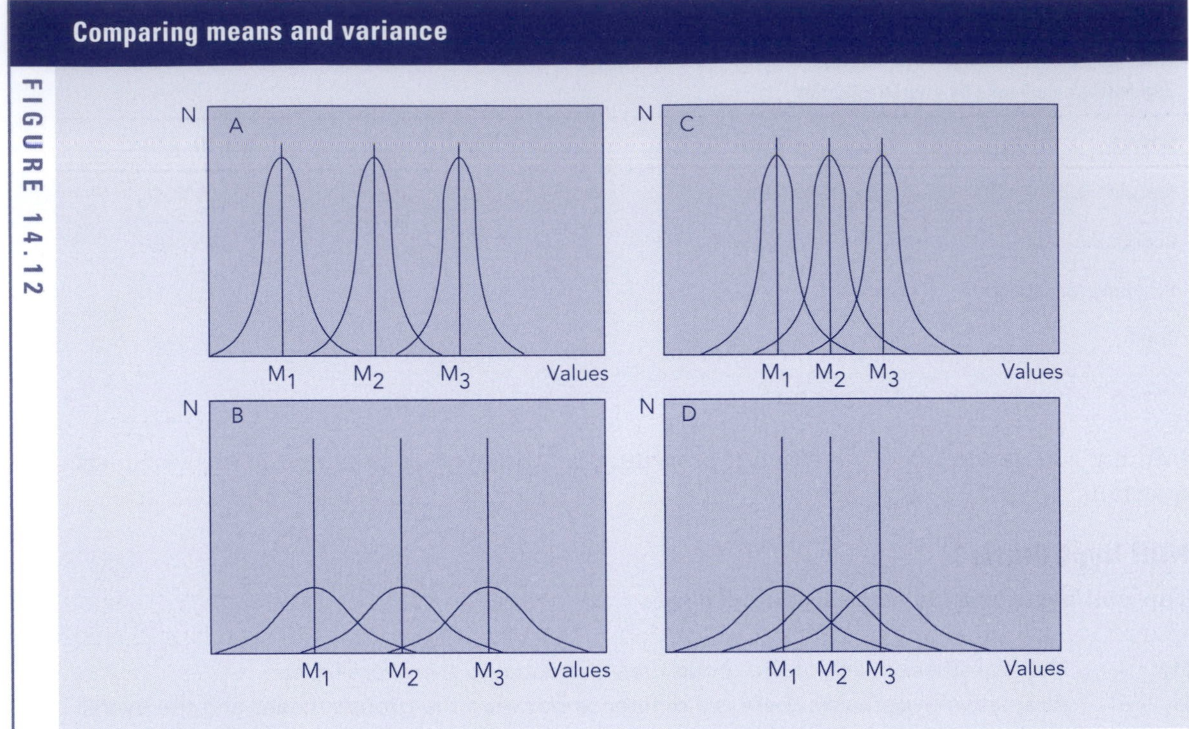

- the spread of the separate subgroup means around the overall mean—the *between groups* variance; and
- the spread of subgroup observations around the means of the subgroups—the *within groups* variance.

The greater the *between groups* variance, the *greater* the likelihood of significant difference. The greater the *within groups* variance, the *less* the likelihood of significant difference. Analysis of variance is based on the ratio of these two measures, which produces a statistic referred to as *F*.

As with the other statistics examined, values of F for a given number of degrees of freedom (based on sample sizes and number of groups) have a known probability distribution in the null hypothesis situation. Low values of F are unlikely and result in the rejection of the null hypothesis.

SPSS procedures and output

Examples of two analyses of variance are shown in Figure 14.13. For *Between Groups* and *Within Groups* the output shows the *Sum of Squares*, the degrees of freedom (df), the *Mean Square* (variance), the *F ratio* and the *F probability* (Sig.) of a significant difference among the means.

The first example compares *cost* (dollars spent on texts) across three different training course groups (*crse*). The means for these subgroups are shown in Figure 14.11. The F ratio is 1.231 and the F probability is 0.301. The latter is greater than .05, so the null hypothesis is accepted. It is concluded that there is no significant difference among the means, that is, expenditure is not related to course type.

FIGURE 14.13

***SPSS* output: one-way analysis of variance**

ANOVA

Expenditure on books by course attended

	Sum of Squares	df	Mean Square	F	Sig.
Between Groups	27 608.757	2	13 804.379	1.231	.301
Within Groups	527 079.723	47	11 214.462		
Total	554 688.480	49			

Income in $'000s per year by course attended

	Sum of Squares	df	Mean Square	F	Sig.
Between Groups	250.341	2	125.170	3.607	.035
Within Groups	1 631.039	47	34.703		
Total	1 881.380	49			

The second example compares income in $'000s per year (*inc*) across the three different training course groups (*crse*). The F probability is 0.035, which is less than 0.05, so in this case the null hypothesis is rejected. It is concluded that there *is* a significant difference among the mean incomes of management trainees enrolled in different training courses.

The first example of a one-way analysis of variance table shown in Figure 14.13 was produced using the following procedure:

- Select **Analyze** from the menu bar, then **Compare Means**, then **One-Way ANOVA**
- Move the variable *cost* to the **Dependent List** box and the variable *crser* to the **Factor** box.
- Click on **OK** to produce the one-way analysis of variance table in **Output** window.

COMPARING GROUPS OF MEANS: FACTORIAL ANALYSIS OF VARIANCE (ANOVA)

As with one-way analysis of variance, factorial analysis of variance deals with *means*. While one-way analysis of variance deals with means of groups determined on the basis of one variable, factorial analysis of variance is designed to test for differences among sets of means grouped by more than one classifying variable, or 'factor'. An example of sets of means grouped by more than one factor is shown in Figure 14.14. The table sets out the means of management trainees' personal expenditure on professional development per annum

FIGURE 14.14

Table of means grouped by two factors

Expenditure on professional development $ per annum by gender and use of career planning service

Used career planning service	Gender	Mean exp.	N	Std. Deviation
No	Male	288.46	13	143.111
	Female	1050.00	5	715.891
	Total	500.00	18	508.169
Yes	Male	874.17	12	435.899
	Female	520.25	20	394.523
	Total	652.97	32	439.459
Total	Male	569.60	25	431.880
	Female	626.20	25	505.382
	Total	597.90	50	466.126

(*devlpt*) broken down by two factors—involvement in career planning (*cp*) and gender (*gender*).

It can be seen from the table that there is little overall difference between the professional expenditure of males ($569.60) and females ($626.20) on development, and not a lot of difference between people who undertook career planning ($652.97) and those who did not take career planning ($500.00). There is, however, a large difference in expenditure between males and females who *did not* undertake career planning ($288.46 and $1050.00 respectively) and also between males and females who *did* undertake career planning ($874.17 and $520.25 respectively). Factorial analysis of variance examines this 'crosstabulation of means' and determines whether the differences revealed are significant. As with the one-way analysis of variance, the procedure examines the differences between group means and the spread of values within groups.

The table shown in Figure 14.14 is produced by the following *SPSS* procedure:

- Select **Analyze** from the menu bar, then **Compare Means**, then **Means**.
- In the **Means** dialog box move the variable *devlpt* to the **Dependent List** box and move the variable *cp* to the **Independent List** box.
- Click on **Next** to select **Layer 2** and move *gender* to the **Independent List** box.
- Click on **OK** and the table will be produced in the **Output** window.

Null hypothesis

The null hypothesis is expressed as follows:

H_0 – Null hypothesis: the level of personal expenditure on professional development per annum by the management trainees *will not* be affected by undertaking career planning or gender.

H_1 – Alternative hypothesis: the level of personal expenditure on professional development per annum by the management trainees *will be* affected by undertaking career planning or gender.

A table of expected values consistent with the null hypothesis can be produced as for the Chi-square example, but the values will be means rather than numbers of cases.

Factorial analysis of variance

Figure 14.15 shows the results of a factorial analysis of variance. The F probabilities (Sig.) in the *Main Effects* part of the output indicate that neither the relationship between *expenditure on professional development* and *career planning* (p = 0.828), nor between *expenditure on professional development* and *gender* (p = 0.118), are significant on their own. However, when both variables are taken into account—in the *2-Way Interactions* part of the table—the F probability is 0.000, which is less than 0.05. The null hypothesis is therefore rejected and it is concluded that the interaction between gender and career planning in relation to personal expenditure on professional development is significant.

The table in Figure 14.15 was produced using the following procedure:

- Select **Analyze** from the menu bar, then **General Linear Model,** then **Univariate.**
- Move the variable *devlpt* to the **Dependent variable** box and *cp* and *gender* to the **Fixed factor(s)** box.
- Click on **OK** and the factorial analysis of variance table will be presented in the **Output** window.

CORRELATION

Correlation can be used to examine the relationships between two or more *ordinal* or *scale* variables. If two phenomena are related in a systematic way they are said to be *correlated.* They can be:

- *positively* correlated (as one variable increases so does the other);
- *negatively* correlated (as one variable increases the other decreases); or
- *uncorrelated* (there is no relationship between the variables).

FIGURE 14.15

***SPSS* output: factorial analysis of variance**

Dependent Variable: DEVLPT

Source	Type III Sum of Squares	df	Mean Square	F	Sig.
Corrected Model	3 303 219.853(a)	3	1 101 073.284	6.897	.001
Intercept	18 204 769.255	1	18 204 769.255	114.040	.000
GENDER	405 004.099	1	405 004.099	2.537	.118
CP	7 631.755	1	7 631.755	.048	.828
GENDER * CP	3 032 835.349	1	3 032 835.349	18.999	.000
Error	7 343 184.647	46	159 634.449		
Total	28 520 625.000	50			
Corrected Total	10 646 404.500	49			

a R Squared = .310 (Adjusted R Squared = .265)

It is often helpful to think of correlation in visual terms. Relationships between income and four variables are shown in Figure 14.16, where a variety of types of correlation are illustrated. The graphics were produced using the *SPSS* **Graphs** and then selecting the **Scatter** procedure. Each point represents one person, case or observation.

Correlation coefficient (r)

Correlation can be measured by means of the *correlation coefficient*, usually represented by the letter *r*. The coefficient is:

FIGURE 14.16

***SPSS* output: relationships between variables**

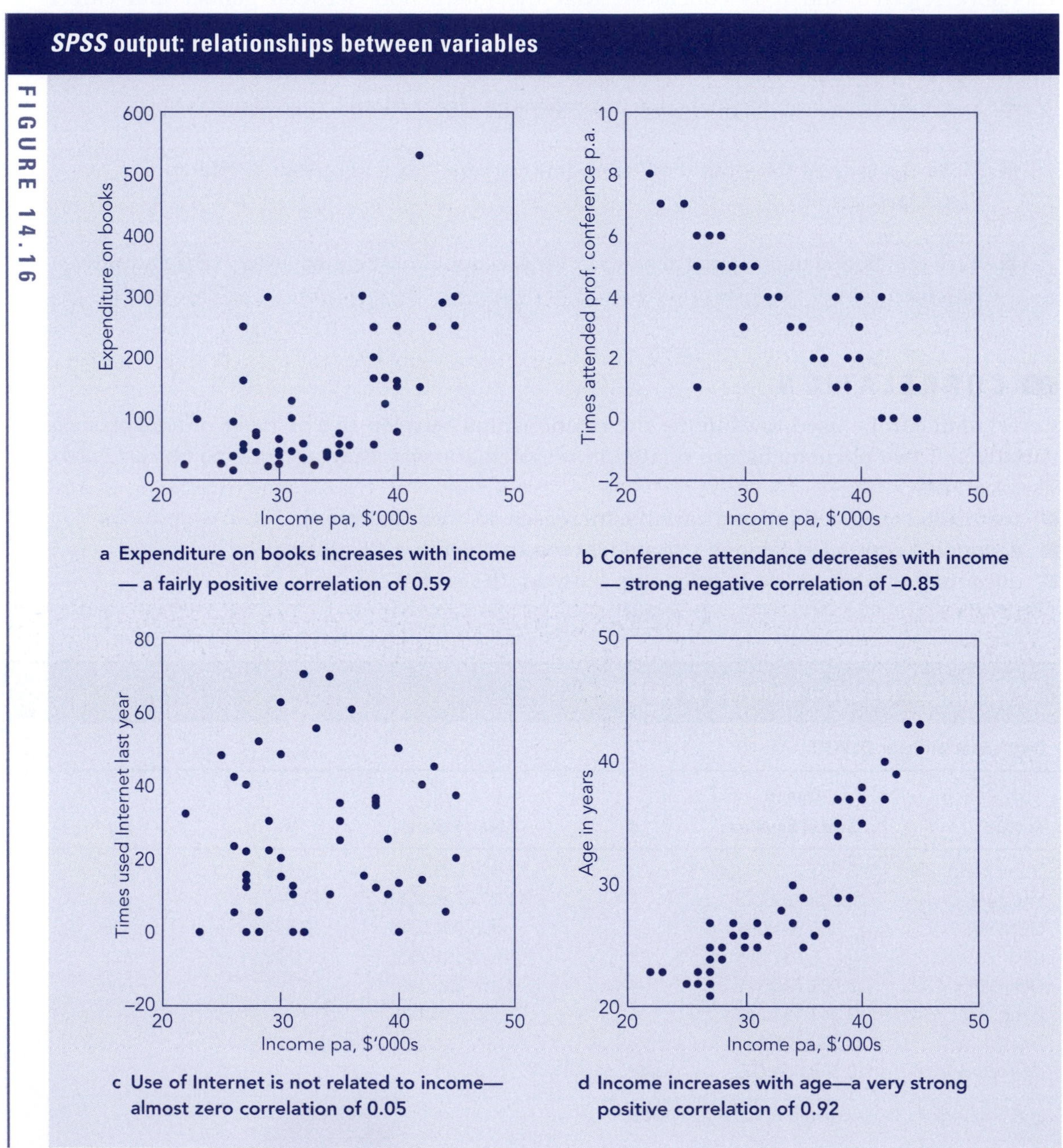

a Expenditure on books increases with income — a fairly positive correlation of 0.59

b Conference attendance decreases with income — strong negative correlation of –0.85

c Use of Internet is not related to income—almost zero correlation of 0.05

d Income increases with age—a very strong positive correlation of 0.92

- zero if there is no relationship between two variables;
- +1.0 if there is perfect positive correlation between two variables (they increase together);
- –1.0 if there is perfect negative correlation between two variables (one increases as the other decreases);
- between 0 and +1.0 if there is *some* positive correlation; or
- between 0 and –1.0 if there is *some* negative correlation.

The closer the coefficient is to 1.0, the greater the correlation. For example, 0.9 is a *high positive* correlation, 0.2 is a *low positive* correlation and –0.8 is a *high negative* correlation.

The correlation coefficient is calculated from a formula that involves measuring how far each data point is from the mean of each variable and multiplying the two differences. In Figure 14.17 it can be seen that the result will be a positive number for data points in the top right-hand and bottom left-hand quadrants (B and C) and negative for data points in the other two quadrants (A and D). The calculations are shown for two of the data points by way of illustration. If most of the data points are in quadrants B and C a positive correlation will result, while if most of the data points are in A and D a negative correlation will result. If the data points are widely scattered in all four quadrants, then the negatives cancel out the positives, resulting in a low value for the correlation. This explains in very broad terms the basis of the positive and negative correlations, and high and low correlations. It is beyond the scope of this book to explain how the 'perfect' correlation is made to equal one, but for those with the requisite mathematics, this can be deduced from the formula for r, which is given in Appendix 5 (p.336).

Significance of r

The *significance* of a correlation coefficient depends on its magnitude (closeness to 1) and the sample size, and is assessed by means of a t-test (see the formula in Appendix 5).

The null hypothesis is expressed as follows:

Correlation

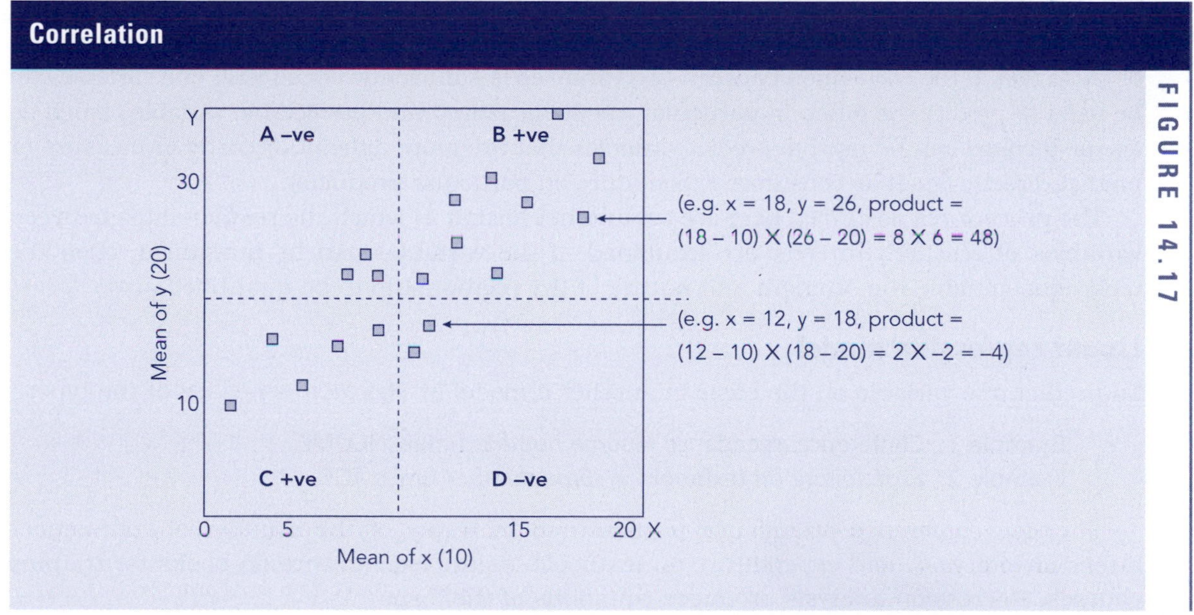

FIGURE 14.17

H_0 – Null hypothesis: the correlation between the variables is *zero*.
H_1 – Alternative hypothesis: the correlation between the variables is *not zero*.

The t-test therefore indicates only whether the correlation coefficient is significantly different from zero. Coefficients that are quite low can emerge as significant if the sample is large enough.

SPSS and correlation

SPSS can be used to produce correlation coefficients between pairs of variables, as shown in Figure 14.18. The output is in the form of a symmetrical matrix so that, for example, the correlation between age and income is the same as between income and age. For each pair of variables the output includes the correlation coefficient, the sample size (N) and p (Sig. 2-tailed), the probability related to the t-test. As with other tests, if the probability is below 0.05 we reject the null hypothesis—therefore only those correlations where the value of p is below 0.05 are significantly different from zero.

The correlation matrix shown in Figure 14.18 was produced using the following procedure.

- Select **Analyze** from the menu bar, then **Correlate**.
- Select **Bivariate** to open the **Bivariate Correlations** dialog box.
- Move the variables *inc, age, prof, cost* and *int* to the **Variables** box.
- Click on **OK** and the correlation matrix will be presented in the **Output** window.

REGRESSION

Linear regression takes us one step further in this type of quantitative analysis—in the direction of *prediction*. If the correlation between two variables is sufficiently consistent, one variable can be used to predict the other. In particular, easily measured and predictable variables (such as age or income) can be used to predict variables that are more difficult or costly to measure or predict directly (such as consumer expenditure on particular products).

The procedures described here are yet another format in which the relationships between variables of research interest are examined. If the variables can be quantified, then the techniques enable the strength and nature of the relationship to be quantified also.

Linear regression model

To predict one variable on the basis of another a model or *equation* is needed of the type:

Example 1: Conference attendance = *some number* times INCOME
Example 2: Expenditure on textbooks = *some number* times AGE

Suppose conference attendance is measured in terms of the number of conferences attended in a year, and expenditure on textbooks as the expenditure on books for training courses. Regression analysis produces equations of the form:

SPSS output: correlation matrix

FIGURE 14.18

		Income pa, $'000s	Age in years	Times attended prof. conf. pa	Expenditure on books	Times used Internet pa
Income pa, $000s	**Pearson Correlation**	1	.917**	−.845**	.587**	.049
	Sig. (2-tailed)	.	.000	.000	.000	.735
	N	50	50	50	50	50
Age in years	**Pearson Correlation**	.917**	1	−.722**	.605**	−.081
	Sig. (2-tailed)	.000	.	.000	.000	.578
	N	50	50	50	50	50
Times attended prof. conference pa	**Pearson Correlation**	−.845**	−.722**	1	−.518**	−.119
	Sig. (2-tailed)	.000	.000	.	.000	.409
	N	50	50	50	50	50
Expenditure on books	**Pearson Correlation**	.587**	.605**	−.518**	1	−.091
	Sig. (2-tailed)	.000	.000	.000	.	.530
	N	50	50	50	50	50
Times used Internet pa	**Pearson Correlation**	.049	−.081	−.119	−.091	1
	Sig. (2-tailed)	.735	.578	.409	.530	.
	N	50	50	50	50	50

** Correlation is significant at the 0.01 level (2-tailed).

Example 1: Number of conferences attended = a + b × INCOME
Example 2: Dollars spent on texts for training courses = a + b × AGE

The *beta coefficients* or *parameters* a and b are determined from examination of existing data using *regression analysis*. Once we have values of a and b we can predict conference attendance on the basis of income and book expenditure on the basis of age. The process of finding out the values of the parameters or coefficients is referred to as *calibration* of the model. In general terms this is represented by the equation:

$$y = a + bx$$

where y stands for conference attendance or dollars spent and x stands for income or age. Note that *conference attendance* and *expenditure on books* are the *dependent* variables here and INCOME and AGE are the *independent* variables.

In visual terms this describes a 'regression line' fitted through the data, with 'intercept' or 'constant' of a and 'slope' of b as shown in Figure 14.19. The regression procedure finds the *line of best fit* by finding the line which minimises the sum of the (squared) differences between it and the data points, and specifies this line by giving values for a and b.

SPSS and regression

Two examples of regression output from *SPSS* are shown in Figure 14.20. The *SPSS* program produces a large amount of output which we are not concerned with here.

FIGURE 14.19

Regression line

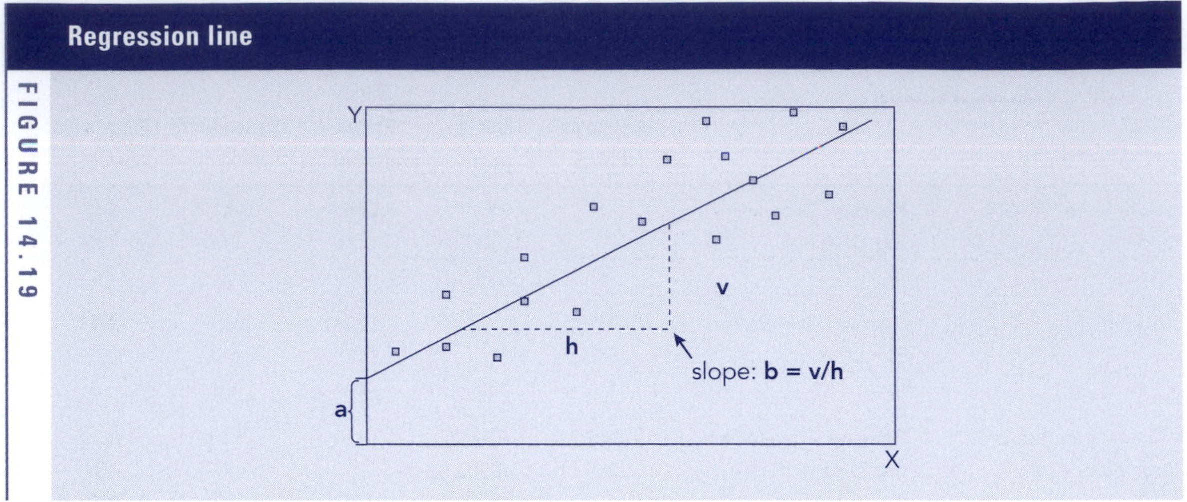

However, the output illustrates the point that regression is an involved process and only the broad outlines are dealt with in this book. The output relates to *multiple* regression, which involves more than one independent variable, as discussed in the next section—but here we have only one independent variable: income.

The items we are interested in are the value of the regression coefficient (R, which is similar to the correlation coefficient) and its test of significance, and the beta coefficients listed under B. For Example 1, the relationship between conference attendance and income, the value of R is 0.845 and its probability (as measured by an ANOVA F test) is 0.000, which makes it significant. The constant (a) is 13.245 and the coefficient or slope (b) for income is –0.286. The regression equation is therefore:

$$\text{Number of conferences attended per annum} = 13.245 - 0.286 \times \text{INCOME (in \$'000s pa)}$$

This regression line can be plotted onto a graph, as shown in Figure 14.21. With this equation, if we knew a management trainee's income we could estimate the number of conferences attended. This can be done by either by reading it off the graph or calculating it. For example, for a student with an income of $30,000 a year:

$$\text{Number of conferences attended per annum} = 13.245 - 0.286 \times 30 = 4.665$$

So we would estimate that the average trainee with such an income would be expected to attend four or five professional conferences a year. Of course we are not saying that *every* trainee with that income will attend four or five professional conferences a year. The regression line/equation is a form of average—it is not precise.

The regression table for Example 1, shown in Figure 14.20, was produced using the following procedure:

- Select **Analyze** from the menu bar, then **Regression**, then **Linear**
- Move the variable *conf* to the **Dependent** box and *inc* to the **Independent(s)** box.
- Click on **OK** and the regression table will be presented in the **Output** window.

SPSS output: regression analysis

FIGURE 14.20

Example 1: Conference attendance and income

Variables Entered/Removed(b)

Model	Variables Entered	Variables Removed	Method
1	Income pa, $'000s(a)	.	Enter

a All requested variables entered
b Dependent Variable: Times attended prof. conference pa

Model Summary

Model	R	R Square	Adjusted R Square	Std. Error of the Estimate
1	.845(a)	.715	.709	1.13

a Predictors: (Constant), Income pa, $'000s

ANOVA(b)

Model		Sum of Squares	df	Mean Square	F	Sig.
1	Regression	153.755	1	153.755	120.268	.000(a)
	Residual	61.365	48	1.278		
	Total	215.120	49			

a Predictors: (Constant), Income pa, $'000s
b Dependent Variable: Times attended prof. conference pa

Coefficients(a)

Model		Unstandardized Coefficients		Standardized Coefficients	t	Sig.
		B	Std. Error	Beta		
1	(Constant)	13.245	.880		15.059	.000
	Income pa, $'000s	–.286	.026	–.845	–10.967	.000

a Dependent Variable: Times attended prof. conference pa

continues

FIGURE 14.20

SPSS output: regression analysis *continued*

Example 2: Expenditure on textbooks and age

Variables Entered/Removed(b)

Model	Variables Entered	Variables Removed	Method
1	Age in years(a)	.	Enter

a All requested variables entered
b Dependent Variable: Dollars Spent on Texts

Model Summary

Model	R	R Square	Adjusted R Square	Std. Error of the Estimate
1	.605(a)	.366	.353	85.58

a Predictors: (Constant), Age in years

ANOVA(b)

Model		Sum of Squares	df	Mean Square	F	Sig.
1	Regression	203 104.348	1	203 104.348	27.729	.000(a)
	Residual	351 584.132	48	7 324.669		
	Total	554 688.480	49			

a Predictors: (Constant), Age in years
b Dependent Variable: **Dollars Spent on Texts**

Coefficients(a)

Model		Unstandardized Coefficients		Standardized Coefficients	t	Sig.
		B	Std. Error	Beta		
1	(Constant)	–182.219	58.558		–3.112	.003
	Age in years	10.425	1.980	.605	5.266	.000

a Dependent Variable: **Dollars Spent on Texts**

Example 2 in Figure 14.20 produces a similar output for the relationship between *dollars spent on texts for training course* and *age*. In this case the regression equation would be:

Expenditure on books for training course = −182.219 + 10.425 × AGE (in years)

A regression line can be shown graphically by selecting *Analyze* then *Curve Estimation* in *SPSS*—resulting in output as shown in Figure 14.21.

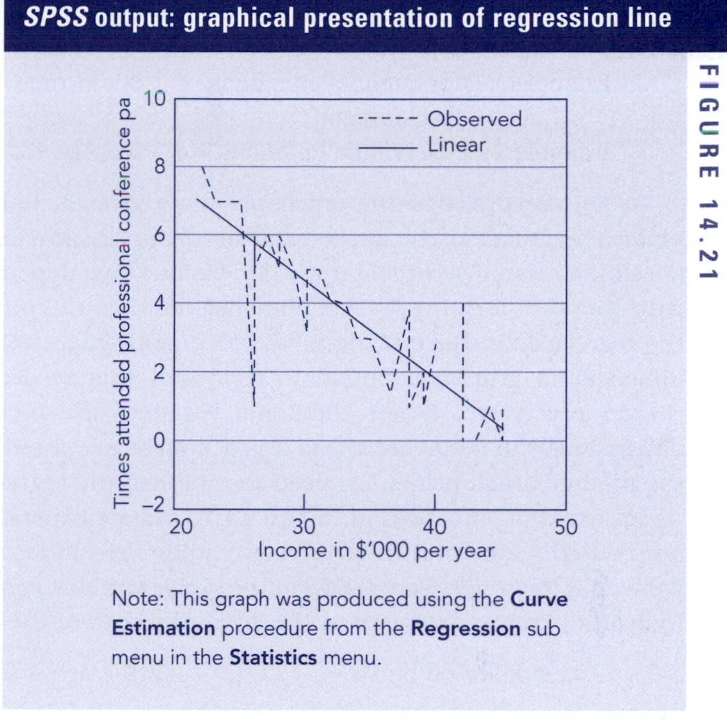

FIGURE 14.21 ***SPSS* output: graphical presentation of regression line**

Note: This graph was produced using the **Curve Estimation** procedure from the **Regression** sub menu in the **Statistics** menu.

Non-linear regression

In Figure 14.22 the relationship between the two variables is *non-linear*, which means that the relationship indicated is curved rather than being a straight line. The standard regression procedure discussed above seeks to fit a straight line to these data, but this would not be an accurate reflection of the relationship. This emphasises the importance of examining the data *visually*, as done here, and not relying just on correlation coefficients. When theory or observation of the data suggests that a *curved line* would better represent the relationship, non-linear methods may be used. These are available in *SPSS* and involve applying logarithms or other formulae to the data, but these techniques are beyond the scope of this book.

Multiple regression

Multiple regression is linear regression that involves more than one independent variable. For example, we might hypothesise that the number of conferences attended per annum is dependent not just on income but also on personal expenditure on professional development, or that dollars spent on texts for a training course is not just dependent on age but

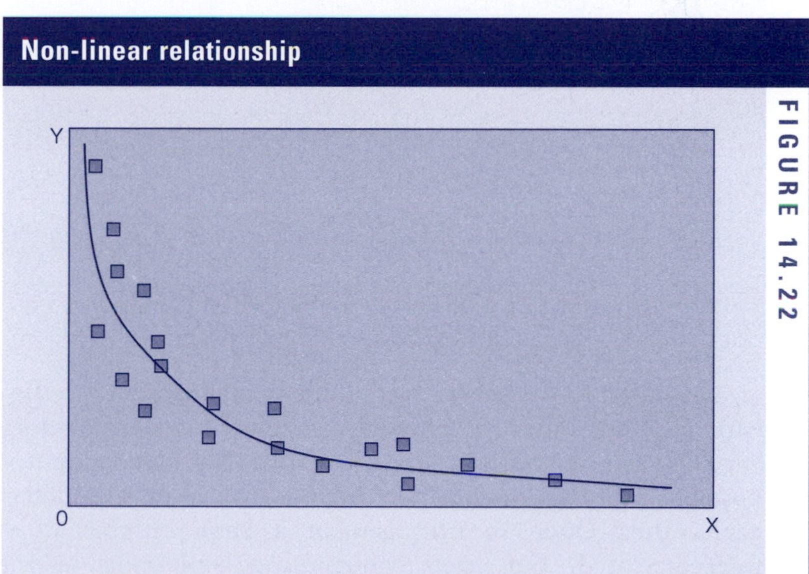

FIGURE 14.22 Non-linear relationship

also frequency of reading the *Financial Review*. Thus our models, or regression equations, would be:

Example 1: Conferences attended = a + b × Income + c × Expenditure on professional development
Example 2: Expenditure on books = a + b × Age + c × Reading *Financial Review*

In *linear* regression the procedure fits a straight line to the data—the line of best fit. In *multiple* regression the procedure fits a *surface* to the data—the *surface of best fit*. It is possible to visualise this in three dimensions (one dependent and two independent variables) with the axes forming a three-dimensional box, the observations suspended in space, and the regression surface being a flat plane somewhere within the box. *SPSS* provides a three-dimensional graphical option to represent this relationship using the *Graphs* and then *Scatter* procedure. When additional variables are included then four, five or even more dimensions will be involved and it is of course not possible to visualise the process. However, the mathematical principles used to establish the regression equation are the same.

An example is shown in Figure 14.23, where expenditure on books for a training course are related to age and frequency of reading the *Financial Review*. It will be noticed that the value of R has risen from 0.605 in the single variable case (Figure 14.20, example 2) to 0.720, indicating an improvement in the 'fit' of the data to the model. The model equation is now:

Expenditure on books = −117.360 + 7.219 × age + 0.754 × reading *Financial Review*

The model/equation is implicit in all multiple regression analyses, but in much social research it is not the model/equation and prediction which is important but simply the relationships between the dependent variable and a range of independent variables. Variables which make a significant contribution to R^2 are included in the analysis and the beta coefficients indicate the respective relationships.

The multiple regression table shown in Figure 14.23 was produced using the following procedure:

- Select **Analyze** from the menu bar, then **Regression**, then **Linear** to open the **Linear Regression** dialog box.

- Select the variable *cost* and move it to the **Dependent** box by clicking on the **right arrow** button.

- In a similar fashion, move the variables *inc* and *finrev* to the **Independent(s)** box.

- Click on the **OK** button and the regression table will be produced in the ***SPSS* Output** window.

It is possible, in theory, to continue to add variables to the equation. This should be done with caution, since it frequently involves *multi-collinearity*, in which the independent variables are themselves intercorrelated. The independent variables should be, as far as possible, just that—independent. Various tests exist to determine their independence from each other. Often in management a large number of variables are involved, many intercorrelated, but each contributing something to the management issue under

FIGURE 14.23

SPSS output: multiple regression

Variables Entered/Removed(b)

Model	Variables Entered	Variables Removed	Method
1	Times read *Financial Review* in last year, Age in years(a)	.	Enter

a All requested variables entered
b Dependent Variable: **Expenditure on books**

Model Summary

Model	R	R Square	Adjusted R Square	Std. Error of the Estimate
1	.720(a)	.519	.499	75.34

a Predictors: (Constant), Times read *Financial Review* in last year, Age in years

ANOVA(b)

Model		Sum of Squares	df	Mean Square	F	Sig.
1	Regression	287 941.206	2	143 970.603	25.367	.000(a)
	Residual	266 747.274	47	5 675.474		
	Total	554 688.480	49			

a Predictors: (Constant), Times read *Financial Review* in last year, Age in years
b Dependent Variable: **Expenditure on books**

Coefficients(a)

Model		Unstandardized Coefficients		Standardized Coefficients	t	Sig.
		B	Std. Error	Beta		
1	(Constant)	–117.360	54.207		–2.165	.035
	Age in years	7.219	1.930	.419	3.741	.000
	Times read *Financial Review* in last year	.754	.195	.433	3.866	.000

a Dependent Variable: **Expenditure on books**

investigation. Multivariate analysis procedures, such as cluster and factor analysis, discussed below, are designed to partly overcome these problems.

FACTOR AND CLUSTER ANALYSIS

Introduction

Factor and cluster analysis are techniques used when the number of independent variables is large and there is a desire to group them in some way. The theoretical counterpart to this is that there are some complex phenomena that cannot be measured by just one or two variables, but require a battery of variables, each contributing some aspect to the make-up of the phenomenon. An example is *organisational commitment*, which can arise from a range of variables such as job satisfaction, income, tenure, age, salary, job level, type of industry, involvement in decision-making, relationship with supervisor, organisational culture, self-esteem, education and family situation. Factor and cluster analysis are ways of grouping variables to jointly account for complex phenomena.

Factor analysis

Factor analysis is based on the idea that certain variables 'go together', in that people with a high score on one variable also tend to have a high score on certain others. For example, people who attend computer training courses might also use the Internet while people with strong pro-environment views might be found working in certain types of organisations. Analysis of this type of phenomenon can be approached using a simple, manual technique involving a correlation matrix of the variables as illustrated in Figure 14.24. Groupings of variables can be shown by indicating which variables have the highest correlations with each other. In Figure 14.24 three groupings of variables are shown where the arrows indicate highest correlations.

This manual procedure only takes account of the highest correlation, with some use being made of the second highest as indicated. Variables will have a range of lower order relationships with each other that this method does not take into account. A number of lower order correlations may cumulatively be more significant than a single 'highest' correlation. From a more sophisticated perspective, factor analysis is a mathematical

FIGURE 14.24 Simple manual factor analysis

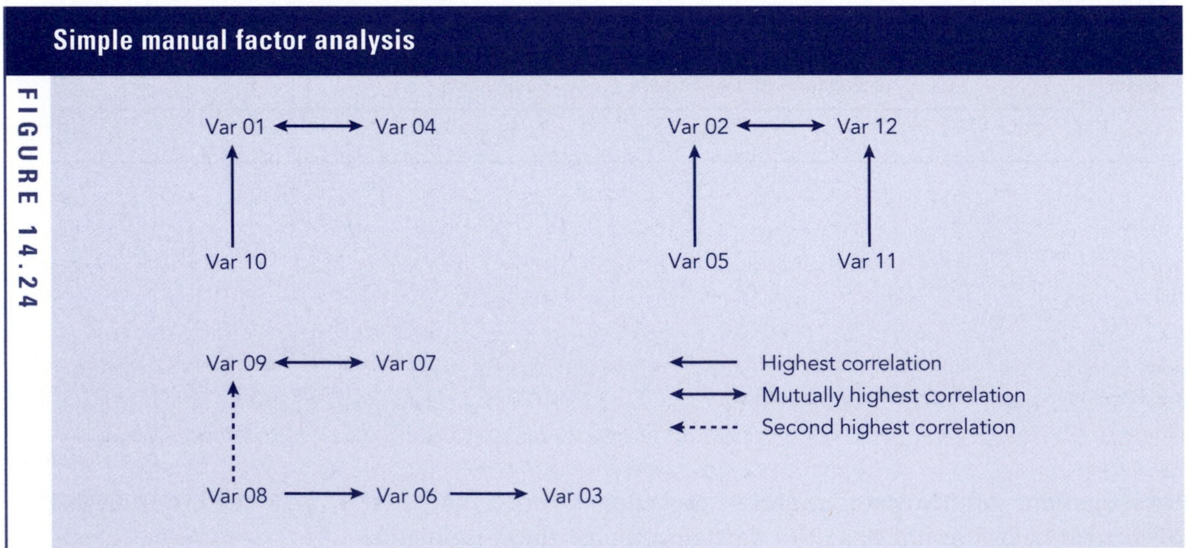

procedure that groups the variables by taking account of *all* the correlations. In essence it is a method for determining the number of underlying factors or groups among a larger number of variables.

Factor analysis can be conducted using the *SPSS* procedure **Factor**. The procedure for producing a matrix of variables and factors involves a range of choices concerning the optimal method for *extracting* the *factors* from the data. However, these decisions are beyond the scope of this book.

The Training Survey does not contain data suitable for factor analysis but an example of the results of an *SPSS* factor analysis from another data set is shown in Figure 14.25. The matrix shows the results of a factor analysis of data from a questionnaire survey of 3132 employees in eighteen Australian organisations. The survey contained fifty questions concerning employees' satisfaction with various aspects of organisational communication (see the Communication Satisfaction Questionnaire, Downs 1988). Understanding the dimensions of *communication satisfaction* is important to management research since it has been shown as a significant predictor for organisational climate, job satisfaction and organisational commitment (Ticehurst & Ross-Smith 1992).

The variables arising from 50 questions are labelled COMSAT4, COMSAT5 etc. in Figure 14.25. Seven factors were extracted using the *SPSS* **Factor** procedure. This suggests that there are seven components or dimensions that make up the *communication satisfaction* construct. The factor matrix shows the *factor loadings* of the fifty variables used in the study on the seven factors. All variables have loadings on all seven factors but for clarity only variables with a factor loading of greater than 0.3 are shown in the table. Values below 0.3 are of little practical interest.

It is not difficult to understand factor loadings. They are similar to correlation coefficients and represent the association between the variables and the factors. They can range in value from –1.00 to +1.00. As a rule of thumb, only variables with a loading of greater than 0.5 should be accepted as loading on a factor. For example, Factor 7 is comprised of 5 variables with loadings all above 0.5. Unfortunately, not all factors are as 'pure' as Factor 7 in the real world of management research. It can be seen that some variables have a loading on more than one factor. For example, the first variable, COMSAT38, has a loading of 0.678 on Factor 1, but is 'contaminated' by a loading of 0.326 on Factor 3. In an effort to identify factors that are uniquely represented by a set of variables, researchers often only accept a variable as loading on a factor if it has a loading of more than 0.5 and a *contamination* of less than 0.3 on another factor.

Factors are usually given names by researchers to reflect the conceptual areas that they represent. For example, if all the variables (questions) making up Factor 7 were concerned with some form of immediate communication with work mates the factor might be labelled 'interpersonal'. As a matter of interest, previous research suggests that some of the factors (dimensions) comprising communication satisfaction are *communication with top management, interdepartmental communication, communication with supervisor, media quality, informal communication, communication climate* and *personal feedback*.

The factor analysis shown in Figure 14.25 was prepared using the following *SPSS* procedure:

FIGURE 14.25

Factor matrix: communication satisfaction

Variable	Factor						
	1	2	3	4	5	6	7
	Factor loadings						
COMSAT38	.678		.326				
COMSAT36	.674		.352				
COMSAT37	.653						
COMSAT31	.590						
COMSAT21	.570						
COMSAT24	.554		.306	.337			
COMSAT28	.541						
COMSAT23	.529		.359	.304			
COMSAT27	.519	.391					
COMSAT30	.507					.311	
COMSAT35	.506	.354					
COMSAT19	.478		.399				
COMSAT33	.469	.342					
COMSAT26	.456	.421					
COMSAT32	.374	.363					
COMSAT20		.836					
COMSAT22		.809					
COMSAT29		.793					
COMSAT25		.763					
COMSAT18		.714					
COMSAT34		.637					
COMSAT48			.799				
COMSAT49			.790				
COMSAT51			.774				
COMSAT47			.766				
COMSAT50			.733				
COMSAT12				.756			
COMSAT13				.727			
COMSAT17				.711			
COMSAT16				.708			
COMSAT6				.620			
COMSAT15				.494			
COMSAT10		.344		.478			
COMSAT5	.350			.397	.388		
COMSAT8					.785		
COMSAT4		.318			.747		
COMSAT7					.684		
COMSAT9		.363			.662		
COMSAT14	.303			.310	.470		
COMSAT11		.382			.437		
COMSAT52						.766	
COMSAT53						.758	
COMSAT54	.319					.739	
COMSAT56	.348					.651	
COMSAT55	.313					.607	
COMSAT45							.826
COMSAT46							.807
COMSAT43							.797
COMSAT42							.788
COMSAT44							.587

Extraction Method: Principal Component Analysis.

Rotation Method: Varimax with Kaiser Normalisation.

- Select **Analyze** from the menu bar, then **Data Reduction**.
- Select **Factor**, then transfer the variables to be included in the analysis to the **Variables** box.
- Click on **Rotation** then, under **Method**, select **Varimax**, and under **Display** select **Rotated solution,** then click on **Continue** to return to the **Factor Analysis** dialog box.
- Click on **Options** then, under **Missing Values,** select **Replace with mean**.
- Under **Coefficient Display Format** select **Sorted by size**. Also select **Suppress Absolute Values Less Than 0.3**.
- Select **Continue**, then click on **OK** to produce a factor matrix table in the **Output** window.

It is important to note that an experienced researcher might select other *SPSS* factor analysis options than those chosen here.

Cluster analysis

Cluster analysis is another 'grouping' procedure that attempts to identify relatively homogeneous groups of cases (or variables) based on selected characteristics. Consider the case of a cable TV company in which management is seeking to determine an optimal programming mix to attract potential customers. The company has collected data concerning two variables—*age* and *hours of TV viewing per week*. The data can be plotted graphically as shown in Figure 14.26. It can be seen that there are three broad 'clusters' of respondents: two young clusters and one older cluster. There is also one value, called an *outlier*, which does not fit in any of the clusters. Each of these clusters might form particular market segments. With just two variables and a few observations it is relatively simple to identify clusters visually. However, with more variables and more cases this is not possible manually and the use of statistical software becomes necessary.

The *SPSS Cluster Analysis* procedure first calculates the 'distances' between data points in terms of a range of specified variables. Those points which are closest together are put into a first round cluster and a new point halfway between the two is put in their place. The process is repeated to form a second round of clustering, and a third and fourth and so on, until there are only two 'points' left. The result is usually illustrated by a *dendrogram* as shown in Figure 14.27. This figure was prepared using the same data used to prepare the scattergram shown in Figure 14.26. The three clusters shown in Figure 14.26 can easily be identified in the dendrogram, as can the outlier value.

The data used to prepare Figures 14.26 and 14.27 are shown in Appendix 6 (p. 337). The cluster analysis dendrogram shown in Figure 14.27 was prepared using the following *SPSS* cluster analysis procedure:

- Select **Analyze** from the menu bar, then **Classify**.
- Select **Hierarchical Cluster**, then transfer the two variables to be included in the cluster analysis to the **Variables** box.
- In the **Cluster** box select **Cases**. In the **Display** box select **Plots**. Do not select **Statistics**.
- Click on **OK** to produce a cluster analysis dendrogram in the **Output** window.

ANALYSIS CONTEXT

As has been stressed throughout this book, a theoretical or evaluative framework should determine the method of data collection and analysis. At the analysis stage the researcher should ideally not be wondering what to relate to what, or be choosing variables and analyses in an *ad hoc* manner. While a certain amount of inductive exploration and even serendipity is inevitable, ideally there should be a basic analysis plan from the beginning. Key variables and the question of relationships between them should have been thought about in advance, for example, as a result of an early 'concept mapping' exercise. Thus, while the examples given in this chapter may appear *ad hoc* and 'data driven', in a real research project the procedures used should be theory driven, problem driven or hypothesis driven.

FIGURE 14.26

Plots of clusters

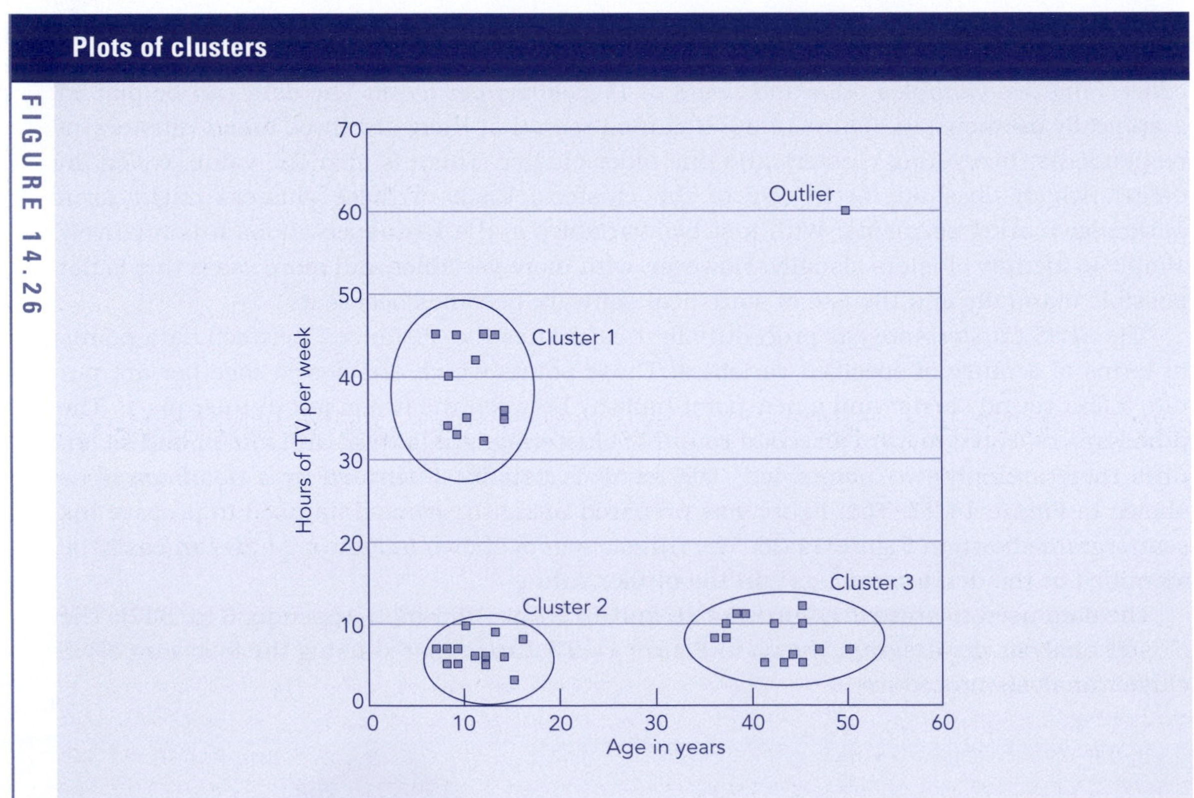

FIGURE 14.27 ***SPSS* output: cluster analysis dendrogram**

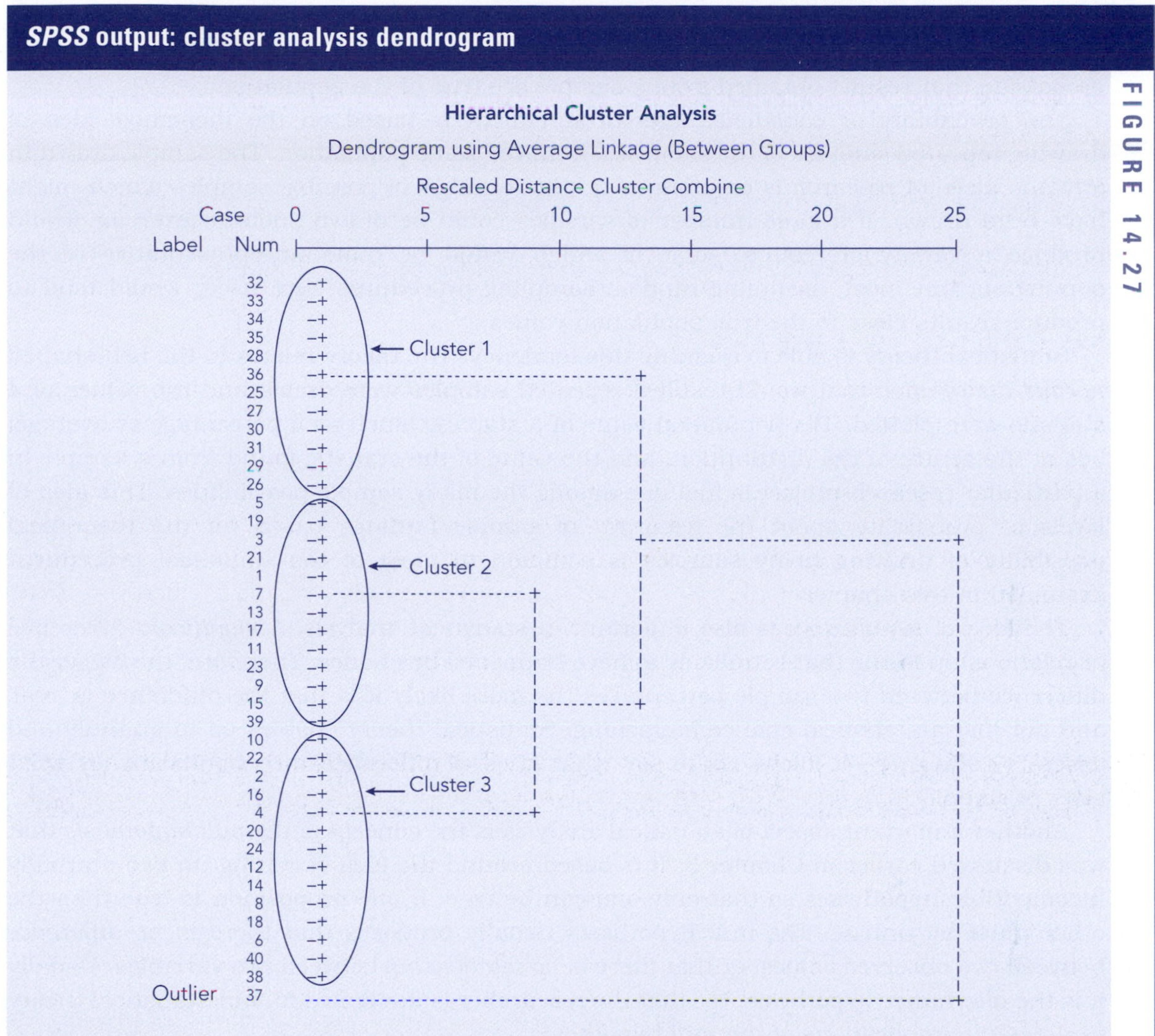

SUMMARY

This chapter provided an introduction to statistical analysis. A number of basic concepts and ideas—including measures of *central tendency* and *dispersion*, *probabilistic statements*, *normal distribution*, *significance*, the *null hypothesis*, and *dependent* and *independent* variables—provide a foundation for statistical analysis.

Central tendency describes how the scores on a variable tend to cluster about the centre of their distribution. Three indexes of central tendency are the *mean*, *mode* and *median*. *Dispersion* describes how the scores on a variable are dispersed or spread across the measurement scale. Three indexes of dispersion are *range*, *variance* and *standard deviation*.

Inferential statistics seeks to make *probabilistic* statements about a *population* on the basis of information available from a sample drawn from that population. The statements are probabilistic because it is not possible to be absolutely sure that any sample is truly representative of the population from which it has been drawn. We can only estimate the *probability* that results obtained from a sample are true of the population.

The probability or *confidence interval* statement is based on the *theoretical* idea of drawing repeated samples of the same size from the same population. The sample drawn in any one piece of research is only one of a large number of possible samples which might have been drawn. If a large number of samples could be drawn such an exercise would produce a variety of results, some of which would be quite unrepresentative of the population, but most, assuming random sampling procedures were used, would tend to produce results close to the true population values.

Statistical theory is able to quantify this tendency. The theory relates to the bell-shaped *normal distribution* that would result if repeated samples were drawn and the values of a statistic were plotted. The population value of a statistic (such as a percentage or average) lies at the centre of the distribution, and the value of the statistic found from a sample in a particular research project is just one among the many sample possibilities. This idea of levels of probability about the accuracy of sample findings based on the theoretical possibility of drawing many samples is common to most of the statistical procedures examined in this chapter.

The idea of *significance* is also important in statistical analysis. A *significant* difference or relationship is one that is unlikely to have happened by chance. Therefore, the bigger the difference between two sample percentages the more likely it is that the difference is 'real' and not just a statistical chance happening. Statistical theory enables us to quantify and assess significance—it allows us to say what sizes of differences are significant for what sizes of sample.

Another important aspect of statistical analysis is the concept of the *null hypothesis* that was discussed earlier in Chapter 3. It is based around the idea of setting up two mutually incompatible hypotheses so that only one can be true. If one proposition is true then the other must be untrue. The null hypothesis usually proposes that there is *no difference* between two observed values, or that there is *no relationship* between two variables. Usually it is the *alternative* hypothesis, H_1, that the researcher is interested in, but statistical theory explores the implications of the null hypothesis.

The concept of *dependent* and *independent variables* was discussed earlier in Chapter 10 in relation to experimental research designs. If there is a relationship between a dependent and an independent variable the implication is that changes in the former are caused by changes in the latter. The independent variable influences the dependent variable.

A number of statistical analysis procedures were outlined in the chapter. These included the *Chi-square test*, the *t-test*, *analysis of variance*, *correlation*, and *linear and multiple regression*. These procedures were illustrated by the use of the *SPSS* statistical analysis software package.

EXERCISES

1 It is suggested that you replicate the various analyses set out in this chapter using the data in Appendix 4 (p. 334) or your own data set.

FURTHER READING

General introduction to research methods: Burns (1994).
Discussion of basic statistics: Spatz and Johnston (1989).
More advanced discussion of behavioural research: Kerlinger (1986).
Statistics in the context of business and management: Keller and Warrack (1991).
Use of SPSS *in social research:* Babbie and Halley (1995), Francis (1996), Gerber and Voelkl (1997), Coakes and Steed (1997) or Green, Salkind and Akey (1997).

CHAPTER 15

Qualitative data analysis

This chapter addresses the task of analysing qualitative data, building on Chapter 7, which deals with the collection of such data. As indicated in the earlier chapter, it is sometimes difficult to separate the collection and analysis processes for qualitative data, at least in a temporal sense; but there is nevertheless a clear difference between certain data collection activities, such as interviewing someone with a tape recorder, and certain analysis activities, such as poring over typed interview transcripts.

Traditionally qualitative data have been analysed by manual means, and this continues, but in recent years computer software has become available to aid the process. Computers replicate and speed-up some of the more mechanical of the manual processes, but, of course, the task of interpretation remains with the researcher. The chapter first discusses the question of data storage and confidentiality; it then considers manual analysis methods and computer-based methods in turn. Since the most common form of qualitative data is interview or focus group transcripts or notes, the following discussions are based on this form of data. Most of the procedures nevertheless apply, in adapted form, to other forms of data, such as printed materials from organisational archives and the media.

DATA STORAGE AND CONFIDENTIALITY

Regardless of whether qualitative data are analysed manually or by computer, consideration should be given to the security and confidentiality of transcripts and tapes, particularly if sensitive material is involved. This raises ethical issues, as discussed in Chapter 3. As a precaution, ideally research material should not be labelled with real names of organisations or people. Fictitious names should be created. If it is felt that it will be necessary to relate tapes and transcripts back to original respondents at some later date, for example, for second interviews, a key relating fictitious to real identities should be kept in a separate, secure place. Of course, actual names mentioned by respondents on tapes cannot easily be erased, and it is a matter of judgement as to whether it is necessary to disguise such names in transcripts—in most cases they should be disguised in any quotations of the material in the research report. In some cases, however, it is necessary to create transcripts which are, in a way, less anonymous than the original. For example, an interviewee might say: 'I find it difficult to get on with John'. The transcript might change 'John' to 'David', but may need to identify John/David's position—for example: 'I find it difficult to get on with David [Supervisor]'.

MANUAL METHODS

Introduction

There are various ways of analysing interview transcripts or notes. The essence of any analysis procedure must be to return to the terms of reference, the conceptual framework and the research questions or hypotheses of the research, as discussed in Chapter 3. The information gathered should be sorted and evaluated in relation to the concepts identified in the conceptual framework, the research questions posed or the hypotheses put forward. In qualitative research, those original ideas may be very tentative and fluid. Questions and/or hypotheses, and the definition and operationalisation of concepts may be detailed or general; the more detailed and specific they are, the more likely they will be to closely influence the analysis. Conversely, the more general and tentative they are the more likely it is that the data analysis process will influence their refinement. Data gathering, hypothesis formulation and the identification of concepts is a two-way, evolving process. Ideas are refined and revised in the light of the information gathered, as described in relation to the *recursive* and *grounded theory* approaches discussed in Chapter 7.

In Chapter 3 it was noted that the development of a conceptual framework and of research questions or hypotheses is the most difficult and challenging part of a research project. In quantitative research involving primary data collection this work must mostly be done in advance of data collection because of the formal, one-off nature of the data collection process. It is therefore based primarily on a reading of the literature. In the case of qualitative research this challenging work may be spread throughout the research process, as indicated in Figure 15.1. This is another way of looking at the induction/deduction distinction discussed in Chapter 2.

In addition to the problem of ordering and summarising the data conceptually, the researcher is faced with the very practical problem of just how to approach the pile of interview notes or transcripts which have been assembled.

FIGURE 15.1 Circular model of the research process in qualitative and quantitative contexts

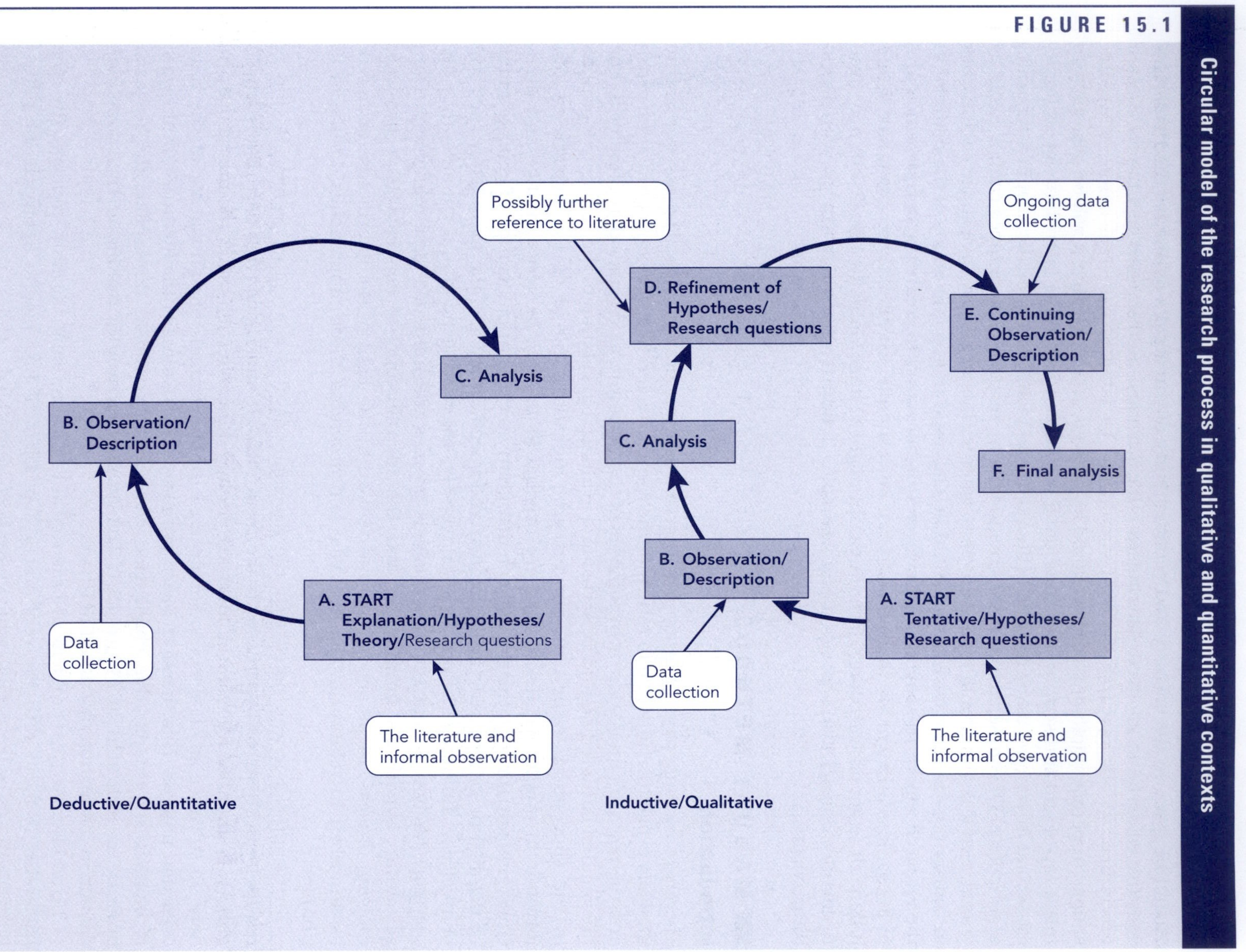

Reading

The basic activity in qualitative analysis is the *reading* of notes, transcripts, documents, or *listening* or *viewing* audio and video materials. In what follows, it is assumed that the material being analysed is text—while practical adaptations are necessary for audio and video material, the principles are the same. The reading process is started in light of research questions and/or hypotheses initially developed and/or those which have evolved during the data collection process.

Emergent themes

A typical approach to qualitative analysis is to search for *emergent themes*—the equivalent of *variables* in quantitative research. The themes may arise from the conceptual framework and research questions, and therefore be consciously searched for in a deductive way, or they may emerge unprompted in a more inductive way. Typically, both processes will be at work. This can be illustrated with an example. Figure 15.2 presents a very simple conceptual framework for studying the relationship between career attitudes and attitudes towards in-service training. It suggests that overall attitudes towards in-service training are made up from a number of factors which may be associated with an employee's basic attitudes towards his or her career. It is deliberately sketchy, with items labelled A, B, C and X, Y, Z, leaving scope for these factors to emerge from the data. Figure 15.3 contains short extracts from interviews with employees enrolled in an in-service course. Themes which emerge from the transcripts are 'flagged' in the left-hand margin. The researcher's judgement of the strength with which the views are expressed is indicated here with one or more plus or minus signs. It is clear that other themes might be identified and alternative terms might be used for the items which are identified, illustrating the personal and subjective nature of qualitative analysis.

The 'developed' conceptual framework presented in Figure 15.4 shows how some of the themes/concepts/factors and relationships emerging from the interviews might begin to be incorporated into the conceptual framework. On the basis of information from abstracts from three interviews, the conceptual framework is *developed* but not *fully* developed; it represents work in progress.

Outline conceptual framework for qualitative study of career and in-service training attitudes

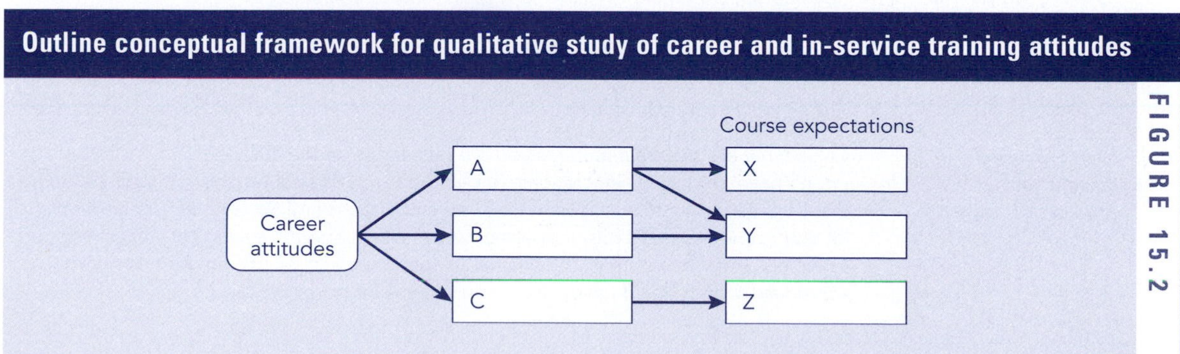

FIGURE 15.2

FIGURE 15.3

Interview transcript extracts

Mark (Age 27, Male, Salary $45K, Marketing)

Codes	Transcript
Career: Strategic *Course: Up-to-date* *Career: Competitive ++*	*Q. What are your main reasons for enrolling in this course?* Well, in my case, it's just a strategic career move really. My first degree was an arts degree, so I felt I should get a basic business qualification. I didn't feel that I really needed it right now—I seem to be able to do the job I'm in OK—but thinking ahead, if I want to move onwards and upwards, sort of thing: I need to keep up-to-date and I may be at a disadvantage compared with people with business qualifications—so here I am!
Course: University Reputation + *Career: Competitive +*	*Q. Why this particular course at this particular university?* I think the main reason is its reputation. Everybody says that with a qualification from this place you can't go wrong. Again, I feel I need to give myself as many advantages as possible, given that I didn't start out with a business degree.
Course: Flexibility +	*Q. So what are the main features you are looking for in the course?* Well, to be honest, I want flexibility so that I can fit it into my schedule—because I'm quite busy at work—and I want it to be challenging but not too tough, so that I can get it out of the way as soon as possible. It's a means to an end. I enjoy the marketing stuff, but some of the rest of it's not too exciting—I want to do some of it in intensive mode if I can.

Anna (Age 32, Female, Salary $52K, HR)

Codes	Transcript
Career: Skills upgrade + *Course: Up-to-date* *Career: Competitive*	*Q. What are your main reasons for enrolling in this course?* It's really to update my skills. I finished my first degree 10 years ago and I just need to get up to date with ideas, computer skills and so on. Even though I've got the experience, some of my new graduate staff know more about some things than I do. I've always prided myself on being ahead of the game and I thought with all these new developments, like e-business, the best way to be on top of things was to take a course.
Course: Up-to-date ++ *Course: Available choice +*	*Q. Why this particular course at this particular university?* I think this place is more on the ball than the other universities around. The marketing professor is always being quoted in the business press and he always sounds impressive to me. I looked at the website and they just project an image of being up there with the latest ideas. The other places seemed a bit staid by comparison. And there's more choice of the sorts of subjects I'm interested in, like e-business and international marketing.

Ben (Age 25, Male, Salary $45K, Accounting)

Codes	Transcript
Career: Company role expectation *Course: Convenience +*	*Q. What are your main reasons for enrolling in this course?* Well, there's a sort of tradition in the company where I work—more or less everybody comes here to do the MBA and the company pays half the cost. So it's a bargain! You can't afford not to really—it's expected if you want to progress. And I work around the corner, so it's very convenient.
Course: Minimal expectations *Course: Skills upgrade*	*Q. So what are the main features you are looking for in the course?* I don't have any fixed expectations, really. I hope it's interesting and not so demanding that I fail things—that would be a bit of an embarrassment! So far I haven't learned a lot that's new—some of it is a repeat of what I heard about 5 years ago—and from the same lecturers! So it's a sort of refresher in some respects—but I hope to get onto some new stuff in due course, else it could get a bit boring.

Partially developed conceptual framework

FIGURE 15.4

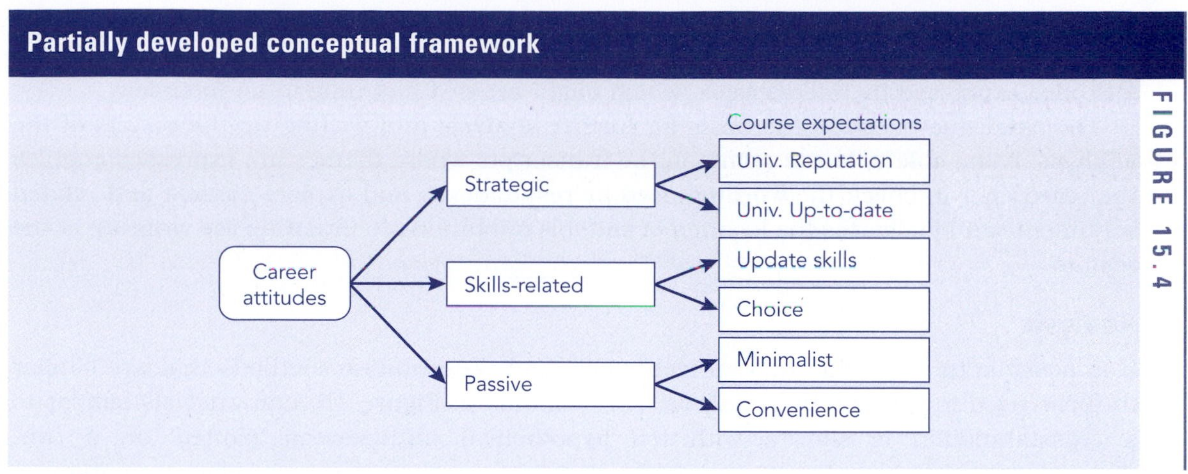

Mechanics

The initial steps in qualitative analysis involve fairly methodical procedures to classify and organise the information collected.

Analysis can be done by hand on hard copy transcripts, which should have a wide margin on one side to accommodate the 'flagging' of themes discussed above. Colour coding can be used in the flagging process and 'Post-it' notes can also be used to mark key sections.

Standard word processing packages can be of considerable assistance in the analysis process. The space for flagging can then be secured using the columns or tables facility in the word processor. Word processing packages also have facilities for:

- adding 'Comments' and for blocking text with colour, underlining or bold;
- 'searching' to locate key words and phrases;
- coding and cross-referencing using indexing or cross-referencing procedures.

It can be seen, therefore, that standard word processing packages have a number of features to aid text analysis, although obviously not as many as the specialist packages discussed later in the chapter.

It can be useful to number the paragraphs in a transcript or use the line numbering facility available in word processing packages. This can facilitate a *cataloguing* process, which might result in something like the following:

Career attitude—strategic:	Mark: p. 2, para. 3, p. 7, para. 4
	Jennie: p. 7, para. 1
Career attitude—skills-based	Anna: p. 3, para. 2
	Ben: p. 4, para. 4
	Jiri: p. 6, para. 2

This method is often necessary to keep track of topics across a number of interviews, but also because topics are typically covered several times in the same interview. A particular focus of the analysis may be related not to particular substantive topics raised by the interviewer, and therefore related to particular questions, but to, for example, underlying attitudes expressed by interviewees, which might arise at any time in an interview.

The catalogue becomes the basis for further analysis and writing up the results of the analysis: being able to locate points in the transcripts where themes are expressed enables the researcher to check the wording used by respondents and explore context and related sentiments and facilitates the location of suitable quotations to illustrate the write-up of the results.

Analysis

It is possible to use data analysis techniques and presentation methods that are similar to those used in quantitative analysis. For example, in Figure 15.5 an analysis similar to a crosstabulation is shown, with ten hypothetical interviewees 'plotted' on a two-dimensional space based on two variables derived from the interviews referred to above; a composite measure of 'career-orientation' and content vs contextual aspects, of courses. The placing of the respondents depends on a qualitative assessment based on the interview transcripts. It can be seen that, in the example, the respondents fall into three groups. Given that this is a qualitative survey and the sample of interviewees is unlikely to be statistically representative, the *numbers* in each group are not important, but simply indicate the existence of three groups. Such a grouping would provide the basis for further analysis of the transcripts (see Huberman & Miles 1994: 437).

Thus analysis of qualitative data has certain parallels with quantitative analysis, with themes corresponding to variables and relationships explored in ways which parallel crosstabulation and correlation. But they are parallels only, not equivalents. Whereas

FIGURE 15.5 Crosstabulation of qualitative data

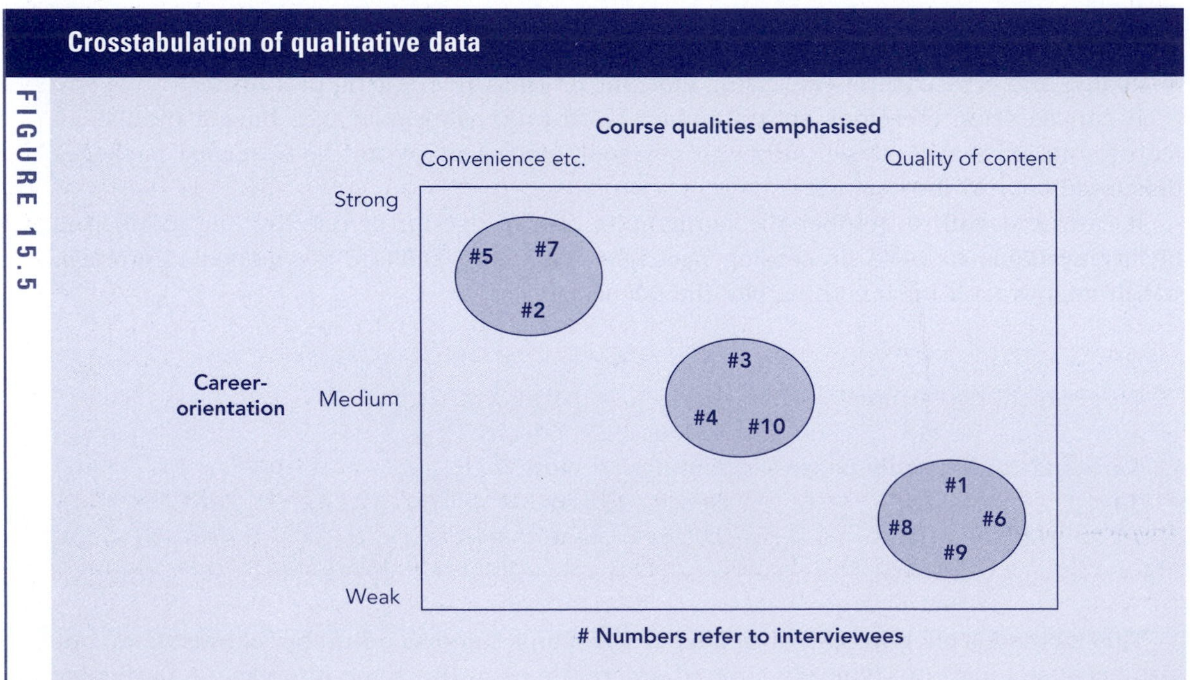

quantitative analysis seeks to establish whether certain observations and relationships are generally true in the wider population on the basis of probability, qualitative analysis seeks to establish the existence of relationships on the basis of what individual people say and do. If only one person or organisation is shown to behave in a certain way as a result of certain forces, this is a valid finding for qualitative research. The question of just how widespread such behaviour is becomes a matter for other types of research.

Detailed analysis may be less important when the purpose of in-depth or informal interviews is to provide input into the design of a formal questionnaire. In that case the interviewer will generally make a series of notes arising from the interview which are likely to be of relevance to the questionnaire design process, and can also provide input to the design process from memory, as long as the questionnaire design work is undertaken fairly soon after the interviews.

USING COMPUTER SOFTWARE

When the researcher is faced with a substantial number of lengthy documents to analyse, the decision may be made to ease the laborious process of coding and analysing by making use of one of the computer-aided qualitative data analysis software (CAQDAS) packages now available. As with statistical packages, it takes time to learn how to use qualitative analysis packages and to set up a system for an individual project, so a decision has to be made, on the basis of the quantity and complexity of the documentary material to be analysed, as to whether that investment of time will result in a net time saving, compared with manual analysis.

Consideration should, however, be given to the fact that, once an analysis system has been set up, more analysis can be relatively quickly undertaken, possibly resulting in a better quality output than may have been possible using manual methods. Further, looking to the future, a computerised analysis system can more easily be returned to at future dates for additional interrogation. Finally, even if the amount of data in a given project may not justify setting up a computerised analysis system, a smaller project may be an easier vehicle for learning to use and gain experience with a package.

We have noted above that standard word processing packages such as *MS Word* offer facilities which can aid in sorting and locating material in transcripts. The standard word processing package is, however, limited in its capabilities for this purpose. A number of purpose-designed CAQDAS packages are now on the market. One of the most commonly used, and the one which is demonstrated here, is *NVivo*. *NVivo* is part of a stable of packages from QSR (Qualitative Solutions and Research Pty Ltd), which includes N6, an updated version of *NUD*IST* which was presented in the first edition of this book, and *XSight* designed for market researchers. Information on the packages can be found on the QSR website, details of which are given at the end of the chapter.

CAQDAS packages involve storage of the primary textual data and assistance in coding, sorting and organising the text. This sorting process is known as *code-and-retrieve* and involves labelling sections of text according to their content or level of interest (*code*) and then collecting together similarly labelled sections in categories (*retrieve*). In these packages an *indexing* system is used to store categories of information, ideas about the various categories, and their interrelationships.

NVIVO

Introduction

NVivo is the one of the most widely used CAQDAS packages. The reasons for its popularity include its ability to assist in shaping and understanding data and its capacity to help form and test theoretical assumptions about the data. *NVivo* is also able to index and coordinate the analysis of text stored as computer files, including primary textual material, such as interview transcripts and field notes, as well as other material, such as newspaper clippings and company reports.

Running *NVivo* software

The material on career and training attitudes presented in the manual analysis section above is used to demonstrate the operation of *NVivo* below. An ideal way for readers to engage with this section is to replicate the processes outlined on a computer. In what follows it is assumed that *NVivo* has been installed on a computer and an *NVivo* icon is displayed on the computer 'desktop'.

It is not possible in a short summary such as this to present all the features of *NVivo*; this is done in the tutorials and 'Help' built into the package, the manuals which accompany the software, and in other specialist texts, such as those by Gibbs (2002) and Bazeley and Richards (2000). Details of support materials are provided on the QSR website (see end of the chapter). Here just six *NVivo* procedures, considered to be sufficient to get someone started with the package, are outlined. They are:

NVivo procedures:

- Starting up
- Creating a Project
- Creating documents
- Document attributes
- Coding documents
- Analysis

Typically, in order to move from step to step in any process, the user of *NVivo* is required to click on such buttons as 'Next', 'Finish' or 'OK'. These instructions are indicated below in square brackets: [Next], [Finish], etc.

Starting up

To begin a *NVivo* session:

- Click on the *NVivo* icon, which opens the *NVivo* 'Launch Pad' window, as shown in Figure 15.6. The user is provided with the opportunity to:
  - Create a [new] Project
  - Open a [existing] Project
  - Open an *NVivo* tutorial [on how *NVivo* works]
  - Exit *NVivo*

***NVivo* Launch Pad**

FIGURE 15.6

Creating a project

To demonstrate the system, we start with **Create a Project**. This involves creating a named location for a research project into which the documents to be analysed, such as interview transcripts, will later be added—rather like setting up a normal Windows 'folder' for storing files.

- Click on **Create a New Project** to reveal the **New Project Wizard**: this offers the user a **Typical** or **Custom** set up—we will deal only with the typical set up here. [Next]

- A dialog box is presented requesting a **Name** and **Description**. Type in 'Careers' as the name and 'Careers and Training Project' as the description. [Next]

- *NVivo* confirms the project name and description and indicates that the details will be stored in a folder located at: C:\QSR Projects\Training. [Finish]

NB.: If you wish to save your project details onto a floppy disk, as is sometimes necessary in a computer laboratory environment, use the 'Custom' set-up, where an alternative file location—eg. A:, can be specified.

- The *NVivo* 'Project Pad' now appears on the screen, as shown in Figure 15.7.

NB.: This screen can also now be obtained by clicking on 'Open a Project' in the Launch Pad and selecting Project Name 'Careers'.

FIGURE 15.7

NVivo Project Pad

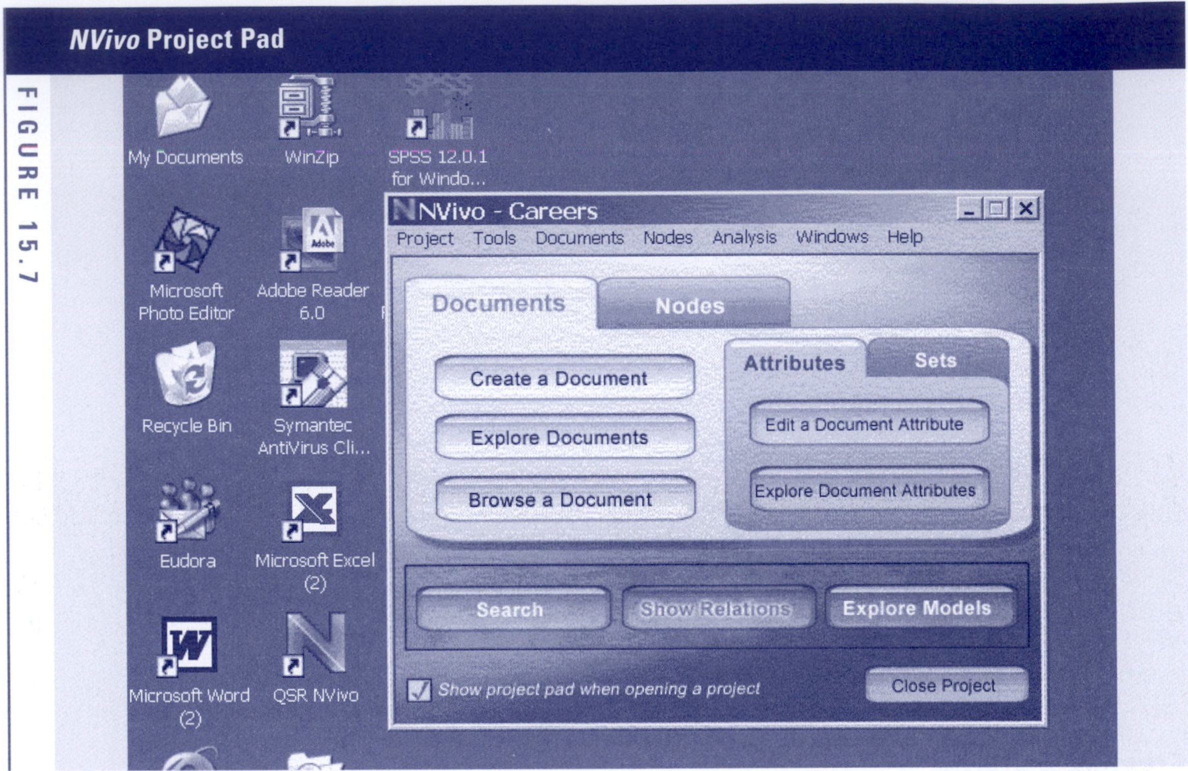

Creating documents

Each of the interviews in Figure 15.3 becomes a separate document. For use in *NVivo* documents must be saved in Rich Text Format (suffix .rtf). This can easily be done in word processors such as *Word* by saving a copy using *Save as* and selecting Rich Text Format in *File type*. A copy of the file will automatically be saved with a suffix: .rtf. The text should be as plain as possible: *Italic* and **bold** and *Word* headings can be used, but more complex formatting, such as tables and columns, should not be used.

For this demonstration, therefore, three files were created, containing the questions and answers, but not the annotations, from Figure 15.3. These were named:

- Int_Mark.rtf
- Int_Anna.rtf; and
- Int_Ben.rtf.

These can be stored on hard disk, floppy disk or CD.

The three documents must be loaded into the 'Careers' *NVivo* project system.

- In the Project Pad, click on **Create a Document**. The **New Document Wizard: Creation** dialog box appears and offers a range of options. For this demonstration, select the first option: **Locate and import readable external file(s)**. [Next]

- Locate the first text file—in this case Int_Mark.rtf—on the hard disk or floppy disk. [Open]

■ The **New Document Wizard: Obtain Name** box offers a range of ways of providing a name and description for the file. In this case, select the first option: **Use the source file name as document name, and first paragraph as description.** [Finish] This means that *NVivo* will refer to this document by the name of: 'Int_Mark.rtf' and, when appropriate, will also use the more detailed description: 'Mark (Age 27, Male, Salary $45K, Marketing)'.

■ Repeat this process for each of the other two interview files.

■ Returning to the Project Pad. Click on **Explore Documents** to reveal the three files listed, as in Figure 15.8.

***NVivo* Document Explorer**

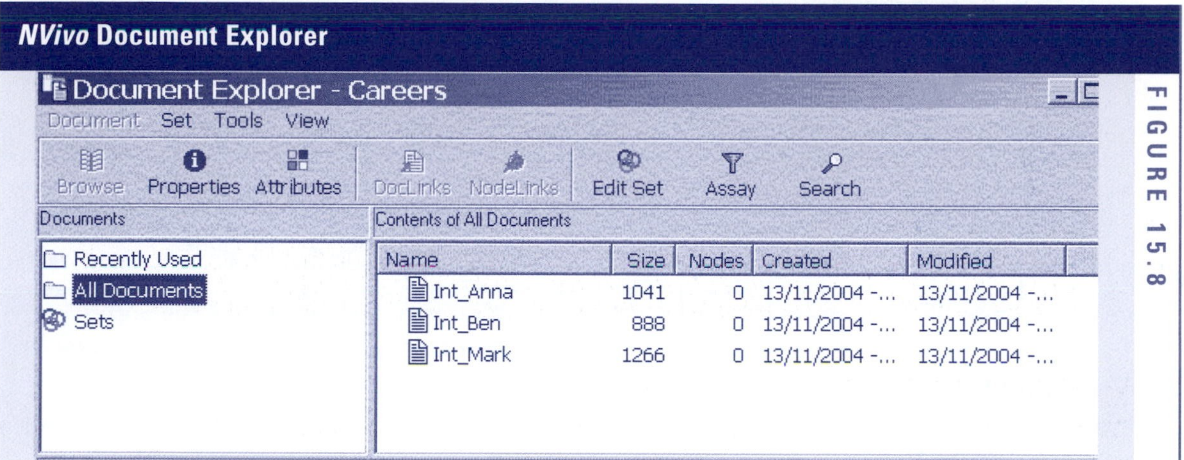

FIGURE 15.8

Document attributes

Attributes of documents can be recorded rather like variables in a quantitative study. This can aid analysis. For example, if one attribute of the interview transcripts is 'Gender of interviewee', results can be divided into male and female for some analysis purposes. We have four items of information for each respondent: age, gender, salary, and sector of management employed in (see Figure 15.9) and these can be recorded as attributes.

■ In the Project Pad, select **Documents** and click on **Edit a Document Attributes**.

■ **Create new Attribute** is highlighted. In the **Type the new attribute name** box, type *Age*, then specify **value type** in this case 'Number'. [Apply]

■ Repeat for *Gender* (Value type: String), *Salary* (Value type: Number) and *Sector* (Value type: String). 'Descriptions' can be added in the space provided if you wish—eg. 'Annual salary, $'000s'.

This defines the attributes to be used—similar to defining variables in *SPSS*. Values for each interviewee/transcript must now be recorded.

FIGURE 15.9

NVivo Document Attributes

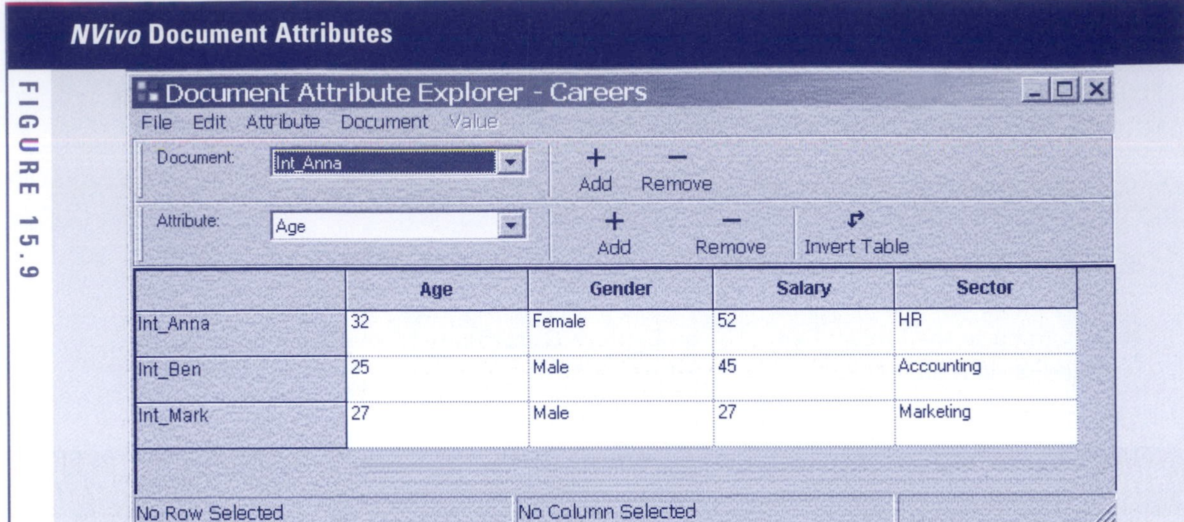
Document Attribute Explorer - Careers
File Edit Attribute Document Value
Document: Int_Anna
Add Remove
Attribute: Age
Add Remove Invert Table

	Age	Gender	Salary	Sector
Int_Anna	32	Female	52	HR
Int_Ben	25	Male	45	Accounting
Int_Mark	27	Male	27	Marketing

No Row Selected
No Column Selected

- In the Project Pad, select **Documents** and click on **Explore Document Attributes**.

- A spreadsheet-style table is presented, with document names down the side and attributes across the top—as in Figure 15.9, but with the table spaces blank.

- To enter the attribute data, in each space right-click, then click on **New Value** and enter the value [OK], as shown in Figure 15.9. Once started, values which have already been used appear in the dialog box—clicking on these values removes the necessity to retype frequently used values—eg. male and female—when a number of documents is involved.

Coding documents

Documents such as interview transcripts must be *coded* before they can be analysed. This involves setting up a *coding system*. A coding system can develop and evolve as the research progresses, but it has to start somewhere. In the section on manual coding above, the 'flagging' process is similar to the coding process involved here. On the basis of an initial conceptual framework (Figure 15.2), and then reading short extracts from three interviews, it was possible to develop a more elaborate coding system (Figure 15.3). In a fully-fledged project the researcher would go on to read and code the full interview transcripts of the three example interviewees and other interviewees as well, and would apply the flagging/ coding system to the other texts read and would further develop the system in an inductive way. Coding systems using *NVivo* are developed in the same way. In the example below, it is assumed that preliminary reading of some of the interview transcripts has pointed to items A and B and X and Y in Figure 15.4. This is the beginning of the coding system to be entered into *NVivo*.

The groupings of related concepts, as shown in Figure 15.4, are referred to in *NVivo* as **Tree Nodes**. Free-floating concepts, which have not been linked to any tree structure, are referred to as **Free Nodes**. The procedures below describe the process for entering *Career* *attitudes* and *A (Strategic)*, *B (Skills-related)*, *X (Reputation)* and *Y (Up-to-date)* into the *NVivo* system.

- In the Project Pad, click on **Nodes**, then on **Create a Node**, then the **Tree** tab—the box shown in Figure 15.10 is displayed.
- Type *Career Attitude* in the **Title** box. [Create]. *Career Attitude* appears in the left-hand box under **Trees**.
- Double click on *Career Attitude* and it moves up into the **Tree Nodes** box.
- Type *Strategic* in the **Title** box and *Strategic approach to career* in the **Description** box (as on p. 300–1). [Create]. *Strategic (1 2)* appears in the left-hand box.
- Double click on *Strategic* and it moves up into the **Tree Nodes** box.
- Type *Reputation* in the **Title** box and *Emphasis on reputation of university* in the **Description** box. [Create]. *Reputation (1 2 1)* appears in the left-hand box.
- Type *Up-to-date* in the **Title** box and *Emphasis on up-to-date courses* in the **Description** box. [Create]. *Up-to-date (1 2 2)* appears in the left-hand box.
- Repeat for **Passive** (Convenience, Minimalist) and **Skills-related** (Choice, Skills update) tree nodes
- Now select the **Free** tab and insert the **Competitive** node.
- A rudimentary coding system has now been created. It can be examined and edited by clicking on **Explore Nodes** in the Project Pad, as shown in Figure 15.11.

Create a Node dialog box

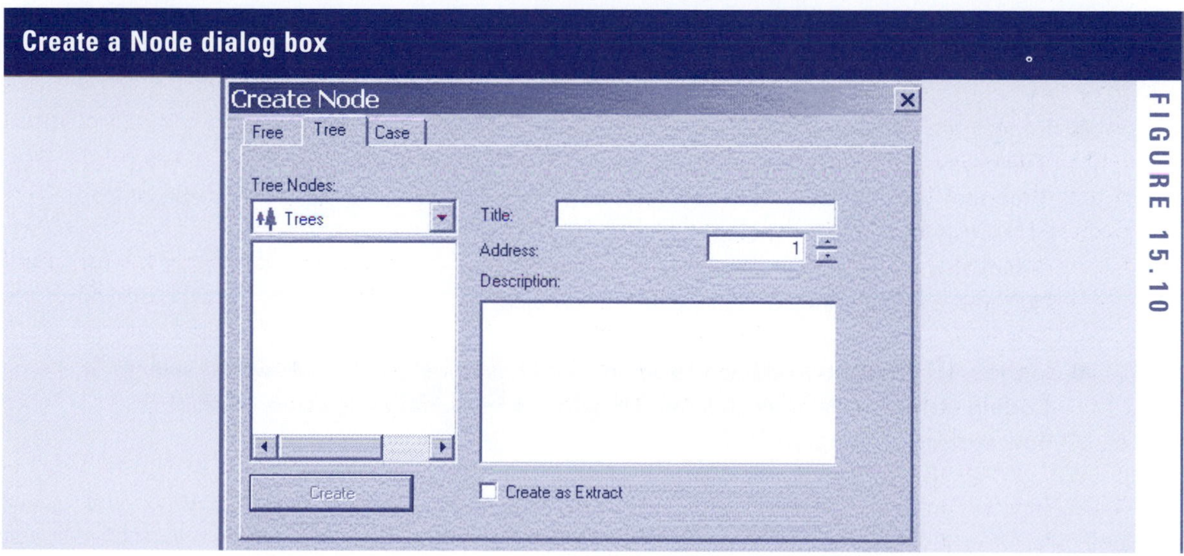

FIGURE 15.10

FIGURE 15.11 Nodes created

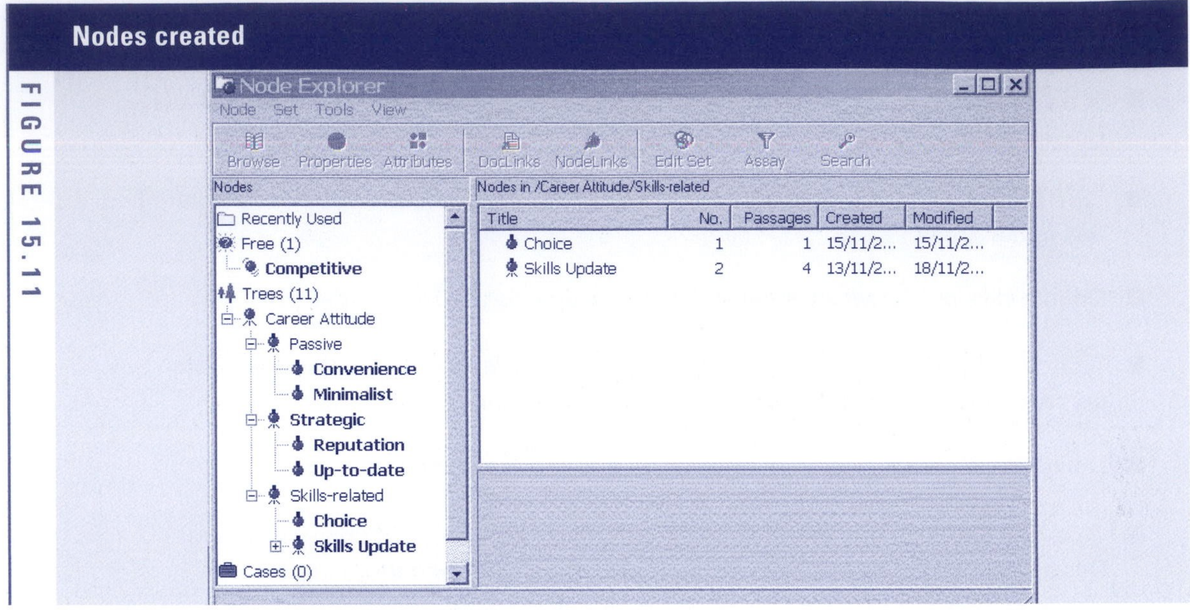

Documents can now be coded using the following procedures.

- In the Project Pad, click on **Documents** and **Browse a document**. The list of document files is presented. Select **Int_Anna**. [OK]. Anna's interview transcript is presented.

- Block in: **'It's really to update my skills. I finished my degree ... computer skills and so on'**. Click on **Coder** at the bottom right of the screen and click on **Career Attitude**, then on **Strategic** and then highlight **Skills-related**. Then click on **Code**. (Note: The speed-coding tool bar at the bottom of the screen can be used to speed up the process when extensive coding is called for.) Repeat this process for **'I think this place is more on the ball than the other universities around ... the latest ideas'**, coding it 'Up-to-date'.

- Repeat the coding process for:
  'I've always prided myself on being ahead of the game' (Competitive)
  'I thought with all these new development, like e-business, the best way to be on top of things was to take a course' (Skills update)
  'I think this place is more on the ball . . . latest ideas' (Up-to-date)
  'And there's more choice . . . marketing' (Choice)

- In order to display the results of coding when it is done, click on **View** and select **Coding stripes**. This replicates the flagging in Figure 15.3. The screen should now appear as in Figure 15.12.

FIGURE 15.12

NVivo coded text

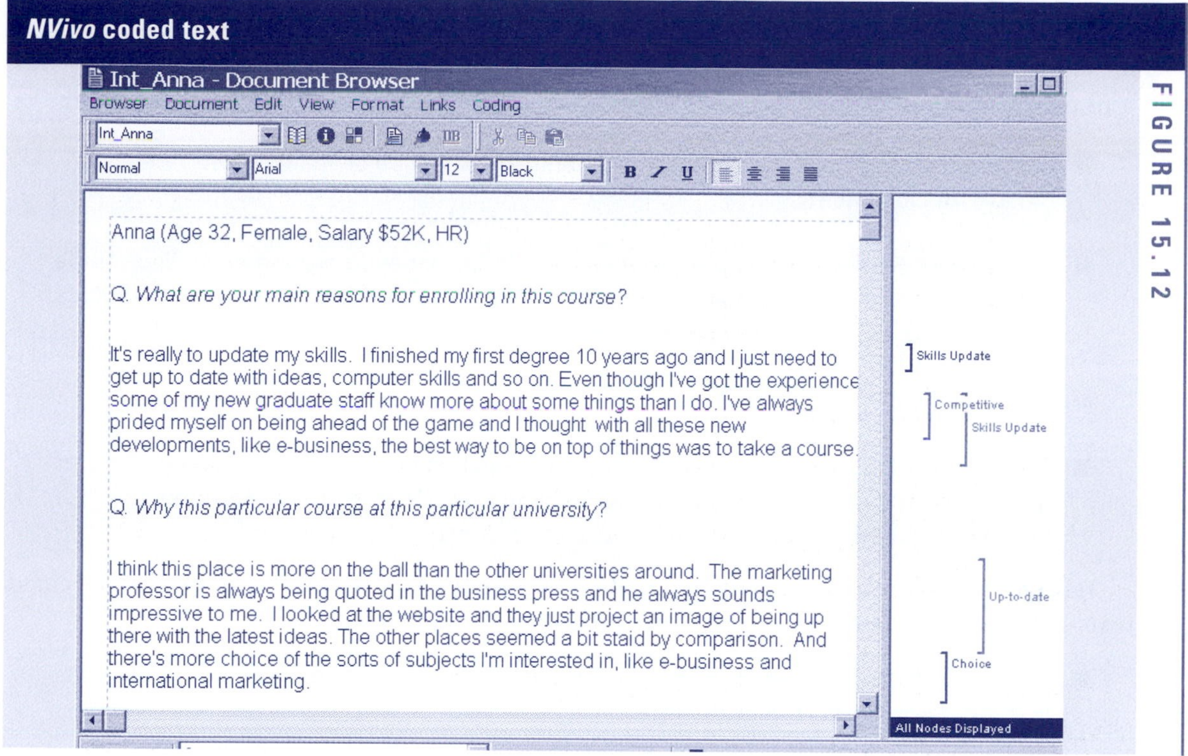

Analysis

Software packages invariably include a large range of procedures which are impossible to cover in a short summary such as this. Here we cover five very basic analysis procedures/ issues which will be sufficient to get the researcher started. These are:

***NVivo* analysis:**

- Searching
- Searching and coding
- Search results
- Selective searching
- Models—conceptual frameworks

Searching

One of the simplest forms of analysis is to obtain a listing of all the sections of text coded in a certain way. Thus a listing of all passages coded with the free node 'Competitive' would be obtained as follows:

- In the Project Pad, select **Search**. The **Search Tool** dialog box is displayed, as in Figure 15.13. This has three sections: **Find, In this Scope** and **And Spread Finds.**

- In **Find:** double click on **Node** to reveal the **Single Node Lookup** dialog box. If *Competitive* is not already displayed, click on the **Choose** button to locate and select it. [OK]

NB.: In the **Single Node Lookup** dialog box: the **Return** box indicates how the results of the search will be stored—keep the default **All finds as a node**. The **Name** box indicates the name of the folder/file in which the results will be stored—keep the default **/Search Results/Single Node Lookup**.

- **In this Scope** indicates the type of documents which will be searched—keep the default **All Documents**.
- **And Spread Finds** indicates the spread of text to be retrieved around each 'find' of the search—for example, a number of characters either side of the find, or the surrounding paragraph—keep the default **No Spread**.
- Click **Run Search**.
- The results of the search are placed in a new 'Search Results' node (see 'Search Results' below). You are given two options to view the results: **Show Node in Explorer** or **Browse Node**. Select the latter—the results are displayed as shown in Figure 15.14.

Rather than searching for a named node it is possible to search for any item of specified text—for example, mentions of the word 'e-business'—as follows:

- Select **Text** instead of **Node** at the second step (In **Find** ..) above and enter the search text (eg. 'e-business') rather than specifying a node.

Search results

Search results are not just displayed on the screen but are stored as *new nodes*. This can be seen as follows:

FIGURE 15.13 *NVivo* Search Tool dialog box

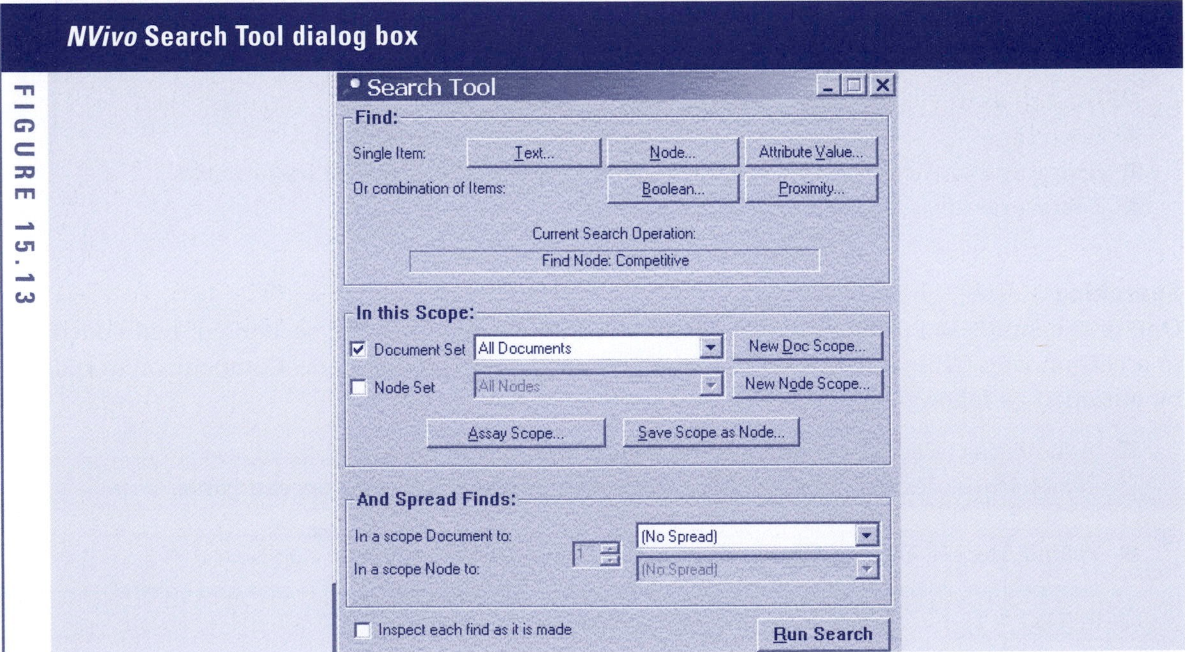

NVivo Search listing of 'Competitive' passages

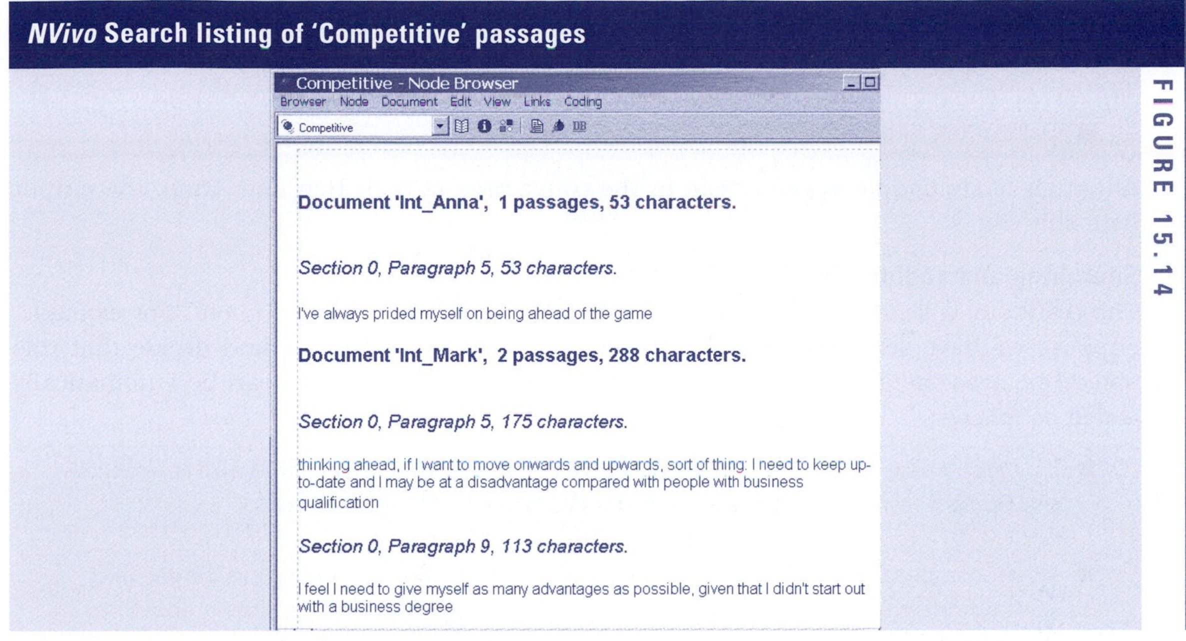

FIGURE 15.14

- In the Project Pad, select **Nodes** and click on **Explore Nodes**.

- In the **Node Explorer:** click on **Trees** and it will be seen that, in addition to the **Career Attitudes** group of nodes, there is now a **Search Results** set of nodes.

- Right click on any search result to:
  - view (**browse**) it;
  - delete if it will not be required in future—this is recommended to avoid confusion with later searches;
  - rename it (**Inspect/Change Node's properties**)

- Incorporate it into the *Career Attitudes* node—see below.

Selective searching

Suppose we would like to list all instances of *Skills update* being mentioned by male respondents—the equivalent to a crosstabulation in quantitative analysis. This can be achieved as follows:

- In the Project Pad, select **Search**.

- In the **Search Tool** window: in **Find, Single item** click on **Node**.

- In the **Single Node Lookup** dialog box, select **Skills update.** [OK]

- Back in the **Search Tool** window: in **Find, Single item** click on **Attribute Value.**

- In **Attribute Value Lookup** dialog box: select **Document Attributes** then **Gender** then **Male**. [OK]

- Back in the **Search Tool** window: Click on **Run Search**.

Although *Skills update* is mentioned in the transcripts of both Ben and Anna, the output lists only Ben's.

Searching and coding

The results of a search can be used to add further coding to the document. For example, suppose we have searched for occurrences of the word 'e-business' and decide that this should be associated with the idea of 'Update skills'. The documents can be automatically coded as follows:

- Conduct a search for occurrences of the text 'e-business' as suggested above—setting the **Spread** to encompass, say, 40 characters either side of the word.

- When complete, enter **Explore Nodes** and locate the **Search Result** and **Single Text Lookup** referring to the 'e-business' search and change its name (as shown above) to 'e-business'.

- Click on **Career Attitude** and **Skills-related** until **Update skills** is displayed.

- Right click **e-business** and paste it on to **Update skills**. Now **e-business** becomes a 'child' node of **Update skills**.

- The result can be seen by going to **Browse a document** and inspecting **Int_Anna**. Viewing 'coding stripes' will show that the two mentions of 'e-business' in the document have been appropriately coded.

Models—conceptual frameworks

One of the principles of qualitative analysis is the inductive development of theory as the research progresses. The sort of conceptual framework presented in Figure 15.4 is just a starting point. New concepts and elements of the conceptual framework can be expected to emerge as the analysis progresses—the 'e-business' example above is a simple example. *NVivo* refers to the conceptual framework as a *Model* and includes a procedure to produce a diagrammatic presentation of the model as it develops. To do this:

- In the Project Pad select **Explore Models**, then **Tools**, then **Add to Model**.

- Select **Node** the **Career Attitudes**. The computer presents a message: **'(1) Career Attitudes: This model has descendants. do you want to add them?'** Select **Yes**.

- The model appears on the screen as shown in Figure 15.15. Note: the layout may be cramped but can be rearranged by selecting and dragging the points on the diagram.

NVivo Model diagram

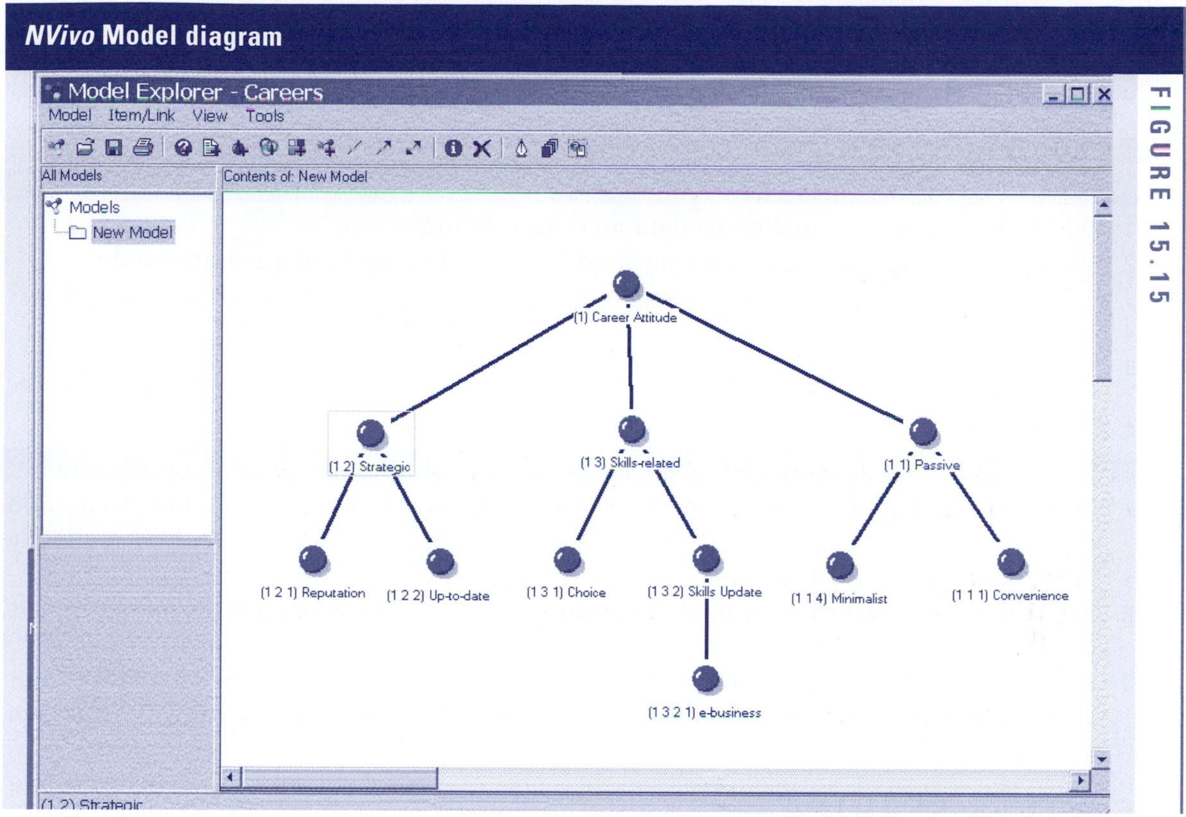

FIGURE 15.15

SUMMARY

This chapter on qualitative data analysis complements Chapter 7, which deals with the collection of qualitative data. First, the issue of storage of qualitative data is discussed—since interviewees may speak frankly and at length on sensitive topics, it is an important ethical issue to ensure confidentiality, both in the security of data storage and in the way interviewees are identified, by the use of pseudonyms. The rest of the chapter is divided into two sections dealing respectively with manual and computer-aided analysis methods.

Manual methods of data analysis involve 'flagging' issues or themes which emerge in texts such as interview transcripts. Such issues or themes may relate to an existing draft conceptual framework, research questions and/or hypotheses, or, in a 'grounded theory' inductive approach, they may be used to build up a conceptual framework from the data. Since texts are invariably available as word-processed files, it is noted that certain features of word processing packages, such as 'search' and 'list' or 'index', can be used to assist in the 'flagging' process. This provides a link to the custom-made Computer Aided Qualitative Data Analysis Software (CAQDAS) packages.

The chapter introduces the *NVivo* package, covering the setting up of a project file and a coding system, coding of data and some elementary analysis procedures. While the package has a large range of capabilities—including the handling of data other than interview transcripts—a limited range of five analysis procedures is presented in this outline; but it is believed this is adequate for the qualitative researcher to make a start with computer-aided data analysis.

TEST QUESTIONS

1 Why is the storage of qualitative data an ethical issue?
2 What are the two major activities involved in manual analysis of qualitative data?
3 What word processing procedures might be used in 'manual' analysis of qualitative data?
4 What is the difference between a 'Node' and a 'Document' in *NVivo*?
5 What is the difference between a 'Tree Node' and a 'Free Node' in *NVivo*?

EXERCISES

1 Type up the three transcript files for the 'Careers' project from Figure 15.3—and replicate the coding and analyses presented in this chapter. This can be done manually or by using *NVivo*.
2 Run the *NVivo* tutorials, particularly exploring features of *NVivo* not presented in this chapter.
3 Conduct interviews with fellow students using the questions in Figure 15.3 and two or three additional questions, and replicate the analysis in this chapter, but with your own coding system.

FURTHER READING

Analysis of qualitative data generally: Miles and Huberman (1994).
Use of computer software packages in qualitative data analysis: Miles and Weitzman (1994); Richards and Richards (1994).
On use of NVivo *software:* Gibbs (2002); Bazeley and Richards (2002); Morse and Richards (2002).
Website for NVivo*:* (www.qsrinternational.com) includes a downloadable bibliography on qualitative data analysis sources.

reporting
PART
4

CHAPTER 16

Reporting research results

This chapter outlines the principles involved in research report writing. It considers the relationship between the *nature of the research project*, the intended *audience* for the report, the appropriate report *style* and the *structure* of the report. The term *report* is used in this chapter to refer to all forms of reporting of research results, including articles, theses, books and consultants' reports to clients.

THE IMPORTANCE OF THE REPORT

Written reports are a key element of the world of business. Feasibility studies, marketing plans, research studies, development proposals, environmental impact assessments and performance appraisals are all produced in the form of written reports. The results of many academic studies are also produced in report format, sometimes referred to *monographs*, although articles and theses are the more typical academic outputs. While the term 'report' is used here, the principles outlined below also apply to other research reporting formats, including articles and theses.

The 'medium is the message' and in this case the medium is the written report. The ability to prepare a report and recognise good quality and poor quality reports are key elements in the skills of the professional manager. Although form is no substitute for good content, a report that is poorly presented can undermine or even negate good content. While most of the researcher's attention should be focused on achieving high quality substantive content, the presentational aspects raised in this chapter also merit serious attention.

ACTUALLY GETTING STARTED

In Chapter 3 it was noted that inexperienced researchers invariably leave too little time for report writing as part of the research process. Even when adequate time has been allocated in the research timetable for writing it is often whittled away by problems encountered in the research process. The inevitable result is that too little time is left for preparing the report, resulting in the 'last minute rush' syndrome which afflicts so many researchers.

There is also a tendency to put off report writing because it is difficult. It is often felt that with a little more data analysis and a little more reading, report writing will be easier. This is rarely the case.

A common practice is for researchers to spend a great deal of their depleted time, with the deadline looming, writing and preparing material which could have been dealt with much earlier in the process. There are large parts of any report that can be written before data analysis is complete or even started. This includes, in many cases: the introduction; statement of objectives; outline of the theoretical or evaluative framework; literature review; and description of the methodology. In addition, time-consuming activities such as arranging production of diagrams, figures, tables and cover designs can be done earlier rather than later.

Report elements:

- Beginnings and endings
  - Cover and title page
  - Table of contents
  - Executive summary/synopsis/abstract
  - Preface/Foreword
  - Acknowledgements
  - Appendices
- Main body of the report
  - Technical aspects
  - Structure and content

Reports include a number of elements as shown above and these provide the structure for the bulk of the discussion in this chapter.

BEGINNINGS AND ENDINGS

Cover and title page

The cover and title pages should include:

- Cover:
  - Title of report
  - Author
  - Institution or publishers (on back cover and spine in the case of books)
- Title page:
  - Title of report
  - Author
  - Institution or publisher, including address and phone numbers*
  - Sponsoring body (for example, 'Report to the Board of Directors')
  - Date of publication*

* sometimes on the reverse of title page

The cover should include minimal information, such as title, author(s), and publisher or sponsor. The quality and design of the cover will vary with the context and the resources available. The title page is the first or second page inside the cover. It may include much the same information as the cover or considerably more detail. In some cases, as in commercially published books, some of the detail is provided on the reverse side of the title page.

If the report is available for sale it should also include an International Standard Book Number (ISBN) on the back cover. All publications in the Western world have a 10 digit ISBN. The first digit '0' indicates that the book is published in an English-speaking country. The second group of digits identifies the publisher. The third group identifies the book. ISBNs are allocated by national libraries, which receive free deposit copies of all publications in their country. The allocation of ISBNs in Australia was previously carried out by the National Library in Canberra, but is now contracted out to a private organisation. The ISBN makes it easy to order publications through bookshops and ensures that the publication is catalogued in library systems around the world.

Table of contents

The table of contents may include chapter titles only, or may include full details of all subsections in the report—although it is not necessary to list in the table of contents all levels of headings (see discussion of 'heading hierarchy' below). Most word processing software now includes procedures for automatically preparing tables of contents and lists of figures and tables. These involve styling each heading appropriately as a level 1, level 2, list, etc. heading and indicating where in the document the table of contents is to be located. The software then, when instructed, compiles the table of contents automatically. This has the advantage of automatically keeping track of sections and page numbers when changes are made to the report. In fact, word processing packages can take care of the whole business of numbering headings and presenting them in the appropriate style, as discussed under 'Section numbering' and 'Heading hierarchy' below. An example of a typical table of contents is shown in Figure 16.1.

Sometimes a draft table of contents forms part of a research proposal, but even if it does not, it can be helpful to draw up such a draft early in a research project. This can help in alerting the researcher of material which needs to be gathered and can help to avoid the 'last minute rush' syndrome discussed above.

FIGURE 16.1

Example of a table of contents

Contents

Executive summary/synopsis/abstract

Executive summary is the term typically used for the summary of a project report, *synopsis* is generally used in the case of theses and *abstract* is generally used for journal articles. The term *executive summary* is used here, but most of the comments also apply to the other forms of summary.

An *executive summary* is sometimes thought of as the summary for the 'busy executive' who does not have time to read a whole report. However, the term really refers to the idea that it should contain information necessary to take *executive action* on the basis of the report.

Executive summary content:

- The background, context or objectives
- Methods and data sources
- Main findings
- Conclusions
- Recommendations where appropriate

An executive summary should contain a summary of the *whole* report, as indicated to the left.

An executive summary is therefore *not* an introduction to the report. It follows that it should only be written when the main report is complete. It should be possible for the executive summary to be read completely independently of the report and to make sense. Thus, for example, it does not typically contain references.

There are no fixed rules on the appropriate length of an executive summary, but an approximate guide is:

Report length	*Executive summary length*
Up to 20 pages	1–2 pages
Up to 50 pages	3–4 pages
Up to 100 pages	4–5 pages
Over 100 pages	5–6 pages

Preface/Foreword

A *Preface* or *Foreword* can be used for a variety of purposes. Usually they explain the origins of the study and outline any qualifications or limitations. They also include acknowledgements of assistance if there is no separate acknowledgements section. They can also be used to convey personal information, such as the personal motivation for undertaking a research project. Sometimes a significant individual, such as the director of an institution, a minister or an eminent academic, is asked to write a Foreword.

Acknowledgements

It is a matter of courtesy to acknowledge any assistance received during the course of a research project. People and institutions that might be acknowledged include:

- funding organisations;
- liaison officers of funding organisations;
- members of steering committees;
- organisations and individuals providing access to information and resources;

- staff employed, including interviewers, coders, computer programmers, word processors, secretarial support, etc.;
- individuals (including academic supervisors) who have given advice, commented on report drafts, etc.; and
- individuals who responded to questionnaires etc. (collectively).

Appendices

An appendix contains material that is too detailed or cumbersome to be included in the body of the report, but should nevertheless be available to the reader. There are examples in this book. Just when material should be considered for presentation in an appendix rather than in the body of the report is a matter for judgement and depends to a large extent on the 'report as narrative' versus 'report as record' ideas discussed later in this chapter.

MAIN BODY OF THE REPORT: TECHNICAL ASPECTS

Section numbering

It is usual to number the major sections or chapters of a report and also the subsections within chapters, as shown in the example in Figure 16.1. As discussed under 'Table of contents' above, this can be managed by word processing packages—for example, in Microsoft *Word* by use of 'Styles'.

Heading hierarchy

In the main body of the report a hierarchy of heading styles should be used with the major chapter/section headings being in the most prominent style and with decreasing emphasis for subsection headings. This convention helps readers to know where they are in a document. When a team is involved in writing a report it is clearly sensible to agree on these heading styles in advance. With modern word processing systems and printers an extensive hierarchy is available and, as already discussed, such software packages can automatically manage heading styles and section numbering.

Paragraph numbering

Paragraphs are individually numbered in some reports. This can be useful for reference purposes when committees are discussing a report. Paragraphs can be numbered in a single series for the whole report or chapter by chapter—for example 1.1, 1.2, 1.3, etc. in Chapter 1, and 2.1, 2.2, 2.3, etc. in Chapter 2, and so on.

Page numbering

One problem in putting together long reports, especially when different authors are responsible for particular sections, is the organisation of page numbering so that it follows on from chapter to chapter. This can be avoided by numbering each chapter separately, for example:

Chapter 1: pages 1.1, 1.2, 1.3, etc.
Chapter 2: pages 2.1, 2.2, 2.3 etc.

Word processing software can produce page numbers in this form automatically.

It is general practice for the title page, contents, acknowledgements and the executive summary to be numbered using Roman numerals, as in this book, and for the report proper to start at page 1 with Arabic numerals. Most word processing software has this capacity.

Typing layout/spacing

Essays and books tend to use the convention of starting new paragraphs by indenting the first line. Report style is to separate paragraphs by a blank line and not to indent the first line. Report style also tends to use more headings. A document typed or word processed in report style usually leaves wide margins, which raises the question as to whether it is necessary to print documents in 1.5 or double space format or whether single spacing is adequate (and more environmentally friendly!).

Tables, graphics and text

When presenting the results of research, an appropriate balance must be struck between the use of tables, graphics and text. In most cases, very complex tables are consigned to appendices and simplified or graphical versions are included in the body of the report. It may be appropriate to place *all* tables in appendices and provide only instantly readable graphics in the body of the report. The decision about which approach to use depends partly on the complexity of the data to be presented, but mainly on the type of audience.

Tables, graphics and text each have a distinctive role to play in the presentation of research findings. Tables provide information and graphics illustrate that information so that patterns can be portrayed visually. The text should tell a story or develop an argument and 'orchestrate' tables and graphics in order to support that task.

Typically then, the text should develop an argument and make reference to the table or graphic to help the argument along. There is little point in using text simply to repeat what is presented in a table or graphic. Even if the text is primarily descriptive, it should draw attention to notable features of the data in a table or graphic—such as the highest, the lowest, the greatest contrast, the lack of contrast or how the patterns relate to a theory, hypothesis or research or management issue.

Presentation of graphics

Diagrams and tables should, as far as possible, be complete in themselves. They should be fully labelled so that the reader can, in most cases, understand them without needing to refer to the text. They should usually indicate the source of data, although, where a report is based primarily on one primary data source, such as a survey, it is not be necessary to indicate this on every table and diagram. However, some commercial consultants tend to label every diagram with the source, including their own name or logo, so that if a user photocopies just one table or diagram then its source is still indicated.

MAIN BODY OF THE REPORT: CONTENT

Structure

The *structure* of a report is of fundamental importance. It needs to be considered and discussed thoroughly before writing starts, particularly when a team is involved in its preparation. While all reports have certain structural features in common, the important aspects concern the underlying argument and how this relates to the objectives of the study and any data collection and analysis involved. This is fundamentally linked to the research objectives, the theoretical or evaluative framework, and the overall strategy, as discussed in Chapter 3.

Figure 16.2 illustrates the idea of linkages between the various elements of the research process, right through to the final report. Conveying these linkages clearly and explicitly makes a report more readable and increases the chances that the reader will understand the message you are trying to convey. A report should:

- clearly state the relationships between the research questions or objectives, the conceptual or theoretical framework used and any literature drawn on;
- indicate the information needs which are necessary to answer the research questions;
- discuss how and why particular data collection and analysis methods were chosen; and
- link the analysis and conclusions clearly and explicitly to the research questions posed.

An outline of the report's structure, similar to the contents page, but with target word or page lengths indicated, should be agreed upon at the start. While such a structure is a necessary starting point for the report, it needs to be flexible. As drafting proceeds it may be found that what was originally conceived as one chapter needs to be divided into two or three chapters, or what was thought of as a separate chapter can be incorporated into another chapter or into an appendix. Consideration needs to be given to the overall length of the report—in terms of words or pages—throughout its preparation.

When a questionnaire survey is involved there is a tendency to structure the presentation according to the sequence of questions in the questionnaire and, correspondingly,

Linkages

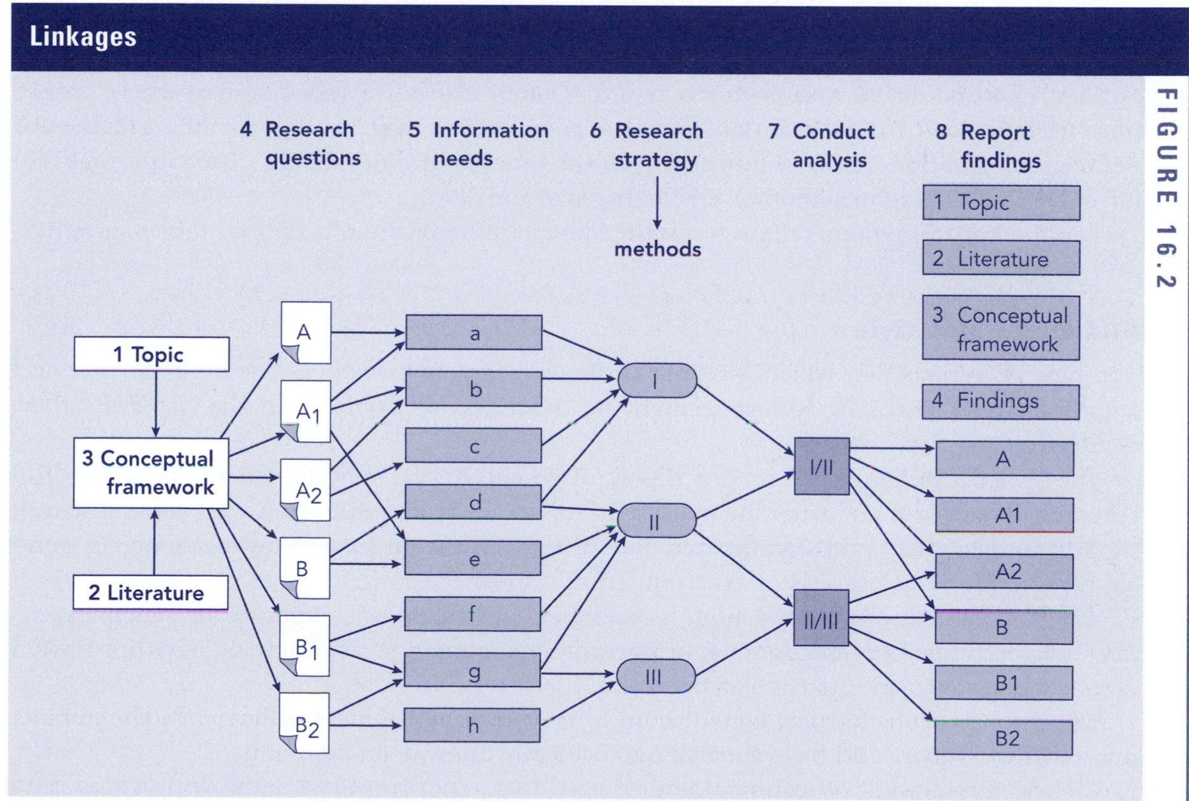

FIGURE 16.2

the sequence of tables as the computer produces them. This is not an appropriate way to proceed. Questionnaires are structured for ease of interview and for the convenience of the interviewer and the respondent—they do not necessarily provide a suitable sequence and structure for a report.

For a researcher to be clear in his or her own mind about structure is one thing, conveying it to the reader is quite another. While the contents page and general organisation of a report should make the reader aware of the structure, this is rarely sufficient. The structure sometimes needs to be *explained* more than once.

It is good practice to provide an outline of the structure of the whole report in the introductory chapter and also to provide a chapter outline in the introduction to each chapter. Summaries are useful at the end of chapters—these can be reiterated at the end of the report when drawing conclusions together. It is advisable to provide numerous references backwards and forwards as reminders to the reader as to where you are in the overall 'story' of the report. When a list of 'factors', 'issues' or 'topics' is about to be discussed one by one, it is useful to list the factors or issues to be discussed and then summarise the conclusions in regard to each factor/issue/topic at the end of the section to indicate what the review of factors/issues/topics has achieved.

Functions of a report

A report can be thought of in two ways: firstly, the *report as narrative* and, secondly, the *report as record.*

Narrative means that a report has to tell a story to the reader. The writer of the report therefore needs to think of the flow of the argument—the 'story'—in the same way that the writer of a novel considers the plot.

The *report as record* means that a report is often also a reference source where people may wish to look for information. Being a good record may involve including extensive detailed information that may interfere with the process of 'story telling'. The latter may call for only simplified information or key features of the data.

Serving both functions requires careful consideration of the role of text, tables, graphics and appendices.

Audiences and style

The type of audience at which a report is directed largely influences the style, format and length of the report. An audience might be described as comprising the *general public, decision-makers* or *experts.*

The *general public* might read a report of research in a newspaper or magazine—full research reports are not generally written for a popular readership. However, some research reports that have a 'campaigning' role may be written with a largely 'lay' audience in mind (eg reports on homelessness or environmental issues).

Decision-makers are groups such as members of boards of companies or senior executives, elected members of councils, or government ministers, who may or may not have a detailed knowledge of a particular field.

Experts are professionals, consultants or academics who are familiar with the subject matter of the report and have the skills to critically analyse its contents.

Clearly the amount of technical jargon used in a report and the detail with which data are presented will be affected by the extent to which the intended audience is made up of these various groups.

The narrative structure

The *narrative structure* of a research report usually develops along the lines shown in Figure 16.3. The items listed may emerge in a variety of chapter or section configurations. For example, sections A and B could be one chapter, or three or four, depending on the complexity of the research project.

The introductory section, A, should reflect the considerations which emerged in the initial planning stages of the project (stages 1, 2 and 6—see Figure 3.1, p. 46). 'Context' includes reference to the environment in which the research is situated, including any initial literature review that may be involved. Section B should reflect steps 3–5 and 7–8 in the research planning process in Figure 3.1 and may include further reference to the literature.

In sections B and C it is important that the relationship between data requirements and the research questions and theoretical or evaluative frameworks is explained, as discussed in Chapters 3 and 8. It should be clear from the discussion why the data are being collected,

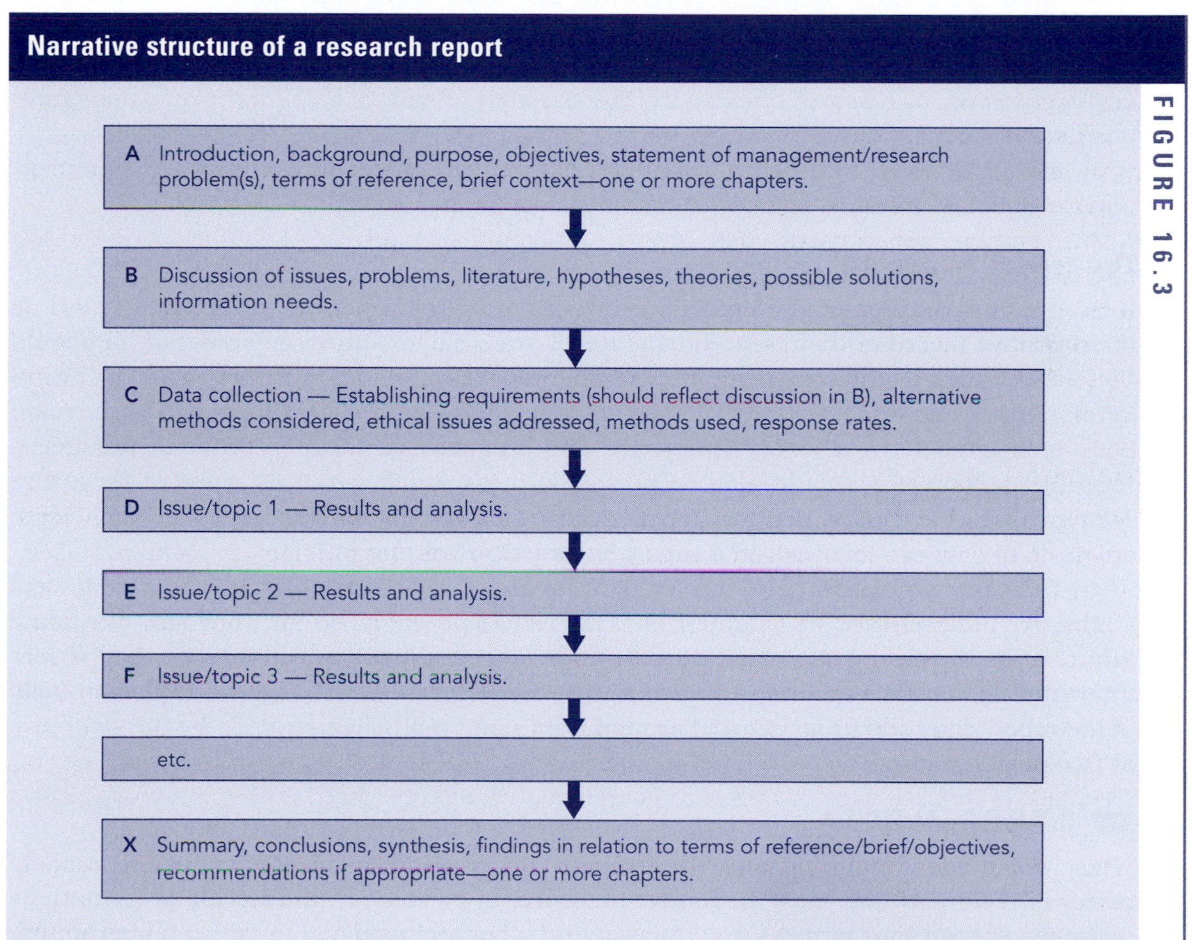

FIGURE 16.3

how this relates to the planning, management or theoretical issues raised and how it was anticipated that the information collected would solve or shed light on the problems or issues raised, or aid decision-making.

In section C the methodology should be described in detail. It should be clear why particular techniques were chosen, how samples were selected and what data collection instruments were used. Any ethical issues faced should be discussed. Where sample surveys are involved, full information should be given on response rates and sample sizes obtained. Some indication should also be given of the implications of the sample size in terms of confidence intervals, as discussed in Chapter 11. These technical aspects of the results of any survey work can be included in the methodology section of the report or in the first of the results sections.

The results and analysis sections—D, E, F, etc—should ideally be structured by the discussion in B, around issues or elements of the research problem. There is a tendency for many research reports to have one 'results' chapter, but a report can look more interesting if results can be divided into more than one chapter, with titles referring to substantive issue/topics in the research, as illustrated in Chapters 4 and 5 in the example in Figure 16.1.

Sometimes conclusions are fully set out in the results and analysis chapter and all that is required in the final chapter is to reiterate and draw them together. In other cases the final chapter includes the final stage of analysis and the drawing of conclusions from the data. In writing the final chapter it is vital to refer back to the *terms of reference*, the brief or the *objectives* or *research questions* of the research to ensure that all the questions have been addressed.

It should be noted that not all research reports include recommendations. Recommendations are most likely to arise from evaluative research.

The report as 'record'

It is wise to think beyond the immediate use of a research report—in terms of a report as the definitive record of the research conducted, available for future consultation. It should therefore contain a summary of all the relevant data collected in a form that would be useful for any future user of the report. This means that, while data may be presented in the main body of the report in a highly condensed and summarised form in order to produce a readable narrative, it should also be presented in as much detail as possible for future reference. Data included 'for the record' can be placed in an appendix or, when large amounts of data are involved, in a separate statistical volume.

In the case of questionnaire survey data it can be a good idea to provide a statistical summary, as discussed in Chapter 14. This would probably be an appendix, including tables from all the questions in the order they appear in the questionnaire. Any reader interested in a specific aspect of the data is then able to locate and use it. The main body of the report can then be structured around issues and not be constrained by the structure of the questionnaire.

OTHER MEDIA

While the written report is still the most common medium for the communication of research results, this is likely to change in future. In particular, multimedia presentations using *PowerPoint* type formats, the Internet and other technology that can combine sound, moving images and the written word are becoming commonplace. Often the researcher is required to present final or interim results of research in person and some sort of audio-visual aids are usually advisable, including:

- handouts;
- posters;
- overhead transparencies;
- slides;
- video clips; or
- computer-based presentations, such as Microsoft *PowerPoint*.

Increasingly, the most common medium is the *PowerPoint* type presentation. It should be noted that different media play different roles—an oral presentation is not intended to present the whole contents of a report. That's what the report is for! The sort of formal detail which *must* be included in a formal written report has no place in a 20-minute oral presentation. Typically, therefore, in the latter it is important to present a *narrative*, but it may not be the whole narrative included in the written report. Because time is often short, it is generally necessary to be *very selective*. Only the basics of the methodology, not the minutiae, can be outlined. Only *key* findings can be presented, and these should be the most important and/or most interesting to the audience. Attention must be paid to the arrangement of tables and graphics which are to be read off a screen by someone at the back of a room. In such a situation, far less information can be presented than on the page of a report. It is better to get two or three points across to an audience in a clear and measured way than to try to present ten points in a rushed and incoherent manner.

The inexperienced presenter should consciously study others' presentations to gain an appreciation of what constitutes good and bad presentation technique.

IN CONCLUSION

Ultimately, the writing of a good research report is an art and a skill that develops with practice. Reports can be improved enormously as a result of comments from others—often because the writer has been 'too close' to the report for too long to be able to see glaring faults or omissions. The researcher/writer can also usually spot opportunities for improvement if he or she takes a short break and returns to the draft report with 'fresh eyes'. Finally, checking and double checking the report for typing, spelling and grammatical errors, both by using spell-checking and grammar-checking programs and your own eyes, is well worth the laborious effort.

Research is a process of systematic careful inquiry that—in the words of Roger Bennett (1991) with which we began this text—aims to 'discover new information or relationships and to expand/verify existing knowledge for some specified purpose'.

It is hoped that this book has provided assistance in that process of inquiry and that the reader will enjoy some of the satisfactions and rewards that can come from worthwhile research.

SUMMARY

This chapter has provided an overview of the principles involved in writing a research report. Report writing and presentation are key elements of the contemporary role of the manager. A research report is an outcome of management research, regardless of whether it is conducted for practical applied purposes or for academic reasons. There are two important components of a research report, namely *presentation* and *content*. Poor presentation will detract from the content of a report and even an excellent presentational style cannot compensate for poor content. Presentation and content both need to be of a high standard. The presentation of the report is usually organised in accordance with well-established practices, including items such as a cover page, contents, executive summary, preface, acknowledgements, numbering of sections and pages, heading hierarchy, and the layout of text, graphics and tables.

The *structure* of a report is of fundamental importance. While all reports have certain structural features in common, the important aspects concern the underlying argument and how this relates to the objectives of the study and any data collection and analysis involved. This is linked fundamentally to the research objectives, theoretical or evaluative framework and overall strategy. Conveying these linkages clearly and explicitly makes a report more readable and increases the chances that the audience will clearly understand the content of the report.

It is also important to recognise the *narrative* role of a report, in that the report needs to tell a coherent story to the audience. At the same time the report needs to be a *record* which can act as a reference source that people can look to for information relevant to the research project. There is sometimes a conflict between these two roles and the author needs to give careful consideration to the balance between these roles. Serving both functions requires close attention to the role of tables, graphics and appendices in the report.

The *type of audience* at which a report is directed largely influences the style, format and length of the report. An audience might be described as comprising the general public, decision-makers or experts, or a combination of these groups. The depth of the report and the technical details to be included will be strongly influenced by the intended audience.

Finally, it is important to allow sufficient time in a project for the preparation and writing of a research report. It is not necessary to wait until the end of the project to begin writing the report. The introduction, statement of objectives, outline of the theoretical or evaluative framework, literature review and description of the methodology can all be written before the data analysis is even started.

FURTHER READING

Preparation of research reports: Anderson & Poole (1994) and Forsyth (1997).

Writing, presentation and evaluation of research reports in management contexts: Davis & Cosenza (1993), Chapter 15, 'Research reporting', and Chapter 16, 'Evaluation of business research', Gay & Diehl (1992), Chapters 14 & 15, 'Preparation and evaluation of a research report'; Kervin (1992), Chapter 18, 'Conclusion, recommendations and reporting'; Leedy (1993), Chapter 12, 'Writing the research report'; Sekaran (1992), Chapter 11, 'The research report'; Zikmund (1991), Chapter 23, 'Communicating research results: Research report, oral presentation, and research follow up'.

Writing style and referencing: Snooks and Co. (2002).

Appendix 1

International and Australian management and business journals

International journals

Academy of Management Journal
Academy of Management Review
Administrative Science Quarterly
Asian Business
Asia Pacific Journal of Management
Asia Pacific Journal of Operational Research
Asia Pacific Journal of Quality Management
British Journal of Management
British Journal of Administrative Management
Business Asia
Business China
Business Europe
Business Information Review
Business Strategy Review
California Management Review
Canadian Journal of Administrative Sciences
Communications International
European Business Journal
European Business Review
European Industrial Relations Review
European Journal of Information Systems
European Journal of Operational Research
European Management Journal
Euroweek
Executive Development
Far Eastern Economic Review
Harvard Business Review
HR Focus
HR Magazine
Health Services Management
Human Resource Management
Industrial and Labor Relations Review
Industrial Management
Industrial Relations Journal
Industrial Relations Review and Report
International Journal of Contemporary Hospitality Management
International Journal of Educational Management
International Journal of Industrial Organization
International Journal of Management
International Journal of Operations and Production Management
International Journal of Project Management
International Journal of Public Administration
International Journal of Public Sector Management
International Journal of Purchasing and Materials Management
International Journal of Service Industry Management
International Journal of Technology Management
International Labour Review
International Management
International Organization
International Review of Strategic Management
Journal of Applied Business Research
Journal of Business
Journal of Business Administration
Journal of Business Communication
Journal of Business Ethics
Journal of Business Research
Journal of Business Strategy
Journal of Consumer Affairs
Journal of Consumer Research
Journal of Educational Administration
Journal of European Industrial Training
Journal of Language for International Business
Journal of Management in Business
Journal of Management in Medicine
Journal of Managerial Psychology
Journal of Operations Management
Journal of Organizational Behavior
Journal of Organizational Behavior Management
Journal of Organizational Change Management
Journal of Product and Brand Management
Logistics Information Management
Long Range Planning
Management Accounting Research
Management Development Review
Management Education and Development

Management Quarterly
Management Research News (MRN)
Management Review
Management Science
Management Today
New Technology, Work & Employment
Organizational Dynamics
Organization Science
Organization Studies
Personnel Journal
Personnel Management
Personnel Psychology
Personnel Review
Project Management Journal
Public Administration Quarterly
Public Administration Review
Public Personnel Management
Public Productivity and Management Review
Purchasing and Supply management
R&D Management
Research-Technology Management
Review of Business
Risk Management
Sloan Management Review
Strategic Management Journal
Supervisory Management
Technology Analysis and Strategic Management
Technology Review
Technovation
TQM Magazine
Training
Training and Development
Training and Management Development Methods
Training Tomorrow
Women in Management Review

Australian journals

Australian Business Monthly
Australian Journal of Communications
Australian Economic Review
Australian Journal of Management
Australian Journal of Psychology
Asia Pacific HRM
Asia Pacific Journal of Human Resources
Asian Studies Review
Australian Journal of Political Science
Australian Journal of Public Administration
Australian Journal of Public Health
Business Review Weekly
Business Sydney
Business Queensland
Canberra Bulletin of Public Administration
Journal of Educational Administration
Journal of Industrial Relations
Labour and Industry
Labour Economics and Productivity
Personal Investment
Reserve Bank Bulletin

Appendix 2

Increasing response rates in mail surveys

In Chapter 8 a number of factors that affect mail survey response rates are listed. They are discussed in more detail below.

INTEREST OF THE RESPONDENT IN THE SURVEY TOPIC

A survey of a local community about a proposal to route a six-lane highway through the neighbourhood would probably result in a high response rate, but a survey of the same community on general patterns of shopping behaviour would probably result in a low response rate. Variation among the population in the level of interest in the topic can result in a biased, unrepresentative response. For example, a survey on the provision of Internet access for employees of a company might evoke a high response rate among those interested in computing and a low response rate among those not interested—giving a false impression of employees' enthusiasm for Internet access. To some extent this can be corrected by weighting (see Chapter 8) if the bias corresponds with certain known characteristics of the population. For example, if there was a high response rate from young people and a low response rate from older people, information from the human resources department on the actual proportions of different age groups in the company could be used to weight the results.

LENGTH OF THE QUESTIONNAIRE

It might be expected that a long questionnaire would discourage potential respondents. It has, however, been argued that other factors such as the topic and the presentation of the questionnaire are more important than the length of the questionnaire. This implies that, if the topic is interesting to the respondent and is well presented, then length is not an issue.

QUESTIONNAIRE DESIGN, PRESENTATION AND COMPLEXITY

Care must be taken in design and physical presentation with any respondent-completed questionnaire. Typesetting, colour coding of pages, graphics and so on may be necessary. Some questionnaires present awesome lists which can look very complicated and demanding to complete: breaking such lists up into shorter lists can help.

ACCOMPANYING LETTER

The letter from the sponsor or researcher that accompanies the questionnaire may have an influence on people's willingness to respond. Does it give a good reason for the survey? Is it from someone, or the type of organisation, whom the respondent trusts or respects?

POSTAGE-PAID REPLY ENVELOPE

It is usual to include a postage-paid envelope for the return of the questionnaire. Some believe that an envelope with a real stamp on it will produce a better response rate than a business reply-paid envelope. Providing reply envelopes with real stamps is more expensive because, apart from the time spent in sticking stamps on envelopes, stamps must be provided for both respondents and non-respondents.

REWARDS

The question of rewards for taking part in a survey can arise in relation to any sort of survey, but it is a device used most often in postal surveys. One approach is to send every respondent some small reward such as a voucher for a firm or agency's product or service, or even money. A more common approach is to enter all respondents in a draw for a prize. Even a fairly costly prize is money well spent if it results in a substantial increase in the response rate. When the cost of the alternative household survey involving face-to-face interviews is considered, a substantial prize that results in a significant increase in responses may be considered good value.

It could be argued that the introduction of rewards causes certain people to respond for the wrong reasons and introduces a potential source of bias in responses. It might also be considered that the inclusion of a prize or reward 'lowers the tone' of the survey and places it in the same category as other commercial junk mail that comes through people's letter boxes every day.

REMINDERS/FOLLOW-UPS

Sensible reminder and follow-up procedures are perhaps the most significant tool available to the researcher. Typically, a postcard reminder might be sent one week or ten days after the initial mailing. After two weeks a letter accompanied by a second copy of the questionnaire ('in case the first has been mislaid') should be sent. A final reminder card can be sent a week or so after that. The effects of these reminders and follow-ups can be seen in Figure 8.3 (p. 150). As noted in Chapter 8, it can be seen that the level of responses peaked after only three days and looked likely to cease after about sixteen days, giving a potential response rate of just 40 per cent. The surges in responses following the sending of the postcard and the second copy of the questionnaire can be seen, and the net result was a 75 per cent response rate, which is very good for this type of survey.

The sending out of reminders means that it must be possible to identify returned questionnaires so that reminders are not sent to those who have already replied. This means that questionnaires or envelopes must have an identifying number that can be matched with the mailing list. Some respondents resent this potential breach of confidentiality, but it cannot be avoided if only non-respondents are to be followed up. There is often a further advantage to being able to identify responses—they can be used to check the representativeness of the response. For instance, the questionnaire itself may not include respondents' addresses, but the geographical spread of the response can be examined if the identity of the responses is known and any necessary weighting can be carried out to correct any geographical bias.

The need for follow-ups must be considered when budgeting for a postal survey, since postage and printing costs are often the most significant item in such budgets.

Appendix 3

Suggested Appendix on Sample Size and Confidence Intervals

(This is a suggested wording for an appendix or note to be included in research reports based on sample data. Suppose the survey has a sample size of 500.)

All sample surveys are subject to a margin of statistical error. The margins of error, or *confidence intervals*, for this survey, with a sample size of 500, are as follows:

Finding from the survey	95% confidence interval
50%	±4.4%
40/60%	±4.3%
30/70%	±4.0%
20/80%	±3.5%
10/90%	±2.6%
5/95%	±1.9%

This means that, for example, if 20 per cent of the *sample* are found to have a particular characteristic, there is an estimated 95 per cent chance that the true *population* percentage lies in the range 20 ±3.5 per cent—that is, between 16.5 per cent and 23.5 per cent.

These margins of error have been taken into account in the analyses in this report.

Appendix 4

Details of *SPSS* data file used in Chapter 14

Question No.	Name	Type	Width	Decimal places	Label
–	qno	Numeric	4	0	Questionnaire number
1	crse	Numeric	1	0	Course enrolled in
2	cp	Numeric	1	0	Used Career Planning/last 6 months
	ment	Numeric	1	0	Used Mentoring/last 6 months
	comp	Numeric	1	0	Used Computer Training/last 6 months
	pa	Numeric	1	0	Used Perf. Appraisal/last 6 mths
3	rep	Numeric	1	0	Good reputation (rank importance)
	access	Numeric	1	0	Easy access (rank importance)
	curr	Numeric	1	0	Curriculum (rank importance)
	fees	Numeric	1	0	Fees paid (rank importance)
	park	Numeric	1	0	Easy parking (rank importance)
4	cost	Numeric	4	0	Cost of books
5	text	Numeric	1	0	Good textbook—importance
	lect	Numeric	1	0	Knowledgeable lecturer—importance
	assg	Numeric	1	0	Easy assignments—importance
6	sug1	Numeric	1	0	Suggestions for improving course—1
	sug2	Numeric	1	0	Suggestions for improving course—2
	sug3	Numeric	1	0	Suggestions for improving course—3
Additional data items					
	costr	Numeric	1	0	Cost recoded
	age	Numeric	2	0	Age in years
	gend	Numeric	1	0	Gender
	inc	Numeric	2	0	Income, $'000s pa
	int	Numeric	2	0	Times used Internet in last year
	lib	Numeric	2	0	Times used library in last year
	finrev	Numeric	3	0	Times read *Financial Review* in last year
	conf	Numeric	1	0	Times attended prof. conference in last year
	devlpt	Numeric	4	0	Personal exp. on prof. development, $pa

Values	Missing	Columns	Alignment	Measure/Data type
None	None	4	Right	Scale
As in Fig. 13.4*	None	4	Right	Nominal
As in Fig. 13.4	None	4	Right	Nominal
as above	None	4	Right	Nominal
as above	None	4	Right	Nominal
as above	None	4	Right	Nominal
None	None	4	Right	Ordinal
None	None	4	Right	Ordinal
None	None	4	Right	Ordinal
None	None	4	Right	Ordinal
None	None	4	Right	Ordinal
None	None	4		Scale
As in Fig. 13.4	None	4	Right	Scale
as above	None	4	Right	Scale
as above	None	4		Scale
As in Fig. 13.4	None	4	Right	Nominal
as above	None	4	Right	Nominal
as above	None	4	Right	Nominal
None	None	4	Right	Ordinal
None	None	4	Right	Scale
1 Male 2 Female	None	4	Right	Nominal
None	None	4	Right	Scale
None	None	4	Right	Scale
None	None	4	Right	Scale
None	None	4	Right	Scale
None	None	4	Right	Scale
None	None	5	Right	Scale

* 'Other' excluded

qno	crse	cp	ment	comp	pa	rep	access	curr	fees	park	cost	text	lect
1	2	1	1	0	0	1	4	2	3	5	100	3	3
2	2	1	1	1	0	1	4	2	3	5	so	2	3
3	3	1	0	0	0	2	5	1	3	4	250	2	2
4	4	0	0	0	0	2	3	1	4	5	25	3	2
5	3	1	0	0	1	1	4	3	2	5	55	3	3
6	3	1	1	1	0	2	4	1	3	5	40	2	3
7	2	1	0	0	0	3	2	1	4	5	150	2	3
8	2	1	0	1	0	3	4	2	1	5	250	1	2
9	4	0	1	0	0	1	5	2	3	4	300	2	3
10	3	1	1	0	0	2	3	1	5	4	100	1	2
11	3	1	1	0	1	2	3	1	4	5	75	2	2
12	2	1	0	1	0	1	4	3	2	5	50	2	3
13	1	1	0	1	0	1	5	2	3	4	55	2	3
14	3	1	1	0	0	2	4	1	3	5	75	3	3
15	1	1	1	0	0	3	2	1	5	4	150	3	3
16	1	1	1	0	1	1	5	3	2	4	49	3	3
17	1	1	0	1	1	1	4	3	2	5	95	2	3
18	1	1	0	1	0	1	5	2	3	4	199	2	2
19	1	1	0	1	0	1	3	2	4	5	250	3	2
20	1	0	0	1	0	1	3	2	4	5	39	3	3
21	1	0	1	1	0	2-11	1	3	4	5,911	2		3
22	1	0	1	0	0	2 1	1 >	5	3	4	165	2	3
23	1	1	1	0	0	2	4	1	3	5	300	1	2
24	1	1	1	0	1	2	4	3	5	1	44	2	3
25	1	1	0	1	1	3	4	1	2	5	56	1	2
26	1	1	0	1	1	3	4	5	1	2	160	2	2
27	2	0	0	1	0	3	5	2	3	4	530	2	3
28	2	0	0	0	0	1	5	4	2	3	21	2	3
29	2	0	1	0	0	1	4	3	2	5	65	3	3
30	2	1	1	1	0	1	4	3	2	5	130	3	3
31	2	1	1	1	1	1	4	2	3	5	290	3	3
32	2	1	1	1	1	1	4	5	3	2	25	2	3
33	2	0	0	0	0	1	4	2	3	5	58	2	2
34	2	0	0	0	0	1	5	3	2	4	164	3	2
35	2	0	0	0	0	1	5	2	3	4	250	3	3
36	3	1	1	0	1	1	5	2	3	4	24	2	3
37	3	1	1	0	0	3	4	1	2	5	75	2	3
38	3	1	1	0	0	3	4	1	2	5	123	1	2
39	3	0	1	0	0	2	4	1	3	5	300	2	3
40	3	0	1	0	1	2	4	3	1	5	16	1	2
41	3	0	1	1	1	2	4	3	1	5	78	2	2
42	3	1	1	1	1	4	5	1	2	3	163	2	3
43	3	1	1	0	1	4	5	1	2	3	250	2	3
44	3	1	1	0	1	2	5	1	2	3	25	3	3
45	3	0	1	1	1	2	4	1	5	3	40	3	3
46	3	0	0	1	0	1	4	1	3	5	45	3	3
47	3	0	1	1	0	1	4	1	3	5	45	2	3
48	3	1	1	1	0	1	4	1	3	5	35	2	2
49	3	1	0	0	0	11	4	3	1	5	36	3	2
50	3	0	0	0	0	1	5	4	3	2	45	3	3

assg	sug1	sug2	sug3	costr	age	gender	inc	int	lib	finrev	conf	devipt
1	1			2	25	2	31	12	10	0	5	500
1	2	1		1	21	2	27	14	10	0	6	500
2	3	4		4	34	1	38	36	5	0	4	900
2	1	2	4	1	22	2	25	48	12	0	7	1000
1				2	26	2	36	60	15	0	2	1000
1	2			1	30	2	34	10	25	0	3	750
2	3			3	38	2	40	0	25	25	3	750
2	4	5		4	37	2	40	0	12	200	2	250
2				4	26	1	29	22	1	25	5	200
1	1	1		2	23	2	23	0	12	0	7	0
1	2	3		2	24	2	28	0	15	0	5	0
1				1	24	2	27	0	25	0	6	550
2	1	2		2	37	2	38	12	25	0	1	1000
2	4			2	35	2	40	13	25	0	2	1500
1	1	2	5	3	40	2	42	14	12	100	4	500
1	1			1	22	2	27	15	12	52	6	400
1	2	1		2	23	2	26	23	22	20	1	850
2	3	4		3	35	1	38	34	2	100	1	0
2	1	2	4	4	41	1	45	37	1	250	0	0
1				1	26	1	30	48	0	0	3	200
1	2			2	26	1	32	0	0	0	4	200
2	3			3	37	1	39	10	0	0	2	200
2	4	5		4	43	1	45	20	0	0	1	1050
2				1	29	1	35	30	0	0	3	1500
1	1	1		2	25	1	27	40	0	0	6	1000
1	2	3		3	35	1	40	50	0	40	4	990
1				4	37	1	42	40	1	160	0	300
2	1	2		1	27	1	29	30	3	0	5	350
2	4			2	26	1	30	20	6	0	5	350
1	1	2	5	3	27	1	31	10	0	64	5	1050
1	1			4	43	1	44	5	0	65	1	1000
1	2	1		1	25	1	30	15	0	0	5	950
2	3	4		2	29	1	35	25	0	0	3	200
2	1	2	4	3	29	1	38	35	0	0	1	200
1				4	39	1	43	45	0	175	0	200
1	2			1	28	2	33	55	0	0	4	50
2	3			2	25	2	35	35	0	0	3	55
2	4	5		3	29	2	39	25	25	1 50	1	850
2				4	27	2	37	15	50	60	2	2000
1	1	1		1	22	2	26	5	40	0	6	1500
1	2	3	4	2	25	2	28	5	32	40	6	500
1				3	27	2	27	12	12	42	6	300
2	1	2		4	23	2	27	22	16	200	6	300
2	4			1	23	2	22	32	10	0	8	300
1	1	2	5	1	23	2	26	42	10	52	5	250
1	1	2		1	24	1	28	52	10	0	6	500
1	2	3		1	25	1	30	62	-0	0	5	200
2	3	4	1	1	27	1	34	69	0	52	3	1100
2	4	5		1	26	1	32	70	0	52	4	950
1	5	3	4	1	27	1	31	0	15	26	5	650

Appendix 5

Statistical formulae

Confidence interval

95 per cent confidence interval for normal distribution for percentage p

$$\text{C.I.} = \pm 1.96\sqrt{\frac{p(100 - p)}{n - 1}}$$

where n = sample size

Chi-square

$$\chi^2 = \sqrt{\Sigma((O - E)/E)^2}$$

t for difference between means

$$t = \sqrt{\frac{(\bar{X}_1 - \bar{X}_2)}{(s_1^2/n_1 + s_2^2/n_1)}}$$

Standard deviation

$$\text{SD} = \sqrt{\frac{\Sigma(X - \bar{X})^2}{n}}$$

Correlation coefficient

$$r = \frac{\Sigma((X - \bar{X})(Y - \bar{Y}))^2}{(s_1^2/n_1 + s_2^2/n_1)}$$

Value of t for correlation coefficient

$$t = r\sqrt{(N - 2)/(1 - r^2)}$$

Appendix 6

Cluster analysis data

TV	Age	TV	Age
7	7	7	9
11	39	8	36
7	8	6	12
10	37	7	50
5	9	45	7
10	45	40	8
10	10	45	9
5	45	35	10
6	11	42	11
8	37	45	12
5	12	45	13
5	43	36	14
9	13	35	14
6	44	34	8
6	14	33	9
11	38	32	12
8	16	60	50
5	41	10	42
5	8	3	15
7	47	12	45

References

Academy of Management 1997, Code of ethical conduct. *Academy of Management Journal*, 40(6), 1469–74.

Adler, P.A. & Adler, R. 1994, Observational techniques. In N.K. Denzin & Y.S. Lincoln (eds), *Handbook of Qualitative Research*. Sage, Thousand Oaks, CA, 377–92.

Adriaans, P. & Zantinge, D. 1996, *Data Mining*. Addison-Wesley, Harlow, Essex.

Alreck, P.L. & Settle, R.B. 1995, *The Survey Research Handbook*. 2nd edn, Irwin, Burr Ridge, IL.

Alvesson, M. & Deetz, S. 1996, Critical theory and postmodern approaches to organizational studies. In S.R. Clegg, C. Hardy & W.R. Nord (eds), *Handbook of Organization Studies*. Sage, London, 191–217.

American Psychological Association 1994, *Publication Manual of the American Psychological Association*. 4th edn, American Psychological Association, Washington, D.C.

Anderson, J. & Poole, M. 1994, *Thesis and Assignment Writing*. 2nd edn, John Wiley & Sons, Brisbane.

Argyrous, G. 1996, *Statistics for Social Research*. Macmillan Education Australia, Melbourne.

Atkinson, R. 1998, *The Life Story Interview*. Sage, London.

Aung, M., Zhang, M., Farhat, H. & Gan, W. 2001, An exploratory study of the smoking issue in restaurants. *Management Decision*, 39(4), 279–84.

Australian Bureau of Statistics 1997, *The Australian Business Longitudinal Survey: 1994–95 and 1995–96*. (Cat. No. 8141.0). ABS, Canberra.

Australian Bureau of Statistics 2002a, *Projections for the Populations of Australia, States and Territories: 1999–2061* (Cat. No. 3222.0). ABS, Canberra.

Australian Bureau of Statistics 2002b, *Attendance at Selected Cultural Venues and Events: 2002* (Cat. No. 4114.0). ABS, Canberra.

Australian and New Zealand Academy of Management 1996, *1996–97 Membership Directory*. Macquarie University, Graduate School of Management, North Ryde, NSW.

Australian Government Publishing Service 1994, *Style Manual for Authors, Editors and Printers*. 5th edn, AGPS, Canberra (For current, 6th edition—see Snooks & Co, 2002).

Babbie, E.R. 1990, *Survey Research Methods*. 2nd edn, Wadsworth, Belmont, CA.

Babbie, E.R. & Halley, F. 1995, *Adventures in Social Research: Data Analysis Using SPSS for Windows*. Pine Forge Press, Thousand Oaks, CA.

Backstrom, C.H. & Hursh-Cesar, G. 1981, *Survey Research*. 2nd edn, Wiley, New York.

Bainbridge, W.S. 1989, *Survey Research: A Computer-Assisted Introduction*. Wadsworth, Belmont, CA.

Barnard, C. 1968 [1938], *The Functions of the Executive*. 30th anniversary edn, Harvard University Press, Cambridge, Mass.

Barney, J.B. & Griffin, R.W. 1992, *The Management of Organizations*. Houghton Mifflin Company, Boston.

Barry, P. 1990, *The Rise and Fall of Alan Bond*. Bantam/ABC Books, Sydney.

Barry, P. 1993, *The Rise and Fall of Kerry Packer*. Bantam/ABC Books, Sydney

Bartunek, J.M., Bobko, P. & Venkatraman, N. 1993, Toward innovation and diversity in management research methods. *Academy of Management Journal*, 36(6), 1362–73.

Bazeley, P. & Richards, L. 2002. *The NVivo Qualitative Project Book*. Sage, London.

Beaubien, J.M. 2003, Comprehensive Meta-Analysis (software review). *Personnel Psychology*, 56(1), 291–293.

Bennett, R. 1991, What is management research? In N. Smith & P. Dainty (eds), *The Management Research Handbook*. Routledge, London, 67–77.

Berdie, D.R., Anderson, J.F. & Niebuhr, M.A. 1986, *Questionnaires: Design and Use*. 2nd edn, Scarecrow Press, Metuchen, N.J.

Berg, B. 1995, *Qualitative Research Methods for the Social Sciences*. 2nd edn, Allyn and Bacon, Boston.

Berry, M.J.A. & Linoff, G. 2004, *Data Mining Techniques: for Marketing, Sales, and Customer Support*. Wiley, New York.

Bertaux, D. (ed.) 1981, *Biography and Society*. Sage, London.

Boote, J. and Mathews, A. 1999, Saying is one thing: doing is another: the role of observation in marketing research. *Qualitative Market Research*, 2(1), 15–23.

Bouma, G.D. 1993, *The Research Process*. Oxford University Press Australia, Melbourne.

Brewer, E.W. & Shapard, L. 2004, Employee burnout: a meta-analysis of the relationship between age or years of experience. *Human Resource Development Review*, 3(2), 102–23.

Bristol, T. & Fern, E.F. 2003, The effects of interaction on consumers' attitudes in focus groups. *Psychology and Marketing*, 20(5), 433–54.

Bruner, G.C. & Hensel, P.J. 1992, *Marketing Scales Handbook: A Compilation of Multi-Item Measures*. American Marketing Association, Chicago, IL.

Bryman, A. 1996, Leadership in organizations. In S.R. Clegg, C. Hardy & W.R. Nord (eds), *Handbook of Organization Studies*. Sage, London, 276–92.

Bryman, A. & Bell, E. 2003, *Business Research Methods*. Oxford University Press, Oxford.

Bulmer, M. (ed.) 1982, *Social Research Ethics: An Examination of the Merits of Covert Participant Observation*. MacMillan, London.

Burns, J.P.A., *et al.* (eds) 1986, *The Adelaide Grand Prix—The Impact of a Special Event*. Centre for South Australian Economics Studies, Adelaide.

Burns, R.B. 1994, *Introduction to Research Methods*. 2nd edn, Longman Cheshire, Melbourne.

Buzan, T. 1994, *The Mind Map Book: How to Use Radiant Thinking to Maximize Your Brain's Untapped Potential*. Dutton, New York.

Bryman, A. 1995, *Disney and his Worlds*. Routledge, London.

Campbell, D.T. & Stanley J.C. 1972, *Experimental and Quasi-Experimental Designs for Research*. Rand McNally, Chicago.

Carty, V. 1997, Ideologies and forms of domination in the organization of the global production and consumption of goods in the emerging postmodern era: a case study of Nike Corporation and the implications for gender. *Gender, Work and Organization*, 4(4), 189–201.

Chen, Z. & Dubinsky, A.J. 2003, A conceptual model of perceived customer value in e-commerce: a preliminary investigation. *Psychology and Marketing*, 20(4), 323–47.

Clarke, T. & Clegg, S. 2000, *Changing Paradigms: The Transformation of Management Knowledge for the 21st Century*. Harper Collins, London.

Clegg, S. 1989, *Frameworks of Power*. Sage, London.

Clegg, S. 1996, Constituting management. In G. Palmer & S. Clegg (eds), *Constituting Management: Markets, Meanings and Identities*. Walter de Gruyter, New York, 1–9.

Clegg, S. & Dunkerley, D. 1980, *Organizations, Class and Control*. Routledge & Kegan Paul, London.

Coakes, S.J. & Steed, L.G. 1997, *SPSS: Analysis Without Anguish: (Version 6.1 for IBM and Macintosh Users)*. John Wiley & Sons, Brisbane.

Conlon, R.M. & Perkins, J. 2001, *Wheels and Deals: the Automotive Industry in Twentieth-century Australia*. Ashgate, Aldershot, UK.

Cooper, D.R. & Emory, C.W. 1995, *Business Research Methods*. 5th edn, Richard D. Irwin Inc, Chicago.

Craig Smith, N. 1991, The case-study: a vital yet misunderstood research method. In N. Smith & P. Dainty (eds), *The Management Research Handbook*. Routledge, London, 145–58.

Critcher, C. & Gladstone, B. 1998, Utilizing the Delphi technique in policy discussion: a case study of a privatized utility in Britain. *Public Administration*, 76(4), 431–49.

Daft, R.L. 1994, *Management*. 3rd edn, The Dryden Press, Orlando, FL.

Daniel, F., Lohrke, F.T., Fornaciari, C.J. & Turner, R.A. 2004, Slack resources and firm performance: a meta-analysis. *Journal of Business Research*, 57(6), 565–74.

David, M. & Sutton, C.D. 2004, *Social research: The Basics*. Sage, London.

Davis, D. & Cosenza, R. M. 1993, *Business Research for Decision Making*. 3rd edn, Wadsworth, Belmont, CA.

Dawson, J. & Hillier, J. 1995, Competitor mystery shopping: methodological considerations and implications for the MRS Code of Conduct. *Journal of the Market Research Society*, 37(4), 417–43.

Denzin, N.K. & Lincoln, Y.S. (eds) 1994, *Handbook of Qualitative Research*. Sage, Thousand Oaks, CA.

Denzin, N.K. & Lincoln, Y.S. 1994, Introduction: entering the field of qualitative research. In N.K. Denzin & Y.S. Lincoln (eds), *Handbook of Qualitative Research*. Sage, Thousand Oaks, CA., 1–17.

Dewhirst, H.D. 1989, Management in Australia: 'No worries'. *Survey of Business*, 25(2), 3–6.

Dex, S. (ed.) 1991, *Life and Work History Analyses: Qualitative and Quantitative Development*. Routledge, London.

Dillman, D.A. 2000, *Mail and Telephone Surveys: The Total Design Method*. 2nd edn, Wiley, New York.

Dodd, C.A., Clarke, I. & Kirkup, M.H. 1998, Camera observations of customer behaviour in fashion retailing: methodological propositions. *International Journal of Retail and Distribution Management*, 26(8), 311–19.

Downs, C.W. 1988, *Communication Audits*. Scott Foresman, Glenview, Ill.

Dreilinger, C. 1994, Why management fads fizzle. *Business Horizons*, 37(6), 11–15.

Duffy, M.E. 1987, Methodological triangulation: A vehicle for merging qualitative and quantitative research methods. *IMAGE: Journal of Nursing Scholarship*, 19, 130–3.

Dunne, S. 1995, *Interviewing Techniques for Writers and Researchers*. A. & C. Black, London.

Easterby-Smith, M., Thorpe, R. & Lowe, A. 1993, *Management Research: An Introduction*. Sage, London.

Enright, M.J. & Roberts, B.H. 2001, Regional clustering in Australia. *Australian Journal of Management*, 26(1), 65–85.

Evered, R. & Reis Louis, M. 1991, Alternative perspectives in organizational sciences: 'inquiry from the inside' and 'inquiry from the outside'. In N. Smith & P. Dainty (eds), *The Management Research Handbook*. Routledge, London, 7–22.

Ferri, E. (ed.) 1993, *Life at 33*. National Children's Bureau, London.

Fetterman, D. 1989, *Ethnography: Step by Step*. Sage, Newbury Park, CA.

Fiedler, F. 1974, The contingency model—new directions for leadership utilisation. *Journal of Contemporary Business*, 3, 65–79.

Fielding, N.G. & Lee, R.M. (eds) 1991, *Using Computers in Qualitative Research*. Sage, London.

Finn, M., Elliott-White, M. & Walton, M. 2000, *Tourism and Leisure Research Methods*. Longman, Harlow, UK.

Flick, J.P., Radomsky, M.C. & Ramani, R.V. 1999, The Penn State approach to site-specific health and safety training. *Professional Safety*, 44(10), 34–38.

Foddy, W. 1993, *Constructing Questions for Interviews and Questionnaires*. University of Cambridge Press, Cambridge.

Foglesong, R.E. 2001, *Married to the Mouse: Walt Disney World and Orlando*. Yale University Press, New Haven, CT.

Forsyth, P. 1997, *How to be Better at Writing Reports and Proposals*. The Industrial Society, London.

Fowler, F.J. 1993, *Survey Research Methods*. 2nd edn, Sage, Newbury Park, CA.

Francis, G. 1996, *Introduction to SPSS for Windows*. Prentice Hall, Sydney.

French, J.R.P. & Raven, B. 1959, The bases of social power. In L. Cartwright & A. Zander (eds), *Group Dynamics Research and Theory*. Tavistock, London.

Frey, J.H. 1989, *Survey Research by Telephone*. 2nd edn, Sage, Newbury Park, CA.

Garcia-Quevedo, J. 2004, Do public subsidies complement business R&D? A meta-analysis of the econometric evidence. *Kyklos*, 57(1), 87–102.

Garratt, S. 1991, *How to be a Consultant*. Gower, Aldershot, UK.

Gay, L.R. & Diehl, P.L. 1992, *Research Methods for Business and Management*. Maxwell Macmillan International, New York.

George, D. & Mallery, P. 1995, *SPSS/PC+ Step by Step: A Simple Guide and Reference*. Duxbury Press, Belmont, CA.

Gerber, S. & Voelkl, K. 1997, *The SPSS Guide to The New Statistical Analysis of Data by T.W. Anderson and Jeremy D. Finn*, Companion volume to the *New Statistical Analysis of Data* by T.W. Anderson & Jeremy D. Finn, Springer, New York.

Ghauri, P.N., Gronhaug, K. & Kristianslund, I. 1995, *Research Methods in Business Studies*. Prentice Hall, London.

Gibbs, G. 2002, *Qualitative Data Analysis: Exporations with NVivo*. Open University Press, London.

Gibson, L.J. & Miller, M.M. 1990, A Delphi model for planning 'preemptive' regional economic diversification. *Economic Development Review*, 8 (2), 34–41.

Giddens, A. (ed.) 1974, *Positivism and Sociology*. Heinemann, London.

Gill, J. & Johnson, P. 1997, *Research Methods for Managers*. 2nd edn, Paul Chapman Publishing, London.

Glaser, B. & Strauss, A.L. 1967, *The Discovery of Grounded Theory: Strategies for Qualitative Research.* Aldine, Chicago.

Glass, G.V., McGaw, B. & Smith, M.L. 1981, *Meta-Analysis in Social Research.* Sage, Beverley Hills, CA.

Glebbeek, A.C. & Bax, E.H. 2004, Is high employee turnover really harmful? An empirical test using company records. *Academy of Management Journal*, 47(2), 277–86.

Goldman, R. & Papson, S. 1998, *Nike Culture: the Sign of the Swoosh.* Sage, London.

Green, S.B., Salkind N.J. & Akey, T.M. 1997, Using SPSS for Windows: Analyzing and Understanding Data. Prentice Hall, Upper Saddle River, NJ.

Greenbaum, T.L. 1998, *The Handbook for Focus Group Research.* 2nd edn, Sage, Thousand Oaks, CA.

Greenbaum, T.L. 2000, *Moderating Focus Groups: A Practical Guide for Group Facilitation.* Sage, Thousand Oaks, CA.

Grichting, W.L. & Caltabiano, M.L. 1986, Amount and direction of bias in survey interviewing. *Australian Psychologist*, 21(1), 69–78.

Grunow, D. 1995, The research design in organization studies. *Organization Studies*, 6, 93–103.

Gummesson, E. 1991, *Qualitative Methods in Management Research.* Sage, Newbury Park, CA.

Hackman J. & Oldham, G. 1975, Development of the job diagnostic survey. *Journal of Applied Psychology*, 60(1), 159–70.

Hague, P.N. 1993, *Questionnaire Design.* Kogan Page, London.

Hammersley, M. & Atkinson, P. 1995, *Ethnography: Principles in Practice.* 2nd edn, Routledge, London.

Hampilos, J. 1988, A four-component self-esteem construct: its measurement and construct validity. *Dissertation Abstracts International*, 49, 4599A, No. 8827581, University Microfilms, Ann Arbor, MI.

Hart, S.J. 1991, A first-time user's guide to the collection and analysis of interview data from senior managers. In N. Smith & P. Dainty (eds), *The Management Research Handbook.* Routledge, London, 190–204.

Harvard Business School (n.d.), Harvard Business School Case Studies, Harvard University, Boston, MA. Available at: (http://harvardbusinessonline/hbsp/harvard/edu/b01/en/cases/cases_home.jhtml).

Hassard, J.S. 1991, Multiple paradigm analysis: a methodology for management research. In N. Smith & P. Dainty (eds), *The Management Research Handbook.* Routledge, London, 23–43.

Healey, M. & Rawlinson, M. 1994, Interviewing techniques. In V. J. Wass & P.E. Wells (eds), *Principles and Practice in Business and Management Research.* Dartmouth Publishing, Aldershot, UK, 123–45.

Hedges, B. 1986, *Personal Leisure Histories.* Sports Council/Economic and Social Research Council, London.

Higgs, J. (ed.) 1997, *Qualitative Research: Discourse on Methodologies.* Hampden Press, Sydney.

Hoinville, G. & Jowell, R. 1978, *Survey Research Practice.* Heinemann, London.

Hormozi, A.M. & Giles, S. 2004, Data mining: a competitive weapon for banking and retail industries. *Information Systems Management*, 21(2), 62–71.

Hosoda, M., Stone-Romero, E.F. & Coats, G. 2003, The effects of physical attractiveness on job-related outcomes: A meta-analysis of experimental studies. *Personnel Psychology*. 56(2), 431–48.

Hubbard, R. & Lindsay, R.M. 1995, 'Caveat emptor' applies to the consumption of published empirical research results, too. *Management Research News*, 18(10/11), 49–55.

Huberman, A.M. & Miles, M.B. 1994, Data management and analysis methods. In N.K. Denzin & Y.S. Lincoln (eds), *Handbook of Qualitative Research*. Sage, Thousand Oaks, CA., 428–44.

Huddleston, P., Whipple, J. & Van Auken, A. 2004, Food store loyalty: application of a consumer loyalty framework. *Journal of Targeting, Measurement and Analysis Marketing*, 12(3), 213–30.

Hudson, S., Snaith, T., Miller, G. & Hudson, P. 2001, Distribution channels in the travel industry: using mystery shoppers to understand the influence of travel agency recommendations. *Journal of Travel Research*, 40(2), 148–54.

Hummels, H. & Timmer, D. 2004, Investors in need of social, ethical, and environmental information. *Journal of Business Ethics*, 52(1), 73–84.

Hussey, J. & Hussey, R. 1997, *Business Research*. Macmillan, London.

Hutton, P.F. 1990, *Survey Research for Managers: How to Use Surveys in Management Decision-Making*. 2nd edn, Macmillan, Basingstoke, Hants.

Iacocca, L.A. 1984, *Iacocca: An Autobiography*. Bantam Books, Toronto.

Jankowicz, A.D. 1991, *Business Research Projects for Students*. Chapman and Hall, London.

Jones, S. 1987, Choosing action research: a rationale. In I.L. Mangham (ed.), *Organisation Analysis and Development*. Wiley, Chichester, Sussex.

Jorgensen, D.L. 1989, *Participant Observation: A Methodology for Human Studies*. Sage, Newbury Park, CA.

Judge, T.A., Colbert, A.E. & Ilies, R. 2004, Intelligence and leadership: a quantitative review and test of theoretical propositions. *Journal of Applied Psychology*, 89(3), 542–52.

Judge, T.A., Erez, A., Bobo, J.E. & Thoresen, C.J. 2002, The core self-evaluations scale: development of a measure. *Personnel Psychology*. 56(2), 303–31.

Kasprzyk, D., Duncan, G., Kalton, G. & Singh, M.P. 1989, *Panel Surveys*. John Wiley & Sons, New York.

Katz, D.R. 1994, *Just Do It: the Nike Spirit in the Corporate World*. Adams Publishers, Holbrook, MA.

Kellehear, A. 1993, *The Unobtrusive Researcher*. Allen & Unwin, Sydney.

Keller, G. & Warrack, B. 1991, *Essentials of Business Statistics*. Wadsworth, Belmont, CA.

Kelly, G.A. 1955, *The Psychology of Personal Constructs*. Norton, New York.

Kelly, J.R. 1980, Leisure and quality: beyond the quantitative barrier in research. In T.L. Goodale & P.A. Witt (eds), *Recreation and Leisure: Issues in an Era of Change*. Venture, State College, PA, 300–14.

Kervin, J.B. 1992, *Methods for Business Research*. Harper Collins, New York.

Kiousis, S. 2004, Explicating media salience: a factor analysis of *New York Times* issue coverage during the 2000 U.S. presidential election. *Journal of Communication*, 54(1), 71–87.

Klein, N. 1999, *No Logo: Taking Aim at the Brand Bullies.* Picador, New York.

Krejcie, R.V. & Morgan, D.W. 1970, Determining sample size for research activities. *Educational and Psychological Measurement*, 30, 607–10.

Kuhn, T. S. 1962, *The Structure of Scientific Revolutions.* Chicago University Press, Chicago.

Kimmel, A.J. 1988, *Ethics and Values in Applied Social Research.* Sage, Newbury Park, CA.

Kraut, A.I. (ed.) 1996, *Organizational Surveys: Tools for Assessment and Change.* Jossey-Bass, San Francisco, CA.

Krueger, R.A. 1994, *Focus Groups: A Practical Guide for Applied Research.* 2nd edn, Sage, Newbury Park, CA.

Kvale, S. 1996, *Interviews: An Introduction to Qualitative Research Interviewing.* Sage, Thousand Oaks, CA.

Ladkin, A. 1991, The life and work history methodology: a discussion of its potential use for tourism and hospitality research. In J. Phillimore & L. Godson (eds), *Qualitative Research in Tourism: Ontologies, Epistemologies and Methodologies.* Routledge, London, 236–54.

Lainsbury, A. 2000, *Once upon an American Dream: The Story of Euro Disneyland.* University of Kansas Press, Lawrence, KS.

Lavrakas, P.K. 1993, *Telephone Survey Methods: Sampling, Selection and Supervision.* 2nd edn, Sage, Newbury Park, CA.

Leedy, P.D. 1993, *Practical Research: Planning and Design.* 5th edn, Macmillan, New York.

Lees-Haley, P.R. 1980, *The Questionnaire Design Handbook.* Rubicon, Huntsville, Ala.

Lester, J.D. 2000, *Citing Cyberspace.* Longman, New York.

Li, X. & Crane, N.B. 1996, *Electronic Style: A Handbook for Citing Electronic Information.* 2nd edn, Information Today, Medford, NJ.

Likert, R.A. 1982, A technique for the measurement of attitudes. *Archives of Psychology*, 140, 44–53.

Linstone, H.A. 1978, The Delphi technique. In J. Fowles (ed.), *Handbook of Futures Research.* Greenwood Press, Westport, Conn., 273–300.

Mahadevan, R. 2004, *The Economics of Productivity in Asia and Australia.* Edward Elgar, Cheltenham, UK.

Mason, J. 1996, *Qualitative Researching.* Sage, London.

Mathews, B.P. & Shepherd, J.L. 2002, Dimensionality of Cook and Wall's 1980, British Organizational Commitment Scale revisited. *Journal of Occupational and Organizational Psychology*, 75(3), 369–75.

Mathieu, J. & Zajac, D. 1990, A review of meta-analysis of the antecedents, correlates and consequences of organizational commitment. *Psychological Bulletin*, 108(2), 171–94.

Maxwell, J. 1996, *Qualitative Research Design: An Interactive Approach.* Sage, Thousand Oaks, CA.

McCall, G.J. & Simmons, J.L. (eds) 1969, *Issues in Participant Observation.* Addison Wesley, Reading, Mass.

McCall, M. & Bobko, P. 1990, Research methods and discovery in industrial/organizational psychology. In M. Dunnette & L. Hough (eds), *Handbook of Industrial and Organizational Psychology.* 2nd edn, Consulting Psychologists Press, Palo Alto, CA., 381–418.

McDonagh, J. & Coghlan, D. 2001, The art of clinical inquiry in information technology-related change. In P. Reason & H. Bradbury (eds), *Handbook of Action Research: Participative Inquiry and Practice.* Sage, London, 372–78.

McNiff, J. & Whitehead, J. 2002, *Action Research: Principles and Practice*. Routledge/Falmer, London.

Metcalfe, M. 1996, *Business Research Through Argument*. Kluwer, Boston.

Miles, M. & Huberman, M. 1994, *Qualitative Data Analysis: A Sourcebook of New Methods*. Sage, Thousand Oaks, CA.

Miles, M. & Weitzman, E. 1994, *Computer Programs for Qualitative Data Analysis*. Sage, Thousand Oaks, CA.

Moos, R.H. & Moos, B.S. 1974, *Manual for the Family Environment Scale*. Consulting Psychologists, Palo Alto, CA.

Morgan, D.L. 1988, *Focus Groups as Qualitative Research*. Sage, Newbury Park, CA.

Morgan, G. & Smircich, L. 1980, The case for qualitative research. *Academy of Management Review*, 5(2), 491–500.

Morse, J. & Richards, L. 2002, *Readme First for a User's Guide to Qualitative Methods*. Sage, Thousand Oaks, CA.

Mowday, R., Steers, R. & Porter, L. 1979, The measurement of organizational commitment. *Journal of Vocational Behaviour*, 14(2), 224–27.

Murray, J.B. 1990, Review of research on the Myer-Briggs Type Indicator. *Perceptual and Motor Skills*, 70(2), 1187–1202.

Newby, R., Watson, J. & Woodliff, D. 2003, Using focus groups in SME research: the case of owner-occupier objectives. *Journal of Developmental Entrepreneurship*, 8(3), 237–46.

O'Brien, S. & Ford, R. 1988, Can we at last say goodbye to social class? An examination of the usefulness and stability of some alternative methods of measurement. *Journal of the Market Research Society*, 30(3), 289–332.

Okazaki, S. & Rivas, J.A. 2003, Beyond the net: cultural values reflected in Japanese multinationals' web communication strategies. *Journal of International Consumer Marketing*, 16(1), 47–70.

Oppenheim, A.N. 1992, *Questionnaire Design, Interviewing and Attitude Measurement*. Pinter, London.

Ouchi, W. 1981, *Theory Z: How American Business Can Meet the Japanese Challenge*. Addison-Wesley, Reading, Mass.

Palmer, I. & Dunford, R. 2002, Managing discursive tension: the co-existence of individualist and collaborative discourses in Flight Centre. *Journal of Management Studies*. 39(8), 1045–70.

Parker, T. 1988, *Red Hill: A Mining Community*. Coronet, London.

Paul, J. 1996, Between-method triangulation in organizational diagnosis. *International Journal of Organizational Analysis*, 4(2), 135–54.

Perlow, L.A. 1998, Boundary control: the social ordering of work and family time in a high-tech corporation. *Administrative Science Quarterly*, 43(2), 328–57.

Perrone, L. & Vickers, M.H. 2003, Life after graduation as a 'very uncomfortable world': an Australian case study. *Education and Training*, 45(2/3), 69–78.

Peters, T.J. & Waterman, R.H. 1984, *In Search of Excellence*. Harper & Row, Sydney.

Peterson, K.I. 1994, Qualitative research methods for the travel and tourism industry. In J.R. Ritchie & C.R. Goeldner (eds), *Travel, Tourism and Hospitality Research*. 2nd edn, John Wiley, New York, 487–92.

Plummer, K. 2001, *Documents of Life 2*. Sage, London.

Preuss, H. 2000, *Economics of the Olympic Games: Hosting the Games 1972–2000.* Walla Walla Press, Petersham, NSW.

Prior, L. 2003, *Using Documents in Social Research.* Sage, London.

Project on Disney 1995, *Inside the Mouse: Work and Play at Disney World.* Duke University Press, Durham, NC.

Punnett, B.J. & Shenkar, O. (eds) 1996, *Handbook for International Management Research.* Blackwell, Cambridge, Mass.

Pyle, D. 2003, *Business Modeling and Data Mining.* Morgan Kaufmann, San Francisco, CA. (See also associated website: (www.modelandmine.com) accessed Nov. 2004.)

Raimond, P. 1993, *Management Projects: Design, Research and Presentation.* Chapman and Hall, London.

Rea, L.M. & Parker, R.A. 1992, *Designing and Conducting Survey Research: A Comprehensive Guide.* Jossey-Bass Publishers, San Francisco, CA.

Reason, P. & Bradbury, H. (eds) 2001, *Handbook of Action Research: Participative Inquiry and Practice.* Sage, London.

Richards, T.J. & Richards, L. 1994, Using computers in qualitative research. In N.K. Denzin & Y.S. Lincoln (eds), *Handbook of Qualitative Research.* Sage, Thousand Oaks, CA., 445–62.

Roberts, B. 2002, *Biographical Research.* Open University Press, Buckingham, UK.

Robbins, S.B., Lauver, K., Le, H. & Davis, D. 2004, Do psychosocial and study skill factors predict college outcomes? A meta-analysis. *Psychological Bulletin,* 130(2), 261–88.

Robbins, S. & Mukerji, D. 1994, *Managing Organisations: New Challenges and Perspectives.* Prentice Hall, Sydney.

Robson, S. & Foster, A. (eds) 1989, *Qualitative Research in Action.* Griffin, London.

Roethlisberger, F.S. & Dickson, W.J. 1939, *Management and the Worker.* Harvard University Press, Cambridge, Mass.

Rose, D. (ed.) 2000, Researching Social and Economic Change: the Uses of Household Panel Studies. Routledge, London.

Rose, H. 1991, Case studies. In G. Allan and C. Skinner (eds), *Handbook for Research Students in the Social Sciences.* Falmer, Brighton, 190–202.

Rosenthal, R. 1966, *Experimenter Effects in Behavioral Research.* Appleton-Century-Crofts, New York.

Roy, D. 1952, Quota restrictions and goldbricking in a machine shop. *American Journal of Sociology,* 57, 427–42.

Sacks, O. 1985, *The Man Who Mistook his Wife for a Hat.* Picador, London.

Sainsbury, M. 2003, *Moral Rights and Their Application in Australia.* Federation Press, Annandale, NSW.

Sanderson, S. & Uzumeri, M. 1995, Managing product families: the case of the Sony Walkman. *Research Policy,* 24(4), 761–82.

Saunders, M.N.K., Lewis, P. & Thornhill, A. 1996, *Research Methods for Business Students.* Pitman, London.

Schein, E.H. 1985, *Organizational Culture and Leadership.* Jossey Bass, San Francisco, CA.

Schneider, B. 1990, *Organizational Climate and Culture.* Jossey Bass, San Francisco, CA.

Schwartzman, H.B. 1993, *Ethnography in Organizations.* Sage, Newbury Park, CA.

Seidman, I.E. 1991, *Interviewing as Qualitative Research: A Guide for Researchers in Education and the Social Sciences.* Teachers College Press, New York.

Sekaran, U. 1992, *Research Methods for Business: A Skill-Building Approach*. 2nd edn, John Wiley & Sons, New York.

Semeonoff, B. 1976, *Projective Techniques*. John Wiley & Sons, London.

Shafritz, J.M. & Oh, J.S. 1987, *Classics of Organization Theory*. 2nd edn, The Dorsey Press, Chicago.

Shaw, R. 1999, *Reclaiming America: Nike, Clean Air, and the New National Activism*. University of California Press, Berkeley, CA.

Sieber, J.E. 1992, *Planning Ethically Responsible Research*. Sage, Newbury Park, CA.

Silverman, D. (ed.) 1997, *Qualitative Research: Theory, Method and Practice*. Sage, London.

Sinacore, A. L. & Akçali, F.O. 2000, Men and families: job satisfaction and self-esteem. *Journal of Career Development*, 27(1), 1–13.

Small, J. 2004, Memory work. In J. Phillimore & L. Godson (eds), *Qualitative Research in Tourism: Ontologies, Epistemologies and Methodologies*. Routledge, London, 255–72.

Small, J. & Onyx, J. (eds) 2001, *Memory-work: A Critique*. School of Management, University of Technology Sydney, Sydney.

Smith, N. & Dainty, P. (eds) 1991, *The Management Research Handbook*. Routledge, London.

Smith, P.C., Kendall, L.M. & Hulin, C. 1975, *The Measurement of Satisfaction in Work and Retirement: A Strategy for the Measurement of Attitudes*. Bowling Green State University, Bowling Green, OH.

Snooks and Co. 2002, *Style Manual for Authors, Editors and Printers*. 6th edn, John Wiley & Sons, Milton, Qld.

Spatz, C. & Johnston, J.O. 1989, *Basic Statistics: Tales of Distribution*. 4th edn, Brooks/ Cole Publishing, Pacific Grove, CA.

Spradley, J.P. 1979, *The Ethnographic Interview*. Holt, Rinehart and Winston, New York.

Spradley, J.P. 1980, *Participant Observation*. Holt, Rinehart and Winston, New York.

Stake, R.E. 1994, Case studies. In N.K. Denzin & Y.S. Lincoln (eds), *Handbook of Qualitative Research*. Sage, Thousand Oaks, CA, 236–47.

Stake, R.E. 1995, *The Art of Case Study Research*. Sage, Thousand Oaks, CA.

Stewart, D.W. & Shamdasani, P.M. 1990, *Focus Groups: Theory and Practice*. Sage, Newbury Park, CA.

Storey, W.K. 2004, *Writing History: A Guide for Students*. Oxford University Press, New York.

Strauss, A.L. 1987, *Qualitative Analysis for Social Scientists*. Cambridge University Press, Cambridge.

Strauss, A. & Corbin, J. 1994, Grounded theory methodology: An overview. In N.K. Denzin & Y.S. Lincoln (eds), *Handbook of Qualitative Research*. Sage, Thousand Oaks, CA., pp. 273–85.

Tanur, J.M. (ed.) 1991, *Questions About Questions: Inquiries into the Cognitive Bases of Surveys*. Russell Sage Foundation, New York.

Taylor, F.W. 1911, *Principles of Scientific Management*. Harper & Brothers, New York.

Templeton, J.F. 1994, *Focus Group: A Strategic Guide to Organizing, Conducting and Analyzing the Focus Group Interview*. Revised edn, Probus Publishing Co., Chicago.

Tesch, R. 1990, *Qualitative Research: Analysis Types and Software Tools*. Falmer Press, New York.

Thorsteinson, T.J. 2003, Job attitudes of part-time vs full-time workers: a meta-analytic review. *Journal of Occupational and Organizational Psychology*, 76(2), 151–77.

Ticehurst, G.W. & Ross-Smith, A. 1992, Communication satisfaction, commitment, and job satisfaction in Australian organisations. *Australian Journal of Communication*, 19(1), 130–44.

Turner, B.A. 1987, The use of grounded theory for the qualitative analysis of organisational behaviour. *Journal of Management Studies*, 20(3), 333–48.

UK Longitudinal Studies Centre (ULSC) 2004, website at: (www.iser.essex.ac.uk/ulsc/), University of Essex, Colchester. Accessed August 2004.

University of California, Berkeley, Library (n.d.), *Walt Disney: A Bibliography of Materials Held in the UC Berkeley Library*. UC Berkeley Library, Berkeley, CA. Available at: (www.lib.berkeley.edu/MRC/disney.html) Accessed Oct. 2004.

Vallaster, C. & Koll, O. 2002, Participatory group observation—a tool to analyze strategic decision making. *Qualitative Market Research*, 5(1), 40–57.

Van Fleet, D.D. 1991, *Contemporary Management*. 2nd edn, Houghton, Mifflin Company, Boston.

Van Maanen, J. 1983, *Qualitative Methodology*. Sage, London.

Vaughn, S.V., Schumm, J.S. & Sinagub, J. 1996, *Focus Group Interviews in Education and Psychology*. Sage, Thousand Oaks, CA.

Veal, A.J. 1997, *Research Methods for Leisure and Tourism*. Financial Times/Prentice Hall, London.

Vecchio, R.P., Hearn, G. & Southey, G. 1992, *Organisational Behaviour: Life at Work in Australia*. Harcourt Brace Jovanovich, Sydney.

Venard, B. & Tsai, T. 1998, Networks as a national competitive advantage: the Singapore case study. *Journal of General Management*, 24(2), 1–18.

Verdurm, A. & Viane, J. 2003, Exploring and modelling consumer attitudes towards genetically modified food. *Qualitative Marketing Research*, 6(2), 95–110.

Von Bertalanffy, L. 1972, The history and status of general systems theory. *Academy of Management Journal*, 15, 407–26.

Waldman, D., Atwater, L. & Antonioni, L.E. 1998, Has 360 degree feedback gone amok? *Academy of Management Executive*, 12(2), 86–94.

Walker, J. 1996, *Columbia Online Style: Apa-style Citations of Electronic Sources*. Rev. 12/96, Vers.1.0. Retrieved June 8, 1998 from: (www.cas.usf.edu/english/walker/apa.html).

Wallach, E. 1983, Individuals and organization: the cultural match. *Training and Development Journal*, 12, 28–36.

Wansink, B. & Van Ittersum, K. 2003, Bottoms up! The influence of elongation on pouring and consumption volume. *Journal of Consumer Research*, 30(4), 455–63.

Ward, A. 2003, *The Leadership Lifecycle: Matching Leaders to Evolving Organizations*. Palgrave MacMillan, Basingstoke, UK.

Wass, V.J. & Wells, P.E. (eds) 1994, *Principles and Practices in Business and Management Research*. Dartmouth Publishing Company Limited, Aldershot, Hants.

Whitehouse, G., Diamond, C. & Lafferty, G. 2002, Assessing the benefits of telework: Australian case study evidence. *New Zealand Journal of Industrial Relations*, 27(3), 257–68.

Whyte, W.F. 1982, Interviewing in field research. In R. G. Burgess (ed.), *Field Research: A Sourcebook and Field Manual*. Allen & Unwin, London, 111–22.

Williams, F. 1986, *Reasoning with Statistics: How to Read Quantitative Research*. 3rd edn, Holt, Rinehart & Winston, New York, NY.

Williamson, J.B., Barry, S.T. & Dorr, R.S. 1982, *The Research Craft*. Little Brown, Boston.

Willig, C. 2001, *Introducing Qualitative Research in Psychology: Adventures in Theory and Method*. Open University Press, Buckingham, UK.

Wilson, A.M. 1998, The use of mystery shopping in the measurement of service delivery. *Services Industry Journal*, 18(3), 148–63.

Yin, R.K. 1994, *Case Study Research: Design and Methods*. 2nd edn, Sage, Newbury Park, CA.

Yin, R.K. 2003a, *Case Study Research: Design and Methods*. 3rd edn, Sage, Thousand Oaks, CA.

Yin, R.K. 2003b, *Applications of Case Study Research*. 2nd edn, Sage, Thousand Oaks, CA.

Young, C.H., Savola, K.L. & Phelps, E. 1991, *Inventory of Longitudinal Studies in the Social Sciences*. Sage, Newbury Park, CA.

Zikmund, W.G. 1991, *Business Research Methods*. 3rd edn, Dryden Press, Orlando, FL.

Zikmund, W.G. 1997, *Business Research Methods*. 5th edn, Dryden Press, Orlando, FL.

Zuber-Skerritt, O. (ed.) 1996, *New Directions in Action Research*. Falmer Press, London.

Index

Page numbers in *italics* refer to figures